meat

meat

A KITCHEN EDUCATION

James Peterson

TEN SPEED PRESS
Berkeley

Published in the United States by Ten Speed Press,
an imprint of the Crown Publishing Group, a division
of Random House, Inc., New York.
www.crownpublishing.com
www.tenspeed.com

Ten Speed Press and the Ten Speed Press colophon are
registered trademarks of Random House, Inc.

Library of Congress Cataloging-in-Publication Data
Peterson, James.
  Meat : a kitchen education / James Peterson. — 1st ed.
    p. cm.
  Includes index.
  1. Cookery (Meat) 2. Meat cuts. I. Title.
  TX749.P485 2010
  641.6′6—dc22

                              2010021759

ISBN 978-1-58008-992-0

Printed in China

Design by Nancy Austin and Katy Brown
Illustrations by Alex Kaluzshner

10 9 8 7 6 5 4 3 2 1

First Edition

CONTENTS

ACKNOWLEDGMENTS

On such a complicated project, there are innumerable people who contribute in large and small ways. Alice Piacenza was the person with whom I worked most closely. She tested recipes, was the hands in the shots, and, most importantly, helped me with the photography. Her assistance was invaluable.

I'd like to thank Joshua Applestone of Fleischer's Meats for generously taking most of a day to show us butchering techniques and for encouraging the appreciation of locally raised animals. Rudi Weid's butchery classes at the Institute of Culinary Education were also extremely helpful. Rudi guided us through the process of breaking down a whole lamb and with fine-tuning the meat charts. Thank you, too, to my dear friend Dennis Malachosky for explaining and demonstrating to me the many complexities of butchering and cooking venison. Much appreciation goes to the gentlemen at Los Paisanos Meat Market for their help, guidance, and courtesy.

I'd also like to thank those at Ten Speed, including my editors Aaron Wehner and Dawn Yanagihara, who worked day in and day out readying the manuscript for publication. Sharon Silva's copyediting was extremely thorough and contributed enormously to the finished text. Nancy Austin's art direction and Katy Brown's expertise were essential for the book's clean design that disguises its production complexity. Thanks to illustrator Alex Kalushner for his charming animal renderings.

Finally, there are those in my personal life who keep me going, who encourage and cajole, and without whom I could not have brought this project to fruition. Elise and Arnold Goodman have been my agents now for 20 years—they have provided advice and have helped me weather the many ups and down of this industry. Sarah Leuze and Joel Hoffman have been steady reminders that I can do what I need to do and have helped me realize so many of my personal goals. Last, I'd like to thank Zelik Mintz for standing behind me for so many years, for spurring me on, and for providing endless encouragement.

INTRODUCTION

Almost thirty years ago, when I owned a restaurant, I was confronted with a strange offer from a regular client. He worked at a laboratory where rabbits were raised for scientific experiments. The trials always included a control group made up of animals to which nothing was done, yet when these rabbits got old, they were "discarded." He asked me if I would like some of these control-group subjects. I was grateful to get my hands on older rabbits—they're perfect for thorough larding and slow braising—so I said yes. I was also eager to save them from a meaningless death.

The following Monday, a large cardboard box arrived. As I lifted the box, I knew from its motion that the rabbits were alive. Given the weight of the box, I expected to encounter about a dozen, so I was shocked to find only two giant rabbits that reminded me of a Monty Python skit. The task was left to me to do them in, which I did with a quick snap of the neck and a slit of the throat. On one hand, the killing wasn't as bad as I had anticipated. But the whole process upset me, especially the sad resignation the rabbits displayed as they seemed to know they were about to die. Never again have I looked at meat in the same way. The experience drove home the fact that an animal has to give its life in order for us to eat meat. I was left convinced that people who consume meat should have to kill for their supper at least once in their lives.

The average American eats more than eight ounces of meat a day, far more than needed for healthy nutrition. Asians eat small amounts of meat with hefty portions of carbohydrates, such as rice or noodles, and have lower rates of heart disease and stroke than Americans. It may seem perplexing to read in a book about meat that we should eat less of it, but this is, indeed, my position. We should eat less and eat better. In France, a good chicken costs twenty dollars or more. But what a chicken it is. Organic and truly free range, it is slaughtered at an older age than American chickens and as a result has a lot more flavor, if a bit more texture. Grass-fed steers in Italy and France develop a better flavor than some of the grass-fed beef in America, again, in part, because they are butchered at an older age. Beef in Japan is a rare luxury, but genuine Kobe beef is considered among the best in the world.

Americans are also enthusiastic consumers of steaks and chops. In other words, we eat high on the hog—literally. Most, though not all, of the tender meat on an animal is found along the back. Meat from the leg and shoulder, despite being the most flavorful, is often neglected. In *Meat*, I have included recipes and techniques that allow the reader to explore some of these underexploited cuts, with braising often taking center stage as the best method for cooking them. Offal, known euphemistically in the United States as variety meats, is also overlooked. How many Americans know the joys of properly cooked kidneys or sweetbreads or even a slice of liver? To the uninitiated, these typically inexpensive cuts are often a delicious revelation.

I have divided the chapters in *Meat* according to the type of animal, with the recipes in each chapter organized by either cooking technique alone or by cut and its appropriate cooking techniques. The emphasis on techniques, all of which are described beginning on page 5, is important because once you learn how to make one recipe, you can apply the same technique to a wide range of possibilities. Many of the recipes are extremely simple, sometimes involving only grilling or sautéing without a sauce or garnish. But what may seem overly simplistic is actually how most of us cook and eat.

You'll find that each chapter is rich in photographs, most of them devoted to either cutting meat into pieces suitable for cooking or to techniques such as larding. These tasks may seem the work of a butcher rather than a cook, but butchers are disappearing, and many of those who remain are reluctant to carry out some of the more labor-intensive techniques. Plus, by doing the work yourself, you'll gain both valuable practice with a knife and beneficial insight into how animals are put together. You'll also save money by buying large cuts and breaking them down into steaks or chops or into pieces suitable for braising. You may even discover that you enjoy cutting up meat, finding it to be surprisingly soothing once you get the knack of it.

Pork, beef, lamb, and veal charts showing where various cuts are located on each animal will further your understanding of how to cut and cook meat. People are anatomically similar to the animals they eat, so it's a good idea to check your own body to locate the various cuts. Once you know the source of each cut, you will recognize which parts are tougher—the more activity the muscle gets, the tougher the meat—and require longer cooking and which can be tossed onto a grill or into a sauté pan for a relatively short time.

Although techniques are at the heart of this book, putting together flavor combinations that both pair well with the meat at hand and share a geographical and seasonal affinity is also important. To help you achieve these successful pairings, I have included several flavor profiles inspired by traditional cuisines (see page 25). For example, if you are thinking Moroccan, you'll find a list that includes olives, preserved lemons, almonds, and saffron, to name only a few of the possibilities. Or, if you prefer Indian flavors, coriander, cumin, fenugreek, cashews, and coconut milk are among the options.

The controversy over how animals are raised and slaughtered for meat has been explored by a number of thoughtful writers, which prompts me to keep my advice on the subject brief: follow your conscience. Needless suffering is inherent in how many animals are raised and slaughtered, and we shoppers must use our wallets (nothing else is as convincing) to let sellers know that we want to buy meat from animals that have been treated humanely. Always ask the butcher the source of the meat he or she sells. A butcher who can provide a specific answer usually has greater concern for the well-being of animals. Plus, the easier it is to learn about the origin of the meat, the more likely it is that the animals have been humanely raised and slaughtered. By insisting on being better informed, we can transform an industry that is opaque and secretive into one that is transparent and, as a consequence, humane.

Even though most of us shop at a supermarket—and, admittedly, nowadays supermarkets are far more interesting than in the past—I recommend finding a high-quality butcher to patronize as often as possible. Not only will you learn from a butcher, but he or she will recognize your genuine concern for the quality and provenance of what is sold. The meat at a butcher shop is often more expensive than at supermarket, but it is also usually of higher quality, and because your butcher will teach you about lesser-known—and often less costly—cuts rarely found at supermarkets, you may actually end up saving money.

Simply put, much of what I'm encouraging is the simple act of tasting, of training your palate to recognize meat of better quality. As you learn to appreciate the flavor of fine meat (and to understand the flavor of what's not so fine), you'll find yourself satisfied with eating less meat. You'll also find more joy in the kitchen as your cooking improves.

BASIC COOKING TECHNIQUES

Meat is usually cooked by one of the following techniques: sautéing, broiling, roasting, braising (which includes stewing), poaching, frying, stir-frying, grilling, smoking, or barbecuing. It can be slowly cooked in its own fat, known as confit, or it may be served raw. The cut of meat determines the best cooking method. Some techniques are relatively quick and heat the meat only until it is warm inside; others are long, to ensure the heat penetrates the meat thoroughly and evenly. Tender cuts—such as those from the loin and some parts of the leg of a cow, pig, or lamb or tender parts of poultry—are suited to quick cooking: sautéing, roasting, frying, stir-frying, grilling, and, in some cases, poaching. Tougher cuts such as shank, shoulder, and certain muscles from the leg, are best barbecued, poached, or braised—techniques that involve cooking for a prolonged period, which breaks down the collagen, a particularly sturdy protein, rendering the meat tender.

Sautéing

Sautéing is cooking in a sauté pan or skillet in a small amount of fat. (The word *panfrying* is sometimes used for the same technique.) The purpose of the fat is to lubricate the meat and prevent it from sticking, and unless the meat is breaded, the fat is not absorbed by the meat. So, if you're counting calories, don't count the fat used to sauté the meat. In fact, the meat is likely to render fat, which means the total number of fat calories actually diminishes.

A wide variety of different fats can be used for sautéing, and because the cooked fat is often patted off sautéed meats (again, when they are not breaded), the type you use isn't that important. What is important is that the fat is hot enough to brown the meat quickly before it overcooks or, worse, before it releases water into the pan. Butter is popular for sautéing because of its flavor and because it helps browning, but it burns at such a low temperature that it is not good for sautéing thin pieces of meat, which must be cooked at a high temperature. It is perfect for sautéing bone-in chicken pieces, however, because chicken can be cooked at a relatively low temperature and can take time to brown. The butter imparts a lovely flavor, not because the chicken absorbs fat, but because caramelized milk solids cling to the meat. For most sautéing, oils, clarified butter, and rendered animal fats are more practical than butter because they burn at higher temperatures. Many chefs and recipes suggest browning in a combination of butter and oil, mistakenly believing the oil prevents the butter from burning. But the milk solids in the butter burn at the same low temperature regardless of whether or not they are surrounded with oil.

I recommend "pure" olive oil for sautéing because of its neutral flavor. Most vegetable oils often have a vague fishy smell and taste when heated, and at the very least fill the kitchen with a weird aroma. Pure olive oil is olive oil that has been stripped of its flavor and is much less expensive than extra virgin olive oil. It would be a waste to use extra virgin olive oil because its delicate flavor is destroyed by the high heat.

Sautéing is sometimes used as an intermediate step in preparations, such as stews, in which the meat is then braised, or small roasts that won't have time to brown in the oven. When sautéing meat for a stew, it's important to keep the fat at a high temperature. The way to achieve this is to add the meat to the hot fat a few pieces at a time. If the meat is added all at once, the temperature will drop and the liquid (a mixture of sugars and proteins but mostly water) the meat naturally releases will ooze out into the pan, instead of caramelizing on the surface of the meat. Once this happens, the meat continues to release more liquid and ends up boiling in its own juices. Likewise, when the meat is turned, flip only a few pieces at a time to prevent the rush of liquid.

The temperature at which you sauté depends on how thick the meat is. Thick pieces, such as chicken on the bone, can be sautéed over low to medium heat because the meat requires a relatively long time to heat through and there's plenty of time for browning to occur. On the other hand, you need high heat for a thin chop so it will brown before it overcooks.

Clarified Butter

Many recipes call for clarified butter, which burns at a much higher temperature than regular butter. The reason for this is that the water and the milk solids (proteins), which burn at a low temperature, are eliminated. There are two ways to clarify butter. If you are working with more than a couple of pounds (unlikely in a home kitchen), simply melt the butter over medium heat, let it sit, and skim off the froth. Then carefully ladle off the clarified butter, which is pure gold and clear. At the bottom you will see the water with additional milk solids dissolved in it. This can be discarded or fed to the cat.

A second method, more appropriate for small amounts of butter, is to boil the butter until all the water it contains evaporates and the milk solids lightly caramelize. This is easy to recognize because brown coagulated milk solids adhere to the bottom and sides of the pan after about 10 minutes. At this point, the cooking must be stopped immediately. The best way to do this is to submerge the bottom of the pan in a bowl of cold water for a second or two before pouring off the clear, gold butter through a fine-mesh strainer.

Making a Pan-Deglazed Sauce

1. Sauté the meat in pure olive oil; regular or clarified butter; rendered duck fat, pork fat, or bacon fat; or grape seed oil or vegetable oil. Remove the meat from the pan and pour off and discard the cooking fat.

2. Return the pan to medium heat and add one of the following aromatics: minced garlic, minced shallot, or finely chopped onion. Stir just until it releases a toasty aroma.

3. Pour in a liquid, such as wine (red or white, sweet or dry), beer, broth, tomato puree, apple cider, or water, and bring to a boil. Deglaze the pan, using a wooden spoon to scrape the caramelized juices into the liquid as it boils.

4. Boil down the liquid to reduce by half, then stir in meat glaze (page 318) and cook until the mixture is reduced to a lightly syrupy consistency.

5. Season with one or more flavorings, such as a finely chopped fresh herb (parsley, chives, or chervil), drained capers, halved or chopped olives, diced tomatoes, chopped reconstituted dried chiles, sautéed fresh or reconstituted dried mushrooms, julienned prosciutto, or chopped fresh truffles.

6. Finish the sauce with an enrichment, such as heavy cream (reduce the sauce further after adding the cream), cold butter (whisked in at the last minute, without allowing the sauce to boil), or mayonnaise or aioli, preferably homemade (again at the last minute and without allowing the sauce to boil).

Choose a pan just large enough to hold the pieces of meat in a single layer without crowding. This prevents their juices from running out onto an exposed (and very hot) section of the pan and burning. Always start cooking the meat with the most attractive side down, so that when you turn the meat, it will be facing up. If you are cooking chicken, sauté the skin side first.

Because both sautéing and sweating call for cooking in a small amount of fat in a sauté pan, they are sometimes confused. Sweating, which is commonly used for vegetables, is cooking over low heat so that the food releases its natural juices, which then caramelize on the bottom of the pan. Sautéing, in contrast, is designed to seal juices within a savory crust.

When meats are properly sautéed, they leave a crust of savory caramelized juices adhering to the bottom of the pan. The juices must be golden brown, not black and burned. (Use a nonstick pan or a shiny-surfaced pan, not a black or dark pan, to sauté; a shiny pan allows you to judge the condition of the juices coating the pan bottom.) This flavorful crust can be deglazed and used to make a delicious pan sauce in just half a dozen easy steps with a handful of ingredients (see above).

Broiling

Unlike sautéing and grilling, which cook meat from the bottom up, broilers cook from the top down. The problem with most home broilers, especially electric broilers, is that they are not hot enough. If the broiler isn't hot enough, the meat will turn gray, and the liquid it releases will drip down and be lost instead of caramelizing into a savory crust. To avoid this, preheat the broiler for at least 10 minutes before using it. Start with the meat almost (but not quite) touching the heat source and monitor the progress closely. If the meat starts to char too fast, lower it. If you can't get it to brown, give up on broiling or get another broiler. And always use a flameproof dish or pan for broiling—not a rimless cookie sheet or a mere piece of foil—so any juices released by the meat are captured and can be served.

Roasting

In the purest sense, roasting means cooking *in front* of the heat source in the open air, not in the oven. The traditional method involves a roaring fire and a spit, with a pan placed under the spit to catch the juices. When meat is roasted in front of a hot fire, it is invariably scented slightly with smoke, instead of with the burning fat fumes that accumulate in an oven, so its flavor is inimitable. Roasting in the open air is also more likely to produce a crust on the meat because, unlike in an oven, no moisture is surrounding the roast. Unfortunately, most of us don't have access to a spit, although the more determined among us can no doubt find one online and rig it up in front of the fireplace. Using small home spits in glass enclosures is no different than cooking in the oven except, perhaps, for ensuring more even browning.

Larger tender cuts, usually from the loin, are roasted, as are the legs of smaller animals; parts of the leg or, occasionally, the shoulder of larger animals; and most birds. Roasting meat in the oven is essentially baking, but it has several goals: the meat should have a savory, golden brown crust; it should be cooked evenly throughout to the desired temperature; and it should provide a jus to accompany each serving.

The most common roasting question is the temperature of the oven. The temperature is important because it affects browning. As a general principle, the smaller the roast, the higher the temperature. If a roast is very small—a quail, squab, or poussin, for example—brown it on the stove top first and then finish it in the oven. Few ovens can be set sufficiently hot to brown small items before they overcook. A large roast, such as a turkey, can be cooked at a relatively low temperature because there will be plenty of time for browning. A chicken, on the other hand, should be roasted at a high temperature so it turns brown and crusty but does not overcook.

A good general principle is to brown a roast at a high temperature and then lower the temperature according to the size and the desired internal temperature of the meat. As noted above, for small roasts, such as a squab or quail, the browning is done on the stove top. But for large roasts, like a big prime rib, start them in a 500°F oven until they are browned and then turn down the oven to 300°F for slow, even cooking. The initial cooking at high temperature ensures a crust will form and any bacteria on the surface of the meat will be killed. In restaurant kitchens equipped with accurate low-temperature ovens, cooks will sometimes roast at a high temperature to form a crust and kill bacteria and then turn the oven down to 125°F, a technique that ensures, even after as long as 24 hours, the meat is perfectly medium-rare throughout. However, don't try this in a home oven, which isn't accurate enough.

Jus and Gravy

Roasting delivers a bonus: the chance to serve jus or gravy. Jus is the drippings released from the roast, but the term is also used for the drippings combined with liquid, such as broth or water. A gravy is the diluted jus thickened, usually with flour or cornstarch. The first step to making either one is never to use a roasting rack. A rack suspends the meat over the roasting pan, which means the juices drip down onto the very hot pan and burn. Instead, choose a heavy roasting pan just large enough to accommodate the roast (an iron skillet is good) and with relatively low sides to ensure good heat circulation. Place the roast directly on the bottom, and surround it with meat trimmings or coarsely chopped aromatic vegetables, such as carrot and onion. Make sure the pan surface is completely covered or the jus could burn on the exposed spots. When roasting a chicken, put the neck and gizzard on the pan bottom and set the bird on them to prevent sticking.

Ironically, if you overcook a roast, it releases plenty of juices to skim and serve as a jus or to convert into a gravy. Frequently, however, a properly cooked roast does not release enough liquid. For example, a prime rib, roasted rare, will give off almost no juice. To circumvent this problem, brown

continued on page 12

Basting

Many recipes for roasts (as well as braises) call for basting. The idea behind basting a roast is to keep the surface of the meat continuously in contact with fat so it doesn't dry out. When roasting poultry this is superfluous since the poultry is already covered with a layer of fat contained in the skin. Meats from other animals should have a layer of fat left on to protect them from drying, or should have a sheet of fatback tied around them to eliminate the need for basting. The main disadvantage to basting is that it lets heat out of the oven. If you're roasting on a spit, then there's no harm in basting—but, frankly, not a whole lot of good either. In principle, basting should only be done with fat, not with liquids such as wine, broth, or the juices from the roast, which cause the roast to steam and inhibit browning. The roast becomes more of a braise.

Basting a braise is something else entirely. Letting heat out of the oven is less of an issue because the high heat needed to form a crust is no longer necessary. Basting a braise with its reduced and defatted braising liquid as the last stage of the braising is an excellent way to coat the meat with a savory glaze and to bring out the flavor of the liquid by exposing it to more oxygen.

In short, when you are braising, basting is a good idea; when you're roasting, it isn't.

Vegetable Prep

Root vegetables are often sectioned and turned or julienned to be used in braises or as accompaniments to roasts. Here are a few tricks:

Julienning a leek

1. Cut the root end off the leek and then cut off the greens. If the white is long, cut it in half crosswise.

2. Cut the leek sections in half lengthwise. Rinse out any sand that may be caught between the layers.

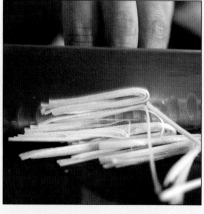

3. Fold the leek halves in half and cut into julienne.

Sectioning and turning a turnip

1. Cut the ends off the turnip.

2. Cut the turnip into sections.

3. Use a sharp paring knife to cut away excess flesh and shape the piece into an ovoid.

Julienning a carrot

1. Cut the peeled carrot into sections.

2. Use a vegetable slicer to slice the carrot lengthwise.

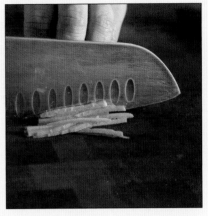

3. Stack the slices and cut them into julienne.

Sectioning a carrot

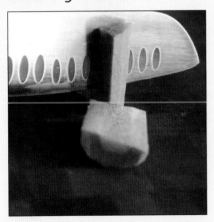

1. Cut the carrot sections into wedges.

2. Snap the core out of each section.

meat trimmings (from your roast or, if your roast has already been trimmed, from the butcher) in the roasting pan in the hot oven; once they are browned, set the roast on top. The trimmings will provide juices, which in turn can be deglazed for a jus or gravy.

There are two kinds of jus: those that have caramelized and those that have not. A jus that has caramelized—cooked until all liquid disappears and only a solid glaze is left adhering to the pan—will have a much more pronounced flavor than one that has not. When dealing with small amounts of jus—especially when red meats are roasted rare—it makes sense to go ahead and caramelize the jus (if it hasn't already caramelized) by boiling it down to a glaze. When dealing with large amounts of jus, such as from a well-done turkey, don't bother to caramelize; it will take you all evening.

Sometimes when roasting a chicken or other small roast, you end up with a few tablespoons of juices and at least an equal amount of fat in the bottom of the pan. How do you get rid of the fat? The best approach is to set the pan on the stove top and boil down the juices until the moisture evaporates and the drippings caramelize and adhere to the pan bottom. At this point, pour off and discard the fat and then deglaze the pan with liquid.

A good way to create a flavorful jus is to deglaze the caramelized drippings in the roasting pan with broth, boil the broth down until it caramelizes, pour off any fat, deglaze with more broth, and caramelize again; repeat until you have the intensity you want, then use only a small amount of broth to dissolve the final caramelized layer. You can repeat this caramelization process as many times as you like, though I usually stop at three.

Once you have a jus, you can thicken it with cornstarch, a roux, cream, or giblets. You can whisk together equal amounts of cornstarch and cold water (usually about 1 teaspoon cornstarch per cup of jus) and slowly stir it into the simmering jus to produce a shiny, glazelike jus called a *jus lié*. You can use flour cooked with a little butter to create a roux to produce a gravy (about 1 tablespoon each flour and butter per cup of jus). The roux can be made directly in the roasting pan with fat released by the roast, supplemented with a little butter, if necessary, or it can be made in a saucepan. In either case, broth, water, or jus is added to the roux to make the gravy. To make a cream gravy, add cream to the gravy at the end, after thickening with roux. There are two ways to make giblet gravy, the French and the American. For the American method, roast the giblets along with the meat, chop them fairly fine, and add them to the gravy at the end. For the French method, puree the raw liver with an equal amount of butter and work the mixture through a strainer. Whisk the puree into the jus just before serving, being careful not to let the jus boil once you've added the giblet butter.

Braising

Braising is basically cooking foods in a relatively small amount of liquid (as contrasted with poaching, which is cooking in a lot of liquid). There are four kinds of braising: brown long, brown short, white long, and white short. Braises and stews are closely related. The primary difference is that stews are made with smaller pieces of meat.

Brown braises require browning the meat before it is braised by sautéing (for stews) or by browning in the oven. Traditional cookbooks explain that this creates a crust that helps seal in juices, but in fact juices continue to escape as the meat is browning. The trick to successful browning is to use heat that is high enough to evaporate the juices the moment they come to the surface of the meat, contributing to the savory crust. Juices that caramelize this way—cook as they are exposed to the air—develop savory compounds that add flavor to the finished dish.

White braising skips the browning of the meat, and instead begins its cooking in liquid. For example, a traditional Provençal daube is made by simmering chunks of beef or lamb in wine without browning them first. Even if the daube is made with red wine, it is still considered a white braise.

Short braising involves cooking meat only long enough to heat it through. The chicken fricassee recipes beginning on page 47 are examples of short braises. Short braises can be brown or white, depending on whether the meat is browned before it is combined with liquid. Beef Stroganoff is an example of a dish that is white short braised: the meat is cooked in liquid just until it is medium-rare. *Long braising* means that the meat has been brought to a relatively high internal temperature (about 190°F) and held there, usually for hours, until the meat breaks down and tenderizes. Like short braises, long braises can be brown or white.

Degreasing

Recipes for braises and broths frequently call for "degreasing" during and after cooking. Degreasing is especially important when braising because the fat should be completely eliminated before the meat is glazed in the oven. The usual way to degrease a liquid is to move a ladle around the perimeter of the pot, with the ladle's opening almost perfectly flat in relation to the surface of the liquid. This degreasing method takes practice to avoid allowing too much of the precious braising liquid into the ladle with the fat. A more efficient and easier method is to chill the liquid and then remove the congealed fat that forms on the top.

The most elaborate braises, brown long braises, involve several steps. A typical long braise uses a single large cut of meat with plenty of internal fat and fat covering the meat. If you are braising something lean, it is best to lard it as shown on the facing page. This is a labor-intensive step and the necessary fatback can be hard to find, but larding is worth both the time and the effort. The pot should match the shape and size of the meat—an oval pot is generally a good choice—as closely as possible. This will keep the amount of cooking liquid needed to a minimum. First, cook the meat with aromatic vegetables until it releases juices that caramelize on the bottom of the pot. This stage is delicate because the juices must be cooked long enough to separate out the fat and to caramelize, but not so long that they burn. If the juices have not caramelized and formed a crust on the pan bottom, you will pour off the flavorful juices when you pour off the fat. The meat must also be cooked to a relatively high temperature—at least 160°F—so it will have released all its juices. If the meat is not heated through and the juices are starting to caramelize, add a small amount of water or broth to the pot to prevent the juices from burning and to give the meat longer to cook. When all the juices have finally caramelized, pour off the fat that has collected on top of the crust. Then add liquid—usually enough to come halfway up the sides of the meat—along with a bouquet garni (page 320) and bring the liquid to a simmer.

Cover the pot with a sheet of aluminum foil, pressing it down slightly in the middle so that moisture condenses on its underside and drips down onto the exposed parts of the meat, and then with a lid. The braising proper now starts—the dish is brought to the simmer on the stove, and the meat is kept at a bare simmer, which should appear as just a ripple on the surface of the liquid, never a boil. The easiest way to keep the braise at the correct cooking temperature is to put it in a 275°F oven and then check it periodically, adjusting the temperature as needed to maintain a bare simmer. You can also braise on top of the stove, but most stoves have self-starters that click infernally if you try to turn the heat down very low. When the meat starts to soften, usually after about 1½ hours, turn it over so any part that was exposed is now submerged. Continue cooking until a skewer slides easily in and out of the meat with no clinging. Depending on the cut, the whole process can take from 1 to 5 hours. Meat that is braised so

continued on page 16

Larding

Many cooks believe that cooking meat in liquid keeps it moist. Liquid, in fact, does nothing to keep meat moist. The addition of fat is what keeps meat moist.

It may seem paradoxical in this fat-conscious age to add fat to meats by larding, which calls for inserting strips of fat directly into the muscles. But there is no other way to add moistness to long-braised meats. Plus, the need to lard meats is particularly true today because meats are generally leaner than in the past.

Traditionally, there are two ways to lard: The first calls for a larder, a long pointed tube with a handle. The fat is inserted into the tube, the tube is driven into the meat, and then the tube is withdrawn, leaving the fat embedded in the meat. The second method uses a larding needle, which looks like a knitting needle with a hinged end for holding the fat. The fat is drawn through the meat, as if sewn. Because both methods can be difficult to master, the method shown here is a hybrid of the two. A larder is driven into the meat and then a larding needle is slid through the tube and into the meat, leaving the fat embedded.

Look for fatback, the thick layer of fat, with or without skin, from a pig's back, for larding. You will probably need to special order it from your butcher. Make sure the layer of fat is nice and thick. Do not make the mistake of buying salt pork, which will make the meat too salty. When cutting the fatback into strips, or lardons, save the rind for adding gelatin to braises. You can also use more expensive Italian *lardo* (pork fat cured with salt and spices), but it is seasoned, so temper your seasoning accordingly.

Larding

1. Larding needle and larder.

2. Cut away the rind attached to the fatback, then cut the fatback into slices about ¹/₄ inch thick.

3. Cut the slices into strips, or lardons, about ¹/₄ inch on each side and as long as the fatback is wide.

4. If the recipe instructs, marinate the strips overnight with parsley and crushed garlic.

5. Attach a strip of fat to a larding needle. Slide a larder into the meat, and slide the larding needle into the tube of the larder.

6. Pull the larding needle through the meat and trim off the ends of the fat.

Garniture

The French have a nomenclature for describing the final garniture, or garnish, for a braise or stew. It's not important to remember the specific terms, but the distinctions they describe are useful for understanding how to put together a braise or stew. When the aromatic garniture—usually onions, carrots, and celery—is left in and becomes part of the braise or stew, the dish is said to be *bonne femme* (housewife's style). When the aromatic garniture is fished out after it has cooked for a while and a new garniture is simmered in the braise or stew during the last hour or so of cooking, the dish is said to be *bourgeoise*. When the aromatic garniture is removed and discarded at the end of cooking and a separate garniture is prepared on the stove top and added just before serving, the dish is said to be part of *la cuisine classique*. A classic boeuf bourguignon, for example, is made by stewing beef with red wine, carrots, onion, celery, and a bouquet garni. The vegetables and bouquet garni are then discarded and the stew is finished with a garniture of bacon (cut into strips called lardons), pearl onions, and sautéed mushrooms.

long that it is practically falling apart is said to be cooked *à la cuillière* (pronounced kwee-YAIR), or "to the spoon," implying that it is tender enough to be served with a spoon or a pair of spoons.

Once the meat is uniformly tender, transfer it to a clean (and ideally smaller) pot. Strain the braising liquid and degrease it (see page 14). Sometimes you will need to reduce it as well. Then pour the liquid back over the meat, return the pot to the oven, and cook, basting often with the braising liquid, for about 30 minutes. As the braising liquid reduces, it covers the braise with an irresistible reddish sheen.

Long braising is reserved for tough, sinewy cuts that release gelatin as they cook. The main danger is that the meat will dry out. The best method for preventing this (other than choosing the right cut to braise) is to lard the meat, as already suggested, or to wrap it in a sheet of fatback, known as a bard. Pork rind can also be added to stews and braises to contribute extra gelatin, and meat glaze (page 318) will contribute both gelatin and savor.

Other than brown and white, short and long, most braises get their identity from several components: the braising liquid, the aromatic garniture (such as the onions, celery, and carrots cooked in most stews), the herbs in the bouquet garni, or the finishing garniture. Keep in mind that the aromatic garniture, which helps flavor the braising liquid, is usually different from the finishing garniture (see above).

When braises are served, the braising liquid is often thickened to give it a lightly syrupy consistency. The best way to achieve this is to add ingredients that provide natural gelatin: concentrated broth, calf's or pig's feet (split lengthwise and blanched), meat glaze (page 318), pork rind (not from bacon), or knucklebones. A common alternative is to thicken the braising liquid—especially if it is made with red wine—with a butter and flour paste called a *beurre manié*. To make the paste, work together equal parts flour and butter with the back of a fork, counting on a tablespoon or two of the mixture per cup of liquid to be thickened. Whisk the *beurre manié* into the braising liquid and bring to a simmer just before serving. The flour and butter can also be cooked into a roux and the braising liquid whisked into it, which results in a liquid with a matte finish reminiscent of a classic gravy. Another method, and the tastiest, is to reduce the braising liquid down to the minimum amount you need, or until it has a lightly syrupy consistency, and then whisk in a little cold butter to finish, which yields a silky, unctuous consistency. Other starches, such as cornstarch or arrowroot, can be whisked with an equal amount of cold water. Then the mixture, called a slurry, can be whisked into the simmering braising liquid, giving it a nice sheen.

A final braising method, a tradition of the French kitchen, originated with hearth cooking. It calls for sealing meat in a pot with luting paste—a pastrylike mixture of flour and water—and then cooking it *sous les cendres*, "under the ashes," often for as long as 24 hours. Little or no liquid is added to meat cooked by this method, known as *à l'étuvée*. The juices in the meat are the only braising liquid. By the time the meat is done, it has released all of its juices, which are undiluted by any braising liquid, and is unbelievably succulent. The technique shares some similarity with barbecuing (see page 23), in which meat is cooked and smoked at the same time.

Stews

Stews are simply braises in which the meat has been cut into small pieces. When selecting meat for a stew, be sure to avoid a cut that is too lean. Many butchers mistakenly advertise "lean stew meat" to shoppers. Instead, you should opt for beef chuck, veal breast, or lamb shoulder.

Most stew recipes call for marinating meat; marinating definitely enhances the flavor, but it isn't essential. It is ideally done overnight in the refrigerator or for 4 hours at room temperature. Garlic does wonders in a marinade, as do onions—both are almost essential.

One technique, often called for in older recipes, is to lard the individual pieces of meat. Most people aren't going to bother with larding these days, but there's no better method for ensuring that the meat will remain moist. If you decide to try it, marinate the strips of lard with garlic overnight before you use them. This will implant a burst of flavor inside each piece of meat. (See page 15 for more about larding.)

Typically, the first instruction in a stew recipe is to brown the meat, which brings out a nice caramelized, meaty flavor, though you can choose to skip this step. If you decide to brown the meat, it should be at room temperature so it doesn't cool down the pan, and you should brown only a few pieces at a time, again so the pan doesn't cool. If the pan cools, browning stops and the meat releases liquid, which, instead of caramelizing on the surface of the meat and on the pan, creates steam. Once steaming begins, the meat will end up in an insipid liquid. If this happens, immediately take the meat out of the pan and wait for the pan to get hot again before restarting the browning. When it is time to turn the meat, don't turn all the pieces at once for the same reason.

Some recipes call for flouring the meat before browning. This is an effective way to both encourage browning and add a thickening agent to the stew. Roll the meat in the flour, coating it evenly, and then pat off the excess. Don't sprinkle the flour onto the meat as it browns, which would allow the flour to mix with the cooked fat and emulsify the fat into the braising liquid, making it greasy.

The braising liquid for a stew ideally contains, in addition to water or broth, some concentrated bouillon to give it body and a few tablespoons of meat glaze (page 318) for flavor and texture. Other than bouillon, the best moistening liquid is the liquid from the marinade, if you used one; wine; or any

Braising Model

Here are the basic components of a braise or stew, drawn from the description of braising, with suggestions for each category. Keep in mind that the lists are starting points only, and that once you begin regularly preparing braises, you will add to the possibilities.

Ingredients for the Marinade
Braising liquids (following), curry powder, garlic, ginger, herbs, miso, saffron, turmeric, soy sauce

Braising Liquids
Apple cider, beer, broth, Cognac, grape juice, Madeira, meat glaze (page 318), port, red wine, rum, tomatoes, verjuice, vinegar, white wine

Ingredients for Bouquet Garni (asterisk designates classic ingredients)
Bay leaf,* chervil, leek greens, lemongrass, marjoram, parsley,* rosemary, savory, tarragon, thyme*

Aromatic Garnitures
Carrots, celery, chiles, fennel, garlic, ginger, leeks, mushrooms (dried or fresh), onions

Thickeners
Arrowroot, *beurre manié*, chiles (reconstituted dried, ground to a paste), chocolate, cornstarch, cream, egg yolks, meat glaze (page 318), nut butter, pig's or calf's foot, pork rind, potatoes, potato starch, pureed aromatic vegetables, roux

Flavors for Finishing Liquid for Serving
Butter; Cognac; herbs such as parsley, chives, tarragon, chervil, or cilantro; vinegar

Finishing Garnitures
Almonds, bacon, carrots (sliced or turned into shapes), cashews, croutons (sautéed in butter, in cubes, or in heart shapes), dried fruits, fava beans, garlic cloves (blanched or roasted), grapes, green beans, olives, parsnips, pearl onions, potatoes, preserved lemons, prunes, raisins, spinach

of the suggestions listed in the box at left. Aromatic vegetables and herbs for the bouquet garni are the same as for any braise (see the box at left).

After a stew has been properly cooked and the fat has been skimmed off during and after braising, it can be served as is or the braising liquid can be reduced or thickened, or both. The advantage to reduction (boiling down) is that the flavor will be concentrated. Be careful to remove any fat on the surface of the liquid as it reduces, and never reduce the liquid at a hard boil, which can cause the fat to emulsify and make the liquid greasy. If you opt to thicken the liquid, it can done in any of the same ways—with *beurre manié*, roux, cornstarch or arrowroot slurry, or butter.

Making Confit

The French verb *confire* means to cook in or impregnate a food with sugar syrup or alcohol (for fruits), vinegar (for vegetables), or fat (for meat), with the result that the food, known as a confit, is preserved without refrigeration. The best-known confit is made by gently cooking duck, goose, or pork completely submerged in its own fat until a skewer slides easily in and out of the meat. In the broadest sense, making confit could be considered a kind of braising because the meat is stewing in its own juices, which are kept inside the meat by the surrounding fat. Others argue that making a confit is analogous to frying because frying calls for submerging foods in hot fat. But that comparison fails to acknowledge the difference in the temperature of the fat. The fat for a confit is kept at a lower temperature than it is for frying and has a tenderizing effect on the meat. The idea of the confit has become trendy, so that nowadays all sorts of things—tomatoes or even seafood—that have no traditional roots are given the name. For more about making confit, see page 79.

Poaching

Unlike braised meats, which are cooked with a minimum of liquid to encourage an interchange of flavors—the meat releases flavor into the surrounding aromatic liquid and then absorbs the aromatic liquid in an ongoing back-and-forth process—poached meats are typically fully submerged in an abundance of liquid, with the flavors that the meat releases becoming so diluted that they have no effect on the meat. Like poaching, boiling calls for a generous amount of liquid, but the liquid for boiling should bubble vigorously, while poaching liquids should just tremble on the surface and never bubble up.

Savory broths are made by poaching meat in a generous measure of water, with the meat sometimes discarded and sometimes served as part of a meal. The reverse is true as well: when the purpose of poaching meat in water is to serve the meat rather than make a broth, the broth can be served with the meat or reserved for another use. Occasionally, however, the distinction between braising and poaching is blurred. For example, the classic *blanquette de veau* calls for poaching pieces of veal in broth and then thickening the broth with a roux, egg yolks, and cream. A stew, which is a type of braise, is nearly identical except that a bit less liquid is used—just enough to cover the meat.

The most famous poached meat dishes are French pot-au-feu, New England boiled dinner (which, despite the name, is poached), and Italian *bollito misto*. All are made by poaching tough cuts of meat in broth to cover generously for several hours until they are fully tenderized. In a pot-au-feu, a variety of beef cuts is used; a *bollito misto* often contain meats from different animals; and a traditional New England boiled dinner features corned beef. When a pot-au-feu or *bollito misto* is served, the broth is usually presented as a first course and the meat follows, though it can also be plated with the meat surrounded by the broth. The corned beef usually makes the broth for a New England boiled dinner too salty to serve.

Although the most famous poached dishes are made by cooking tough cuts of meat for long hours, another poaching technique, known as *à la ficelle*, calls for poaching tender cuts just long enough to heat them through to the desired temperature. *Ficelle* means "string" and refers to tying string around a piece of meat, perhaps a section of beef fillet, submerging it in the ever-present simmering pot on the farmhouse stove or hearth, and then retrieving it with the string when it's cooked to a uniform rare or medium-rare. *Boeuf à la ficelle*, made with tenderloin, is the best known *à la ficelle* dish, but the technique can also be used to poach a duck breast, a leg of lamb, a pork loin, or tender cuts of veal such as top round. The poached meat is then sliced and served surrounded with the poaching broth and the aromatic vegetables, such as carrots or onions, included in the broth.

Frying

There are two kinds of frying: shallow frying and deep-frying. Shallow frying is usually done in a sauté pan with high sides and with only enough hot fat to come halfway up the sides of the foods to be fried. Deep-frying calls for a large pot or deep fryer, and the food is submerged in the oil. In recent years, fried foods have been much maligned because of the presumption that they contain excessive fat. But if they are properly cooked, with an eye toward the ideal heat and depth for the oil, they will absorb very little fat. Also, if you use a vegetable oil rather than the more traditional animal fat, you won't be introducing any cholesterol.

Freezing Meat

Freezing meat is less than desirable—thawed, frozen meat seems to cook from rare to overdone in a split second—but sometimes it is necessary. Two factors help diminish the damaging effects of freezing: tight wrapping and rapid freezing. When wrapping meat for freezing, first tightly enclose it in plastic wrap and then cover it completely in aluminum foil to prevent freezer burn. Refrigerate the meat so it goes from cold to frozen very quickly. Set the freezer temperature control to the lowest setting—around zero is ideal—before putting the meat into the freezer.

Always exercise caution when frying. The pan should be at least twice the depth of the oil, and the oil should come no more than halfway up the sides of the pan. Put the pan on the back of the stove so you, or someone else, don't jostle it and cause the oil to splash. When adding foods to the hot oil, don't use your hands (the oil can spatter). Instead, use a wire skimmer or slotted spoon.

Frying is a relatively straightforward technique, though a few general rules apply: The smaller the item to be fried, the hotter the oil should be. This is because heat penetrates quickly to the center, so prolonged frying in oil that is not hot enough will overcook the inside of the item without browning the outside. Conversely, if you're frying chicken, for example, in oil that is too hot, the chicken will brown and even burn before the heat penetrates to the center.

Most fried foods are covered with some type of batter or other coating before they are plunged into the oil. These can be as simple as a mixture of flour and water or plain flour. More elaborate batters contain egg, sometimes with beaten egg whites.

Stir-Frying

Unlike frying, stir-frying is accomplished with a minimum of hot fat, usually peanut oil or another vegetable oil, and nearly continuous motion. A wok is traditionally used, though you can use a large sauté pan with high sides. It is an ideal technique for cooking relatively small pieces of meat that will brown quickly on contact with hot fat.

Before adding the meat to the pan, always heat the oil over high heat until it just begins to smoke. Then add the meat and stir and toss to brown it evenly and seal in the flavor.

Grilling

Often confused with barbecuing (see page 23) and sometimes even with smoking (see page 22), grilling is cooking food directly above the heat source—charcoal or gas—on a grill rack. In an ideal situation, none of the smoke generated by fat or juices dripping onto the heat source comes up and touches the grilling meat. Sophisticated European grills even have vents with fans to pull away any smoke generated by the meat. On the other hand, many of us like our grilled foods to be lightly scented with smoke.

Just as for frying, the thinner the piece of meat being grilled, the hotter the heat should be. When buying a grill, choose one that allows you to adjust the height of the rack. That way you can grill chicken or other slow-cooking meats high above the heat source and thin steaks just a few inches from it.

Ideally, grilling should be done in the open air. Cooking in a covered grill isn't true grilling; instead, it is a combination of grilling and smoking or grilling and roasting.

Sometimes it is convenient to grill with indirect heat—in other words, with the meat not placed directly over the heat source. To set up a charcoal grill for indirect-heat grilling, build a hot fire on one side of the grill bed and leave the other side with no fire or with a cooler fire. If using a gas grill, preheat all the burners on high, then turn off the burner(s) directly under the meat. This technique is especially useful when grilling a large cut, such as a leg of lamb. The lamb is grilled directly over the heat only until browned, and then it is moved to the side without direct heat, the grill is covered, and the lamb continues to cook on the interior—in essence, roast—without burning on the exterior. This is when a covered grill comes in handy. It is also useful if you want your food to have a smoky flavor. If you are using a charcoal grill, you can sprinkle the hot coals with a handful of wood chips that have been soaked in water for at least an hour, or you can place a small sheet of aluminum foil over the coals and top it with a handful of sawdust. If you have a gas grill, you don't need to soak the chips. Some gas grills have specially designed smoker boxes for holding the chips or sawdust. If yours doesn't, put them in a perforated aluminum foil packet and place it directly on the burner.

It's important to avoid flare-ups when grilling, as they can leave greasy soot clinging to the food. Chicken is especially tricky because of the fat in the skin. Some cooks start the chicken flesh side down over relatively high heat and then cook it skin side down over lower heat. Sometimes it is necessary to move foods around to prevent flare-ups. If you still end up with bits of soot on the food, you can wipe them off with a towel before serving.

Smoking

Smoking is occasionally confused with grilling because the latter can involve using exotic woods to build the fire or adding soaked wood chips to the fire to generate smoke. Barbecuing and smoking are similar except that barbecuing has a form of braising going on at the same time.

There are two kinds of smoking, cold and hot. Cold smoking is done with smoke that has been allowed to cool so that it doesn't cook the food. Most cold-smoked foods have been cured first, such as smoked salmon. The smoke adds flavor and works as a preservative. Cold smoking at home is a rather elaborate process because you must devise a way to cool off the smoke. I made my own cold smoker by attaching a length of stovepipe to the chimney hole of my hot smoker, which directs the smoke into a large cardboard box. I then put the food to be smoked, typically salmon, in the box and seal up the box tight.

Hot smoking is easier and can even be done on the stove top with equipment you probably already have on hand: Place a little mound of wood chips in the center of a wok, cover the chips with a small square of aluminum foil, and set a circular cake rack in the wok. Then set the food on the rack, cover the wok, making sure the seal is tight (see recipe for smoked duck breast, page 75), and place the wok over the heat. Or, you can buy a good-quality stainless-steel or cast-iron stove-top smoker that is not too costly.

You can use also a covered grill for hot smoking: Prepare a fire on one side of the grill bed, cover the fire with soaked wood chips (or put unsoaked chips in a smoker box or perforated foil packet if using a gas grill), put the food on the grill rack over the fire, and cover the grill. Once the meat has browned, move the food to the side with no fire to complete the cooking.

If you decide you want to pursue the world of hot-smoked foods, you may want to invest in an outdoor hot smoker, essentially a large, tall metal box with a hot plate on the bottom. Some hot smokers can also be adapted for cold smoking; they can produce smoke that is cooled before being introduced into another chamber.

Barbecuing

Barbecuing is closely related to both braising and smoking. It is, in fact, a kind of uncontained braise in which the smoke carries the heat of the fire and the liquid for the braise is the moisture naturally contained in the meat. Some recipes for barbecuing call for braising the meat first (and ideally incorporating the braising liquid into the sauce); others cook the meat entirely in a covered grill. The best meats for barbecuing are the tougher cuts of beef, pork, lamb, or game, many of which are also ideal for braising.

The grill is set up for barbecuing the same way it is set up for indirect-heat grilling, with the heat under one side of the grill rack and no heat under the other side, and the meat is placed on the latter for all or most of the cooking. This ensures the fire provides the gentle heat needed for generating smoke and for braising. For meats that cook for a long time, you will need to add charcoal to the fire every hour or so to keep it going. Wood chips or sawdust are sometimes added to generate smoke (see Grilling, page 21).

The flavor in barbecued foods comes primarily from the smoke, though a marinade and a sauce, which are sometimes one and the same, are also important elements. The sauce is the source of one serious controversy in the barbecue world: some purists say you must never brush the meat with sauce as it cooks, and others insist on applying it.

IMPROVISING INTERNATIONAL FLAVORS

When improvising in the kitchen, it helps to be inspired by a traditional cuisine. Time-honored cooking has a natural logic: it combines ingredients from the same region that also share a growing season. Foods that grow together do naturally well together in the kitchen and have helped establish centuries-old cooking styles. By combining these ingredients judiciously (you have to understand how they work), it is possible to invent within the style of a particular cuisine. Adherence to long-established collections of ingredients helps guide our creativity and keeps us from coming up with illogical combinations and questionable fusions.

This is not an exhaustive list of the cuisines of the world. Instead, I have chosen those that best illustrate the techniques for cooking meat. Once the techniques are mastered, it's a simple matter to plug in various ingredients and flavor combinations.

A Note about Herbs

Most herbs are divided into two types. The first consists mostly of water and has a flavor that is delicate and fleeting. These herbs do not dry well and should be added to dishes near the end of cooking. They include parsley, chervil, chives, tarragon, basil, dill, cilantro, and mint. Other herbs, especially those that grow in hot climates, contain a great deal of oil, which means they dry well. They should be added to dishes near the beginning of cooking so they release their strong flavors slowly and discreetly. These include thyme, bay leaf, marjoram, oregano, sage, and epazote (used in Mexican cooking).

Morocco

Many of the spices used in Moroccan cooking are similar to those used in medieval European cooking. Experiment with adding them to braising mixtures and you'll come up with typical Moroccan flavors, best characterized as having a gentle yet complex spiciness. Use the herbs and aromatics the same way you would use onions and carrots in traditional braises. Add fresh ginger to a classic mirepoix (onions, carrots, and celery) at the beginning and then add saffron to the liquid near the end of cooking and your braise will have an unmistakable Moroccan character. Another touch is to finish dishes with a mixture of cilantro, parsley, garlic, lemon juice, paprika, and cumin. Lamb is the most popular meat in Moroccan cooking, and garnishes often include preserved lemons and olives. *Harissa* (see right), a pungent sauce made from chiles, is often passed at the table.

> **Harissa**
>
> Soak 8 assorted dried chiles, such as ancho, guajillo, or chilhuacle negro, in hot water to cover for about 30 minutes, or until softened. Drain and seed the chiles, then chop finely. Mince 2 garlic cloves, crush to a paste with the side of a large knife, and combine with the chiles in a small bowl. Peel, seed, and chop 1 tomato, add to the chile mixture, and season with salt and pepper.

HERBS AND AROMATICS: Cilantro, garlic, ginger, mint, orange flower water, parsley

SPICES: Cinnamon, coriander, cumin, paprika, saffron, turmeric

GARNITURES AND OTHER FLAVORINGS: Almonds, argan oil (rich cooking oil made from seeds of a native tree), chickpeas, couscous, eggplant, honey, lemons (fresh and preserved), olives, prunes, raisins, *smen* (type of aged clarified butter), tomatoes

Italy

Many Italian stews, soups, and sauces begin with a *soffrito*, a mixture of onions, carrots, celery, and often prosciutto or pancetta and herbs, sweated in butter or olive oil. Italian cooks are fond of sage and use it in much the same way the French use thyme. It's often cooked in butter and the perfumed butter then used as a sauce. Basil is another popular herb of the Italian kitchen and should only be added near the end of cooking. Oregano, marjoram, rosemary, and thyme can be included in a bouquet garni, or they can be dried and sprinkled over foods to be grilled. Rosemary has an aggressive flavor that easily takes over, however, so be careful not to add too much. Don't hesitate to use marjoram whenever possible. It gives foods an unmistakable—and pleasant—aroma and flavor.

HERBS: Basil, marjoram, mint, oregano, parsley, rosemary, sage, thyme

AROMATICS: Carrots, celery, fennel, garlic, onions, tomatoes

COOKING FATS: Butter, lard, olive oil

FLAVORINGS: Mushrooms (dried and fresh; especially porcini), olive oil, Parmesan cheese, truffles, wine

France

French cooks are masters in the use of herbs and employ a wide variety of them in their cooking. Thyme, bay leaf, and parsley make up the classic bouquet garni, and chervil, tarragon, parsley, and chives are combined for fines herbes, a traditional mixture used for finishing sauces, especially for white meats and fish. Stronger herbs, such as oregano, marjoram, and thyme, are dried and smeared on foods before grilling.

Since the seventeenth century, when French cooks stopped relying on imported spices, local products available in abundance, have been central to French cuisine. Cooks employ wild mushrooms and especially truffles when they can afford them. The late food scholar Waverly Root once said that the cooking of a country or region can be defined by the kind of cooking fat used. France can be divided into four parts: the northeast, where lard is traditionally the principal cooking fat; the northwest, where butter is used; the southwest, where duck and goose fat are important; and the southeast, where olive oil is favored.

HERBS: Bay leaf, chervil, chives, marjoram, oregano, parsley, rosemary, sage, tarragon, thyme

SPICES: Cloves, curry powder, mace, nutmeg, pepper, saffron

AROMATICS: Carrots, celery, garlic, leeks, mushrooms (cultivated and wild), onions, truffles

COOKING FATS: Butter, duck and goose fat, lard, olive oil

Mexico

Mexican cooks employ a broad mix of flavorings in their savory dishes. While French cooks are masters of manipulating herbs, and Indian cooks of spices, Mexican cooks have mastered the subtle flavors of a vast array of chiles. It's worth experimenting with a variety of dried chiles to learn the subtle differences of flavor among them: soak them in hot water for 30 minutes; seed and chop them; and then infuse them in hot cream, which acts as a carrier for the flavor. Chiles are combined with cinnamon and sometimes chocolate to make the country's celebrated moles. Tomatillos, related to gooseberries, are another iconic Mexican ingredient. When simmered and then pureed, they produce a tangy, pleasantly sour sauce that is irresistible atop nearly any grilled or sautéed meat.

HERBS: Avocado leaves, cilantro, epazote, marjoram, Mexican oregano, thyme

SPICES: Achiote seeds, allspice, cinnamon, cloves, coriander, cumin

AROMATICS: Garlic, onions

FLAVORINGS: Almonds, avocados, chiles (dried and fresh), chocolate, sesame seeds, tomatillos, tomatoes

India

Most Indian cooks roast and grind their spices each time they cook. Every region, and even every household, has its own version of such traditional spice mixtures as garam masala, *chaat masala*, *panch phoron*, and *sambaar* powder. Indian cooks also use unusual cooking fats, including ghee (toasted clarified butter; made as described on page 6), mustard oil, sesame oil, and coconut oil. When Indian cooks prepare a braised dish, they routinely begin by sautéing such aromatic ingredients as onions, garlic, chiles, and fresh ginger in one of these fats. Or, they may sweat a spice mixture along with the aromatic ingredients to bring out its flavor. To moisten the braise, they will typically use broth, tomatoes, coconut milk, or yogurt, and then mix in additional flavorings, such as curry leaves or a spice. Indian cooks also like to add an acidic ingredient—vinegar, lime juice, tamarind, mango powder—to impart a tang. Some dishes are finished with a mixture known as a *tadka* (as well as by other names), which is added just before serving. It contains whole spices—cumin, brown mustard seeds, cloves—and sometimes aromatic vegetables—chiles, garlic, onions—which are fried together in oil or ghee. Finally, the sauce is sometimes thickened with a nut butter, such as cashew or almond butter, and given a last flavor boost with a chopped herb, such as cilantro, mint, or basil.

> **SPICES:** Asafetida, black salt, brown mustard seeds, cardamom, cinnamon, cloves, coriander, cumin, fenugreek, garam masala, ginger powder, mustard powder, nutmeg, *sambaar* powder
> **HERBS:** Basil, cilantro, cinnamon leaf, curry leaf, mint
> **GARNITURES AND THICKENERS:** Almonds (whole or ground to butter), cashews (whole or ground to butter), sesame seeds (whole or ground to butter)
> **MOISTENING LIQUIDS AND FINISHES:** Broth, coconut milk, cream, tomatoes, yogurt

Southeast Asia

The cuisines of Thailand, Laos, Vietnam, Myanmar, and other Southeast Asian countries are enormously complex, yet certain flavorings are sufficiently common among them to give a brief description. One of the most important flavorings is fish sauce—*nam pla* in Thailand, *nuoc mam* in Vietnam, *nam pa* in Laos, *patis* in the Philippines, and so on—which is used as a flavoring in soups, sauces, stir-fries, and braises and as a table condiment. In Thailand, cooks finely grind together herbs and spices to make the country's famed curry pastes, the best known of which are red, green, or yellow. Shrimp paste, made by drying shrimp in the sun and letting it ferment, is almost universal in Southeast Asian cooking. Although it carries a sharp, pungent—some would say unpleasantly pungent—flavor, don't be tempted to leave it out of your cooking, or your dishes will lack an authentic Southeast Asian flavor. (Stirring it into dishes at the end of cooking, rather than heating it at the beginning, will attenuate its odor.) Lemongrass and kaffir lime leaves are used to give dishes a lemony flavor. Galangal, a rhizome related to ginger, also has a faintly citrusy flavor, but with a hint of pine. Acidity, instead of coming from lemons or other citrus, usually comes from tamarind, available as blocks of gooey, tarlike pulp or as fresh pods.

(It is the sticky substance surrounding the seeds in the pods, not the seeds themselves, that contain the characteristic acidity.) Several types of mint, including spearmint and peppermint, and of basil, all of them with a more intense licorice note than familiar sweet (Italian) basil, are also used.

> **HERBS AND SPICES:** Basil, cilantro, coriander, galangal, ginger, kaffir lime leaf, lemongrass, mint, nutmeg
>
> **FLAVORINGS:** Coconut milk, curry pastes, fish sauce, kaffir lime juice, shrimp paste, tamarind

Japan

Much of Japanese food is flavored with *dashi*, a broth made from dried bonito flakes and seaweed. It has an alluring smoky flavor that makes it a superb backdrop for all manner of savory foods. Japanese cooks also rely heavily on the soybean to provide an array of savory ingredients. The most famous is soy sauce, but of equal importance is miso paste, used in marinades, soups, and stews. Japanese cooks use sake and mirin, as well, the latter a slightly syrupy sweet rice wine used only in cooking. Much of the savor of Japanese cooking comes from the judicious juxtaposition of sweet and salty, with perhaps teriyaki sauce, a mixture of soy sauce and mirin, the best-known example.

> **SPICES:** Mustard, wasabi, 7-spice mixture
>
> **HERBS AND SEAWEED:** *Hijiki* (sea vegetable), *konbu* (large black seaweed), nori (black seaweed in thin sheets, for sushi), *sansho* powder (spicy; related to Sichuan pepper), *shiso,* wakame (brown sea algae)
>
> **AROMATICS:** Chiles, garlic, ginger (young and mature), miso, mushrooms, onions, sesame seeds, *yuzu* (type of citrus)
>
> **OILS AND FLAVORFUL LIQUIDS:** Dashi, mirin, plum vinegar, sake, soy sauce, tamari, toasted sesame oil

China

Encapsulating Chinese cooking in a few sentences is absurd, but there are certain ingredients that come up over and over again and can be used to lend a distinctly Chinese character to stir-fries, braises, or other dishes. One characteristic of Chinese cooking is its dependence on a wide array of prepared sauces, all of which have been made commercially for centuries and that have the stand-by status of American mustard, ketchup, and mayonnaise. Also, often by using just three ingredients—ginger, toasted sesame oil, and soy sauce—it's possible to give a dish a Chinese flavor.

> **AROMATIC INGREDIENTS AND SPICES:** Cinnamon, cloves, garlic, ginger, orange peel, Sichuan pepper, star anise
>
> **PREPARED SAUCES AND CONDIMENTS:** Chile oil, chile paste, hoisin sauce, oyster sauce, rice vinegar, rice wine, soy sauce, toasted sesame oil

CHICKEN
AND TURKEY

In 1950, Americans consumed about twenty pounds of chicken per capita. In 2009, that figure had grown to almost 125 pounds per capita. But while the quantity eaten is now six times greater, the status of the chicken has diminished. No longer does it carry the esteem that prompted Henry IV to declare that every French peasant should have a chicken in the pot on Sundays, or pushed the U.S. Republican Party in the 1920s to promise a chicken in every pot and a car in every backyard.

The reason for this downfall is simple: the chickens most of us eat nowadays are a pale reflection of the birds of seventeenth-century France or early-twentieth-century America. Instead, they are battery raised, that is, they spend their lives—sometimes no longer than fifty days—confined to small cages in crowded warehouselike structures, where they dine on feed guaranteed to fatten them up fast. Indeed, sometimes these caged birds are fattened so quickly that their legs are too spindly to support their weight.

To avoid these factory birds, many shoppers opt for chickens labeled "free range." According to U.S. law, free-range chickens must be allowed access to the outdoors, though neither the range nor the conditions are specified. In other words, producers may decide that the outdoors is as little as a two-foot square of gravel. That means that some free-range chickens are going to be better than others. Other farmers raise heirloom birds the old-fashioned way, allowing them to wander freely, to peck and scratch in the grass at will, and to live much longer lives than their caged or even free-range cousins. Although most of us are quick to proclaim we favor these traditionally reared chickens above all others, we may actually be disappointed with our purchase. An older chicken that has run around a lot is typically tougher than one that hasn't.

Four other labels are routinely encountered when shopping for chicken, all defined by law: "natural," "no hormones added," "no antibiotics added," and "organic." If a bird is labeled "natural," it means it has been minimally processed and contains no artificial flavorings or colorings or chemical preservatives—all good things to know, but only a narrow indication of quality. The use of hormones in the raising of chickens is prohibited by law, so the claim is acknowledging only what the law already stipulates. In contrast, producers can administer antibiotics, but they must stop giving them to the chickens well before the birds are processed, so they are free of antibiotic residue at the time they are slaughtered for sale. However, because many consumers prefer to buy birds that have never been given antibiotics, nearly all farmers raising free-range chickens are also keeping them antibiotic free from birth. Finally, chickens labeled "organic" have been fed an exclusively organic diet.

Dry plucking is another sign of a superior chicken. Nearly all the chickens raised in the United States are wet plucked, which means they are first plunged into boiling water to loosen the feathers and then held against a kind of rubber wheel that spins, taking the feathers with it. The danger of wet plucking is that the water cools down to a temperature that allows the growth of bacteria. Wet plucking also causes the bird to absorb up to 7 percent of its weight in water, leaving it with slimy skin that encourages bacterial growth. Dry plucking is considerably more labor-intensive, requiring up to an hour of hard work per bird. But it leaves the skin dry, so that it crisps up better in the oven or sauté pan.

Ideally, then, the chicken you purchase will be an heirloom breed, truly free range, at least two months old, and organic. It will have never been given antibiotics, and will have been dry plucked. The best place to look for this top-quality bird is at better butcher shops and farmers' markets. But even at what seems like the ideal source, it is always a good idea to ask the butcher or market vendor how the animal was raised and processed to ensure the tastiest purchase.

=====

Turkey comes in a wide variety of sizes, weighing from 8 or so pounds to well over 20. Connoisseurs claim that smaller turkeys have better flavor, but this is debatable. In any case, buy a turkey that will feed your guests (figure on about 1 pound per person) and leave you plenty of leftovers (consider doubling the amount you need for your first dinner). For example, a 20-pound turkey serves 10 people and ensures that there will be plenty of leftovers with which to improvise meals in the days to follow.

When buying turkey, it is ideal to buy a fresh turkey that has never been frozen. If your only option is a frozen one, be sure to give it plenty of time to thaw (about two days in the refrigerator). You can invest (and "invest" is the operative word) in an organic free-range turkey—you will likely pay about four times the price for it as you would for a mass-produced turkey. Heirloom breeds of turkey are beginning to appear around the holidays; if your guests prefer white meat, keep in mind that these birds often have a smaller amount of breast meat.

Roast Chicken

Every cook has his or her own favorite approach to roast chicken, ranging from the straightforward—put it in the oven and let it cook—to the complex, which can include everything from elaborate schemes for turning the chicken at various stages to browning it on the stove top before slipping it into the oven. Although my approach is among the simplest, it does call on a few tricks to help browning, to prevent sticking, and to ensure the breast and thighs cook at the same rate.

The first trick is to dispense with a roasting rack. A rack keeps the chicken suspended above the roasting pan so that when it releases juices, the juices hit the hot pan and burn. Also, if you've added aromatic vegetables to the roasting pan, they are more likely to burn with a rack because they are scattered over a large surface area and can easily overheat. Instead, use a roasting pan about the size of the chicken—a cast-iron skillet works well—place a few pieces of chopped onion and carrot and/or the chicken neck, gizzard, and liver in the pan to prevent the chicken from sticking and place the chicken on top. By cooking the giblets in this way, you can then use them for giblet gravy (see page 64). To keep the chicken looking neat and to help it roast evenly, so all the meat is done at the same time, truss it as shown on the facing page.

Basic Roast Chicken

When you are roasting a chicken, remember that its quality makes all the difference. Follow the tips on pages 32 and 33 for selecting a superior bird, tracking one down at a good butcher shop or farmers' market. If you are pressed for time and end up at a supermarket, a kosher chicken is a good choice.

MAKES 4 MAIN-COURSE SERVINGS

1 chicken, about 4 pounds
Salt
Pepper
Butter

Preheat the oven to 500°F. Select a heavy roasting pan or skillet just large enough to hold the chicken. If the giblets were included with the bird, put the neck and gizzard on the center of the pan. Season the outside of the chicken with salt and pepper, then truss it as shown on the facing page. Place it in the pan, resting it on top of the neck and gizzard, if used. Fold a sheet of aluminum foil to create a triple thickness, making it just large enough to cover the breast. Rub butter evenly on one side of the folded foil, then place it, buttered side down, over the breast. This will help to slow down the cooking of the breast meat.

Roast the chicken for about 20 minutes, or until the thighs brown. Remove the foil and continue to roast for about 30 minutes more, or until an instant-read thermometer slid between a thigh and breast without touching bone reads 145°F. If you do not have a thermometer, tilt the chicken slightly so some of the juices run out of the cavity. The chicken is ready if the juices are clear but streaked with red. (The juices in the cavity go through three stages: murky pink, or underdone; clear streaked with red, or perfect; and clear, or overdone.)

Remove the pan from the oven, and transfer the chicken to a cutting board in a warm spot. Tent loosely with foil and let rest for 15 minutes before carving (see page 37).

Trussing and roasting a chicken

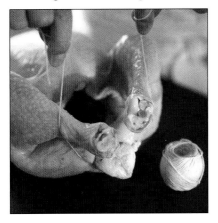

1. Cut a 3-foot length of string, and slide the center under the cavity end of the chicken.

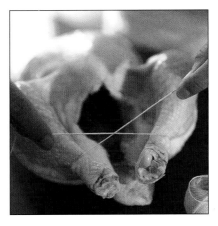

2. Pull the string in opposing directions to form an X.

3. Pull the string on the left under the right drumstick and the string on the right under the left drumstick, and then pull tight.

4. Pull the string back along the sides of the chicken.

5. Pull the string up, hooking the string under the wings.

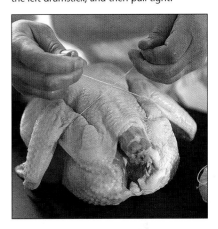

6. Pull the ends across the back and tie together into a knot.

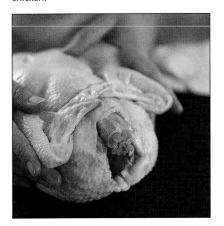

7. Tuck the wings behind the back.

8. Place the chicken on a bed of vegetables, and place a triple sheet of buttered aluminum foil over the breast.

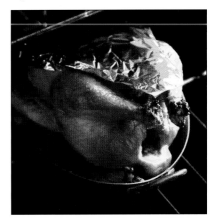

9. Roast until the thighs are well browned. Remove the foil and continue to roast until the juices in the cavity are clear with streaks of red.

Preparing a jus

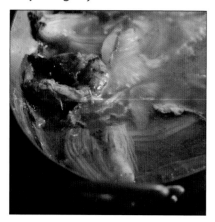

1. Place the roasting pan on high heat and boil down the juices until they caramelize and the fat floats on top in a clear layer.

2. Pour the fat out of the roasting pan.

3. Deglaze the pan with water or broth.

4. With the pan on high heat, scrape the bottom with a wooden spoon.

5. Strain the liquid.

Preparing a Chicken Jus

A jus is a gravy that has not been thickened. To make a successful jus, the juices on the bottom of the roasting pan must be caramelized, or cooked down until all of the liquid is gone and a savory golden crust has formed. If the juices haven't caramelized, put the roasting pan on the stove top and move it between medium and high heat until the juices boil down and caramelize and a layer of fat floats on the top. Discard the fat and add about 3/4 cup broth or water to the pan. Deglaze over high heat, scraping up the crust with a wooden spoon. Strain through a fine-mesh strainer into a saucepan or warmed sauceboat.

Carving a roast chicken

1. Slide a knife between the thigh and the breast.

2. Pull the thigh away from the breast with a carving fork.

3. Slide the knife into the breast meat just above the wing and cut through the wing joint; remove the wing.

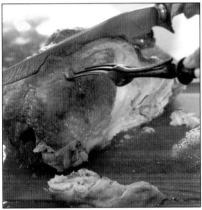

4. Slide the knife along the breastbone on the side with the thigh removed.

5. Pull the breast meat away from the bone. Repeat on the other side.

6. Serve the jus with the carved roast chicken in soup plates because the jus is very liquid.

Roast Chicken with Ricotta and Sage

Any number of ingredients can be stuffed under the skin of a chicken: chopped mushrooms (sautéed until tender and the moisture has evaporated), spinach (blanched and coarsely chopped), fresh cheeses, mornay sauce (thick béchamel with cheese), herb sprigs. All of these stuffings, except the herbs, help to protect the breast meat from overcooking.

MAKES 4 MAIN-COURSE BREAST SERVINGS AND 4 MAIN-COURSE LEFTOVER THIGH SERVINGS

Two 15-ounce tubs ricotta cheese

Salt

Pepper

8 fresh sage leaves, chopped, or 1 tablespoon chopped fresh marjoram

2 chickens, about 4 pounds each

Line a fine-mesh strainer with paper towels, place over a bowl, and spoon the ricotta into the strainer. Cover and refrigerate for at least 4 hours or up to overnight. Transfer the drained cheese to a bowl, season with salt and pepper, and stir in the sage.

Preheat the oven to 450°F. Select a heavy roasting pan or pans just large enough to hold the chickens without crowding. Using your fingers and starting at the cavity, carefully loosen the skin over the breasts of 1 chicken. Gently slide half of the ricotta mixture under the skin, covering the meat evenly, then pat the skin back into place. Repeat with the remaining ricotta mixture and the second chicken. Season the chickens on the outside with salt and pepper. If the giblets have been included with the chickens, place the neck and gizzard from each one in the roasting pan, and place the chickens on top.

Roast the chickens for about 1 hour, or until an instant-read thermometer slid between a thigh and breast without touching bone reads 145°F. If you do not have a thermometer, tilt a chicken slightly so some of the juices run out of the cavity. The chicken is ready if the juices are clear but streaked with red.

Remove the pan(s) from the oven and transfer the chickens to a cutting board (preferably one with a moat to catch juices) in a warm spot. Tent loosely with foil and let rest for 15 minutes before carving. Cut off the thighs and reserve for leftovers. Slide a knife along the breastbone, carefully lifting off the breast meat with its stuffing and crispy skin. Serve each diner a breast.

A Note on Doneness Temperatures

Most recipes for chicken, including those on store packaging, suggest far higher internal doneness temperatures than the ones I give in this chapter. In fact, salmonella and most harmful bacteria are killed at 137°F. Keep in mind, also, that most contamination from bacteria is on the surface of the chicken, not inside the tissues. For this reason, as long as the chicken spends enough time in a hot oven for the surface to get hot (including the surface in the cavity), the chicken is safe. A certain amount of pink on the thigh is normal in a properly cooked chicken. Also, directions that say to cook a chicken until the juices run clear will result in overcooking. The juices in the cavity should be clear but streaked with red.

Roast chicken with ricotta and sage

1. Stuff the ricotta under the skin on the breast of the chicken.

2. Chicken stuffed with ricotta.

3. Roast stuffed chicken.

Stuffing a Chicken

When you stuff the cavity of a chicken, you have to roast the chicken long enough for the stuffing to reach at least 137°F, the temperature at which most harmful bacteria are killed. This means that the meat of the chicken is much hotter and is invariably overdone. A better system is to stuff a flavorful mixture under the skin of the chicken, spreading it over the meat, or to slide herb sprigs, such as tarragon or parsley, between the skin and the meat. A substantial stuffing, such as the one in Roast Chicken with Ricotta and Sage (opposite), protects the breast meat from overcooking and encourages the formation of a crispy skin. The ideal way to serve these stuffed chickens is to give each diner a breast with its stuffing and reserve the thighs for another meal. If you have a stuffing you like that you typically stuff into the cavity, put it in a baking dish, cover the dish with aluminum foil, and cook it with the chicken. Then, if you like, spoon it into the cavity to serve it.

4. A serving of chicken breast stuffed with ricotta and with jus.

Roast Capon

A capon is a rooster that has been castrated at a young age. Such a bird is less aggressive than a rooster and develops tender flesh—and lots of it. Capons, especially when they are organic and free range, tend to be expensive, but their rich poultry flavor makes the extra investment well worth it. Capons should be roasted like small turkeys—started in a hot oven and finished in a moderate oven—and never allowed to overcook or they'll dry out. Make sure the capon you buy includes its giblets, which can often be found in a small bag tucked into the cavity or in the neck end.

MAKES ABOUT 12 MAIN-COURSE SERVINGS

1 capon, about 10 pounds
Salt
Pepper
Butter
1¹/₂ cups chicken broth (page 316), or as needed
2 tablespoons flour

Preheat the oven to 450°F. Select a heavy roasting pan just large enough to hold the capon. Put the liver, neck, and gizzard on the center of the pan. Season the outside of the capon with salt and pepper and place it in the pan, resting it on top of the liver, neck, and gizzard, if used. Fold a sheet of aluminum foil to create a triple thickness and so it is just large enough to cover the breast. Rub butter evenly on one side of the folded foil, then place it, buttered side down, over the breast. This will help to slow down the cooking of the breast meat.

Roast the capon for about 1 hour. Remove the foil and continue to roast for about 40 minutes more, or until a thermometer inserted between the thigh and the breast reads 140°F. If you do not have a thermometer, tilt the capon slightly so some of the juices run out of the cavity. The capon is ready if the juices are clear but streaked with red.

Transfer the capon to a platter, tent loosely with foil, and keep it in a warm spot while you make the gravy.

Remove the liver, gizzard, and neck from the pan and set the pan aside. Strip the meat from the neck and discard the skin and bones. In a food processor, combine the liver, gizzard, and neck meat and process until finely chopped, stopping before a paste forms. Set aside.

Check the juices in the roasting pan. If you have a lot of juices, transfer them to a glass pitcher, skim off the fat with a ladle, return 2 tablespoons of the fat to the pan, and discard the remaining fat. Set aside the pitcher holding the juices. If there is only a small amount of juices in the pan, place the pan on the stove top over high heat and boil down the juices until they caramelize on the bottom of the pan, forming a golden crust with a layer of fat on top. Pour off all but 2 tablespoons of the fat. If you have set aside a pitcher of juices, add broth to the juices to total 1¹/₂ cups. If you have caramelized the juices, measure out 1¹/₂ cups broth. Return the roasting pan to medium-high heat, add the flour to the fat, and cook, stirring, for 1 minute to cook the starch out of the flour. Pour in the broth or jus/broth mixture and stir constantly until the roux and the caramelized juices dissolve into the gravy and the gravy thickens to a nice consistency. Add the giblets, heat through, and season with salt and pepper. Pour into a warmed sauceboat.

Carve the capon as you would a turkey (see page 66) and serve with the gravy.

Poached Chicken

The secret to successful poached chicken is to have a pot in which the chicken fits as snugly as possible. Oval braising pots are best, but tall, narrow pots also work well. The reason for the exiguous pot is to use a minimum of liquid and thus dilute it as little as possible so the broth ends up concentrated.

The most classic rendition of poached chicken is the French *poule au pot*, the chicken that Henri IV declared every farmhouse family should enjoy on Sunday afternoons. History aside, the most simple approach to the dish was to submerge the chicken in the ever-present pot of long-cooking meat and vegetables, the pot-au-feu (page 177), and serve it with the broth and the usual aromatic vegetables (leeks, carrots, and celery). If you don't happen to have a pot-au-feu on the fire and want to make a simple poached chicken, find a container that fits the chicken, nestle the chicken in it, pour in enough broth just to cover, and add vegetables and a bouquet garni. To serve four people, use a 4-pound broiler-fryer. If serving six, use a larger roasting chicken.

You can use water or a simple broth to poach chicken. The ideal is to use the same poaching liquid repeatedly to poach successive chickens, freezing it between uses.

Poached Chicken with Spring Vegetables

This is a perfect dish to make when baby vegetables are in farmers' markets. Simply replace the large vegetables called for below with baby vegetables, using 12 each of carrots and turnips. When using large vegetables, I suggest removing the woody core from the carrots, a tedious task. Feel free to omit this step.

MAKES 6 MAIN-COURSE SERVINGS

1 roasting chicken, about 6 pounds
3 large carrots, peeled and cut into 2-inch sections
6 leeks, white and pale green parts only
2 large turnips
Bouquet garni (page 320)
4 quarts chicken broth (page 316), or as needed
40 fresh tarragon leaves
Salt
Pepper

Remove the chicken from the refrigerator, truss it (see page 34), and let it come to room temperature.

Meanwhile, prepare the vegetables. Stand each carrot section on one end and cut it into wedges—2, 3, 4, or 5, depending on the girth of the carrot. Cut the core out of each wedge (see page 11) and discard. Cut each leek in half lengthwise and rinse out any sand. Tie the leeks in a bundle with string. Cut off the root and stem ends of each turnip, then cut the turnip into wedges about 3/4 inch wide at the thicker end. Trim away the peel and excess flesh to create ovoid shapes (see page 10).

Put the chicken in a pot in which it fits snugly. Add the vegetables and bouquet garni, then pour in enough broth just to cover the chicken completely. Bring to a gentle simmer over high heat, skimming off any froth that forms on the surface with a ladle. Immediately reduce the heat to maintain a gentle simmer. Cook, uncovered, for about 1 hour, or until a skewer inserted into the breast causes only clear liquid to be released (you'll need to lift the chicken a little out of the poaching liquid).

Remove the chicken from the pot and place on a cutting board. Remove and discard the bouquet garni from the broth. Add the tarragon to the hot broth and season the broth with salt and pepper.

Pull the skin off the chicken and discard, then carve the chicken as shown on page 37. Divide the pieces among warmed soup plates. Using a slotted spoon, lift the vegetables out of the broth and arrange around the chicken, then ladle some of the hot broth over each serving.

Poached chicken with spring vegetables

1. Leeks cut in half lenthwise.

2. Poaching chicken with vegetables

3. Remove the skin from the chicken before serving.

Sautéed Chicken

You need to know only three secrets to make perfect sautéed chicken: use a good chicken, sauté it in butter or other flavorful fat, and don't overcook it. The flavor of sautéed chicken depends a lot on the cooking fat you use. The most tasty is butter or, for a more esoteric choice, goose or duck fat. Olive oil also imparts a good flavor but not as dramatic as that of butter. Butter delivers the best taste because the milk solids in the butter (where much of the flavor is) end up clinging to the chicken and caramelizing. Because sautéing skin-on chicken actually takes fat out of the chicken—the skin releases fat in the heat of the pan—rather than adding it, cooking in butter is a good way of getting the flavor of butter without the fat. The fat stays behind in the pan.

Sautéed Chicken

One of the great things about sautéed chicken is its versatility. While you can serve it plain straight from the skillet, you can make any number of sauces from the juices in the pan (see page 44). Take the bone out of each thigh as shown on page 45, so the thighs and breasts will be done at the same time.

MAKES 4 MAIN-COURSE SERVINGS

1 chicken, about 4 pounds, cut into 6 pieces (as shown on pages 45 and 46)
Salt
Pepper
4 tablespoons butter

Season the chicken pieces on both sides with salt and pepper. Select a skillet just large enough to accommodate the pieces in a single layer, without crowding. A nonstick pan is preferable because otherwise the skin sometimes sticks to the pan.

Melt the butter in the pan over medium heat. When it froths, add the chicken pieces, skin side down, and cook for about 12 minutes, or until the skin is browned and crispy. Turn the chicken over, flesh side down, and continue to cook for about 10 minutes more, or until the pieces feel firm to the touch. If you are not using a nonstick pan and the chicken sticks when you try to turn it, cook it a little longer. It often loosens on its own when the skin cooks a bit more. Serve the chicken immediately.

Sauces for Sautéed Chicken

Two approaches can be used to sauce your sautéed chicken. You can make a sauce independent of the cooking process, such as a mayonnaise (page 172), salsa, or relish, or you can deglaze the pan with wine, broth, or water and add flavorful ingredients to the liquid. Here are a few ideas; each recipe makes 4 servings unless otherwise noted.

WHITE WINE SAUCE WITH FRESH HERBS: Deglaze the pan used to cook the chicken with $1/2$ cup each dry white wine and concentrated chicken broth (page 316) and boil down to reduce by about two-thirds. Lower the heat to medium, add 1 tablespoon meat glaze (page 318), if available, and stir with a whisk until dissolved. (If you have used the meat glaze, you can omit the broth for deglazing.) Add 2 teaspoons finely chopped fresh marjoram or tarragon, then whisk in 4 tablespoons cold butter, cut into 4 slices, if desired. Do not allow the sauce to boil once the butter has been added. Season with salt and pepper.

FRESH TOMATO SAUCE: Deglaze the pan used to cook the chicken with $1/2$ cup dry white wine. Add 4 tomatoes, peeled, seeded, and chopped, and simmer over medium heat until the sauce has the consistency you like. Stir in 1 tablespoon finely chopped fresh tarragon or basil and season with salt and pepper. For a richer, more unctuous sauce, add $1/4$ to $1/2$ cup heavy cream with the tomatoes.

MUSHROOM SAUCE: Slice 1 pound mushrooms, preferably cremini. In a separate skillet, melt 2 tablespoons butter over medium heat. Add the mushrooms, raise the heat to high, and sauté for about 10 minutes, or until well browned. Deglaze the chicken pan with $1/2$ cup dry white wine or Madeira, then whisk in 1 tablespoon meat glaze (page 318). If the sauce starts to get too thick, thin it with some broth or water. Add the mushrooms to the sauce

and add 1 tablespoon chopped fresh tarragon or parsley. Season with salt and pepper. You can use wild mushrooms for this dish; if you use small mushrooms such as morels, leave them whole.

RED WINE SAUCE: Deglaze the pan in which the chicken was cooked with 1 cup dry red wine. Add 2 tablespoons meat glaze (page 318) and stir with a whisk to dissolve. Or, omit the meat glaze and add 1 cup broth. Boil down the sauce to a lightly syrupy consistency, then whisk in 4 tablespoons cold butter, cut into 4 slices. Do not allow the sauce to boil once the butter has been added. Season with salt and pepper.

SIMPLIFIED MEXICAN MOLE: This sauce tastes similar to a mole but is much simpler because it contains none of the traditional spices, nuts, or pumpkin seeds. In a bowl, combine 4 assorted dried chiles, such as ancho, guajillo, pasilla, and/or mulato, with hot water to cover and let stand to soften for 30 minutes. In a large skillet, warm 3 tablespoons olive oil over medium heat. Add 1 large onion, minced, and 3 cloves garlic, minced, and let sweat for about 10 minutes, or until the onion is translucent. Add 3 pounds tomatillos, papery skins removed and quartered, reduce the heat to medium-low, and cook, stirring every few minutes, for about 20 minutes, or until the tomatillos soften and break apart. Drain, seed, and mince the reconstituted chiles and add to the pan along with 2 chipotle chiles in adobo sauce, rinsed, seeded, and minced. Cook, stirring occasionally, for 5 minutes to blend the flavors. Process until smooth in a food processor and pass through a strainer. Return to the skillet, reheat gently, and add 1 bunch cilantro, finely chopped. Season with salt. Makes 8 servings, enough to sauce a double recipe of Sautéed Chicken. Top with sour cream or crumbled *queso fresco*, if desired.

Cutting up a chicken

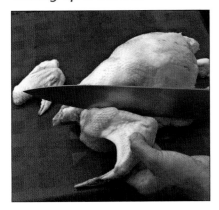

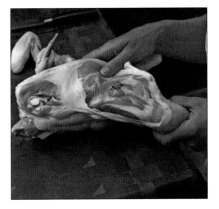

1. With the chicken breast side down, cut off each wing where it joins a breast. Cut around and out from the joint so you don't damage the breast meat.

2. Turn the chicken breast side up. Cut through the skin on the top of the thigh where it joins the breast. Cut through the skin along the side of the thigh.

3. Once you have cut through the skin, snap out the thigh joint. The thigh will still be attached to the body.

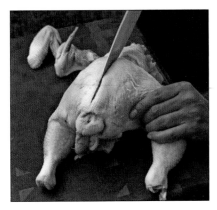

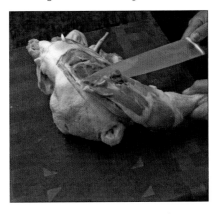

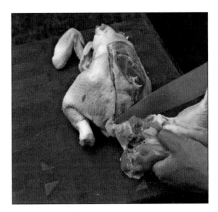

4. Make a cut along the center of the back where the thigh joins the rest of the body.

5. Cut under the thigh where it attaches to the body, being sure to leave the "oyster" attached to the thigh.

6. Continue cutting the thigh away from the back until the leg is fully detached.

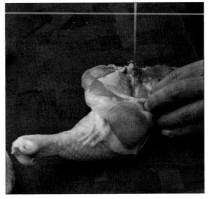

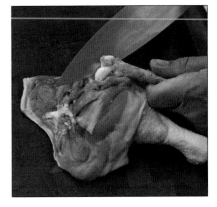

7. Repeat with the other thigh.

8. To remove the thigh bone from the leg, slide a knife under and around it.

9. Cut through the joint and remove the thigh bone.

continued

Cutting up a chicken, continued

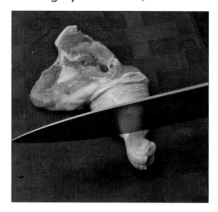

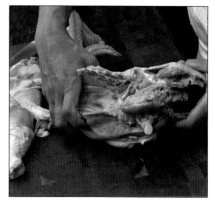

10. Remove the "nub" from the ends of the legs by hammering on a knife with a mallet or rolling pin.

11. Hold the chicken on end, with the breast-bone pointing up, and cut through the ribs to separate the back from the whole breast.

12. Snap the back away from the breasts.

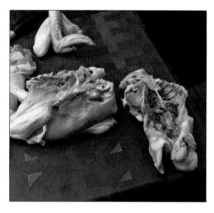

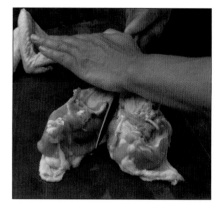

13. Cut the back to separate it from the breast.

14. With the knife held vertically, cut through the cartilage that separates the breasts.

15. Press down to break through the breast-bone and separate the breast into two halves.

16. Chicken cut up into 6 serving pieces.

Chicken Fricassee

A chicken fricassee is a specific dish—chicken simmered with broth, cream, mushrooms, and pearl onions, and the sauce thickened with egg yolks—but it also describes a specific technique: cooking partly in fat, partly in liquid. The chicken is lightly sautéed on both sides until it barely begins to brown, the cooking fat is thrown out, and liquid is added. The chicken finishes cooking in the simmering liquid, and the liquid, usually based on broth, is converted into a sauce. Fricasseeing made more sense when chickens were older and required long cooking to become tender. Nowadays, a fricasseed chicken is almost impossible to distinguish from a sautéed one.

Chicken with Sherry and Mushrooms

You can use nearly any wine or good white wine vinegar to make this dish. You can also use hard cider or a mixture of equal parts cider vinegar and sweet (apple) cider in place of the wine. Although I have given the option of sautéing the chicken in olive oil, butter will result in a better flavor.

MAKES 4 MAIN-COURSE SERVINGS

1 chicken, about 4 pounds, cut into 6 pieces (as shown on pages 45 and 46)
Salt
Pepper
4 tablespoons butter or olive oil
¹/₂ cup dry sherry
10 ounces button mushrooms or larger mushrooms, sliced if large
¹/₂ cup heavy cream
2 tablespoons meat glaze (page 318), optional

Season the chicken pieces on both sides with salt and pepper. Select a skillet just large enough to accommodate the pieces in a single layer, without crowding. A nonstick pan is preferable because the skin sometimes sticks to the pan.

Melt the butter or heat the olive oil in the pan over medium heat. When the butter froths or the oil ripples, add the chicken pieces, skin side down, and cook for about 7 minutes, or until the skin barely begins to brown. Turn the chicken over, flesh side down, and continue to cook for about 5 minutes, or until lightly browned. Transfer the chicken pieces to a platter, and pour the fat out of the pan.

Return the chicken pieces to the pan, add the sherry and mushrooms, and place over low heat. Cover and simmer gently for about 20 minutes, or until the chicken is just firm to the touch. Transfer the chicken to a platter, cover, and place in a warm spot.

Add the cream and meat glaze to the liquid in the pan, stir with a whisk to dissolve the glaze, and boil down over high heat for 3 to 5 minutes, or until the sauce forms a lightly syrupy consistency. Season with salt and pepper.

Spoon the sauce over the chicken and serve immediately.

Chicken with Wild Mushrooms

This is one of the most delicious dishes you can make with chicken. The only disadvantage is the high cost of the wild mushrooms. You can also use fresh mushrooms in place of the dried mushrooms. Purchase 12 ounces, rinse and dry them well, and slice them if large or, if they're small, leave whole. Sauté in butter until well browned then add to the sauce just before serving.

MAKES 4 MAIN-COURSE SERVINGS

2 legs and 2 breasts from one 4-pound chicken
Salt
Pepper
4 tablespoons butter
1 cup (1 ounce) dried morel mushrooms, soaked
   in warm water just to cover for 30 minutes
3/4 cup (0.7 ounce) dried porcini mushrooms,
   soaked warm water just to cover for 1 hour
1/2 cup dry sherry
1 cup heavy cream

Season the chicken pieces on both sides with salt and pepper. Select a skillet just large enough to accommodate the pieces in a single layer, without crowding. A nonstick pan is preferable because the skin sometimes sticks to the pan.

Melt the butter in the pan over medium heat. When the butter froths, add the chicken pieces, skin side down, and cook for about 7 minutes, or until the skin barely begins to brown. Turn the chicken over, flesh side down, and continue to cook for about 5 minutes, or until lightly browned. Transfer the chicken pieces to a platter, and pour the fat out of the pan.

Meanwhile, lift the mushrooms out of their soaking water and squeeze them gently to release any water back into the bowls. Return the chicken to the pan, add the mushrooms and sherry, and then carefully pour in the soaking water, leaving any grit behind in the bowls. Cover and simmer gently for about 20 minutes, or until the chicken is just firm to the touch. Check from time to time to make sure that the liquid has not evaporated. Add water as needed to prevent scorching. Transfer the chicken to a platter, tent with foil, and place in a warm spot.

Add the cream to the pan and simmer for about 5 minutes, or until the sauce is a consistency you like. Spoon the sauce over the chicken.

Moroccan-Style Chicken with Almonds, Dried Apricots, and Chickpeas

You won't find this exact dish in Morocco, but the delicate interplay of spices and textures makes it reminiscent of Moroccan cooking at its best. I use only chicken thighs here because they can cook longer than breasts without drying out. Don't be alarmed if the yogurt seems to have curdled; this is normal.

MAKES 4 MAIN-COURSE SERVINGS

4 large chicken legs

Salt

Pepper

1/4 cup olive oil

4 tablespoons butter

1 large onion, finely chopped

2 tablespoons grated fresh ginger

1/2 teaspoon ground cinnamon

Pinch of saffron threads, soaked in 1 tablespoon hot water for 30 minutes

1 cup plain Greek-style yogurt

2 cups chicken broth (page 316) or water

One 14 1/2-ounce can chickpeas, drained and rinsed

1/4 pound dried apricots, halved

3 tablespoons finely chopped fresh cilantro

2/3 cup slivered blanched almonds, toasted

Season the chicken thighs on both sides with salt and pepper. Select a skillet just large enough to accommodate the pieces in a single layer, without crowding. A nonstick pan is preferable because the skin sometimes sticks to the pan.

Heat the olive oil in the pan over medium to high heat. When the oil ripples, add the chicken thighs, skin side down, and cook for about 7 minutes, or until the skin barely begins to brown. Turn the chicken over, flesh side down, and continue to cook for about 5 minutes, or until lightly browned. Transfer the chicken thighs to a platter, and pour the fat out of the pan.

Return the pan to medium heat and add the butter. When the butter melts, add the onion and cook, stirring every minute or two, for about 7 minutes, or until translucent. Add the ginger, cinnamon, and saffron and its soaking water and then whisk in the yogurt. Cook for 1 minute more, then return the thighs to the pan. Add the broth, chickpeas, and apricots and cover the pan. Simmer gently for about 20 minutes, or until the chicken is just firm to the touch.

Sprinkle the cilantro over the chicken and season with salt and pepper. Transfer the chicken to warmed plates and spoon the sauce over the top. Sprinkle with the almonds and serve right away.

Moroccan-style chicken with almonds, dried apricots, and chickpeas

1. Brown the chicken on both sides in oil.

2. Simmer the chicken with the yogurt, broth, chickpeas, and apricots.

3. Finished Moroccan-style chicken.

Chicken Potpies

These potpies appear here because, like the other recipes in this section on fricasseeing, the chicken is simmered in liquid just until cooked through, or short braised. Most potpies suffer from a soggy bottom crust. To avoid this, I make them in large ramekins and put the pastry only on the top. I have used puff pastry here, but regular pie pastry will also work. Tarragon is delicious with chicken, but feel free to substitute other herbs, such as marjoram, chives, parsley, or oregano. If you don't have shiitake mushrooms, use white or cremini mushrooms. For a splurge, add as many sliced black truffles as you can afford to each ramekin. The pastry traps the aroma of the truffle, which is released at the moment the diner cuts into the pie.

MAKES 6 MAIN-COURSE SERVINGS

3 boneless, skinless chicken breasts, cut into
   $3/4$-inch cubes
$1/2$ pound shiitake mushrooms, stems removed
   and caps thinly sliced
Salt
Pepper
3 thin carrots, peeled and thinly sliced
Leaves from 1 bunch tarragon
2 cups chicken broth (page 316)
1 cup heavy cream
Two 1-pound packages all-butter puff pastry,
   thawed overnight in the refrigerator if frozen
1 egg, beaten with 1 teaspoon salt

Divide the chicken evenly among six 1-cup ramekins. Sprinkle the mushrooms evenly over the chicken, dividing them evenly. Season with salt and pepper. Sprinkle the carrots over the top and finally the tarragon. Press down on the filling in each ramekin so none of the ingredients rise above the rim. (If the ingredients touch the pastry, the pastry will tear.) Pour $1/3$ cup of the broth and $2^{1}/_2$ tablespoons of the cream evenly over each filled ramekin. Season again with salt and pepper.

Preheat the oven to 375°F. On a lightly floured work surface, roll out the pastry about $1/8$ inch thick. Cut out 6 rounds about 2 inches larger in diameter than the rim of the ramekins. Using a sharp paring knife, and working from the center to the edge, make a series of arcs, like spokes, on the surface of each round, being careful not to cut through the dough. Flip each round, brush with the beaten egg, then invert a round over each ramekin (the scored side will be facing up). Press the dough firmly against the sides with your palms until it adheres securely. Brush the pastry with the beaten egg. Place the pies on a sheet pan.

Slide the pan into the oven and bake the pies for about 35 minutes, or until the crust is golden brown and has puffed. Serve at once.

Chicken potpies

1. Cut the chicken into cubes.

2. Put the chicken in large ramekins.

3. Add the remaining ingredients to the ramekins.

4. Cut the pastry into rounds, and make a series of arcs, like spokes, on each round.

5. Lay a pastry round over the top of a ramekin, and press securely against the sides.

6. Finished potpies.

Long-Braised Chicken

When chicken is cooked in a fricassee, it is short braised, which means that the meat has been simmered in liquid just long enough for it to cook through (see page 13). In contrast, long braising involves extended cooking to break down the tough muscle and sinew you find in an old hen or a rooster. Although it is rare nowadays to encounter these more mature birds for sale in a grocery store, it's helpful to understand the technique once used to cook them. The technique also works for chicken thighs.

Coq au Vin

For this traditional dish, I braise a rooster in red wine, but other wine will work as well, as will a broth made from wine and chicken parts (see Cooking Chicken in Red Wine, page 54). The classic garnish for coq au vin—the vegetables or other foods that you serve on top of or around the bird—is included here: pearl onions, bacon, and button mushrooms, but feel free to use one of your own invention (wild mushrooms are wonderful). If using chicken thighs, reduce the simmering time to $1^1/_2$ hours.

MAKES 8 MAIN-COURSE SERVINGS

1 rooster, 7 to 10 pounds, or 8 large chicken thighs
3 cups dry red wine or red wine broth (see note)
1 onion, sliced
1 large carrot, peeled and sliced
3 cloves garlic, crushed
Bouquet garni (page 320)
$^3/_4$ pound thick-cut bacon slices
Salt
Pepper
2 tablespoons meat glaze (page 318), optional
$1^1/_4$ pounds button mushrooms, left whole, or
    larger mushrooms, quartered vertically
Two 10-ounce packages pearl onions, blanched
    in boiling water for 1 minute, drained, rinsed
    under cold water, and peeled
3 tablespoons butter
3 tablespoons flour

If using a rooster, cut it into 6 pieces as shown on pages 45 and 46. Cut each breast piece in half crosswise. Turn each leg skin-side down and cut along the line of fat between the thigh and drumstick to separate the two. You will have a total of 8 pieces.

If time permits, put the rooster pieces in a large bowl and add the wine, onion, carrot, garlic, and bouquet garni. Cover and marinate overnight in the refrigerator. If you don't have time to marinate, have the marinade ingredients ready for adding later.

Cut the bacon slices into lardons, or strips about 1 inch long and $^1/_4$ inch wide and thick. In a deep sauté pan large enough to hold the chicken pieces in a single layer, cook the bacon over medium heat, stirring occasionally, for about 10 minutes, or until it renders its fat and is lightly crispy. Remove the pan from the heat and, using a slotted spoon, transfer the bacon to a bowl and reserve.

Take the rooster pieces out of the marinade, reserving the marinade. Pat the pieces dry and season on both sides with salt and pepper. Return the pan to medium to high heat. When the bacon fat is hot, add the rooster pieces, skin side down, and cook for about 8 minutes, or until browned on the first side. Turn the pieces flesh side down and cook for another 8 minutes, or until browned on the second side. Transfer the pieces to a plate, and discard the fat from the pan.

continued

Coq au vin

1. Combine wine, aromatic vegetables, and a bouquet garni for marinating the rooster.

2. Cut the bacon into lardons.

3. Render the lardons in a sauté pan over medium heat.

4. Season the rooster pieces and brown in the rendered bacon fat.

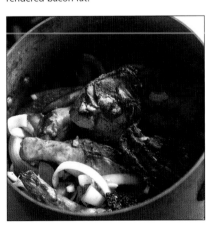

5. Put the browned rooster pieces in a pot, pour the marinade ingredients over the top, cover, and simmer gently.

6. Finished coq au vin.

Place the rooster pieces in a clean pot in which they fit snugly. Pour the marinade ingredients over the pieces and stir in the meat glaze. Cover the pot with a sheet of aluminum foil, pressing it down slightly in the middle so that moisture will condense on its underside and drip down onto the rooster pieces, and then with a lid. Bring to the simmer over high heat and then turn down the heat to maintain at the barest simmer. Simmer for about 3 hours, or until a knife slides easily in and out of a thigh.

One hour into the cooking, remove about $1/4$ cup of the braising liquid and put it in a saucepan with the mushrooms. Place over low heat, cover, and steam for about 12 minutes, or until the mushrooms are tender. (Or, you can sauté the mushrooms in butter.) Pour the mushroom liquid back into the pan with the rooster, and set the mushrooms aside. At the same time, remove about $1/4$ cup of the braising liquid and put it in a saucepan with the pearl onions. Place over medium-low heat, cover partially, and cook for about 15 minutes, or until a knife easily slides through an onion. If the liquid evaporates before the onions are done, add a few tablespoons more braising liquid. Pour the onion liquid back into the pan with the rooster, and set the onions aside.

When the rooster is done, transfer the pieces to a warmed platter or individual plates, cover, and set aside in a warm place. Strain the braising liquid through a fine-mesh strainer into a saucepan, and boil down until reduced to about $1 1/2$ cups. Work the butter and flour together with the back of a fork to make a smooth paste, or *beurre manié*. Whisk half of the paste into the simmering liquid, simmer the liquid briefly, and check the consistency, adding more paste if needed to achieve a good consistency. Season with salt and pepper.

To serve, spoon the thickened braising liquid over the rooster pieces, and then spoon the garnishes—mushrooms, pearl onions, bacon—on top and around the rooster pieces.

VARIATIONS: You can use dry white wine in place of the red wine and give the dish the name of the wine, such as *coq au Riesling*. The garnish of pearl onions, bacon, and mushrooms can be replaced with spring vegetables, wild mushrooms, artichoke hearts, or any of the suggestions on page 18.

Cooking Chicken in Red Wine

Unless you are making an authentic coq au vin (page 52), chicken with a red wine sauce made by simmering the chicken in the wine doesn't cook long enough to eliminate the harsh acidity and tannins in the wine. One way to attenuate this harshness is to simmer the wine with an equal amount of broth, or with 3 tablespoons meat glaze (page 318), per bottle of wine for 3 hours before you combine it with the chicken. But the best technique is to make a red wine broth by browning chicken parts as if making chicken broth (page 316) and replacing the water with red wine. Once you have this broth in hand, use it in a fricassee to finish cooking the chicken or use it to deglaze a pan in which you have sautéed chicken.

Breaded Chicken Breasts

Many of us eat boneless, skinless chicken breasts because we think they're good for us, but we also complain about their lack of flavor. The best trick for keeping the breasts flavorful is to cook them with the bone and skin intact and then peel off the skin and remove the bones—a towel helps with this—once the breasts are cooked. If you're going to sauté a boneless, skinless breast, it's best to bread it lightly and cook it in butter.

Most of us have tasted foods that have been breaded unsuccessfully; the breading is soggy, oily, tastes burnt, and/or slides off the food. To prevent sogginess and to keep the breading intact, bread the breasts just before you cook them, be careful not to overcook them, and serve them the moment they are cooked. If you let the breaded breasts sit before you cook them, the coating will absorb moisture, which will cause it to turn soggy and slip off in the pan. Overcooking produces the same result because the breasts release liquid, turning the breading soggy. Also, don't follow the advice common in many cookbooks that instruct you to pound the breasts until they are very thin. This breaks down the tissue and makes it harder to avoid overcooking. It's better to pound the breasts only lightly, using the side of a cleaver to flatten the thicker part of the breast until it is the same thickness as the thinner part.

Another way to ensure success is to make sure the breading is thin. Use fresh bread crumbs and work them through a drum sieve or fine-mesh strainer so they are very fine. This guarantees they will absorb minimal fat. Cook the breasts in butter or extra virgin olive oil (the heat is gentle enough not to destroy the flavor of the oil). If you are using butter, it's best to use clarified butter (page 6), so specks of milk solids don't cling to the surface of the breading and burn.

Chicken Breasts à la Milanaise

The French are forever naming dishes after countries and cities. When bread crumbs alone are used as a coating on chicken cutlets, the dish is known as *à l'anglaise*; when the same chicken is garnished with cooked egg whites and yolks, capers, and parsley, it becomes *à la viennoise*. These chicken breasts, coated with fresh bread crumbs and Parmesan cheese, are called *à la milanaise*.

MAKES 4 MAIN-COURSE SERVINGS

5 slices slightly stale, dense-crumb white bread, crusts removed

2 ounces Parmigiano-Reggiano cheese, finely grated

4 boneless, skinless chicken breasts

Flour

1 egg

Salt

Pepper

4 tablespoons butter, preferably clarified (page 6), or extra virgin olive oil

Optional Sauce

4 tablespoons butter or extra virgin olive oil

4 fresh sage leaves

continued

Tear the bread into pieces, place in a food processor, and pulse to form crumbs. Pass the crumbs through a fine-mesh strainer or a drum sieve so the crumbs are uniformly fine. Work the cheese through the strainer and combine with the bread crumbs on a plate.

Using the side of a cleaver, lightly pound each breast until the thicker part of the breast is the same thickness as the thinner part. Spread some flour on a plate. In a shallow bowl, beat the egg until blended, then season generously with salt and pepper. Working with 1 chicken breast at a time, coat evenly on both sides with the flour, patting off the excess. Next, dip the breast in the egg, and then, holding the breast above the bowl by one end, wipe off the excess egg by sliding a thumb and index finger along its length. Finally, lay the breast on the bread crumb mixture, turn to coat both sides, and transfer to a plate. Repeat with the remaining chicken breasts.

Select a skillet or sauté pan just large enough to hold the breasts in a single layer and preferably nonstick. Place over low to medium heat and melt the butter. Gently place the breaded breasts in the pan—don't use tongs; use your fingers so as not to tear through the breading—in a single layer. Cook, moving the pan every minute or so to ensure the breasts cook evenly, for about 6 minutes, or until golden brown on the first side. Using a spatula or your fingertips, turn the chicken over and cook for about 6 minutes on the second side, or until golden brown and just firm to the touch. Transfer the breasts to warmed plates and serve immediately, or set aside in a warm place if preparing the sauce. Pour the fat out of the pan.

If making the sauce, return the pan to medium heat and add the butter and sage leaves. When the butter melts, heat for a minute or two until the sage releases its fragrance and the butter froths.

Place a sage leaf on each breast and spoon the butter over the top. Serve at once.

Chicken Breasts with Capers and Lemon

Capers and lemon cut the richness of these breasts and provide a bright, unexpected note that lightens the whole effect.

MAKES 4 MAIN-COURSE SERVINGS

10 slices slightly stale, dense-crumb white bread, crusts removed
4 boneless, skinless chicken breasts
Flour
2 eggs
Salt
Pepper
4 tablespoons butter, preferably clarified (page 6)
¹/₂ cup (1 stick) butter
3 tablespoons capers, drained
Juice of ¹/₂ lemon

Tear the bread into pieces, place in a food processor, and pulse to form crumbs. Pass the crumbs through a fine-mesh strainer or a drum sieve so the crumbs are uniformly fine. Spread the bread crumbs on a plate.

Using the side of a cleaver, lightly pound each breast until the thicker part of the breast is the same thickness as the thinner part. Place some flour in a shallow bowl. In a second shallow bowl, beat the eggs until blended, then season generously with salt and pepper. Working with 1 chicken breast at a time, coat evenly on both sides with the flour, patting off the excess. Next, dip the breast in the egg, and then, holding the breast above the bowl by one end, wipe off the excess egg by sliding a thumb and index finger along its length. Finally, lay the breast on the bread crumbs, turn to coat both sides, and transfer to a plate. Repeat with the remaining chicken breasts.

Chicken breasts with capers and lemon

1. Cut the crusts off the bread slices.

2. Pulse the bread in a food processor to form crumbs, and work the crumbs through a fine-mesh strainer or drum sieve.

3. Working one at a time, coat the breasts with the flour. Then, dip the flour-coated breasts in the egg.

4. Finally, coat the breasts with bread crumbs.

5. Cook the breasts until golden brown and firm to the touch.

6. Finished chicken breasts with capers and lemon.

Select a skillet or sauté pan just large enough to hold the breasts in a single layer and preferably nonstick. Place over low to medium heat and add the clarified butter. When the butter begins to ripple, gently place the breaded breasts in the pan—don't use tongs, which can tear through the breading; use your fingers—in a single layer. Cook, moving the pan every minute or so to ensure the breasts cook evenly, for about 6 minutes, or until golden brown on the first side. Using a spatula or your fingertips, turn the chicken over and cook for about 6 minutes on the second side, or until golden brown and just firm to the touch. Transfer the breasts to warmed plates and set aside in a warm place. Pour the fat out of the pan.

Return the pan to medium heat and add the 1/2 cup butter. When the butter has melted, add the capers and lemon juice and heat until the butter froths. Spoon the sauce over the breasts and serve right away.

Fried Chicken

In the old days, chicken was fried with beef suet, the rendered fat from around the kidneys of a steer, but nowadays most of us use vegetable oil for frying. Vegetable oil has its advantages. It contains no cholesterol and has a high smoke point. However, it also has no flavor or, worse, a vague fishy taste. A better alternative is so-called pure olive oil, commonly referred to as olive oil. Admittedly, it has little flavor, but the flavor it does have is inoffensive and the oil is inexpensive. Don't use extra virgin olive oil for frying. The high heat destroys its flavor, so it isn't worth the expense. Three other good choices for frying are duck or goose fat or peanut oil.

Some of the best fried chicken is made by flouring the chicken, patting off the excess flour, and then plunging the chicken into the hot oil. You can also make a light batter. Whisk together flour and water until you have a mixture with the consistency of heavy cream, then let the batter stand for an hour before you use it. (This relaxes the gluten so the batter doesn't shrink and expose patches of the chicken during frying.) You can also make the buttermilk batter shown below. Whatever batter you decide to use, avoid eggs or at least egg yolks. They'll give the chicken a burnt egg flavor and smell.

Buttermilk Fried Chicken

Here, each chicken is cut into 10 pieces—each half breast is cut in half and the thighs and drumsticks are separated—so the portions are easier to manage. The simple batter, a mixture of buttermilk and flour, can be given a spark of heat with the addition of cayenne pepper.

MAKES 8 MAIN-COURSE SERVINGS

2 chickens, about 4 pounds each
Salt
Pepper
3 cups buttermilk
2 cups flour
1 teaspoon cayenne pepper, optional
Olive oil for frying

Cut each chicken into 6 serving pieces as shown on pages 45 and 46, but leave the bones in the thighs. Cut each breast piece in half crosswise. Turn each leg skin-side down and cut along the line of fat that runs between the thigh and drumstick to separate the two. Each chicken will yield 10 pieces.

Season the chicken pieces on both sides with salt and pepper. Place the pieces in a bowl, pour over the buttermilk, toss to coat, and refrigerate for at least 4 hours or up to overnight

Combine the flour and cayenne in a large baking dish or a rimmed sheet pan.

Line a platter with paper towels. Pour the olive oil to a depth of at least 4 inches into a deep fryer or deep, heavy pot and heat to 350°F. Drain the chicken pieces and pat dry with paper towels. One at a time, dip the chicken pieces into the flour mixture and lower them into the hot oil. Fry, turning the pieces gently every couple of minutes, for about 10 minutes, or until evenly golden brown. Using tongs, transfer to the paper towel–lined platter to drain briefly. Serve immediately.

Buttermilk fried chicken

1. Soak the chicken in buttermilk for at least 4 hours or up to overnight.

2. Drain the chicken, pat dry, and coat evenly with flour.

3. Immerse the chicken, one piece at a time, in the hot oil.

Sauces for Fried Chicken

Many people are surprised to discover that fried chicken was popular in eighteenth-century France and that it was always served with a sauce. *Sauce poivrade*, made by infusing pepper with vinegar and the cooking juices from the chicken trimmings, was particularly common. Fried chicken is also delicious served with a flavored homemade mayonnaise, such as aioli, aioli with saffron, curry mayonnaise, mustard mayonnaise, mayonnaise with chopped grilled peppers, mayonnaise with chiles, or herb mayonnaise. Or, set out an assortment of mayonnaises to accompany fried chicken.

4. Serve the chicken with a flavored mayonnaise, if desired.

Stir-Fried Chicken

Chicken is a good candidate for stir-frying because it cooks quickly and remains tender. At the same time, any vegetables cooked with chicken keep their crunch and fresh flavor. To ensure a stir-fry cooks rapidly, all the components are cut into small pieces of about the same size. Stir-frying was favored originally as a way to conserve fuel, but now the technique has been embraced because of its healthfulness. Be sure to have the wok or sauté pan very hot before adding any food.

Stir-Fried Chicken with Snow Peas, Orange, and Cashews

This dish (pictured on page 24) is an interesting study in textures, as each element has its own identity. To achieve thin, uniform onion slices, use a mandoline or other vegetable slicer, if possible. Accompany the stir-fry with steamed white rice.

MAKES 6 MAIN-COURSE SERVINGS

2 pounds boneless, skinless chicken breasts

1 tablespoon cornstarch

1 orange

1 clove garlic, minced

1 tablespoon toasted sesame oil

$^1/_4$ cup soy sauce

3 tablespoons canola oil

3 slices fresh ginger, about $^1/_8$ inch thick

1 onion, thinly sliced

2 serrano chiles, seeded and minced

1 cup roasted cashews

2 bell peppers, seeded and cut lengthwise into narrow strips or crosswise into narrow rounds and the rounds halved

$^1/_2$ pound snow peas, ends trimmed

Salt

Pepper

Cut the chicken breasts on the diagonal across the grain into strips about $^3/_4$ inch thick. Place in a bowl, add the cornstarch, and toss to coat evenly.

Using a paring knife, remove 2 strips of zest, each 2 inches long, from the orange. Then halve the orange, and squeeze the juice into the bowl holding the chicken. Add the garlic, sesame oil, and soy sauce and toss to mix well.

In a wok or large sauté pan, heat the canola oil, ginger, and orange zest strips over medium heat for 2 minutes, or until fragrant, then raise the heat to high. After the ginger and orange zest have sizzled for a minute or two, add the onion. Toss and stir constantly for about 5 minutes, or until the onion slices begin to soften. Drain the chicken, reserving its marinade, and add to the pan with the chiles. Stir-fry for about 2 minutes, or until the chicken begins to turn opaque. Add the cashews, bell peppers, and snow peas and toss and stir for about 3 minutes, or until the chicken pieces feel firm to the touch. Stir in the marinade and continue to stir for about 30 seconds, or until the sauce thickens slightly. Serve at once.

Grilled Chicken

Few foods take better to the grill than chicken. Two precautions prevail, however: be careful not to overcook the chicken or it will be dry, and always cook the flesh side first to prevent flare-ups. (If you are using a gas grill, grill the flesh side over high heat, and then turn down the heat to medium to cook the skin side.) The chicken is done when it is just firm to the touch, no longer. The timing will vary, depending on the size of the chicken pieces and the intensity of the fire. For more on grilling, see page 21.

Grilled Wine-and-Herb-Marinated Chicken

In this dish, the chicken is marinated (unless you're in a hurry) to provide extra flavor. The wine does not tenderize the chicken, as many people assume, but it does flavor it. The only foods that truly tenderize chicken are certain tropical fruits, such as papaya and pineapple, that contain an enzyme that breaks down protein. Never allow the chicken to remain in one of these fruit marinades for too long, or the meat will turn mushy.

MAKES 4 MAIN-COURSE SERVINGS

1 cup dry white wine

1 small onion, sliced

10 thyme sprigs

1 imported bay leaf

1 chicken, about 4 pounds, cut into 6 pieces
   (as shown on pages 45 and 46)

Salt

Pepper

To make the marinade, in a large bowl, combine the wine, onion, thyme, and bay leaf. Add the chicken and turn to coat with the marinade. Cover and refrigerate for at least 4 hours or up to overnight.

Prepare a medium-hot fire for direct grilling in a grill (see page 21). Take the chicken pieces out of the marinade, pat dry, and season on both sides with salt and pepper.

Place the chicken pieces, flesh side down, on the grill rack and grill for 12 to 15 minutes, or until well browned. Turn the chicken skin side down and move it over medium heat to prevent flare-ups. (In a charcoal grill, this lower heat will be the automatic result of letting the coals sit long enough to become covered with ash. If using a gas grill, turn down the heat to medium.) Cook for 12 to 15 minutes, or until the skin is golden brown and the chicken is just firm to the touch. (Alternatively, insert an instant-read thermometer into the thickest part of a breast without touching bone; it should read 140°F.) Transfer to a platter and serve.

Sautéed Chicken Livers

Chicken livers are one of the least expensive—and tastiest—meats you can buy. Look for moist, shiny livers free of dry patches, and use them right away, as they sour quickly. Always sauté them on the highest possible heat to ensure they brown nicely, and keep in mind that they spatter during cooking, so stand back to avoid burns.

Sautéed Chicken Livers with Thyme

Chicken livers are especially prized for making a rich, creamy mousse (page 310) for spreading on toast or crackers, but they are also good sautéed and served with a pan-deglazed sauce. Be sure to pat them thoroughly dry before you cook them so they will brown well.

MAKES 4 FIRST-COURSE SERVINGS

8 large chicken livers

Salt

Pepper

1/4 cup olive oil

1 shallot, minced

Leaves from 3 thyme sprigs, or 1/4 teaspoon
  dried thyme

1/3 cup red vermouth

1 tablespoon meat glaze (page 318), optional

2 tablespoons Cognac or Armagnac, optional

3 tablespoons cold butter, cut into 3 slices

Using a paring knife, trim away and discard any white membranes or green patches from the livers. Pat them dry and season well with salt and pepper.

Line a plate with paper towels. In a skillet just large enough to accommodate the livers, heat the olive oil over high heat. When it starts to smoke, add the livers and cook for 2 to 3 minutes, or until browned. Turn the livers over and cook on the second side for about 2 minutes, or until they are browned and just firm to the touch. Transfer the livers to the paper towel–lined plate. Pour off the fat from the pan.

Return the pan to medium heat. Add the shallot and thyme to the hot pan and stir until they release their fragrance. Add the vermouth, meat glaze, and Cognac and stir with a whisk to dissolve the meat glaze. Stand back from the pan, as a fire can ignite easily, especially if you have a gas stove. If the sauce starts to get too thick, add a little water, a tablespoon at a time, to thin to a good consistency. Whisk in the butter until emulsified. Do not allow the sauce to boil. Season with salt and pepper.

Divide the livers among warmed plates and spoon the sauce over the top. Serve at once.

Turkey

Many of us only cook turkey for holiday dinners. But these big birds are a great value—a single roast provides leftovers for days—making them well worth cooking the rest of the year.

The biggest worry when cooking a turkey is that you will overcook it. Here are three secrets to a perfectly roasted bird: First, following the advice of most cookbooks or magazine or newspaper articles—to say nothing of the directions on the turkey package or the folly of those plastic pop-up thermometers—on the correct doneness temperature is a guarantee of disaster. If you don't want to sit down to a dry bird, the temperature of the inner part of the turkey, where the thigh meets the back, should never measure more than 140°F. Second, cover the breast meat with a triple layer of aluminum foil for half of the roasting time. This slows down the cooking and prevents the meat from drying out. Third, forgo stuffing the turkey. Otherwise, you will be obliged to cook the bird long enough to heat the stuffing through, which means the meat will overcook. Stuffing also absorbs precious juices that are better suited to making gravy.

Unfortunately, a properly cooked bird doesn't release a lot of juices for making gravy. If you do end up with enough juices, skim off the fat and thicken them with a roux (1 tablespoon each flour and butter per 1 cup juices) to make a gravy. Then, if you like, supplement the gravy with giblets cooked in the roasting pan with the turkey.

Roast Turkey with Giblet Gravy

Order your turkey far enough in advance to make sure you get a fresh, rather than frozen, bird. Buy it from someone whom you trust, as lying about whether a bird has ever been frozen is common. It makes sense to buy a bird that's larger than you need so you'll have plenty left over for sandwiches, creamed turkey, soup, and the like. Take the bird out of the refrigerator 3 to 4 hours before it is scheduled to go in the oven. A room-temperature turkey will roast more quickly and evenly.

MAKES 12 MAIN-COURSE SERVINGS WITH LEFTOVERS

1 turkey with giblets, about 20 pounds, at room
   temperature
Salt
Pepper
Butter
3 tablespoons flour
3 cups chicken broth (page 316), or as needed

Season the turkey on the outside with salt and pepper, and place it, breast side up, in a heavy roasting pan just large enough to accommodate it. Arrange the liver, neck, and gizzard around the turkey. (The giblets are often in a little package hidden in the neck end of the bird.) Fold a sheet of aluminum foil to create a triple thickness, making it just large enough to cover the breast. Rub butter evenly on one side of the folded foil, then place it, buttered side down, over the breast.

Slide the bird into the oven and turn on the oven to 350°F (there is no need to preheat). Roast for about 1 hour. Remove the foil and continue to roast the turkey for about $1^1/_2$ hours longer, or until a thermometer inserted into the space between the thigh and the breast without touching bone reads 140°F. Transfer the turkey to a platter, tent loosely with aluminum foil, and let rest in a warm spot for at least 20 minutes before carving.

To make the gravy, remove the liver, gizzard, and neck from the roasting pan. Remove the meat from the neck and discard the bones. Place the neck meat, gizzard, and liver in a food processor and pulse until finely ground. Do not process to a paste. Set the giblets aside.

Check the juices in the roasting pan. If you have a lot of juices, transfer them to a glass pitcher, skim off the fat with a ladle, and return 3 tablespoons of the fat to the pan. If you have very few juices, place the pan on the stove top, boil down the juices until they caramelize on the bottom of the pan and separate from the fat, and pour off all but 3 tablespoons of the fat. Add the flour to the fat in the pan over medium heat and stir together for 1 minute to cook the flour and form a roux. If you have degreased juices, add broth to the measuring pitcher to total 3 cups. Gradually stir in the broth or broth-juices mixture and continue to stir over medium to medium-high heat until the roux and the caramelized juices dissolve into the gravy and the gravy is smooth and has thickened to a nice consistency. Add the ground giblets, stir well, and season with salt and pepper. Pour the gravy into a warmed sauceboat.

Carve the bird as shown on page 66 and serve with the gravy.

Roasting a turkey and making gravy

1. Cover the turkey breast with buttered foil and roast for 1 hour.

2. Remove the foil so the breast will brown and continue to roast.

3. While the roasted turkey is resting, put the roasting pan with the juices on the stove top.

4. Boil down the juices until they caramelize and form a brown crust.

5. If there are more than 3 tablespoons fat in the roasting pan, remove the excess. Add flour to the roasting pan.

6. Stir the flour around to toast it, then stir in the broth.

7. When the gravy is smooth and nicely thickened, stir in the giblets.

Carving a turkey

1. Cut between the thigh and the breast down to the joint.

2. Pull the thigh back with the fork.

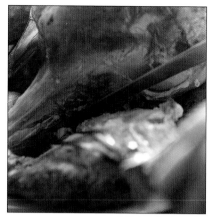

3. Cut around the joint and detach the thigh.

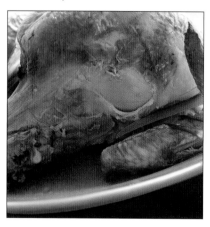

4. Make a horizontal cut into the breast meat just above the wing. Cut in as deeply as you can. This makes it easier to remove the slices from the breast.

5. Slice off the breast meat.

6. After you have carved the breast meat, cut into the wing joint and remove the wing.

7. Cut between the thigh and the drumstick and detach the drumstick.

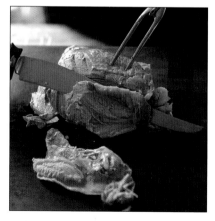

8. Slice the meat off the thigh.

9. Slice the meat off the drumstick.

Sautéed Turkey Cutlets

Turkey cutlets are cooked in the same way as veal cutlets or boneless, skinless chicken breasts—very quickly in butter. Ideally, they are breaded with bread crumbs and/or Parmigiano-Reggiano cheese to prevent their juices from being released. Most recipes for cutlets suggest slicing the cutlets very thin and then pounding them. The problem with this is that they cook in about 15 seconds and never have time for a protective seal to form that prevents the juices from running out. A better approach is to cut them about 1/4 to 1/2 inch thick and dispense with the pounding.

MAKES 4 MAIN-COURSE SERVINGS

6 slices slightly stale, dense-crumb white bread,
　　crusts removed
Flour
1 egg
Salt
Pepper
4 turkey cutlets, each about 6 ounces
　　and 1/4 to 1/2 inch thick
4 tablespoons butter, preferably clarified (page 6)

Tear the bread into pieces, place in a food processor, and pulse to form crumbs. Pass the crumbs through a fine-mesh strainer or a drum sieve so the crumbs are uniformly fine. Spread the crumbs on a plate.

Spread some flour on a plate. In a shallow bowl, beat the egg until blended, then season generously with salt and pepper. Season the cutlets on both sides with salt and pepper. Working with 1 cutlet at a time, coat it evenly on both sides with the flour, patting off the excess. Next, dip the cutlet in the egg, and then, holding the cutlet above the bowl by one end, wipe off the excess egg by sliding a thumb and index finger along its length. Finally, lay the cutlet on the bread crumbs, turn to coat both sides, and transfer to a plate. Repeat with the remaining cutlets. (See photos for breaded chicken breasts, page 57).

Select a skillet or sauté pan just large enough to hold the cutlets in a single layer and preferably nonstick. Place over low to medium heat and melt the butter. Gently place the breaded cutlets in the pan—don't use tongs; use your fingers so as not to tear through the breading—in a single layer. Cook, moving the pan every minute or so to ensure the cutlets cook evenly, for 5 to 12 minutes, or until golden brown on the first side. (Regulate the heat according to the thickness of the cutlets: the thicker the cutlet, the lower the heat setting so that the bread crumbs brown at the same rate that the cutlet cooks through.) Using a spatula or your fingertips, turn the cutlets over and cook for about 5 minutes on the second side, or until golden brown and just firm to the touch.

Transfer the cutlets to warmed plates and serve immediately.

FOWL, RABBIT AND HARE, AND VENISON

In the United States, wild game cannot be sold, only used for personal consumption. But today, many birds such as duck, squab (pigeon), quail, partridge, and pheasant are farm-raised. The same cooking methods are used to prepare most birds, though they are typically modified for two reasons: some birds have only dark meat (duck and squab) and others only white (pheasant), and birds range enormously in size (a duck versus a quail). Birds with dark meat are cooked to a lower internal temperature than those with white (except when braised), and larger birds are roasted at a lower temperature than small birds because they have longer to brown.

Many of us think of the rabbit that we buy from the butcher as game, but it is not. Only if it has been wild-hunted is it authentic game. Hare, on the other hand, is always wild (it is available for purchase only if it has been frozen) and, unlike rabbit, it has red meat. Because of this, it is always cooked rare to medium rare, whereas rabbit is cooked all the way through, in the same way as chicken.

The venison we buy has a delicate flavor surprisingly similar to wild venison that subsist on a diet of field corn. Both farm-raised and wild venison have red meat; certain cuts can be cooked much like lamb, and others like veal.

Duck

Most Americans have access to only one kind of duck, the so-called Pekin duck (sometimes labeled "Long Island"), a small, fatty variety with a name easily confused with the crisp-skinned roast Peking duck of Chinese banquets. Americans living on the coasts (or who shop online) are able to buy Moulard ducks, which are a cross between a Muscovy and a Pekin and are huge, fatty, and used for making foie gras. Americans who hunt or who have friends who hunt can enjoy wild ducks. Also available are Muscovy ducks, sometimes called "barbary ducks," that are originally from South America. Muscovy ducks are leaner than the other two varieties and are often roasted whole. They tend to be very expensive.

Unlike wild ducks, which are best roasted whole at a high temperature for a relatively short time, American domestic ducks (except Muscovy ducks) don't take well to cooking whole because they have a thick layer of fat. By the time you have cooked the duck long enough to render the fat, the meat is overcooked. The solution is to break the ducks into parts—legs (actually the thigh-and-leg combination labeled "duck legs" in the market) and breasts—and to cook them using different methods. The breasts are best sautéed and the legs can be braised, slow roasted (a form of braising), or cooked as confit. An ideal system is to braise the legs and use the braising liquid as a sauce or as the base for a sauce for both the breasts and thighs.

Sautéed Duck Breasts

The ideal sautéed duck breast has crisp, savory skin and pink, rare to medium-rare meat. That is hard to achieve because you can easily overcook the meat before the fat layer has rendered and turned crisp. Of course, you can peel off the skin before you cook the breast (duck meat is leaner than chicken) to the perfect degree of doneness, but the delicious effect of the fatty, rich, savory skin juxtaposed to the lean meat is lost. What you need to do is to render the fat as quickly as possible so the meat doesn't overcook. The solution is to score the skin in two directions: using a sharp knife, slash it about 20 times in one direction, and then, at a 90-degree angle to the first slashes, slash it again about 20 times, always being careful not to cut into the flesh. That way you will expose as much of the skin to the pan as possible, which will hasten the rendering of the fat and limit the time the breast spends cooking.

Always sauté duck breasts over medium heat. If the heat is too high, the skin will brown before it renders its fat. If it is too low, the meat will overcook by the time the fat has rendered. Start with the breasts skin side down, and leave them that way for almost the entire cooking time. Once the fat is rendered and the skin is thin and crisp, flip them over and cook them on the meat side for just a minute or two.

Sautéed Duck Breasts with Cherries and Kirsch

When buying kirsch, don't skimp. Except for a few boutique distilleries, most of the kirsch made in the United States tastes more like almonds (or cherry pits) than it does like cherries. The best brands of this double-distilled brandy are from Switzerland and Germany and may be the most expensive liquor on your shelf. You will probably seldom reach for the bottle except when making fondue or when an un-usually sophisticated friend is visiting and asks for a small glass of it served ice cold. Fortunately, this dish is perfectly good without it, and can also be adapted to a variety of berries—raspberries, blackberries, blueberries—or fresh red or black currants.

MAKES 4 MAIN-COURSE SERVINGS

4 boneless Pekin or Muscovy duck breasts, about ¹/₂ pound each, or 2 boneless Moulard duck breasts, about 1 pound each

Salt

Pepper

1 tablespoon sugar

¹/₄ cup balsamic vinegar, or as needed

1 cup duck broth (page 316), chicken broth (page 316), or braising liquid from braised duck legs (page 76)

2 tablespoons duck glaze (page 316) or meat glaze (page 318)

¹/₂ pound cherries, pitted and halved

1 tablespoon kirsch

3 tablespoons cold butter, cut into 3 slices

Using a thin-bladed, sharp knife, score the skin on the duck breasts in two directions as shown on the facing page, cutting about 20 times in one direction, and then cutting about 20 times at a 90-degree angle to the first cuts. Hold the knife at a slight angle so you can score as deeply as possible without cutting all the way through to the meat. Season the breasts on both sides with salt and pepper.

Place the breasts, skin side down, in a sauté pan just large enough to hold them in a single layer. Place over medium heat and sauté for about 12 minutes for Pekin breasts or about 20 minutes for Moulard breasts, or until the skin is golden brown. If the skin appears to be darkening too much before the breasts have time to cook, turn down the heat slightly. Turn the breasts over and cook for 2 minutes more over medium to high heat for Pekin breasts or 3 minutes more for Moulard breasts. The flesh side will be browned. Set the breasts on a plate and keep them warm while you make the sauce. Pour the fat out of the pan.

Return the pan to medium heat. Add the sugar and stir until it melts and turns golden brown. Add the vinegar and deglaze the pan, scraping up any browned bits with a wooden spoon. If all or nearly all of the vinegar evaporates, add more vinegar so about 2 tablespoons are left in the pan. Add the broth and stir in the glaze. Add the cherries, bring to a simmer, and simmer for about 2 minutes, or until the cherries release some of their juice. Using a slotted spoon, transfer the cherries to a bowl. Continue to simmer the sauce over high heat for about 5 minutes, or until it has a lightly syr-upy consistency. Stir in the kirsch and simmer the sauce for a few seconds.

Return the cherries to the pan, then whisk in the butter until emulsified. Do not allow the sauce to boil. Season with salt and pepper.

Slice the duck breasts, cutting Pekin breasts on the diagonal and Moulard breasts crosswise. Arrange the slices on warmed plates, and spoon the sauce over the slices.

Sauces for Sautéed Duck Breasts

You can construct a sauce for sautéed duck breasts in the classic way (see page 7), by deglazing the sauté pan with a liquid such as wine or vinegar; adding broth or meat glaze (page 318) and then one or more flavorings, such as thyme, parsley, or chervil; and finishing the sauce with butter. This same method is used for making fruit sauces. Fruit sauces are common—and delicious—and can be as simple as infusing citrus zest in the deglazing liquid and then reducing some citrus juice along with the broth in the pan sauce described above, or relatively complex and include a *gastrique*. A *gastrique* (see page 131) is caramel made by caramelizing sugar and then adding vinegar to it. This sweet-and-sour mixture is mixed into the sauce base just before the butter is added. Berry sauces are easily made by cooking the berries in the sauce base, taking them out, reducing the sauce to make up for the liquid released by the fruit, and then returning the fruit to the sauce at the end. Eaux de vie, such as kirsch, mirabelle, framboise, or any of the myriad other varieties available on the shelves of specialty liquor or wine stores, make a perfect finish to the sauce, though they are by no means necessary.

Sautéing duck breasts

1. Score the skin of the breasts in two directions with a sharp knife.

2. Sauté the breasts, skin side down, over medium heat until almost completely cooked through. Cook for only a minute or two on the flesh side.

3. Finished sautéed duck breasts.

Cutting up a duck

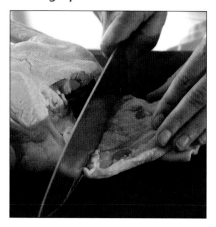

1. Cut off the flap of fat and skin on the neck end of the duck. Save it for fat.

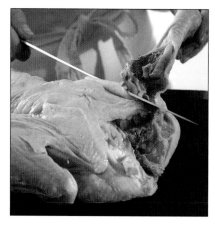

2. With the duck breast side down, cut the wings off where they join the body.

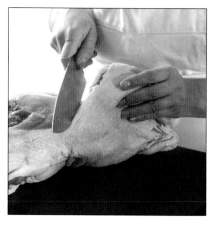

3. Cut through the skin along the side of the thigh.

4. Cut through the skin, separating the thigh.

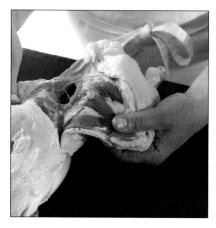

5. Snap out the joint holding the thigh attached to the back.

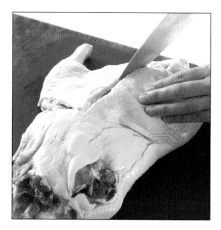

6. Cut through the skin along the center of the back to help disconnect the thigh.

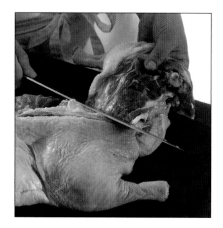

7. With the knife against the back, cut along the back as you peel away the thigh, eventually detaching it.

8. Repeat with the other thigh.

9. Cut along one side of the breastbone and under the wishbone to detach the breast.

Wok-Smoked Duck Breasts

In this recipe, the duck breasts are immersed in a simple brine before they are cooked, which seasons them and keeps them moist. After brining, they are sautéed and then treated to aromatic wood smoke in a covered wok. This same smoking method can be used for duck legs that have been braised or made into confit.

MAKES 6 MAIN-COURSE SERVINGS

For the brine

2 cups salt

1 cup sugar

4 cups hot water

6 boneless Pekin or Muscovy duck breasts, about
¹/₂ pound each, or 3 boneless Moulard duck
breasts, about 1 pound each

Pepper

¹/₂ cup fruit or other hardwood chips such as
hickory, maple, alder, apple, cherry, or peach

To make the brine, in a large crock or other vessel large enough to hold the duck breasts submerged in the brine, combine the salt, sugar, and hot water and stir until the salt and sugar dissolve completely. Refrigerate until cold.

Using a thin-bladed, sharp knife, score the skin on the duck breasts in two directions as shown on page 73, cutting about 20 times in one direction, and then cutting about 20 times at a 90-degree angle to the first cuts. Hold the knife at a slight angle so you can score as deeply as possible without cutting all the way through to the meat. Place the breasts in the brine, immersing them completely, and let soak for 30 minutes for Pekin breasts or 45 minutes for Moulard breasts.

Remove the breasts from the brine and pat dry. Season both sides with pepper. Place the breasts skin side down in a sauté pan just large enough to hold them in a single layer. Place over medium heat and sauté for about 10 minutes for Pekin breasts or about 15 minutes for Moulard breasts, or until the skin is golden brown and crisp. If the skin appears to be darkening too much before the breasts have time to cook, turn down the heat slightly. Immediately transfer the breasts to a sheet pan and slide the pan into the freezer to stop the cooking; leave them in the freezer until completely cool.

continued

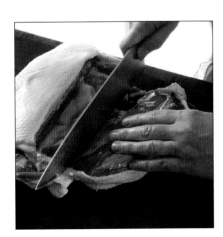

10. Keep the knife against the bone while pulling the breast away from the body.

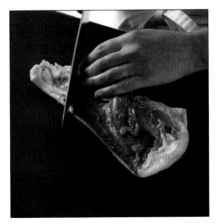

11. Trim excess fat that surrounds the breast meat.

12. Two legs and two breasts.

Line a wok with a double layer of aluminum foil. Place the wood chips in the bottom, and cover the chips with a square of aluminum foil. Place a round cake rack over the foil, and set the duck breasts, skin side up, in a single layer on the rack. Cover the wok, place on the stove top, and turn on the heat to high. When smokes starts to emerge from the sides of the wok—open the windows— turn down the heat to medium. Smoke for about 7 minutes for Pekin duck breasts or about 12 minutes for Moulard duck breasts.

Slice the duck breasts, cutting Pekin breasts on the diagonal and Moulard breasts crosswise. Arrange the slices on warmed plates and serve.

Braised Duck Legs

Duck legs can be braised two different ways: slow roasted skin side up, so that the juices in the duck are the only braising liquid, or browned and then braised in a liquid such as wine. The advantage to the slow-roasting method is its ease; the advantage to the liquid method is that you end up with beautifully glazed duck legs and a sauce.

Slow-Roasted Duck Legs

Despite the recipe name, these duck legs are actually braised using a method the French call *à l'étuvée*, in which no liquid is added. In essence, the braising liquid is in the duck itself. The trick is to get the duck legs hot enough so that their juices are released, and then to keep the juices in the duck long enough to soften the meat to tenderness. As noted earlier, the method is remarkably easy, but you will have no braising liquid for glazing the legs or to use as a sauce. Mango chutney (not pickle) is great with duck in place of a sauce.

MAKES 4 MAIN-COURSE SERVINGS

8 Pekin duck legs, or 4 Moulard duck legs
Salt
Pepper

Trim off the excess fat from the duck legs and season on both sides with salt and pepper. Put the legs, skin side up, in a heavy roasting pan just large enough to hold them in a single layer.

Slide the pan in the oven and turn the oven to 300°F (there is no need to preheat). Roast for about $1^1/_2$ hours for Pekin legs or $2^1/_2$ hours for Moulard legs, or until a knife slides easily in and out and the skin is nicely browned. Serve on warmed plates.

Roast Pears to Accompany Braised Duck Legs

Both pears and apples make a delicious accompaniment to braised duck legs. Apples are best cut into wedges and gently sautéed in butter. Pears should be halved and roasted with a little sugar and butter. To prepare any variety of pears, peel, halve, core, and remove the stems from 2 underripe pears. Place 4 tablespoons butter, cut into small pieces, in a shallow saucepan or a baking pan just large enough to hold the pear halves in a single layer, then add the halves, flat side down. Sprinkle the pears with 1 tablespoon sugar. Roast in a preheated 400°F, basting every 10 minutes with the butter, for about 40 minutes, or until easily penetrated with a knife. Cut each pear half in half lengthwise for serving. Makes 4 side-dish servings.

Slow-Roasted Duck Legs with Sauerkraut

Shredded cabbage or sauerkraut is a delicious accompaniment to duck legs that are slow roasted in the oven. If you opt for sauerkraut, the best choice is the type sold in plastic bags, usually in the dairy section of the supermarket.

MAKES 4 MAIN-COURSE SERVINGS

Slow-Roasted Duck Legs (opposite)
Two 1-pound bags sauerkraut, well drained, or
    1 small head red cabbage, cored and shredded

Roast the legs as directed until they are about 45 minutes short of being done. While the legs are roasting, put the sauerkraut in a roasting pan just large enough to hold both the sauerkraut and the legs in a single layer.

When the legs are ready, remove them from the oven, arrange them on top of the sauerkraut, cover the pan, and slide the pan into the 300°F oven. Continue to cook the legs for about 45 minutes, or until a knife slides easily in and out. Serve the legs on a mound of sauerkraut on warmed plates.

Duck Legs Braised with Red Wine

You can use virtually any liquid, including water, to braise duck legs. Feel free to experiment with good wine vinegar, white wine, sherry, Madeira, or just plain broth, ideally duck broth. Keep in mind, however, that the end result will always be better if you add a little meat or duck glaze or use concentrated broth. A single Moulard leg makes an excellent main-course serving, but one Pekin leg is a little skimpy and serving two is a bit generous. One solution is to serve one Pekin leg with a half of a sautéed Pekin breast or a fourth of a Moulard breast.

MAKES 4 MAIN-COURSE SERVINGS

1 onion, thinly sliced
1 large carrot, peeled and thinly sliced
3 cloves garlic, crushed
8 Pekin duck legs, or 4 Moulard duck legs
Salt
Pepper
3 cups full-bodied red wine
1 cup duck broth (page 316) or chicken broth
    (page 316), preferably concentrated, optional
$^{1}/_{4}$ cup duck glaze (page 316) or meat glaze
    (page 318), optional
Bouquet garni (page 320)

Preheat the oven to 400°F. Arrange the onion, carrot, and garlic in a heavy pan just large enough to hold the duck legs in a single layer. Trim any excess fat off the legs—especially Moulard legs, which are typically very fatty—and season on both sides with salt and pepper. Arrange the legs, skin side up, over the vegetables.

Slide the pan into the oven and roast the legs for about 45 minutes, or until the skin is golden brown. After 30 minutes, check to make sure the vegetables are browning without burning. If they start to burn, add $^{1}/_{2}$ cup water to the pan.

Remove the pan from the oven, tilt it, and spoon or pour out as much of the fat as you can. (Save the fat for sautéing.) Turn down the oven to 300°F. Place the pan on the stove top over high heat and add the wine, broth, and duck glaze. Nestle the bouquet garni around the duck legs. When the wine comes to the simmer, turn down the heat to maintain a slow simmer. Cover the pan with a sheet of aluminum foil, pressing it down slightly in the middle so that moisture will condense on its underside and drip down into the pan, and then with a lid.

continued

Duck legs braised with red wine

1. Season the duck legs with salt and pepper and place them, skin side up, on a bed of vegetables.

2. Roast the duck legs until the skin is golden brown.

3. Holding the legs in place, spoon or pour out the fat in the pan.

4. Add wine, broth, and duck glaze.

5. Add the bouquet garni.

6. Cover the pot with aluminum foil and a lid and braise on the stove top or in the oven.

7. Transfer the legs to a clean pan.

8. Skim the fat off the braising liquid, then strain the liquid over the duck legs.

9. Continue to cook, basting the duck legs every 10 minutes, until covered with a syrupy glaze.

Slide the pan into the oven and braise for 1 hour for Pekin legs or 2 hours for Moulard legs, or until tender when pierced with a paring knife.

Remove the pan from the oven and gently transfer the legs to a clean pan. Turn up the oven to 400°F. Using a ladle, skim off as much fat as possible from the braising liquid, then strain the liquid over the legs. (Or, transfer the legs to a plate for overnight storage, strain the braising liquid into a clean container, cover, and refrigerate overnight. The next day, lift off the congealed fat in a single layer, pour the liquid over the duck, heat on the stove top, and then continue as directed.)

Slide the pan, uncovered, into the oven and cook the duck, basting it every 10 minutes with the braising liquid, for about 30 minutes, or until the duck is covered with a shiny glaze and the braising liquid has a lightly syrupy consistency.

Place the duck legs on warmed plates and spoon the braising liquid over them. If the liquid is thin, serve the duck legs in soup plates.

Homemade Duck Confit

Making confit is a centuries-old method for preserving duck, goose, and pork in their own fat. The meats are slowly cooked until they render their fat and are perfectly tender. Then they are stored, covered with their own fat, for months in a cool place. Nowadays, cooks prepare confit because of its wonderful flavor, rather than out of necessity. Duck legs make especially good confit. If you use Moulard legs, they will render plenty of fat for cooking and storing. If you use Pekin duck legs, you will need to augment the fat they render with extra fat you have saved up from trimming ducks or duck parts or with rendered duck fat you buy.

Once you have the confit, you can serve it as is (it is wonderful with beans or lentils as on page 82); you can shred it, combine it with fat, and turn it into

rillettes (page 308); or you can cut it into chunks, sauté it with wild mushrooms, and serve it over greens (page 81).

MAKES 8 MAIN-COURSE SERVINGS

8 Moulard duck legs, or 8 Pekin duck legs and
    2 cups duck fat trimmings or rendered duck fat
Leaves from 1 bunch thyme, finely chopped
6 cloves garlic, minced and then crushed to a paste
Salt
Pepper

Trim off the excess fat from the legs and set it aside. Rub the duck legs on both sides with the thyme, garlic, salt, and pepper, rubbing the seasonings into the flesh side for a minute or two. If time permits, place the legs in a bowl, cover, and refrigerate overnight. If you have to skip this step, the duck confit will still be good.

Put the reserved fat and the 2 cups duck fat trimmings, if using, in a food processor and process until the fat looks like cake frosting. Place the duck legs, skin side down, in a heavy pot and scoop the duck fat from the processor over the top. (If you have purchased already-rendered duck fat, add it to the top at this point as well.)

Place the pot over medium heat. As the duck fat heats and then begins to cook, it will slowly render and cover the duck. Don't worry if the rendered fat doesn't cover the duck right away. The duck legs will render fat of their own and they will gradually shrink, so they will soon enough be covered with fat. Cook them, uncovered, for about 3 hours, or until the fat turns clear and the duck is easily penetrated with a fork. Adjust the heat as needed to keep the pot at a gentle simmer, with just a bubble or two breaking on the surface every second or so.

Gently transfer the duck legs to a metal or heatproof plastic container. Strain the rendered fat, and

continued

Homemade duck confit

1. Trim off excess fat from the duck legs.

2. Rub the duck legs on both sides with seasonings.

3. Add the fat to a food processor.

4. Process the fat until it looks like frosting.

5. Put the duck legs in a heavy pot and top with the fat. Cook over medium heat.

6. The duck fat will slowly melt and turn clear. Store the legs completely covered with fat.

Wilted salad with duck confit and wild mushrooms

1. Sauté wild mushrooms in duck fat.

2. Pour the sautéed mushrooms, confit, olive oil, and vinegar over salad greens and toss.

3. Finished duck confit and wild mushroom salad.

then pour the hot fat over the duck. Make sure no duck meat is exposed above the fat. Cover and store in the refrigerator for up to 6 months. When you remove any duck legs from the container, always make sure that what remains is covered with fat. If you expose any of the meat, transfer the contents of the container to a saucepan and bring to the simmer. Simmer gently for 10 minutes and return to the container, again making sure no meat is protruding above the surface.

Wilted Salad with Duck Confit and Wild Mushrooms

Once you have made the duck confit, this salad goes together quickly. All you do is sauté wild mushrooms with chunks of confit in duck fat, add olive oil and vinegar, pour the hot mixture over mixed greens, toss, and serve. When preparing the mushrooms, keep them whole or cut them into relatively large pieces, following their natural contours so they maintain their shape. Porcini (cèpes), chanterelles, and black trumpets are good choices here. If you can't find wild mushrooms or your choices are limited, fill out your selection with cultivated mushrooms such as shiitake or oyster.

MAKES 4 MAIN-COURSE SERVINGS

2 confit duck legs (page 79)

4 large handfuls of mixed salad greens

$1/4$ cup rendered duck fat

2 pounds assorted wild mushrooms, washed, dried, and left whole or cut into manageable but large pieces

Salt

Pepper

$1/4$ cup extra virgin olive oil

$1/4$ cup sherry vinegar, or as needed

Pull the duck meat away from the bones and cut it into chunks about $1/2$ inch on each side. Put the greens in a large bowl and set aside.

In a large sauté pan, heat the duck fat over high heat until it ripples but not until it smokes. Add the mushrooms and sauté for about 5 minutes, or until they soften and any water they release evaporates. Add the confit, season with salt and pepper—be careful because the confit is salty—and sauté just until heated through. Add the olive oil and vinegar and bring to a boil.

Remove from the heat, pour over the greens, and toss. Taste a leaf and add more vinegar if needed, then serve.

Ostrich

Ostrich has red meat, like duck, and it can be cooked much like duck. However, it has less fat than duck (indeed, it is regularly promoted as a particularly lean, healthful meat), so you must be careful not to overcook it—no more than medium-rare—or it will be dry and tough. The breasts can be broken down into steaks and sautéed or grilled or they can be roasted whole. The legs can be roasted as well, but because the meat tends to be slightly tough, it should be thinly sliced for serving.

Duck Confit with Warm Lentil Salad

When preparing this salad, be careful not to over-cook the lentils so they end up mushy. Once they are cooked, season them with duck fat or olive oil, vinegar, and, of course, salt and pepper. Serve them warm with a confit duck leg reheated in the oven or microwave. Regular brown lentils work fine for this dish, but if you want to experiment, try using tiny, deep green Le Puy lentils, imported from France, which hold their shape the best, or red or pink lentils.

MAKES 4 MAIN-COURSE SERVINGS

1^1/$_2$ cups lentils, picked over for grit and stones
    and rinsed
3 cups water, or more as needed
4 confit duck legs (page 79)
^{1}/$_2$ cup extra virgin olive oil
3 tablespoons rendered duck fat, melted (optional)
^{1}/$_4$ cup sherry vinegar, or as needed
Leaves from 1 bunch parsley, finely chopped
Salt
Pepper

In a pot, combine the lentils and water, bring to a boil, adjust the heat to maintain a steady simmer, and cook, uncovered, for 20 to 40 minutes, or until tender; add water as needed to keep the lentils moist.

While the lentils are cooking, heat the duck legs in a microwave on high for about 4 minutes, or in a 300°F oven for 15 minutes.

Transfer the lentils to a bowl and add the olive oil, duck fat, vinegar, parsley, salt, and pepper. Toss well, taste, and adjust the seasoning.

Mound the lentils on warmed plates and place a duck leg on top of each portion. Serve immediately.

Roast Wild Duck

Those of us lucky enough to encounter wild ducks are either hunters or have friends who are hunters. They have an incomparable flavor that is entirely different from that of a domestic duck. They also have no layer of fat to protect the meat, unlike their domestic cousins. That means the best way to cook and serve them is to brown them on the stove top, slip them into a hot oven for a very short time, and present them rare.

MAKES 4 MAIN-COURSE SERVINGS

4 dressed wild ducks, 1^1/$_2$ to 2 pounds each
Salt
Pepper
^{1}/$_4$ cup olive oil

Preheat the oven to 450°F. Season the ducks on the outside and inside with salt and pepper.

In a large ovenproof sauté pan, heat the olive oil over high heat. When it is almost smoking, add the ducks and brown well on all sides. Slide the pan into the oven and roast for about 12 minutes, or until the first signs of blood show up in the cavities.

Transfer to warmed plates and serve.

Squab

A squab is a pigeon, albeit not one taken from a public park, but one raised specially to be eaten. Unlike many other game birds, squab has red flesh and a distinct gamy flavor reminiscent of real game felled by a hunter. The easiest method for preparing a squab is to brown it on the stove top and then roast it in a hot oven for a relatively short time. It should be allowed to rest before carving and can be served with a simple jus made by deglazing the roasting pan.

Another method, one that eliminates the need for last-minute carving, is to cut the bird into thighs and boneless breasts and then sauté only these parts for serving. For the best flavor and texture, the meat should be rare to medium-rare. A sauce can be based on broth made from the squab carcasses and used along with wine or vinegar to deglaze the pan. The broth can also be reduced ahead of time into a glaze, or the broth can be dispensed with altogether and meat glaze or duck glaze added to the sauce instead.

Sautéed Squab with Madeira and Vinegar Sauce

The advantage to this dish is that you can do most of the work ahead of time and just sauté the squab parts and make the sauce at the last minute. The cooked birds do not require that they be carved for serving.

MAKES 4 FIRST-COURSE OR 2 MAIN-COURSE SERVINGS

2 squabs, about 1 pound each

Salt

Pepper

1 tablespoon butter for sautéing

1 tablespoon olive oil

1/2 cup Madeira

1/4 cup balsamic vinegar or sherry vinegar

2 tablespoons duck glaze (page 316) or meat glaze (page 318)

4 tablespoons cold butter, cut into 4 slices, for finishing sauce

Remove the legs and wings from the squabs and cut away the breasts as shown on page 84. Reserve the wings for making broth, if desired. Season the squab parts on both sides with salt and pepper. If not cooking right away, reserve the parts in the refrigerator, but let sit at room temperature for about 1 hour before you sauté them.

In a sauté pan just large enough to hold the squab parts in a single layer, melt the 1 tablespoon butter with the olive oil. (Alternatively, use two pans.) When the butter froths, add the squab breasts and legs, skin side down. Sauté for about 2 minutes, until the skin is golden brown. Turn the pieces over and sauté for about 2 minutes, or until the breast meat is well browned and just springs back to the touch. Transfer to a plate lined with paper towels. Pour the fat out of the pan.

Return the pan to high heat. Pour in the Madeira (stand back in case it ignites) and deglaze the pan, scraping up any brown bits on the bottom of the pan with a wooden spoon. Boil to reduce the wine by about three-fourths. Add the vinegar and boil to reduce by about one-half. Whisk in the duck glaze

continued

and stir until it dissolves. If the sauce is too thick, add a little water, 1 tablespoon at a time, until thinned to a good consistency. Whisk in the cold butter until emulsified. Do not allow the sauce to boil. Season with salt and pepper.

Arrange the squab breasts and legs on warmed plates. Pour the sauce over the top and serve.

VARIATION: If the squabs you buy include their liver, you can make a butter with the livers for finishing the sauce. With a large knife, chop the livers with an equal amount of butter, and then force the mixture through a fine- or medium-mesh strainer with the back of a spoon. Whisk the mixture into the sauce in place of the plain butter. This same butter can be used for finishing a roasting jus.

Cutting up a squab

1. Cut through the skin that separates the thigh from the breast.

2. Unfold the thigh and cut through the joint that attaches it to the body.

3. Cut through the joint that attaches the wing to the body.

4. Slide a knife along the breastbone between the meat and the cartilage.

5. Slide the knife along the breastbone to separate the meat from the body.

6. Repeat the steps on the other side of the squab. The cut-up squab.

Sautéed squab with Madeira and vinegar sauce

1. Brown the squab parts, skin side down, in hot oil and butter.

2. Brown the squab on the flesh side until well browned.

3. Pour the fat out of the pan and add Madeira to deglaze the pan.

4. Add vinegar and boil down to reduce.

5. Add duck glaze and stir to dissolve.

6. Add butter and whisk until emulsified.

7. Pour the sauce over the squab.

8. Finished squab with Madeira and vinegar sauce.

Roast Squab

The trick to roasting a squab is to get the bird nicely browned without overcooking it. Unless you have an extremely hot oven, the best way to accomplish this is to brown the squab in oil or clarified butter before sliding it into the oven.

MAKES 4 MAIN-COURSE SERVINGS

4 squabs, about 1 pound each
Salt
Pepper
4 tablespoons olive oil or clarified butter (page 6)

Preheat the oven to its highest temperature. If it has a convection feature, turn it on. Season the squabs on the inside and outside with salt and pepper.

In a sauté pan just large enough to hold the squabs in a single layer, heat the olive oil over high heat. When it begins to ripple, add the squabs and brown well on all sides. When they are evenly browned, slide the pan into the oven and roast for about 10 minutes, or until the birds barely begin to feel firm to the touch.

Transfer to a platter, tent loosely with aluminum foil, and let rest for about 10 minutes. Carve as shown below.

Cooking Poultry by Color

Poultry should be cooked according to whether it has white meat, like chicken or pheasant, or red meat, like duck or squab. As a general rule, white-meat birds are best roasted until the breasts register about 140°F; in contrast, red-meat birds should be roasted to a relatively low internal temperature, 125°F to 130°F. Or, you can break down red-meat birds into breasts and legs, and sauté the breasts to rare or medium-rare and braise the legs until tender when pierced with a knife tip.

Carving roast squab

1. Cut through the joint to remove each wing.

2. Cut through the joint to remove each thigh.

3. Slide the knife against the breastbone and cut away the breast meat.

Quail

Quail are small birds that are sometimes sold with their skin off. They can be simply roasted—they must be browned first on the stove top—or the legs and breasts can be removed and cooked in a sauté pan. This is probably the best method because it gives you the carcasses for making a flavorful broth or a jus for serving with the roast quail.

Roast Quail

Keep in mind that when you are "roasting" a quail, much of the cooking happens on the stove top during browning. This is because only the very hottest oven (hotter than most home ovens) is capable of browning a quail before overcooking it. Unlike squab, which has red meat, quail has white meat, which must be cooked all the way through.

MAKES 4 FIRST-COURSE SERVINGS

4 quail, about $1/4$ pound each

Salt

Pepper

$1/4$ cup olive oil or clarified butter (page 6)

Preheat the oven to its highest temperature. If it has a convection feature, turn it on. With a small piece of string, truss each bird to help hold its shape. Season all over with salt and pepper.

In an ovenproof sauté pan just large enough to hold the quail in a single layer, heat the olive oil over high heat. When it is almost smoking, add the quail and brown well on all sides. When they are evenly browned, slide the pan into the oven and roast for about 10 minutes, or until the birds feel firm to the touch.

Transfer to a platter, tent loosely with aluminum foil, and let rest for about 10 minutes. Carve as shown for squab on the facing page.

Roasting quail

1. Whole quail, ready for trussing.

2. Brown the quail on all sides in hot oil or butter.

3. When evenly browned, roast in the oven.

Sautéed Quail Breasts and Thighs with White Wine Sauce

As when preparing squab, it is easiest to eliminate the need for last-minute carving by cutting up the quail and sautéing the breasts and thighs. If you like, make a broth with the quail carcasses, using chicken or duck broth, a little onion or leek, some carrot, and a bouquet garni. (Follow the directions for making duck broth on page 316.) Simmer the broth until it is reduced to $^1/_2$ cup to concentrate its flavor, then set it aside to use for making the sauce.

MAKES 4 FIRST-COURSE SERVINGS

4 quail, about $^1/_4$ pound each

Salt

Pepper

1 tablespoon butter for sautéing

1 tablespoon olive oil

$^1/_4$ cup dry white wine

$^1/_2$ cup quail broth (see note), duck broth (page 316), or chicken broth (page 316), preferably concentrated

3 tablespoons cold butter, cut into 3 slices

Remove the legs from the quail and then cut away the breast meat. (Follow the directions for cutting up a squab on page 84.) Reserve the carcasses for making broth, if desired (see note). Season the breasts and thighs with salt and pepper. If not cooking right away, reserve in the refrigerator.

In a sauté pan just large enough to accommodate the quail parts in a single layer, melt the 1 tablespoon butter with the olive oil over high heat. Add the quail breasts and thighs, skin side down, and sauté for about 2 minutes, or until the skin is golden brown. Turn the pieces over and cook for about 1 minute, or until the breast meat feels firm to the touch. Transfer the quail pieces to a plate lined with paper towels. Pour out the fat in the pan.

Return the pan to high heat. Pour in the wine and broth and deglaze the pan, scraping up any brown bits on the bottom of the pan with a wooden spoon. Boil to reduce the liquid by three-fourths. Whisk in the cold butter until emulsified. Do not allow the sauce to boil. Season with salt and pepper.

Arrange the quail breasts and thighs on warmed plates and spoon the sauce over the top.

Quail Chaud-Froid

A *chaud-froid* is an aspic with cream in it. Although the word *aspic* instills horror in those familiar with the gelatinized concoctions of 1950s cooking, a well-made natural aspic is actually just cold consommé. When properly prepared, it is one of the most delicious things you can serve. There are two kinds of *chaud-froid*: white made from white broth, and brown made from brown broth. A brown *chaud-froid* is more flavorful and tastes almost as if it is hot when it is used to coat breast meat. The best approach is to make a broth with the quail carcasses, reduce it, combine it with cream, and then use it to coat the chilled breasts. The coated breasts are such an elegant dish that they can be presented alone, with perhaps a little bit of chopped aspic (without the cream in it) on the side. Or, accompany them with a salad.

MAKES 4 MAIN-COURSE SERVINGS

4 quail, about $1/4$ pound each

$1/4$ cup olive oil

1 small onion, chopped

1 small carrot, peeled and chopped

Bouquet garni (page 320)

4 cups chicken broth (page 316), or as needed

Salt

Pepper

$1/2$ cup heavy cream

Remove the legs from the quail and then cut away the breast meat. (Follow the directions for cutting up a squab on page 84.) Set aside the quail carcasses and the thighs for the broth. Remove the skin from the breasts. Reserve the breasts in the refrigerator until needed.

Break up the quail carcasses. In a saucepan, heat 2 tablespoons of the olive oil over high heat. Add the quail carcasses, thighs, onion, and carrot and cook, stirring occasionally, for about 10 minutes, or until browned. Add the bouquet garni, and then add the broth as needed to cover all the solids. Simmer, uncovered, skimming fat and froth that float to the top, for 3 hours.

Remove from the heat and strain through a fine-mesh strainer into a small saucepan. Place the pan over medium heat and simmer until the broth is reduced to 1 cup. Skim off any fat that floats to the top. Remove the pan from the heat and nest it in a bowl of ice water, or refrigerate it. When the broth has congealed (the natural gelatin in the quail pieces will cause it to set), lift off and discard the layer of fat from the surface.

Season the quail breasts on both sides with salt and pepper. In a sauté pan just large enough to accommodate the breasts in a single layer, heat the remaining 2 tablespoons olive oil over high heat. When the oil is almost smoking, add the breasts and sauté for about 1 minute on each side, or until they feel firm to the touch. Transfer the breasts to a plate, pat the oil off them with paper towels, cover, and refrigerate until chilled.

Place the pan of congealed broth over low heat and heat just until the broth melts. Remove from the heat, add the cream, and stir to combine. Season with salt and pepper and chill again, either in a bowl of ice water or in the refrigerator, just until the aspic is at the point of congealing.

Arrange the breasts, skinned side up, on a cake rack set over a clean sheet pan. Spoon a thin layer of the barely congealed aspic over the breasts, and then return the breasts to the refrigerator until the aspic has set. Continue to add thin layers of aspic, moving the breasts in and out of the refrigerator as needed, until you have used all of the aspic in the pan. Then, melt the aspic that has dripped onto the sheet pan, chill it until it begins to congeal, spoon it onto the breasts, and chill the breasts a final time.

Arrange the breasts on plates and serve chilled.

Goose

Geese, like ducks, have a thick layer of fat between the skin and meat that must be rendered during cooking, or the skin will be flabby and inedible. The standard method of roasting a whole goose in a moderately low oven for a very long time slowly renders out the fat, and the skin turns wonderfully crisp and crackling-like. The leg meat becomes meltingly tender, but the breast meat invariably ends up overcooked and dry. (Like duck, goose has red meat—the legs are best braised until fully tender, and the breasts cooked only until medium-rare.)

Another approach—and the one I prefer—is to remove the legs and boneless breasts from the whole goose and cook the parts separately: the thighs are slow-roasted in the oven and the breasts are sautéed relatively quickly on the stove top. The breasts spend most of their cooking time skin side down so that the fat renders and the skin crisps.

When buying goose, look for an organic free-range bird that has been minimally processed. Such geese tend cook up moister and more tender than ones that have been conventionally grown and processed.

Slow-Roasted Goose Legs and Sautéed Breasts

As they cook, the goose legs and breasts will release an enormous quantity of fat. This fat should be saved for sautéing and frying—and for spreading on crusty bread. Put into a clean container and refrigerated, the goose fat will keep for 1 month. Sauerkraut makes a great accompaniment.

MAKES 6 MAIN-COURSE SERVINGS

1 organic free-range goose, 10 to 12 pounds
Salt
Pepper

Remove the legs and wings from the goose and cut away the boneless breasts as shown for squab on page 84. Set aside the carcass and wings for making broth, if desired. Trim away the excess fat on the breasts. Using a thin-bladed, sharp knife, score the skin on the breasts in two directions as shown on the facing page without cutting all the way through to the meat. Reserve the breasts in the refrigerator until needed. Season the legs on both sides with salt and pepper. Put the legs, skin side up, in a heavy roasting pan just large enough to hold them in a single layer.

Slide the pan in the oven and turn the oven to 300°F (there is no need to preheat). Roast for about 5 hours, or until a knife slides easily in and out and the skin is nicely browned.

After the legs have roasted for about 4^1/$_2$ hours, season the breasts on both sides with salt and pepper. Place the breasts skin side down in a sauté pan just large enough to hold them in a single layer. (Alternatively, use two pans.) Place over medium to low heat and cook for about 20 minutes, or until the skin is crisp and golden and the meat plumps up. Turn the breasts over and cook them for about 5 minutes over medium to high heat, or until the flesh browns.

Carve the breasts as shown on the facing page. Carve the legs or arrange them whole on a platter and carve at the table.

Slow-roasted goose legs and sautéed breasts

1. Trim the excess fat from the breasts.

2. Score the skin on the breasts in two directions with a sharp knife.

3. Sauté the breasts, skin side down, over medium to low heat for about 20 minutes.

4. Turn the breasts over and cook for about 5 minutes on the meat side.

5. Remove the tenderloin from each breast and slice the meat on the diagonal.

6. Finished goose.

Guinea Hen

The guinea hen, which is native to Africa and is far more popular in Europe than in the United States, has a relatively mild taste reminiscent of chicken. It is also about the same size as a chicken and can be cooked the same way. Because some cooks consider the flavor of the guinea hen to be a bit more aggressive than that of chicken, they sometimes couple it with more robust flavors, such as bacon or vinegar.

Braised Guinea Hen with Balsamic Vinegar, Capers, and Olives

It would be cost prohibitive to cook a guinea hen in a cup of authentic aged balsamic vinegar, so I have created an "improved" balsamic vinegar by boiling down an inexpensive brand to concentrate its flavor.

MAKES 4 MAIN-COURSE SERVINGS

1 guinea hen, about 4 pounds, or 2 guinea hens, about 4 pounds each, quartered

Salt

Pepper

$1/4$ cup olive oil

1 cup dry white wine

2 cups balsamic vinegar, boiled down to 1 cup

3 tablespoons capers, rinsed

$1/2$ cup Niçoise olives, pitted

1 slice prosciutto, $1/8$ inch thick, cut into tiny dice

4 tomatoes, peeled, seeded, and chopped

1 cup chicken broth (page 316)

2 tablespoons finely chopped fresh parsley

Season the guinea hen pieces on both sides with salt and pepper. In a heavy pot large enough to hold the guinea hen pieces in a single layer, heat the olive oil over high heat. When the oil ripples, add the hen pieces, skin side down, and cook for about 12 minutes, or until browned. Turn the pieces over and cook for about 12 minutes longer, or until browned. Transfer the hen pieces to a platter. Pour out the oil from the pot.

Return the hen pieces to the pot and add the wine, vinegar, capers, olives, prosciutto, tomatoes, and broth. Place over high heat and bring to a simmer. Adjust the heat to maintain a gentle simmer, cover, and cook for about 15 minutes, or until the breasts feel firm to the touch (remove a breast from the pot to test).

Transfer the hen pieces to a platter and keep warm. Boil down the braising liquid, with the liquid boiling only on one side of the pot, until it thickens to a good sauce consistency. Skim off any fat and froth that float to the top. Stir in the parsley. Return the hen pieces to the liquid to heat through.

Divide the hen pieces among warmed plates. Spoon the sauce over the top and serve.

Pheasant

If farm-raised pheasant is all you can find, don't buy it. It has little, if any, game flavor. Wild pheasant, in contrast, is rich and gamy and a delightful luxury.

If you're lucky enough to have shot a pheasant or been given a just-shot pheasant, the first thing you need to do is to hang it, still in its feathers, by its feet in a cool place for a few days. Old books recommend hanging it for two weeks, but that's dangerously long. Three days is the standard recommendation, although if the weather is cold, you might be daring and leave it for a couple of days longer. Aging the pheasant this way definitely brings out its flavor.

Roast Pheasant

A pheasant is all white meat, which means it should be roasted more or less like a chicken. It does not have the fatty skin to protect the meat that chicken has, however, so it is a good idea to cover the breasts with a sheet of fatback or with pieces of *lardo* for the first 20 minutes of roasting. Or, you can slow down the cooking of the breasts by covering them with a triple thickness of aluminum foil.

MAKES 2 GENEROUS MAIN-COURSE SERVINGS

1 pheasant, 4 pounds
Salt
Pepper
About 1/4 pound fatback (weight not including rind) or *lardo*, cut to cover breasts, optional

Hang the pheasant as directed in the introduction (above), then pluck its feathers. To gut the bird, using a sharp knife, make a slit along the neck between the vertebrae and the windpipe. Insert your fingers into the slit and reach around in the cavity of the bird along the inside wall to loosen the lungs. Make a slit in the rear end of the bird and reach in the cavity and pull out the innards. To rid the bird of pin feathers, hold it by its feet over a stove-top flame to singe them off. Cut the toenails off the feet with a knife or scissors. Truss the bird as shown for chicken on page 35, leaving on the feet as Europeans do, unless you are afraid their presence will put off your dinner guests. If you want to leave the head on (to really put off your guests), tuck it in the trussing so that it stays securely along the side of the bird during roasting. Otherwise, chop it off.

Preheat the oven to 500°F. Season the pheasant with salt and pepper and cover the breast meat with fatback, *lardo*, or a sheet of aluminum foil folded to create a triple thickness. Roast for 20 minutes, or until the thighs brown. Remove the fat or foil and continue to roast for about 20 minutes more, or until an instant-read thermometer slid between a thigh and breast without touching bone reads 140°F. If you do not have a thermometer, tilt the pheasant slightly so some of the juices run out of the cavity. The bird is ready if the juices are clear but streaked with red. Don't wait until the red disappears or you will have overcooked the bird. If the juices remain cloudy, the bird isn't done.

Transfer the pheasant to a platter, tent loosely with foil, and let rest for 20 minutes. Carve as directed for a chicken (see page 37).

Rabbit and Hare

Most Americans have an aversion to eating rabbit, probably because they have been exposed to too many Easter bunny, Peter Rabbit, and Bugs Bunny stories. Rabbits also have a confusing anatomy that makes them difficult to eat if you are unfamiliar with their structure. One way to avoid the anatomy problem is to bone the confusing part, which is the saddle. A small rabbit is enough for two servings, and a large rabbit will serve three or four. Once you have boned the saddle, you can season it, flavor it with herbs, or fill it with a delicate stuffing. No one explains how to bone a saddle of rabbit better than Richard Olney in his classic *Simple French Food*.

Most of the rabbits we find in grocery stores are young and should be cooked only until they are heated through, just like chicken. If you're lucky enough to find older rabbits that weigh 5 pounds dressed (that is, readied for cooking), you'll be able to make a delicious rabbit stew with long, slow braising.

Many people assume that rabbit and hare are the same thing or are at least closely related. Although they have a similar anatomy, they are from different species. A greater distinction, however, is that a species of rabbit has been domesticated for sale as meat, but no species of hare has been domesticated. Rabbits are also smaller and have white meat; hares have red meat and a full gamy flavor and are among the most delicious of all wild game. Most of the hare for sale in the United States comes frozen from Scotland. The freezing does little to damage the meat. Remember, though, meat that has been frozen goes from rare to overcooked quickly, so you have to be careful when roasting hare.

Short-Braised Rabbit Stew with Mustard and White Wine

The ideal broth for this stew is made from the forequarters of the rabbit, but you can use chicken broth instead. Or, you can forgo the broth all together and just cook the rabbit in white wine diluted with a little water (1 cup wine to $1^1/_2$ cups water).

MAKES 4 MAIN-COURSE SERVINGS

2 dressed rabbits, 3 to 4 pounds each
4 cups chicken broth (page 316), if not making
   rabbit broth
Salt
Pepper
2 tablespoons butter
2 tablespoons olive oil or rendered bacon fat
$^1/_2$ cup dry white wine
$^1/_2$ cup heavy cream
1 tablespoon Dijon mustard

Cut each rabbit into 2 thighs, 1 saddle, and the forequarters as shown on the facing page. Cut the forequarters into roughly 2-inch pieces and reserve for broth. If you like, bone the saddles as shown on page 96. Whether you have boned them or not, season the saddles with salt and pepper, roll, and tie them as shown on page 96. Cut each saddle into 2 pieces. If making broth from the rabbit forequarters and rib cage, refrigerate the thighs and saddle pieces until needed.

To make the broth, place the forequarter pieces in a pot, add water to cover, and bring to a boil, skimming off any froth from the surface. Adjust the heat to maintain a gentle simmer and simmer, uncovered, for 2 hours. Strain the broth through a fine-mesh strainer. Pour 4 cups of the strained broth into a clean saucepan (reserve the remainder for another use), bring to a simmer, and simmer until reduced to 2 cups. If using the chicken broth, simmer to reduce to 2 cups the same way.

Season the rabbit thighs and saddle pieces all over with salt and pepper. In a sauté pan just large enough to hold the rabbit pieces in a single layer, melt the butter with the olive oil over medium heat. Add the rabbit pieces and brown well on both sides. Transfer the rabbit pieces to a plate. Pour the fat out of the pan.

Return the pan to high heat. Add the wine and the reduced broth and then return the rabbit pieces to the pan. Bring the liquid to a simmer, turn down the heat to low, and simmer, covered, for about 10 minutes, or until the rabbit is firm to the touch. Transfer the rabbit to a plate, cover, and set aside in a warm place.

Simmer the liquid in the pan over medium-low heat to reduce to about 1 cup and then add the cream. Continue to simmer for about 10 minutes, or until lightly thickened. Whisk in the mustard and season with salt and pepper.

Return the rabbit to the sauce and reheat until hot. Snip the strings around the saddle pieces. Divide the rabbit among warmed plates, giving each diner a thigh and half of a saddle. Spoon the sauce over the top and serve.

Cutting up a rabbit

1. Whole rabbits.

2. Start cutting a thigh away where it joins the back.

3. Continue cutting through the joint where the thigh joins the back.

4. Repeat on the other side.

5. Hack off the protruding tailbone where you removed the thighs.

6. Remove the rib cage by cutting through the ribs, about 6 ribs up from the loin, on both sides.

Boning and tying a saddle of rabbit

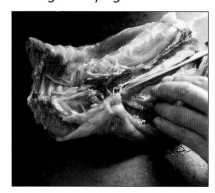

1. Slide a boning knife under the tenderloins on the inside (concave) part of the saddle.

2. Slide the knife around under the bone that supported the tenderloins on both sides. Continue to scrape against bone and pull away the meat.

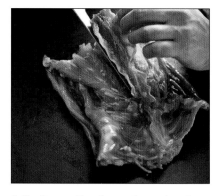

3. Continue cutting the meat away from bone until you get to the bone that runs along the back and clings to the meat. Do not try to cut the meat away from this bone.

4. Slide a knife under the ribs, detaching them from the flap of meat and tissue that covers them.

5. Holding the saddle on end, cut through the bones where the saddle is attached along the back of the vertebrae. Do not hesitate to leave a tiny amount of bone embedded in the skin.

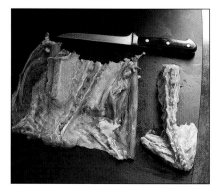

6. The boned saddle and vertebrae (which can be used for broth).

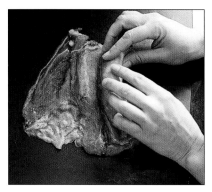

7. Season the inside of the saddle (this is the point at which you can add herbs and/or a stuffing) and roll it up into a sausage shape.

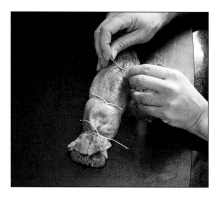

8. Tie the rolled saddle with string.

9. The thighs and saddles from 2 rabbits.

Long-Braised Rabbit Stew

Large and older rabbits need to be long braised by slow, gentle cooking; you will also need to lard them. While rabbit prepared in this way is perhaps the most delicious rabbit of all, it can be hard to find the requisite older rabbit.

MAKES 4 MAIN-COURSE SERVINGS

1 large dressed rabbit, 5 to 7 pounds

1 pound fatback (weight not including rind)
or *lardo*

Salt

Pepper

1 cup dry white wine

3 cloves garlic, crushed

5 thyme sprigs

1 imported bay leaf

1 onion, thinly sliced

1 carrot, peeled and thinly sliced

2 tablespoons butter

2 tablespoons olive oil or rendered bacon fat

4 cups chicken broth (page 316), if not making rabbit broth

1/4 cup meat glaze (page 318), optional

1 cup heavy cream, optional

Cut the rabbit into 2 thighs, 1 saddle, and the forequarters as shown on page 95. Cut the forequarters into roughly 2-inch pieces and reserve for broth. If you like, bone the saddles as shown on the facing page. Cut the fatback into sheets about 1/4 inch thick, then cut the sheets lengthwise into strips, or lardons, about 1/4 inch on each side. Using a hinged larding needle, pull the strips through the thighs and the saddle. Whether you have boned it or not, season the saddle with salt and pepper, roll, and tie it as shown on the facing page. Season the larded thighs and saddle all over with salt and pepper.

In a shallow dish large enough to hold the rabbit pieces, stir together the wine, garlic, thyme, bay leaf, onion, and carrot. Add the rabbit pieces, turn to coat evenly, cover, and marinate overnight in the refrigerator.

To make the broth, place the forequarter pieces in a pot, add water to cover, and bring to a boil, skimming off any froth from the surface. Adjust the heat to maintain a gentle simmer, and simmer, uncovered, for 2 hours. Strain the broth through a fine-mesh strainer. Set aside 4 cups of the strained broth. Reserve the remainder for another use.

Drain the rabbit, reserving the marinade, and pat dry. In a sauté pan just large enough to hold the rabbit pieces in a single layer, melt the butter with the olive oil over medium heat. Add the rabbit pieces and brown well on both sides. Transfer the rabbit pieces to a plate. Pour the fat out of the pan.

Return the pan to high heat. Return the rabbit pieces to the pan along with the marinade, the 4 cups broth, and the meat glaze. Bring to a simmer, turn down the heat to low, cover, and simmer gently for 3 hours, or until the meat is tender when pierced with a skewer or small knife.

Preheat the oven to 400°F. Transfer the rabbit pieces to a smaller clean ovenproof pot. Strain the braising liquid into a glass pitcher and skim off the fat with a ladle. (Or, you can refrigerate the braising liquid, then lift off the congealed fat with a spoon.) Pour the degreased liquid over the rabbit.

Slide the pot, uncovered, into the oven. Cook the rabbit, basting it every 10 minutes with the liquid, for about 40 minutes, or until the braising liquid is syrupy and the rabbit is covered with a shiny glaze. Add the cream and season with salt and pepper. Return the pot to the oven and cook just until the cream is heated through.

Carve the meat off the thighs. Snip the strings around the saddle and cut the saddle crosswise into quarters. Divide the thigh meat and the saddle pieces evenly among warmed soup plates. Spoon the braising liquid around and over the rabbit and serve.

Hare with Red Wine–Black Pepper Sauce

Unlike rabbit, which in most cases should be cooked to the equivalent of medium, hare is best roasted rare. The saddle of the hare is the most desirable part, as the thighs can be quite tough. The ideal approach is to braise the thighs and then use the braising liquid as the base for a sauce for both saddle and thighs. To further enhance the sauce, make a broth from the forequarters and rib cage and use as the braising liquid.

MAKES 4 MAIN-COURSE SERVINGS

1 dressed hare, about 5 pounds
Salt
Pepper
1 onion, chopped
1 large carrot, peeled and chopped
2 cups dry red wine
3 cloves garlic, crushed
1 imported bay leaf
5 thyme sprigs
1/4 cup sherry vinegar or balsamic vinegar
10 peppercorns, crushed under a saucepan
4 tablespoons cold butter, cut into 4 slices

Preheat the oven to 400°F.

Cut the hare into 2 thighs, 1 saddle, and the forequarters as shown for the rabbit on page 95. If you like, bone the saddle as shown for the rabbit on page 96. Whether you have boned it or not, season the saddle with salt and pepper, roll, and tie as shown on page 96.

Cut the forequarters into roughly 2-inch pieces. Transfer the forequarter pieces to an ovenproof pot, add the onion and carrot, and place in the oven until well browned. Remove from the oven, add water to cover and bring to a simmer, skimming off any froth from the surface. Simmer, uncovered, for

4 hours. Strain through a fine-mesh strainer and set aside.

While the broth is simmering, in a shallow bowl, stir together the wine, garlic, bay leaf, and thyme. Add the thighs, turn to coat, cover, and marinate in the refrigerator for at least 4 hours or up to overnight.

The next day, transfer the thighs and the marinade to a pot and add enough broth to come halfway up the thighs. Bring to a simmer on the stove top. Cover the pot with a sheet of aluminum foil, pressing it down slightly in the middle so that moisture will condense on its underside and drip down into the pot, and then with a lid. Simmer gently for 3 hours, or until a knife slides easily in and out of the thighs.

Transfer the thighs to a plate. Strain the braising liquid through a fine-mesh sieve into a clean saucepan. Bring to a simmer and simmer, skimming off any froth that rises to the surface, until reduced to 1 cup.

Meanwhile, preheat the oven to 500°F. Place the saddle in a roasting pan just large enough to hold it and slide the pan into the oven. Roast for about 15 minutes, or until barely firm to the touch. Transfer the saddle to a cutting board, tent loosely with aluminum foil, and let rest for 15 minutes before carving.

While the saddle is roasting, in a clean saucepan over medium heat, combine the reduced braising liquid, vinegar, and peppercorns, and simmer until slightly reduced. Just before serving, whisk in the butter until emulsified. Do not allow the liquid to boil.

Carve the meat off the thighs. Snip the strings around the saddle and cut the saddle crosswise into quarters. Arrange the thigh meat and saddle pieces on a warmed platter or warmed plates. Spoon the braising liquid over the top and serve.

Venison

Unless you hunt or are lucky enough to know a hunter, all venison that you are likely to eat will have been farmed. Venison has red meat and a flavor that varies enormously depending on what the animal has been fed. Wild venison from farm country is likely to have been fattened on corn and have a delicate flavor like farmed venison. Venison hunted in more distant reaches may have lived on pine needles and will have an off, almost kerosene-like flavor.

Some hunters prefer their venison butchered much like lamb, and others like their venison completely off the bone. The choice should depend on how strongly flavored the meat is. Because meat that is cooked on the bone has a more robust flavor, meat with a strong taste should be cooked off the bone and more delicate meat should be left on.

Venison also shares cooking characteristics with lamb. In other words, the shoulder meat is best braised or stewed, the rib and loin sections roasted, and the leg roasted, braised, or cut up for stewing. The top round, the dome-shaped muscle in the leg, can also be sliced into scaloppine and lightly sautéed, in the style of veal (page 243).

Roast Saddle of Venison with Jus

A saddle of venison is treated the same way you treat a saddle of lamb: roasted at a high temperature for a relatively short amount of time. Venison is leaner than lamb, so you must be careful not to overcook it, or you will be left with gray, dry meat. The meat should always be crimson—rare or medium-rare—when served.

MAKES 4 TO 6 MAIN-COURSE SERVINGS

1 untrimmed saddle of venison (including flaps), about 10 pounds
Salt
Pepper
1/2 onion, coarsely chopped
2 cups chicken broth (page 316)

Let the saddle come to room temperature. Preheat the oven to 450°F.

Working carefully to avoid damaging the loin muscle, cut the flaps off the saddle as shown for a saddle of lamb on page 279. Cut the flaps into strips about 1/2 inch wide. There will probably be no more than a thin layer of fat covering the meat. If there is more, trim the excess fat. Season the saddle all over with salt and pepper. Spread the flap strips and onion in a roasting pan just large enough to accommodate the saddle. Place the saddle, fat side up, on top.

Slide the pan into the oven and roast the saddle for about 25 minutes, or until an instant-read thermometer inserted into the center without touching bone reads 125°F or the meat feels firm when you press both ends of the saddle. Check the tenderloins on the bottom by pressing to see if they are firm to make sure they are done, too. If not, turn the saddle over and roast for a few minutes longer.

Transfer to a platter, tent loosely with aluminum foil, and let rest for 15 minutes before carving.

continued

While the saddle is resting, make the jus. Put the roasting pan on the stove top over high heat and stir around the pieces of meat until the meat is browned and any juices caramelize on the bottom of the pan. Spoon out any fat. Deglaze the pan with $^1/_2$ cup of the broth, scraping up any brown bits on the bottom of the pan with a wooden spoon. Boil down the broth until it caramelizes into a crusty layer with a layer of clear fat on top. Spoon out and discard the fat and deglaze the pan with a second $^1/_2$ cup broth, again boiling it down. Deglaze the pan with the remaining 1 cup broth, and then strain the liquid through a fine-mesh strainer into a warmed sauceboat.

To carve the roast lengthwise, cut along one side of the backbone to free the loin muscle. Slice the loin lengthwise with the knife held sideways, as shown for a lamb saddle on page 280. Repeat with the other loin muscle. Turn the saddle over and carve the tenderloins the same way. (Alternatively, cut the loins and tenderloins away from the chine bone and slice crosswise.) Pass the jus at the table.

Roast Rack of Venison with Jus

Even though nowadays farm-raised venison is increasingly available fresh, most shoppers will find only frozen venison in their markets. Fortunately, when properly cooked, frozen venison holds up well, and most diners cannot detect a difference in taste from fresh. A rack of venison is easy to cook and makes a handsome centerpiece on any menu. As with the saddle, make sure you do not overcook this tender cut.

MAKES 4 MAIN-COURSE SERVINGS

1 rack of venison (8 chops), about 2 pounds
Salt
Pepper
1 pound venison stew meat, cut into $^1/_2$-inch strips
$^1/_2$ onion, coarsely chopped
2 cups chicken broth (page 316)

If desired, french the ribs as shown for a rack of pork on page 125. Season the rack all over with salt and pepper and let come to room temperature. Preheat the oven to 450°F.

Spread the stew meat and onion over the bottom of a roasting pan just large enough to hold the venison. Place the venison on top and roast for about 25 minutes, or until an instant-read thermometer inserted into the rack without touching bone reads 125°F for rare or 130°F for medium rare, or the meat feels firm when you press both ends of the rack.

Transfer the rack to a cutting board, tent loosely with aluminum foil, and let rest for 15 minutes before carving.

While the roast is resting, make the jus. Put the roasting pan on the stove top over high heat and stir around the pieces of meat until any juices caramelize on the bottom of the pan. Deglaze the pan with $^1/_2$ cup of the broth, scraping up any brown bits on the bottom of the pan with a wooden spoon and boiling down the broth until it caramelizes into a crusty brown layer. Deglaze the pan with another $^1/_2$ cup of the broth, again boiling it down. Deglaze the pan with the final cup of broth, and then strain the liquid through a fine-mesh strainer into a warmed sauceboat.

Carve the roast, slicing between the ribs. Pass the jus at the table.

Venison Loin Steaks with Juniper Berries

If you are a hunter and you have your venison butchered to include boneless cuts, this is a great way to use the loin. Always cook the loin to rare or medium-rare. If you cook it longer, it will be tough and chewy. The juniper berries enhance the gaminess of the meat; be sure to crush and chop them before using to release their flavor.

MAKES 4 MAIN-COURSE SERVINGS

8 slices venison loin, each about 2 ounces
    and $^1/_2$ inch thick
Salt
Pepper
3 tablespoons olive oil
$^1/_2$ cup Madeira
5 juniper berries, crushed under a saucepan and
    finely chopped
2 tablespoons meat glaze (page 318)
2 tablespoons cold butter, cut into 2 slices

Season the venison with salt and pepper and let come to room temperature.

In a sauté pan just large enough to hold the venison slices, heat the olive oil over high heat. When the oil begins to smoke, add the venison slices and cook for about 1 minute for rare or slightly longer for medium-rare, or until browned on the first side. Turn the slices over and cook on the second side the same way. Transfer to a warmed platter lined with paper towels to absorb any oil, and pat off the burnt oil from the tops with more paper towels. Pour the fat out of the pan.

Return the pan to high heat. Add the Madeira and juniper berries and stir in the meat glaze. Boil down until the sauce has a lightly syrupy consistency. If it becomes too thick, thin it with a little water. Whisk in the butter until emulsified. Do not allow the sauce to boil. Season with salt and pepper.

Place 2 loin slices on each warmed plate. Spoon the sauce over the top and serve.

VARIATIONS: This is a luxurious dish and it warrants a little chopped, sliced, or julienned truffle if you happen to have a truffle on hand. You can also add a little cream to the sauce to give it a silky texture.

Caribou and Moose

Both the caribou and the moose are large animals, and if they are not cooked properly, they can be tough. They are best hung for about three weeks in a cold place (about 34°F), during which enzymes break down the muscle tissue, increasing tenderness. Because the meat of both animals has a strong flavor, it is best marinated. A simple marinade of soy sauce, garlic, and thyme, held in contact with the meat for 12 hours in the refrigerator, will attenuate the gamy flavor. Steaks can be cooked in the same way as beef steaks (see page 181), and cuts suitable for braising—these animals make great pot roasts—can be prepared like beef chuck (see page 147). The rack and the loin can be roasted whole, or they can be broken down, the rack into chops and the loin into steaks.

PORK

T he average American eats fifty-one pounds of pork a year, putting this generally modestly priced meat third behind beef and chicken in popularity. Elsewhere, it is more highly prized. Easy to raise and yielding a wealth of meat and fat, the pig is the primary source of animal protein in dozens of cultures around the world.

A butchered pig is broken down into four primal cuts—the shoulder, belly, loin, and ham—from which smaller pieces are cut for sale. The shoulder, which contains from four to seven ribs, depending on how the animal was butchered, is divided into the Boston butt, which is the upper part, and the picnic ham, which is the arm. The belly, which lies below the upper back, usually weighs close to 20 pounds. It is the source of spareribs and of what becomes bacon and salt pork after smoking or curing. The loin is a long series of muscles that runs from the shoulder all the way back to the leg (the ham). It is divided into three parts: the blade end, which contains the shoulder blade; the center cut, which is where you find tender center-cut chops and the rack of pork; and the blade center sirloin, which is nearest the ham and is the source of loin chops. The loin is also the source of the tenderloin, the most tender muscle on the pig. The ham is the largest cut of the pig, typically tipping the scales at 20 pounds. It is often sold divided in half, with the halves marketed as shank end and sirloin end.

In recent decades, pigs in the United States have been bred to have a much lower fat content than they did in the past. That means you must cook these modern lean pork cuts carefully to prevent them from drying out. Only the relatively fatty parts, namely the shoulder and spareribs, can be braised. The balance are roasted, sautéed, or grilled.

PORK CUTS

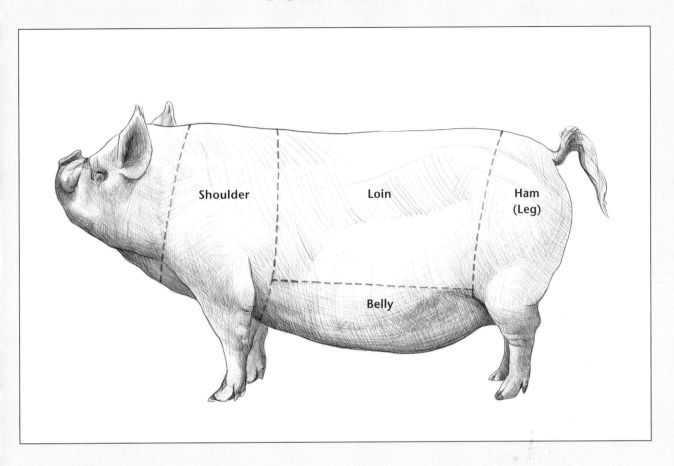

Shoulder
Boston butt: roast, sauté (slices), braise, barbecue
Picnic ham: roast, sauté (slices), braise, barbecue
Shank, hock: braise, poach
Shoulder chops: grill, sauté, braise

Loin
Baby back ribs: roast, barbecue
Loin: roast, grill
Loin chops: sauté, grill
Rack: roast
Tenderloin: roast, sauté, grill, broil (slices)

Belly
Belly: braise, barbecue, cure
Spareribs: roast, braise, barbecue

Ham (Leg)
Ham (leg): roast
Shank, hock: braise, poach

Shoulder

The shoulder is sold in three cuts: the Boston butt, sometimes labeled "pork shoulder" or "pork butt"; the picnic shoulder, which is typically marked "picnic ham"; and the shoulder piece from the shoulder end of the loin. The latter is sometimes sold with the rest of the shoulder and sometimes as part of the loin. All three shoulder cuts can be roasted or braised.

Roast Boston Butt

When you roast a Boston butt, it turns out similar to a fresh ham. But because it is smaller, it is more practical than a fresh ham if you are serving fewer people.

MAKES 10 MAIN-COURSE SERVINGS

1 bone-in Boston butt, about 7 pounds
Salt
Pepper
1 carrot, peeled and cut into 3-inch sections
1 onion, quartered
2 cups pork broth (page 319) or other broth
   or water if making jus

Preheat the oven to 450°F. Trim the rind off the Boston butt and save it in the freezer for flavoring a braise. Trim off the excess fat, and then cut out the shoulder blade as shown on the facing page. Season the meat all over with salt and pepper, and then tie it with kitchen string to make it more compact. Put the roast in a heavy ovenproof pot just large enough to hold it. Arrange the carrot and onion around the meat.

Slide the pot into the oven and roast the pork for about 30 minutes, or until browned. Turn down the oven temperature to 300°F and continue roasting for about 2 hours, or until an instant-read thermometer inserted into the thickest part reads 135°F (it will rise to 140°F while it rests).

Transfer to a cutting board, tent loosely with aluminum foil, and let rest for about 15 minutes before slicing.

If you like, make a jus. Put the pan on the stove top over high heat and boil down the juices until they evaporate and form a crusty brown layer with a layer of clear fat on top. Pour off the fat, return the pan to high heat, and deglaze with the broth, stirring with a wooden spoon until the crust has dissolved into the liquid. Strain the liquid through a fine-mesh strainer into a warmed sauceboat.

Snip the strings and slice the pork across the grain. Arrange the slices on warmed plates. Pass the jus at the table.

Roast Boston butt

1. Boston butt top.

2. Boston butt bottom.

3. After trimming off excess fat, cut out the shoulder blade.

4. Put the tied roast in a pan with aromatic vegetables.

5. Roast to an internal temperature of 135°F.

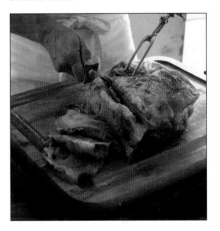

6. Slice the roast pork across the grain.

Slow-Roasted or Barbecued Boston Butt with Marjoram or Thyme

When pork shoulder is cooked in a covered pot in the oven at a very low temperature, it braises in its own juices. Because no liquid is added to the pot, I call it slow roasting. The same effect is created when the shoulder is cooked in a covered grill. Serve the cooked pork as is—it will be tender enough to scoop up with a spoon—or use it in tortillas or pulled pork sandwiches. This pork is particularly delicious if you season it with fresh marjoram, but thyme will do if you can't find marjoram.

MAKES 10 MAIN-COURSE SERVINGS

1 boneless Boston butt, about 4 pounds, or bone-in Boston butt, about 7 pounds
Salt
Pepper
1 bunch marjoram or 1/2 bunch thyme, leaves finely chopped

continued

Trim the rind off the Boston butt and save it in the freezer for flavoring a braise. Rub the pork all over with salt and pepper and then with the marjoram. Tie it with kitchen string to make it more compact. Place the pork in a heavy ovenproof pot just large enough to hold it. Cover the pot with a sheet of aluminum foil, pressing it down slightly in the middle so that moisture will condense on its underside and drip down onto the exposed parts of the meat, and then with a lid.

Slide the pot into the oven and turn on the oven to 200°F (there is no need to preheat). Slow roast for 7 hours, or until the meat is tender when pierced with a skewer or small knife.

To barbecue the pork, trim it and rub it with the seasonings as directed. Prepare a fire for indirect grilling in a covered grill (see page 21). Sprinkle the coals with a handful of soaked wood chips, or put a small sheet of aluminum foil over the coals and top with a handful of sawdust. (If using a gas grill, put unsoaked chips in a special smoker box, or in a perforated foil packet and place directly over the heat.) Place the pork over the cool side of the grill and cook for 7 hours, or until the meat is tender when pierced with a skewer or small knife. Add soaked chips or sawdust and lighted charcoal to the coals (or unsoaked chips or sawdust to the smoker box or foil packet) every 30 minutes or so to keep the fire and the smoke going.

Transfer the pork from the pot or the grill to a warmed platter and serve.

Boston Butt with Sauerkraut

Sauerkraut makes the perfect foil for the rich meatiness of pork shoulder. Here, Boston butt is poached and then served surrounded with sauerkraut. You can expand this dish by cooking homemade sausages (page 296) in the broth and serving them with the sauerkraut. Or, you can omit the sauerkraut and instead simmer 1 small head red or green cabbage, cored and shredded, in the poaching liquid for about 40 minutes.

MAKES 8 MAIN-COURSE SERVINGS

1 boneless Boston butt, about 4 pounds
1 large carrot, peeled and cut into 1-inch sections
1 onion, quartered
Bouquet garni (page 320)
Two 1-pound bags sauerkraut, well drained

Trim the rind off the Boston butt and save it in the freezer for flavoring a braise. Tie the pork with kitchen string to make it more compact. Put it in a pot just large enough to hold it and deep enough for it to be covered with water. Nestle the carrot, onion, and the bouquet garni around the pork and add cold water to cover.

Place the pot on the stove top and bring to a gentle simmer. Cook, skimming off any fat or froth as it rises to the surface, for about 3 hours, or until a knife or skewer easily slides in and out of the pork.

Using the strings, carefully lift the meat out of the pot and place on a warmed platter. Cover and set aside in a warm place. Fish out and discard the vegetables and the bouquet garni, and then boil down the poaching liquid until it is reduced by half. Add the sauerkraut to the broth, lower the heat to a gentle simmer, and cook for 20 minutes.

Snip the strings on the pork and slice it across the grain. Spoon the sauerkraut onto warmed soup plates and arrange the pork slices on top.

Braised Picnic Ham

A fresh picnic ham is one of the tastiest and most economical of all the pork cuts, and braising is the best way to bring out its flavor. If you are able to purchase a boneless picnic ham, get one weighing about 4 pounds. If you can't find a boneless ham, boning it yourself is easy.

MAKES 8 MAIN-COURSE SERVINGS

1 bone-in picnic ham (picnic shoulder),
   about 7 pounds
Salt
Pepper
1 large carrot, peeled and sliced
1 large onion, sliced
1 turnip, peeled and diced
3 tablespoons meat glaze (page 318), optional
1 cup dry white wine
6 cups pork broth (page 319) or other broth or
   water, or as needed
Bouquet garni (page 320)

Preheat the oven to 400°F.

Cut the rind off the picnic ham and reserve it. Bone the picnic ham, then season it thoroughly with salt and pepper, and tie it with kitchen string to make it compact (see page 110). Place the rind, skin side up, in the bottom of a heavy ovenproof pot just large enough to hold the pork and cover it with the carrot, onion, and turnip. Place the ham on top.

Slide the pot, uncovered, into the oven and cook for about 1 1/2 hours, or until the pork releases its juices and the juices boil down and caramelize on the bottom of the pan. Watch to make sure the juices don't burn.

Remove from the oven and, using a large spoon, scoop out and discard any fat from the surface of the caramelized juices. Be careful not to scoop out any juices. Put the pot on the stove top and add the meat glaze, wine, and enough broth to reach

halfway up the sides of the meat. Tuck in the bouquet garni. Cover the pot with a sheet of aluminum foil, pressing it down slightly in the middle so that moisture will condense on its underside and drip down over the exposed parts of the meat, and then with a lid. Place the pot on the stove top, bring to a gentle simmer, and simmer for 1 1/2 hours. After about 30 minutes, remove the lid and lift the foil to make sure the liquid is still at a gentle simmer— you want only a bubble or two to break on the surface every minute or so. When the meat has simmered for 1 1/2 hours, uncover, turn the meat over, re-cover with the foil and lid, and simmer gently for 1 1/2 hours longer, or until a knife or skewer easily slides in and out of the meat.

Transfer the meat to a clean (and smaller) ovenproof pot. Strain the braising liquid into a glass pitcher and skim off the fat with a ladle. Or, ideally, refrigerate the meat and the braising liquid at this point and then lift the congealed fat off the liquid in a single layer. Pour the degreased liquid into a saucepan, bring to a simmer, and simmer, skimming off any fat or froth that rises to the surface, for about 30 minutes, or until reduced by about half. Meanwhile, raise the oven temperature to 400°F.

continued

Pour the reduced liquid over the meat. Slide the pot into the oven and cook the pork, basting it every 10 minutes with the liquid, for about 30 minutes, or until the pork is covered with a shiny glaze.

Transfer the meat to a warmed serving dish, then serve with two spoons or slice with a knife. Spoon the braising liquid over the top.

VARIATIONS: Once you have a braised picnic ham in hand, it can be varied with an almost infinite number of additions. Potatoes can be added to the pot during the last 40 minutes or so of cooking (peel small potatoes and leave whole; peel and section large potatoes). Root vegetables, such as carrots, turnips, and celeriac, cut into pieces or sections, can be added to the braising liquid during the final glazing process, as can mushrooms and sectioned artichoke hearts. You can soak, seed, and puree dried chiles and add them to the braising liquid, turning the dish into a kind of faux mole. Fresh herbs, such as chives, parsley, tarragon, or chervil, can also be added to the braising liquid at the very end, or you can stir in a little heavy cream to add richness.

Braised picnic ham

1. Picnic ham, rind side.

2. Picnic ham, underside.

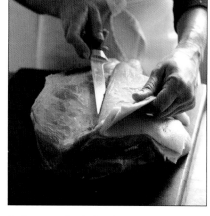

3. Cut away the rind and save it for the braising pot.

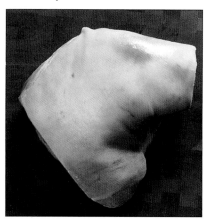

4. Bone the picnic ham.

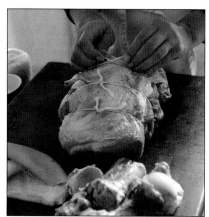

5. Tie the boneless roast with kitchen string.

6. Place the pork on a bed of aromatic vegetables and roast.

7. When the juices have caramelized, add wine and broth.

8. Nestle a bouquet garni in the pot and then braise the pork.

9. Turn the pork over halfway through the braising.

10. Put the pork in a smaller pot.

11. Pour the degreased braising liquid over the pork. Here, the liquid has been refrigerated.

12. If the meat and liquid have been refrigerated, bring the braising liquid to a gentle simmer on the stove top before moving it to the oven. Baste the pork as it braises uncovered.

13. Serve the pork with two spoons.

Pork shoulder chops braised with tomatoes and white wine

1. Uncooked pork shoulder chop.

2. Brown the chops on both sides in hot oil.

3. Pour out the burnt fat and replace it with clean fat, such as butter.

4. Sweat aromatic vegetables until they caramelize.

5. Pour the vegetables over the chops and add the liquids and the bouquet garni.

6. Braise the chops until the meat is easily penetrated with a skewer.

7. Strain the braising liquid and degrease it. Here, the liquid has been refrigerated and the fat has congealed.

8. Reduce the braising liquid and braise the chops in it again.

9. Add optional cream and continue braising.

Pork Shoulder Chops Braised with Tomatoes and White Wine

For this dish, ask the butcher to cut fairly thick chops—about 1 inch thick—preferably from the shoulder end of the whole bone-in pork loin. Chops from the shoulder end have more natural fat, which keeps them moist during braising. Each chop should weigh close to a pound.

MAKES 4 MAIN-COURSE SERVINGS

4 pork shoulder chops, each 12 to 16 ounces and about 1 inch thick
Salt
Pepper
$1/4$ cup olive oil
4 tablespoons butter
2 carrots, peeled and chopped
2 onions, chopped
1 celery stalk, chopped
1 cup dry white wine
1 cup concentrated chicken broth (page 316) or pork broth (page 319), or as needed
Bouquet garni (page 320)
5 tomatoes, peeled, seeded, and chopped
1 cup heavy cream, optional

Season the chops on both sides with salt and pepper. In a large, heavy sauté pan just large enough to hold the chops, heat the olive oil over high heat. When the oil begins to smoke, add the chops and brown well on both sides. Transfer the chops to a plate, and pour the fat out of the pan.

Return the pan to medium heat and melt the butter. Add the carrots, onions, and celery and sweat them, stirring occasionally, for about 10 minutes, or until the vegetables are lightly caramelized. Remove from the heat.

Put the chops in a pan in which they fit as snugly as possible, either a wide pan that will hold them in a single layer or a tall, narrow pot in which you can stack them. Spoon the vegetables over the chops and add the wine, broth, bouquet garni, and tomatoes. Add more broth as needed to cover the chops.

Bring to a simmer over high heat, then reduce the heat to low, cover, and simmer gently for about 3 hours, or until a skewer slides easily in and out of a chop. (Alternatively, slide the covered pot into a 275°F oven and cook for about 3 hours to the same end.)

Transfer the chops to a shallow ovenproof pan in a single layer and set aside. Strain the braising liquid into a glass pitcher and skim off the fat with a ladle. Or, ideally, refrigerate the meat and the braising liquid at this point and then lift the congealed fat off the liquid in a single layer. Pour the strained liquid into a saucepan, bring to a simmer, and simmer, skimming off any fat or froth that rises to the surface, for about 20 minutes, or until reduced by about half. Meanwhile, raise the oven temperature to 400°F.

Pour the reduced liquid over the chops. Slide the pan, uncovered, into the oven and cook the pork, basting every 10 minutes with the liquid, for about 30 minutes. Pour the cream over the chops and continue to cook, basting once or twice, for about 5 minutes longer, or until the liquid is slightly thickened.

Serve the chops in wide soup plates surrounded with the braising liquid.

Potée Auvergnate

A *potée* is much like a pot-au-feu (page 177)—meat cooked by long, gentle simmering—but instead of the meat being primarily beef, it is pork. In this *potée* from the Auvergne, I have used Boston butt and fresh homemade sausages. Feel free to use store-bought sausages, such as sweet Italian sausages.

MAKES 8 MAIN-COURSE SERVINGS

1 boneless Boston butt, about 4 pounds

2 carrots, peeled and cut into 1-inch sections

8 leeks, white part only, tied with kitchen string
   in 2 bundles

1 large onion, quartered

1 turnip, peeled and cut into wedges as shown
   on page 10

Bouquet garni (page 320)

4 quarts chicken broth (page 316), or as needed
   to cover

2 pounds new potatoes

8 medium-sized fresh sausages such as Italian-Style
   Pork Sausage with Marjoram (page 296)

Trim the rind off the Boston butt and save it in the freezer to flavor a braise. Using kitchen string, tie the pork into a more compact shape. Put it in a pot large enough to hold it and the other ingredients with enough headroom so that the ingredients can be fully submerged in broth. Add the carrots, leeks, onion, turnip, and bouquet garni, and pour in the broth to cover.

Bring to a simmer over high heat, then reduce the heat to low and simmer gently, uncovered, for about 2 hours, or until a skewer slides easily in and out of the meat. Add the potatoes and sausages and continue to simmer for about 30 minutes longer, or until the potatoes are easily penetrated with a knife and the sausages are cooked through.

Remove the pork from the pot, snip the strings, and carve into 8 servings. Serve the *potée* in wide soup plates, giving each diner a piece of pork, a sausage, and an assortment of the vegetables. Ladle over enough broth to come about halfway up the slices of pork.

Poached Pork: The Potée

Generations of peasants around the world have sustained themselves with various takes on poached pork. The French *potée* is perhaps the best known of these preparations, and every region in France has its own version. A *potée* typically calls for cooking large pieces of pork shoulder with the usual aromatic vegetables (onions, carrots, and often a leek and/or celery) and something sustaining, such as cabbage, dried beans, lentils, or potatoes. Sometimes the pork is ground and used to stuff cabbage, and sometimes the cabbage is fermented into sauerkraut and served with pork as *choucroute garnie*.

Pork-Stuffed Cabbage

The genius behind this dish lies in the layer of slowly cooked vegetables doused with white wine (to balance the richness of the pork) that caps each serving before it goes in the oven. The pork stuffing is further enhanced with bacon and juniper, and lightened with bread crumbs softened in milk. You can serve these potted stuffed cabbage leaves the day you bake them or you can hold them in the refrigerator for up to 5 days and then reheat them.

MAKES 6 MAIN-COURSE SERVINGS

1 head Savoy cabbage, about 2 pounds

Salt

2 onions, sliced into rings

5 carrots, peeled and sliced

$1/2$ cup olive oil

4 tomatoes, peeled, seeded, and chopped

20 juniper berries

5 cloves garlic

Leaves from 1 bunch parsley

4 slices stale dense-crumb white bread,
    crusts removed

$1/2$ cup milk

$13/4$ pounds boneless pork shoulder, ground
    (ask the butcher to grind it for you)

$1/2$ pound bacon, cut into $1/4$-inch dice

1 egg

1 teaspoon chopped fresh thyme, or 1 tablespoon
    chopped fresh marjoram

1 teaspoon pepper

1 cup dry white wine

Select a pot large enough to hold the head of cabbage immersed in water. Fill the pot with water and bring to a rapid boil. Meanwhile, pull off and discard the outermost leaves of the cabbage. Submerge the cabbage in the boiling water and leave it for 5 minutes, then pull it out by stabbing it with a long fork. Put it in a colander and rinse it with cold running water. Reserve the boiling water. Pull away as many leaves as will come off easily and immerse the cabbage head again in the boiling water for 5 minutes. Remove, rinse, and pull off more leaves the same way. Repeat the process until all the leaves have come away from the head. Throw some salt into the boiling water, add the cabbage leaves, lower the heat to maintain a simmer, and cook for 5 minutes. Drain in a colander. Trim away the ribs or hard pieces from the leaves.

In a large sauté pan, combine the onions, carrots, and olive oil and gently sweat the vegetables over medium heat for about 30 minutes, or until soft. Add the tomatoes and cook until the mixture is dry except for the oil. Remove from the heat.

Place the juniper berries on a cutting board and crush under a saucepan. Add the garlic and parsley and finely chop together. In a bowl, combine the bread and milk and work together to form a paste. Add the juniper berry mixture, the pork, bacon, egg, thyme, 1 tablespoon salt, and the pepper to the bowl and work the mixture with your hands to distribute the ingredients evenly. Don't overwork the mixture or it will be heavy.

Preheat the oven to 350°F. Line six 10- to 12-ounce ovenproof bowls—preferably bowls with lids—with the drained cabbage leaves, leaving enough cabbage overhanging the sides of the bowls to fold over and cover the stuffing. Divide the stuffing evenly among the bowls, and fold over the overhanging cabbage leaves, sealing in the stuffing. Divide the tomato mixture, including its oil, evenly among the bowls, spreading it over the cabbage. Drizzle the wine over the top, again dividing it evenly among the bowls. Put the lids on the bowls, or seal the tops with a double thickness of aluminum foil. Arrange the bowls on a sheet pan. Slide the sheet pan into the oven and bake for 1 hour. You can serve these stuffed cabbage leaves right away, but they taste even better if cooled, covered, and refrigerated for a couple of days, and then reheated in a 350°F oven for about 30 minutes.

Pork Mole

When most people think of mole, they think of chocolate. In fact, most recipes for mole don't contain any chocolate at all. Instead, their distinctive flavor is the result of using a mix of fresh and dried chiles. By playing with the number and variety of chiles, you can come up with interesting variations. Don't hesitate to substitute one or more of your favorite chiles for the chiles suggested here. Accompany the mole with rice.

MAKES 10 MAIN-COURSE SERVINGS

3 poblano chiles

4 ancho chiles, soaked in hot water to cover
    for 30 minutes, drained, and seeded

2 chipotle chiles, soaked in hot water to cover
    for 30 minutes, drained, and seeded

3 tomatoes, peeled, seeded, and chopped

$^{1}/_{2}$ pound tomatillos, papery skins removed
    and halved

1 cup dry-roasted peanuts

$^{1}/_{2}$ teaspoon ground cinnamon

6 cups chicken broth (page 316) or water

1 bone-in Boston butt, about 7 pounds

$^{1}/_{4}$ cup canola oil

Bouquet garni (page 320)

If you have a gas stove, one at a time, put the poblano chiles over the flame and turn as needed to blacken evenly. If you don't have a gas stove, preheat the broiler, put the poblano chiles on a sheet pan, slip under the broiler, and broil, turning as needed to blacken evenly. Transfer the chiles to a bowl, cover with plastic wrap, and let stand for about 10 minutes to steam to simplify peeling. Rinse the peppers under cold running water and peel away the skin with your fingertips. Scrape off any stubborn patches with a small knife. Seed the chiles and chop coarsely.

Coarsely chop the softened ancho and chipotle chiles and add to a blender with the poblanos, tomatoes, tomatillos, peanuts, cinnamon, and 3 cups of the broth. Process until smooth. Add the remaining 3 cups broth and process until combined. Set aside.

Trim the rind off the Boston butt and save it in the freezer for flavoring a braise. Trim off the excess fat and bone the pork as shown on page 107. Cut the pork into 2-inch cubes.

In a heavy sauté pan, heat the canola oil over high heat. When the oil begins to smoke, working in batches to avoid crowding, add the pork and brown well on all sides. Transfer the pork to a heavy pot and pour in the chile mixture. Nestle the bouquet garni in the pot. Bring to a gentle simmer. Cover the pot with a sheet of aluminum foil, pressing it down slightly in the middle so that moisture will condense on its underside and drip down into the pot, and then with a lid.

Simmer for about 3 hours, or until a piece of meat is easily penetrated with a skewer. After about 30 minutes, remove the lid and lift the foil to make sure the liquid is still at a gentle simmer—you want only a bubble or two to break on the surface every second or so. (Alternatively, slide the pot into a 275°F oven and cook for about 3 hours to the same end.)

Spoon the mole onto warmed plates to serve.

Pork Goulash

Essentially a stew containing plenty of onions and flavored with paprika and caraway seeds, goulash is often served with sauerkraut, noodles, or steamed new potatoes, each of which helps to cut the stew's richness.

MAKES 6 MAIN-COURSE SERVINGS

3 pounds boneless pork shoulder, cut into
   2-inch cubes

Salt

Pepper

$1/4$ pound bacon, cut into $1/2$-inch dice

3 tablespoons olive oil

2 large onions, thinly sliced

2 tablespoons tomato paste

4 cloves garlic, minced

$1/4$ cup sweet paprika

2 tablespoons hot paprika

2 teaspoons caraway seeds

Bouquet garni (page 320)

One 12-ounce bottle dark beer

4 cups chicken broth (page 316), or as needed

4 teaspoons cornstarch

$1^{1}/_{2}$ tablespoons water

2 tablespoons chopped fresh dill, optional

Sour cream for serving

Season the pork cubes on all sides with salt and pepper and set aside.

Put the bacon in a heavy pot over medium heat and cook for about 12 minutes, or until the fat is rendered. Using a slotted spoon, transfer the bacon to a bowl and reserve. Raise the heat to high. Working in batches to avoid crowding, add the pork and brown well on all sides. Transfer to a plate and set aside. Pour the fat out of the pot.

Return the pot to medium heat. Add the olive oil and then the onions and sweat the onions, stirring every few minutes, for about 30 minutes, or until they have reduced to about one-tenth of their original volume and have started to caramelize on the bottom of the pan. Add the tomato paste and cook, stirring, for 2 minutes. Add the garlic, the sweet and hot paprika, and the caraway seeds and sweat for 2 minutes longer. Add the pork, nestle the bouquet garni in the pot, and pour in the beer and enough broth to cover the pork. Cover and simmer gently for about $2^{1}/_{2}$ hours, or until a piece of meat is easily penetrated with a skewer. As the stew cooks, uncover the pot occasionally and skim off any fat or froth that forms on the surface.

In a small bowl, stir together the cornstarch and water. Whisk the cornstarch mixture into the stew and bring back to a simmer. Stir in the dill. Spoon the stew into warmed soup plates and serve. Pass the sour cream at the table.

Belly

The belly, the fatty section that stretches along the bottom of the body, below the loin, is used for making such popular preserved pork preparations as slab bacon and pancetta. Sometimes labeled "side pork," it is used fresh in baked beans and cassoulet, and is braised with cabbage. It is also a popular cut in Chinese, Korean, and other Asian cuisines. You can use it for making homemade salt pork, which can then be cooked and combined with lentils for making the classic French dish *petit salé aux lentilles* (page 120). If you have trouble finding pork belly at your regular butcher shop, look for it in a Chinese or other Asian butcher shop.

Homemade Salt Pork

Tastier than what you can buy at the store, this salt pork is handy to have around because you can render it and use it for sautéing or sweating vegetables. You can control the saltiness by leaving it coated with salt for more or less time than given here.

MAKES 2 POUNDS

1 cup coarse sea salt

$1/3$ cup firmly packed brown sugar

6 juniper berries, crushed under a saucepan

2 teaspoons pepper

$1/2$ teaspoon ground ginger

$1/4$ teaspoon ground nutmeg

$1/8$ teaspoon ground cloves

2 imported bay leaves, torn in half

1 piece boneless pork belly, about 2 pounds, or bone-in pork belly, $2^1/2$ to 3 pounds

In a bowl, mix together the salt, sugar, juniper berries, pepper, ginger, nutmeg, cloves, and bay leaves until well combined. Trim the rind off the pork belly and save it in the freezer to flavor a braise. Place the pork belly in a baking dish, and rub the salt mixture thoroughly onto both sides.

Cover and refrigerate for 2 days. Turn the pork belly over, re-cover, and return to the refrigerator for 2 days longer. Rinse the salt mixture off the pork belly and pat dry with paper towels. Use immediately, or wrap airtight and refrigerate for up to 2 weeks or freeze for up to several months.

Homemade salt pork

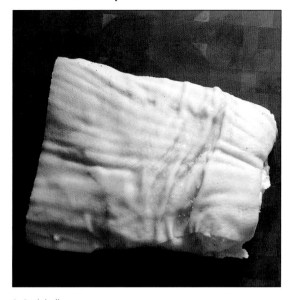

1. Pork belly.

2. Remove the rind from the pork belly.

3. If using bone-in pork belly, cut away the ribs.

4. Rub the pork with the salt mixture.

Salt Pork with Lentils

This traditional French dish, known as *petit salé aux lentilles*, is typically made with the tiny deep green lentils grown around Le Puy, in south-central France, but common brown lentils or even pink or red lentils can be used. The cooking times are similar, though Le Puy lentils may take about 5 minutes longer.

MAKES 6 MAIN-COURSE SERVINGS

Homemade Salt Pork (page 118)
1 large onion, quartered
1 large carrot, peeled and sliced
1 celery stalk, sliced
2 imported bay leaves, torn in half
1 teaspoon peppercorns
3 cups Le Puy lentils, picked over for grit and stones
    and rinsed
3 cups water
Dijon mustard for serving

Put the salt pork in a bowl with water to cover by about 2 inches. Let soak overnight, changing the water once or twice.

Drain the pork, put it in a pot, and add water to cover by about 2 inches. Add the vegetables, bay leaves, and peppercorns and bring to a gentle simmer. Simmer for about 2 1/2 hours, or until the pork is easily pierced with a cooking fork. Remove from the heat and let cool in the cooking liquid.

In a pot, combine the lentils with 3 cups of the cooking liquid from the salt pork and the 3 cups water. (Don't use all of the cooking liquid or the lentils will be too salty.) Bring to a gentle simmer and cook, uncovered, for about 30 minutes, or until tender.

Slice the pork into 6 thick slices, cutting it as if it were a slab of bacon. Spoon a mound of lentils onto each warmed plate. Prop a slice of pork against each mound. Pass the mustard at the table.

Salt pork with lentils

1. Soak the salt pork in water overnight, then simmer for about 2 1/2 hours.

2. Simmered salt pork.

3. Slice the salt pork and serve over the lentils.

Spareribs and Baby Back Ribs

Three types of pork ribs are sold. Spareribs are what is left over when the portion used for bacon is cut away from the belly. These ribs can be somewhat fatty and are usually trimmed into more presentable rectangles called St. Louis ribs. They are a good value because they have a lot of meat on them. Baby back ribs are the ribs that the butcher cuts off when you order a boneless loin of pork. Despite the fact that they are quite bony, they cost about the same per pound as the meat from the loin. If you are up to doing the butchering yourself, it makes sense to buy the rib portion from a whole pork loin, and then cut out the loin muscle yourself, so you have the ribs at a lower price. Finally, country-style ribs are the chops taken from the shoulder end of the loin. They are usually butterflied and are best grilled.

Barbecued Spareribs

The trick to good spareribs is a gentle fire that generates plenty of smoke. Keep in mind that a barbecue is actually a braise (it is the moisture in the ribs that creates the moist cooking environment) and requires slow gentle heat.

MAKES 6 MAIN-COURSE SERVINGS

3 cloves garlic, minced and then crushed to a paste
2 tablespoons firmly packed dark brown sugar
2 tablespoons chili powder
2 tablespoons salt
1 tablespoon pepper
2 teaspoons ground cumin
2 racks spareribs, about 3 pounds each
Barbecue sauce of choice

In a small bowl, stir together the garlic, sugar, chili powder, salt, pepper, and cumin. Rub the slabs of spareribs evenly on both sides with the mixture. Cover and refrigerate, preferably overnight or, if you are in a hurry, for 2 hours.

Prepare a fire for indirect grilling in a covered grill (see page 21). Sprinkle the coals with a handful of soaked wood chips, or put a small sheet of aluminum foil over the coals and top with a handful of sawdust. (If using a gas grill, put unsoaked chips in a special smoker box, or in a perforated foil packet and place directly over the heat.) Place the spareribs over the cool side of the grill and cook for about 2 hours, or until the meat on the ribs offers no resistance when you poke at it with a fork. Control the heat and smoke by opening (for greater heat) or closing the vents on the grill. Add soaked chips or sawdust and charcoal to the coals (or unsoaked chips or sawdust to the smoker box or foil packet) every 30 minutes or so to keep the fire and the smoke going.

Brush the ribs with your favorite barbecue sauce, re-cover, and smoke for a minute more to encourage the sauce to cling, and then serve. Pass extra sauce at the table.

Braised Spareribs with Spices and Red Wine

This dish was inspired by a recipe in Lynne Rossetto Kasper's *The Splendid Table.* She suggests serving the ribs with polenta.

MAKES 6 GENEROUS MAIN-COURSE SERVINGS

5 pounds spareribs

5 tablespoons olive oil

1 large onion, finely chopped

1 bunch parsley, finely chopped

2 imported bay leaves

1 clove garlic, minced

$1/4$ teaspoon ground cloves

$1/4$ teaspoon ground cinnamon

$1/4$ teaspoon ground allspice

$1/4$ teaspoon pepper

1 cup dry red wine

8 tomatoes, peeled, seeded, and chopped, or two 28-ounce cans tomatoes, drained, seeded, and chopped

$1/2$ cup Niçoise olives, pitted

3 tablespoons finely chopped fresh basil

Salt

Cut the racks of ribs into individual ribs. In a heavy pot just large enough to hold all of the ribs later, heat 3 tablespoons olive oil over high heat. When the oil begins to smoke, working in batches to avoid crowding, add the ribs and brown well on both sides. The browning will take about 15 minutes total. Transfer the ribs to a platter. Pour the fat out of the pan.

Add the remaining 2 tablespoons olive oil to the pan, add the onion, and cook over medium heat, stirring occasionally, until the onion is translucent, about 15 minutes. Add the parsley, bay leaves, garlic, and all the spices and cook, stirring, for about 1 minute, or until the spices release their aroma. Add the wine and tomatoes and return the ribs to the pot. Cover, reduce the heat to low, and braise for about $13/4$ hours, or until the meat is easily pulled away from the bone.

Transfer the ribs to a platter and tent with aluminum foil. Skim off the fat from the braising liquid. Simmer the braising liquid over medium heat until reduced to a thick sauce, about 20 minutes. Return the ribs to the pot and simmer for 5 to 10 minutes, or until heated through. Just before serving, stir in the olives and basil and season with salt. Serve the ribs on warmed plates and spoon sauce over each portion.

Baby Back Ribs with Hoisin and Brown Sugar

A number of Chinese recipes cook pork ribs with ginger, hoisin sauce, and sugar. This recipe is my take on that tradition. The heat caramelizes the sugar and meat juices into a delicious accent.

MAKES 6 MAIN-COURSE SERVINGS

2 racks baby back ribs, 2 to 3 pounds each

Pepper

1/4 cup firmly packed brown sugar

2 tablespoons soy sauce

2 tablespoons hoisin sauce

2 tablespoons ketchup

1 teaspoon toasted sesame oil

2 tablespoons dry sherry

Preheat the oven to 350°F or prepare a fire for indirect grilling (see page 21). If you are using the oven, place the ribs in a single layer, rounded side up, in a heavy roasting pan and cook for 20 minutes. Turn the ribs over, brush with one-third of the sauce, and cook for 20 minutes. Turn again, brush with more sauce, and cook for 20 minutes. Turn the ribs a final time, brush with the remaining sauce, and cook for 20 minutes longer, or until the meat pulls away from the bone.

Season the racks liberally with pepper. In a small bowl, stir together the sugar, soy sauce, hoisin sauce, ketchup, sesame oil, and sherry.

If you are using the grill, place the ribs directly over the fire and grill for about 15 minutes. Move the ribs to the cool side of the grill, brush with one-third of the sauce, and grill for 20 minutes. Turn the ribs over, brush with more sauce, and grill for 20 minutes. Turn again, brush with the remaining sauce, and grill for 20 minutes longer, or until the meat pulls away from the bone.

Cut the racks into portions of several ribs each and serve immediately.

Baby back ribs with hoisin and brown sugar

1. If using an oven, cook the ribs for about 1 hour, brushing with sauce every 20 minutes.

2. To serve, cut between the rib bones.

3. Finished ribs.

Loin

A whole loin of pork is almost three feet long and includes twelve ribs. The four ribs nearest the shoulder are shoulder chops and the remaining eight ribs are center-cut chops. The chops cut from the back end of the loin end are loin chops. Often, the loin is boned and is sold in sections that can range from a few inches to over a foot long. A rack of pork cut from the center-cut section of a bone-in loin makes an elegant roast that is much tastier than boneless pork loin.

Roast Boneless Pork Loin

Usually, a boneless pork loin cooks in 35 minutes in a 400°F oven, regardless of how long it is. Ideally, it should be browned on the stove top before roasting, but this isn't essential. Roast it until it feels firm to the touch, no longer, or until an instant-read thermometer stuck into the center reads 135°F. The temperature will rise to 140°F while it rests.

MAKES 4 TO 8 MAIN-COURSE SERVINGS

1 boneless pork loin section, 4 to 8 inches long
Salt
Pepper
2 tablespoons olive oil

Preheat the oven to 400°F. Unless the butcher did it, trim off the silver skin that runs along the top of the loin (see page 129). Season the loin all over with salt and pepper. In an ovenproof sauté pan just large enough to hold the loin, heat the olive over high heat. When the oil begins to smoke, add the loin and brown well on all sides. Slide the pan into the oven and roast for about 35 minutes, or until firm to the touch.

Remove from the oven, tent loosely with aluminum foil, and let rest for 10 minutes before carving. Cut into slices $1/2$ inch thick. Serve 2 slices to each diner on warmed plates.

Gherkin-Mustard Sauce

This tangy sauce makes the perfect accompaniment to grilled and roasted meats, especially pork roasts.

In a small saucepan, combine 3 shallots, minced, and $3/4$ cup dry white wine and simmer gently over low heat until the wine is reduced by about half. Add 2 tablespoons meat glaze (page 318) and whisk until it dissolves. Add 10 small sour gherkins (cornichons), cut into julienne or chopped, and then whisk in 1 tablespoon Dijon mustard until combined. Raise the heat to medium and whisk 4 tablespoons cold butter, cut into 4 slices, until emulsified. Do not allow the sauce to boil. Serve hot. Makes 1 cup.

Frenching a rack of pork

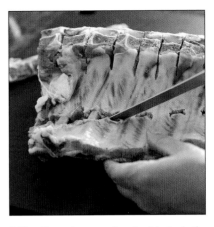

1. Slice along the outside of the rack, about 1 inch in from the end of the ribs, all the way down to the bone.

2. Slide the knife between the ribs and scrape against the bone on both sides to detach the meat and any membrane that might be adhering to the bone.

3. Turn the rack over and again slide the knife between the ribs and across the thin membrane that adheres to the bone.

4. Cut the membrane that adheres to the bone in a straight line parallel to the bone. Push the tissue to each side of the bone with the knife. Don't cut through the tissue.

5. Grip the piece of meat attached to the end of the ribs with a towel and pull it away.

Roast Rack of Pork with Vegetables

Unlike a rack of lamb, which usually comes whole, obliging you to buy the whole thing, you can buy a rack of pork that includes from 4 to 8 ribs, and plan on 1 rib per serving. Tell the butcher you want a roast from the loin end of the rib section (center cut), and ask him or her to cut off the chine bone to make the roast easier to carve. If you roast the rack in a hot oven (450°F), you can get by without browning the roast on the stove top first.

A roast rack of pork is most attractive when you have frenched the ends of the ribs as shown on page 125. Here, a rack of pork is roasted with vegetables—cored carrot sections, turnip wedges, baby potatoes, pearl onions—that have been tossed in melted butter and used to line the bottom of the roasting pan. Gherkin-Mustard Sauce (page 124) makes a fine accompaniment to the roast.

MAKES 6 MAIN-COURSE SERVINGS

1 rack of pork with 6 ribs, about 4 pounds
Salt
Pepper
2 large carrots, peeled and cut into 1¹/₂-inch
    sections
2 turnips, peeled and cut into wedges as shown
    on page 10
12 small fingerling or other small potatoes
1 pint or two 10-ounce packages pearl onions,
    blanched in boiling water for 1 minute, drained,
    rinsed under cold water, and peeled
4 tablespoons butter, melted

Season the pork all over with salt and pepper and let come to room temperature. Preheat the oven to 450°F.

Cut the carrot sections lengthwise into wedges and, if you like, cut away the core from each wedge as shown on page 11. Toss the carrots, turnips, potatoes, and pearl onions with the melted butter and spread over the bottom of a roasting pan just large enough to hold the pork. Place the pork on top and roast for about 1 hour, or until an instant-read thermometer inserted into the center without touching bone reads 135°F. The temperature will rise to 140°F while it rests.

Transfer the rack to a cutting board, tent loosely with aluminum foil, and let rest for 15 minutes before carving. Carve between the ribs, or if you can't cut between the ribs, cut the whole loin muscle away from the ribs and then slice the loin crosswise. Serve with the roasted vegetables.

Roast pork with vegetables

1. Put the seasoned roast in a roasting pan over a layer of vegetables.

2. Finished roast.

3. Carve the roast between the ribs.

Pork Loin Medallions with Red Currant Jam and Sour Gherkins

These medallions are cut from a boneless loin, lightly pounded, and then lightly floured and sautéed in butter. The sauce for this dish, called *sauce charcutière*, is one of the great classics. If you can't find sour gherkins, also known as cornichons, you can leave them out or substitute another sour pickle.

MAKES 4 MAIN-COURSE SERVINGS

1 boneless pork loin section, 1^1/$_2$ pounds

Salt

Pepper

Flour

5 tablespoons butter

^{1}/$_2$ cup dry or semidry white wine

1 cup heavy cream

1 tablespoon Dijon mustard

1 tablespoon red currant jam

^{1}/$_4$ cup julienned sour gherkins (cornichons)

Cut the pork into 8 medallions. Using the side of a cleaver, pound each medallion to flatten slightly. Season the medallions on both sides with salt and pepper and then coat them with flour and pat off the excess. Let come to room temperature.

In a large sauté pan just large enough to hold the pork medallions in a single layer, melt the butter over high heat. When it froths, add the medallions and brown, turning once, for about 2 minutes on each side, or until firm to the touch. Transfer to a warmed platter and set aside in a warm spot. Pour the fat out of the pan.

Return the pan to high heat. Add the wine and boil until it is reduced by half. Add the cream and boil just until the mixture begins to thicken. Whisk in the mustard, jam, and gherkins and season with salt and pepper.

Arrange 2 medallions on each warmed plate and spoon the sauce over the top.

Tenderloin

The tenderest of all pork cuts, the tenderloin, which is the muscle that lies under the loin, is a great value, especially when compared to the same cut from other animals. It is best cooked in one of two ways: browned on the stove top and roasted in the oven, or cut into small rounds (called *noisettes*) and sautéed.

Roast Pork Tenderloin

Most pork tenderloins weigh about 1 pound, which means that one is a bit much for two people and not enough for three. Just plan on having leftovers.

MAKES 4 MAIN-COURSE SERVINGS

2 pork tenderloins, about 1 pound each

Salt

Pepper

3 tablespoons olive oil

3/4 cup water

Preheat the oven to 400°F. Trim the silver skin off the tenderloins. Season the tenderloins all over with salt and pepper. In an ovenproof pan, heat the olive oil over high heat. (Alternatively, use two ovenproof pans.) When the oil begins to smoke, add the tenderloins and brown well on all sides. Slide the whole pan in the oven and roast for about 10 minutes, or until the tenderloins feel firm to the touch or an instant-read thermometer inserted into the center of a tenderloin reads 140°F.

Remove from the oven, tent loosely with aluminum foil while still in the pan, and let rest for 10 minutes. (Leave the tenderloins in the pan so the juices they continue to release end up in the pan.) Transfer the tenderloins to a warmed platter, tent again, and set aside in a warm place.

To create a jus, put the pan on the stove top over high heat and boil down the juices until they evaporate and form a crusty brown layer with a layer of clear fat on top. Pour off the fat, return the pan to high heat, and deglaze with the water, stirring with a wooden spoon until the crust has dissolved into the liquid. Strain the liquid through a fine-mesh strainer into a warmed sauceboat.

Slice the tenderloins and arrange the slices on warmed plates. Pass the jus at the table.

Roast pork tenderloin

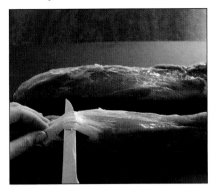

1. Slip a knife under the edge of the silver skin and, while holding the skin taut with one hand, slide the knife under the skin, cutting it away.

2. Brown the tenderloin well on all sides.

3. Roast to an internal temperature of 140°F.

Pork noisettes with prunes (recipe follows)

1. Soak the prunes in white wine.

2. Remove the silver skin from the tenderloins.

3. Cut the tenderloins into rounds.

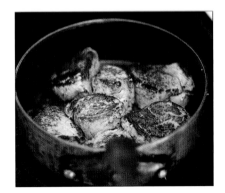

4. Brown the pork rounds on both sides until firm to the touch.

5. Add the prunes and wine to the pan, then add meat glaze and cream and simmer to a nice sauce consistency.

Sautéed Pork Tenderloin with Prunes

To sauté pork tenderloins, cut them into rounds (*noisettes*) about 3/4 inch thick, brown them over high heat, and then continue cooking them until they are firm to the touch. Here, they are served with a sauce made with prunes soaked in wine, a little meat glaze (if you have it), and some cream.

MAKES 4 MAIN-COURSE SERVINGS

1 cup dry or semisweet white wine

1/2 pound pitted prunes

2 pork tenderloins, about 1 pound each

Salt

Pepper

3 tablespoons olive oil

2 tablespoons meat glaze (page 318), optional

1/2 cup heavy cream

In a small bowl, pour the wine over the prunes and let soak for at least 1 hour or up to overnight.

Trim the silver skin off the tenderloins as shown on page 129. Cut the tenderloins into rounds about 3/4 inch thick. Season the rounds on both sides with salt and pepper.

In a sauté pan just large enough to hold the rounds, heat the olive oil over high heat. When it smokes, add the pork rounds and brown, turning once, for about 3 minutes on each side, or until they feel firm to the touch. If they start to get too brown, turn down the heat. Transfer the pork rounds to a warmed platter and set aside in a warm spot. Pour the fat out of the pan.

Drain the prunes, reserving the wine and prunes separately. Measure out 1/2 cup of the wine. Return the pan to high heat and add the 1/2 cup wine and the prunes. Deglaze the pan, scraping up any brown bits on the bottom of the pan with a wooden spoon, then stir in the meat glaze, if using. Boil until the wine is reduced by about half; if you have added the glaze, the sauce will develop a lightly syrupy consistency. Add the cream and boil until reduced to a light sauce consistency. Season with salt and pepper.

Arrange the pork rounds on warmed plates and spoon the sauce and prunes over the top.

Pork Tenderloin with Fresh Apricots

Nearly any fresh or dried fruit—peaches, cherries, raspberries—can be paired with pork. The trick to these combinations is to prepare a *gastrique,* a sweet-and-sour element that complements the mild flavor of the meat and the sweetness of the fruit.

MAKES 4 MAIN-COURSE SERVINGS

2 pork tenderloins, about 1 pound each

Salt

Pepper

3 tablespoons olive oil or clarified butter
(page 6)

1 cup chicken broth (page 316)

4 apricots, halved, pitted, and halves cut
into wedges

1/4 cup *gastrique* (below)

2 tablespoons meat glaze (page 318)

2 tablespoons cold butter, cut into 2 slices

1 teaspoon kirsch, optional

Trim the silver skin off the tenderloins as shown on page 129, and cut the tenderloins into rounds about 1 inch thick. Season on both sides with salt and pepper.

In a sauté pan just large enough to hold the rounds, heat the olive oil over high heat. When it begins to smoke, add the pork rounds and brown, turning once, for about 4 minutes on each side, or until they feel firm to the touch. If they start to get too brown, turn down the heat. Transfer the pork rounds to a warmed platter and set aside in a warm spot. Pour the fat out of the pan.

Return the pan to high heat. Add the broth, apricots, half of the *gastrique*, and the meat glaze and bring to a simmer, stirring to dissolve the meat glaze. Continue to simmer until the mixture reduces to a lightly syrupy consistency. Taste and add more *gastrique* if the sauce needs to be sweeter. Whisk in the butter until emulsified, then whisk in the kirsch. Do not allow the sauce to boil.

Arrange the pork rounds on warmed plates and spoon the sauce and apricots over the top.

Gastrique

Sweet-and-sour sauces made in the French tradition often contain a vinegar-caramel mixture called a *gastrique.* The classic method for making a *gastrique* involves combining vinegar and sugar and then cooking the mixture until it caramelizes. Here is a better method, which calls for caramelizing the sugar and then adding vinegar.

In a small, heavy saucepan, melt 1/4 cup sugar over medium heat, stirring constantly with a wooden spoon so the sugar doesn't burn. The sugar should turn golden brown and then red. As soon as it turns red, add 1/2 cup good-quality wine vinegar, standing back to avoid spatters. Stir the mixture until any hardened sugar dissolves. Makes about 1/4 cup.

Chops

Pork chops from the loin come in three well-known types: shoulder chops taken from the shoulder end of the loin, center-cut chops taken from the center, and loin chops taken from the loin end. Sirloin pork chops, which are taken from the muscles near the hip, are less commonly available. They are often a good value, however, because they are as tender as center-cut chops but less expensive—and less pretty to look at.

The chops taken from the shoulder end of the whole loin include the shoulder blade (for this reason, they are called blade chops) and have considerably more fat than center-cut or loin chops. The higher fat content makes these chops particularly well suited to braising (see recipe, page 113).

Center-cut chops, which come from the section of the loin where the ribs are compact, are easy to cook and eat. You must be careful not to overcook them, however; unlike shoulder chops, they can dry out easily.

Pork Chops with Vermouth and Mustard Sauce

Pork chops can be sautéed and then finished with any of the pan sauces made following the model on page 7. Here, the pan is deglazed with vermouth and the sauce is finished with mustard, which cuts the richness of the pork. You can use thick or thin chops for this recipe, adjusting the heat as needed.

MAKES 4 MAIN-COURSE SERVINGS

4 center-cut pork chops, about 8 ounces each and 1 inch thick
Salt
Pepper
3 tablespoons olive oil
1/2 cup white vermouth
2 tablespoons meat glaze (page 318), optional
1 to 2 tablespoons Dijon mustard

Season the pork chops on both sides with salt and pepper. In a sauté pan just large enough to hold them, heat the olive oil over high heat if cooking thick chops or medium heat if cooking thin chops. When the oil ripples, add the chops and cook, turning once, for about 5 minutes per inch of thickness on each side, or until the chops feel firm to the touch. Transfer the chops to a warmed platter and set aside in a warm spot. Pour the fat out of the pan.

Return the pan to high heat. Add the vermouth and deglaze the pan, scraping up any brown bits from the bottom of the pan with a wooden spoon. Stir in the meat glaze, if using, then simmer until the vermouth is reduced by half; if you have added the glaze, the sauce will develop a lightly syrupy consistency. Whisk in the mustard to taste and season with salt and pepper.

Arrange the chops on warmed plates and spoon the sauce over the top.

Grilled Pork Chops with Fresh Sage

You can try these chops with other herbs, but sage has just the right pungency to hold up to the chops and the lightly smoky flavor from the grill.

MAKES 4 MAIN-COURSE SERVINGS

4 center-cut pork chops, about 8 ounces each and 1 inch thick

Salt

Pepper

8 fresh sage leaves

3 tablespoons extra virgin olive oil

Season the pork chops on both sides with salt and pepper, and press 2 sage leaves on top of each chop. Coat the chops on both sides with the olive oil and let stand for an hour or two to allow the sage to flavor the meat.

Prepare a hot fire for direct grilling in a grill (see page 21). Place the chops on the grill rack and grill, turning once, for about 5 minutes on each side, or until the chops are firm to the touch, or an instant-read thermometer inserted through the side of a chop without touching bone reads 140°F. Serve immediately on warmed plates.

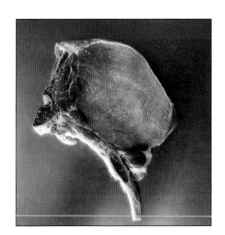

Center-cut chop.

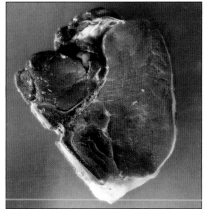

Loin chop.

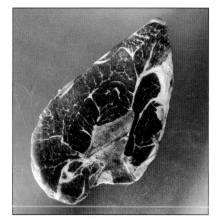

Sirloin chop.

Ham

Hams come in several forms, from the sublime to the banal. The term *ham* refers to a leg of pork, which can be purchased in a variety of forms, including fresh, cured and sometimes smoked, and even precooked and in some cases glazed—so-called supermarket hams.

A fresh ham—a leg of pork with nothing done to it—offers good value. You can brine it before cooking, which I do in the recipe on the facing page, though this is optional. Because a whole leg of pork is a giant piece of meat sufficient for serving twenty or so diners, it is often sold halved, so that you can buy either the butt end or the shank end. Butchers often cut out the best inner slices to sell as ham steaks, however, so if you can swing it, it makes good sense to buy the whole thing.

The most famous hams are cured with salt, sometimes smoke, and sometimes spices for relatively long periods so the meat dries out. Although it is possible to cook these hams, they are often best served raw. Among the best-known of these cured hams are prosciutto from Italy—*prosciutto di Parma* and *prosciutto di San Daniele* are the best-known labels—and *serrano* from Spain. The most celebrated *serrano* is *jamón ibérico de bellota*, made from a special black-footed pig that feasts on acorns (*bellotas*). Ibérico ham from the town of Jabugo, in Huelva Province, is particularly renowned. Bayonne ham from southwestern France; Westphalian ham, a heavily smoked ham from Germany; and American cured hams, known as country hams, are also prized. Smithfield ham, named for Smithfield, Virginia, is probably the most widely recognized of the American hams, but small makers dot the South, so that it is possible to find cured and sometimes smoked hams from Kentucky, Tennessee, the Carolinas, and elsewhere in Virginia. Don't thickly slice these hams; they are too rich and too salty. Instead, slice them thinly and serve as a main course or appetizer or on top of veal, as in the saltimbocca on page 240. They are also good cooked, as the recipe for a baked country ham on page 136 illustrates.

Most hams you encounter at the supermarket are of the banal sort: precooked and in a can and meant to be cooked again. They have been brined by injecting them with brine, instead of patiently waiting for the brine to penetrate on its own, and when they are smoked, they spend very little time in the smokehouse, unlike a genuine country ham, which is sometimes smoked for days. You'll also find spiral-cut hams at the supermarket, which only need to be reheated. They are usually covered with an overly sweet commercial glaze that does nothing to improve their flavor.

Some stores and mail-order operations carry partially cooked hams, often labeled "traditional" hams. These hams need to be cooked to an internal temperature of 140°F before serving.

Roast Leg of Pork

In this recipe, I brine the leg of pork for 2 weeks to make the meat moister, but the brining is optional—roast fresh ham is good without it. If you are using only part of the leg—the butt half or the shank half—cut the brining time to 1 week. Cut the rind off the ham and make a crisscross design in the fat. If there is not enough brine, increase the amounts of the ingredients proportionately.

MAKES ABOUT 20 MAIN-COURSE SERVINGS, IF USING A WHOLE LEG, OR 10 MAIN-COURSE SERVINGS, IF USING A HALF LEG

24 quarts water (6 gallons)

6 cups kosher salt

2 cups firmly packed brown sugar

Ice

1 whole leg of pork (fresh ham), about 20 pounds, or $1/2$ leg of pork, about 10 pounds

In a very large pot, combine 8 quarts of the water, salt, and sugar and bring to a simmer, stirring to dissolve the salt and sugar. Remove from the heat and let cool, then transfer to a vessel large enough to hold the pork submerged in brine. Pour in the remaining 16 quarts water. Add enough ice just to chill the brine.

Trim the rind off the pork leg, leaving a thick layer of fat. Using a sharp knife, score the fat with a crisscross pattern without cutting all the way through to the meat. This will help with brine absorption and fat rendering in the oven. Submerge the leg in the brine, cover, and refrigerate for 2 weeks for a whole leg or 1 week for a half leg. Remove the pork from the brine, discard the brine, and then refrigerate the pork for 3 days before you roast it. This gives the brine time to distribute itself within the leg.

Preheat the oven to 350°F. Place the pork in a roasting pan just large enough to hold it. Roast a whole leg for about 4 hours or a half leg for about 3 hours, or until an instant-read thermometer inserted into the thickest part without touching bone reads 135°F.

Transfer the pork to a platter, tent loosely with aluminum foil, and let rest for 20 minutes. Pour the juices in the roasting pan into a glass pitcher, skim off the fat with a ladle, and reheat the juices just before serving.

Carve the ham into thin slices and serve. Pass the juices at the table.

Brining

Many cooks have taken to brining meats, especially pork to compensate for some of the natural fat that has been bred out of pigs in recent decades. A good basic brine is 1 cup salt to 4 quarts water. You can also add flavorings like fresh thyme, peppercorns, juniper berries, coriander seeds, and bay leaves. Some people like to add something sweet, such as brown sugar, honey, or maple syrup, although maple syrup is a bit expensive for such a project. How long you brine foods depends on their size. Pork chops should be brined for a couple of hours; a whole pork loin can remain for a couple of days. Don't brine any meat too long or it will get mushy. A brine is typically made by bringing the ingredients to a simmer for a few minutes to dissolve the salt and to get any other ingredients to release their flavor. It is then allowed to cool completely before adding the meat.

Baked Glazed Ham

This recipe is for the kind of ham you'll find at the supermarket, ham that's already been cooked. In essence, when you bake it, you are just reheating it.

MAKES ABOUT 20 MAIN-COURSE SERVINGS, IF USING A WHOLE HAM, OR 10 MAIN-COURSE SERVINGS IF SERVING A HALF HAM

1 fully cooked whole boneless ham, about 12 pounds, or $1/2$ fully cooked ham, about 6 pounds

$1/2$ cup Dijon mustard

1 cup firmly packed brown sugar

1 cup chopped pineapple with its syrup

$1/4$ cup cider vinegar or white wine vinegar

Preheat the oven to 350°F. Score the fat covering the ham in a crisscross pattern. Place in a roasting pan just large enough to hold it.

Slide the pan into the oven and bake for about 3 hours, or until an instant-read thermometer inserted into the thickest part reads 130°F.

Remove the ham from the oven, and raise the oven temperature to 400°F. In a small bowl, stir together the mustard, sugar, pineapple and syrup, and vinegar until well combined to make a glaze. Spoon enough of the glaze over the ham to coat it well. Return the ham to the oven and continue to bake the ham, spooning the glaze over the top every few minutes, for about 20 minutes, or until the glaze is browned and well caramelized.

Transfer the ham to a platter, tent loosely with aluminum foil, and let rest for 20 minutes before serving. Carve into slices to serve.

Baked American Country Ham

You won't find an American country ham at the supermarket, but you will be able to track one down at a gourmet shop or online. These hams are delicious, but they have a high salt content. If you are cooking them, you must first reduce their saltiness by soaking them in water for a few days and then blanching them. Even then, the ham will still be salty and should be served thinly sliced. If you are serving the ham raw, it does not need to be soaked but it does need to be sliced paper-thin.

MAKES ABOUT 20 MAIN-COURSE SERVINGS

1 American country ham, about 12 pounds

2 cups firmly packed light brown sugar

Select a vessel large enough to hold the ham covered with water. Trim the rind off the ham, then score the fat in a crisscross pattern. Place the ham in the vessel, add water to submerge, cover, and refrigerate for 3 days, changing the water every 8 hours.

Rinse the ham under cold running water. Put the ham in a pot and add cold water to cover. Bring to a simmer and simmer gently—a bubble should rise to the surface every second or so—for 10 minutes. Drain, re-cover with cold water, and return to the stove top. Bring back to a gentle simmer and simmer for about $1^1/2$ hours, or until an instant-

American Country Ham with Figs

The best way to enjoy a country ham is to eat it raw. You will need to slice it very thin, which will take a little practice. Use a knife with a long, thin, flexible blade. Slice off the fat near where you are cutting away the meat, and then slice the ham along its length, pressing the blade against the meat to keep the blade flat. The salty ham is wonderful simply served with sweet fresh figs.

Slice the ham as thinly as possible as shown on page 138 and arrange on a platter or plates. Surround with 12 ripe fresh figs. Makes 4 first-course servings.

read thermometer inserted into the center without touching bone reads 110°F.

Remove the ham from the pot and place in a roasting pan just large enough to hold it. Preheat the oven to 400°F. Spread the sugar over the ham and slide the ham into the oven. Bake for about 30 minutes, or until an instant-read thermometer inserted into the center without touching bone reads 130°F.

Transfer the ham to a platter, tent loosely with aluminum foil, and let rest for 20 minutes before carving. Cut into thin slices to serve.

Croque-Monsieur with Country Ham

A *croque-monsieur* is a griddled ham and cheese sandwich that has been dipped in béchamel sauce and cooked in butter. A *croque-madame* is a *croque-monsieur* with a fried egg on top.

MAKES 4 SANDWICHES

$1/2$ **cup (1 stick) butter**
$1/4$ **cup flour**
2 cups whole milk
Pinch of ground nutmeg
Salt
Pepper
8 slices firm-crust, dense-crumb white bread
$1/2$ **pound American country ham, very thinly sliced if raw (see page 138), thinly sliced if cooked**
$1/2$ **pound Gruyère cheese, thinly sliced into strips**

In a small saucepan, melt 4 tablespoons of the butter over medium heat. Whisk in the flour and cook, whisking constantly, for about 3 minutes, or until the mixture is smooth (see page 138). Whisk in the milk and then bring to a simmer, whisking constantly. Whisk for about 5 minutes, or until smooth and thickened. Season with the nutmeg, salt, and pepper. Pour into a square baking dish large enough to hold the sandwiches in a single layer.

Lay 4 bread slices on a work surface. Top with the ham and then the cheese, dividing them evenly. Put the remaining bread slices on top. Place the sandwiches in the béchamel, turning to coat both sides.

In a sauté pan large enough to hold the sandwiches in a single layer, melt the remaining 4 tablespoons butter over medium heat. When the butter froths, add the coated sandwiches and cook, turning once, for about 5 minutes per side, or until golden brown.

Cut each sandwich in half and serve hot.

Croque-monsieur.

Croque-madame.

Croque-monsieur with country ham

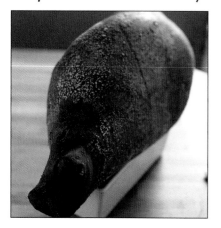

1. Whole country ham.

2. Trim the rind off the ham.

3. Slice the ham with a long, flexible knife.

4. The sliced ham.

5. Cook together flour and butter to make a roux.

6. Add milk and whisk until smooth to make a béchamel. Bring to a boil, then season.

7. Arrange the ham and cheese between slices of white bread.

8. Dip the sandwiches in the béchamel sauce.

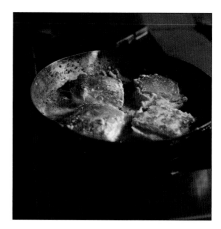

9. Cook the sandwiches in butter.

Ham Hocks

Ham hocks, which are smoked shanks, need long, slow cooking—at least a couple of hours—to release their flavor and for the meat to become tender enough to eat. They are great in soups, especially those made with dried beans or lentils. The best approach when making a soup is to coordinate the cooking of the hocks with the legumes. If the beans take the same time to cook as the hocks, they can be cooked together. If you are cooking lentils, which take less time, the hocks will need to be cooked first in broth or water. Then, when you cook the lentils, use the hock cooking liquid and include the cooked hocks in the pot. When the hocks and beans or lentils are done, pull the meat off the hocks and mix it into the soup.

Smoky Bean and Ham Hock Soup

Adjust the cooking time for this soup to the type of bean you are using. Black beans take the longest, with up to 5 hours for Indian gram beans and up to 3 hours for other black beans. Most dried beans take 2 to 2^1/$_2$ hours, or a little longer if they have not been soaked. Cannellini, *borlotti*, or navy beans are a few of the possibilities.

MAKES 8 FIRST-COURSE SERVINGS

2 cups dried beans (see note), picked over for grit
    and stones and rinsed
2 quarts chicken broth (page 316) or water
Bouquet garni (page 320)
2 ham hocks, ^{1}/$_2$ to 1 pound each
2 tablespoons olive oil
1 large onion, finely chopped
2 cloves garlic, finely chopped
4 jalapeño chiles, seeded and finely chopped
1 cup dry sherry
2 tablespoons chopped fresh cilantro
Salt
Pepper
Tabasco sauce for serving
Sour cream for serving

In a large bowl, soak the beans in cold water to cover for 4 hours. Drain and put into a pot. Add the broth, bouquet garni, and ham hocks and bring to a gentle simmer. Cover and cook for about 2^1/$_2$ hours for most beans or longer for black beans, or until the beans are tender and the meat easily pulls away from the hocks.

While the beans are cooking, in a sauté pan, heat the olive oil over medium-low heat. Add the onion, garlic, and chiles and sweat them, stirring occasionally, for about 10 minutes, or until soft. Remove from the heat.

When the beans and hocks are ready, remove the hocks from the pot. Pull the meat off the hocks, cut into bite-size pieces, and return them to the pot along with the onion mixture and the sherry. Simmer for 5 minutes, then add the cilantro and season with salt and pepper.

Ladle the soup into warmed bowls and serve. Pass the Tabasco sauce and sour cream at the table.

VARIATION: To make a pureed soup, remove the ham hocks and puree the soup with an immersion blender or stand blender. Shred the meat from the hocks and add it to the pureed soup.

Bacon

Most of us find it hard to imagine life without bacon. Its smoky, savory flavor and aroma are hard to resist. Bacon is made from the belly of the pig, which is cured with salt and then smoked. It can be served alone or used, cut into thin strips, as a garnish for stews and braised dishes.

Canadian bacon comes from the loin, not the belly, and is not smoked. Its most popular use is for eggs Benedict, but it can also be sautéed in a little butter or oil and served as you would smoked bacon.

Sautéed Bacon

The trick to sautéing bacon is to use medium heat. If the heat is too low, all of the fat in the bacon will render out before the bacon is cooked. If the heat is too high, the bacon will brown or even burn before it has rendered enough fat.

Look for bacon that has been naturally smoked, rather than "smoke flavored." Also, if you buy slab bacon, it will keep better and you can slice it to any thickness you like. Keep in mind that most slab bacon is sold with the rind intact, so you are getting less edible bacon per pound. Keep slab bacon wrapped in a kitchen towel in the refrigerator. Don't wrap it in plastic wrap or it will quickly sour.

MAKES 4 BREAKFAST SERVINGS

$1/2$ pound slab bacon (weight not including rind)

If your bacon has a rind, remove it as shown below. Slice the bacon to the desired thickness.

Put the bacon in a sauté pan (there is no need to add fat) just large enough to hold it. Put the pan over medium heat and cook for about 5 minutes on the first side, or until the bacon begins to curl. The timing will depend on the thickness. Turn the bacon over with a fork and cook for about 2 minutes, or until cooked to your liking.

Sautéed bacon

1. To detach the rind, slide a sharp, flexible knife blade between the rind and the flesh and work the knife away from you, while pulling on the rind.

2. Cut the bacon to the desired thickness.

3. Sauté the bacon over medium heat.

Eggs Benedict

It's easy to improvise variations on this classic. The Canadian bacon can be replaced with thin pieces of sautéed ham or bacon. Spinach or sliced asparagus or other sliced vegetables can be added, which go on the English muffin underneath the egg. The hollandaise can be changed to béarnaise, or the sauce can be flavored with dill.

MAKES 4 MAIN-COURSE SERVINGS

2 egg yolks
2 tablespoons water
1¹/₂ cups clarified butter (page 6), melted
Salt
Pepper
Fresh lemon juice
4 tablespoons butter, or as needed
8 slices dense-crumb white bread, cut into
    3- to 4-inch rounds with a cookie cutter
8 thin slices Canadian bacon
8 poached eggs (right)

To make the hollandaise, combine the egg yolks and water in a heatproof bowl, place over (not touching) simmering water in a saucepan, and whisk vigorously. At first the mixture will become frothy. Continue to whisk rapidly until the mixture is stiff. Remove the bowl from over the heat and gradually add the clarified butter, a tablespoon at a time, whisking constantly until a smooth, thick sauce forms. Season to taste with salt, pepper, and lemon juice. Place the bowl over the pan of water off the heat to keep warm until using.

In a sauté pan, melt the 4 tablespoons butter over medium heat. Add the bread rounds and cook, turning once, for about 3 minutes per side, or until pale brown. Transfer to warmed plates and set aside in a warm spot.

Add the Canadian bacon to the pan over medium heat and sauté, turning once, for about 3 minutes

on each side or until lightly browned on both sides. Place a slice of Canadian bacon on each bread round, and set a poached egg on top. Spoon the hollandaise sauce over the eggs. Serve at once.

Poaching Eggs

Buy the freshest eggs you can find because they will hold their shape better in the hot water. Pour water into a sauté pan to a depth of 2 inches and bring to a bare simmer. Holding each egg as close to the surface of the water as possible, crack the eggs into the barely simmering water and poach for 3 to 5 minutes. A 3-minute egg will have a medium-firm yolk; adjust the time according to how you like your eggs cooked. If the eggs start to stick to the bottom of the pan, don't try to dislodge them until you are ready to remove them from the pan or you might break the yolks. Using a slotted spoon, remove the eggs from the water and put them in a bowl of ice water until you are ready to serve them. Then, drain off the cold water, add boiling water to cover, and let stand for 1 minute. Remove with the slotted spoon, pat dry on a towel, cut away any ragged white, and serve.

BEEF

Buffalo

A buffalo carcass looks somewhat like a steer carcass but with considerably less fat. Because of this, and because buffalo meat contains no marbling, it is important not to overcook tender cuts such as the rack (or steaks from the rack), the loin (or loin chops), or the leg. When braising buffalo for a pot roast or stew, the meat should ideally be larded (see page 15) because it is so lean. Buffalo has a surprisingly delicate flavor, making a marinade unnecessary.

Beef is the most popular meat in America, with the average per capita consumption weighing in at sixty pounds annually, as compared to just a half pound of lamb. Americans have a long history of raising cattle, and western ranchers once sent their livestock as far east as New York for slaughtering. Nowadays, most beef is slaughtered in the West, where it is usually broken down into individual cuts and shipped in Cryovac (see page 177) to markets all over the country.

High-quality beef comes from steers, which are castrated males. Dairy cows that have gotten too old to produce milk are also processed, but typically their meat goes to fast-food restaurants, not to supermarkets and butcher shops. All beef must be inspected by the United States Department of Agriculture (USDA) before it can be sold, but grading is voluntary. However, most meat processors opt to have their beef graded at the same time as it is inspected. Grading is based on flavor, juiciness, and tenderness, qualities directly related to how much marbling, or intramuscular fat, is present. The highest grade is prime, followed by choice, select, and standard. (Four additional lower grades are used for meat that is not retailed to the public.) Most of us encounter only choice meats, which have a moderate amount of marbling, and occasionally select meats, with somewhat less marbling. Only "uptown" butchers carry prime beef, rich in marbling and butter tender. These same butchers are also likely to dry age their beef themselves, ideally for about six weeks. Dry aging causes enzymes to break down the meat, which both tenderizes it and gives it flavor. Don't confuse meat that's been "aged" in Cryovac, which does nothing to the meat, with authentic dry aging.

Before the animal is reduced to the cuts you find at the store, it is halved lengthwise, and each half is divided into primal cuts: the chuck, which is the shoulder; the rib, which is the back of the rib cage; the loin (including the flaps that are the flank steaks); the breast, which contains the brisket and plate; and the round, or hindquarter including the shanks. Most of the tender cuts come from the loin and rib sections, though a few tender muscles are also found elsewhere on the animal.

BEEF CUTS

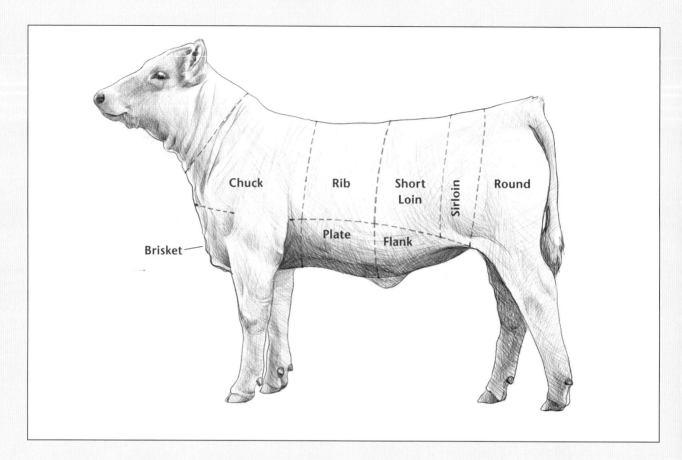

Chuck
Chuck: braise
Chuck round steak: sauté, grill, broil
Short rib: braise, poach, barbecue

Rib
Prime rib: roast
Rib steak: sauté, grill, broil

Short Loin
Porterhouse steak, T-Bone steak: sauté, grill, broil
Shell (bone-in) steak, New York strip (boneless) steak: sauté, grill, broil
Shell (bone-in), strip (boneless): roast, grill
Tenderloin (sliced): sauté, grill, broil
Tenderloin (whole): roast, poach

Sirloin
Sirloin steak: sauté, grill, broil
Tri-tip: sauté, grill, broil

Round
Bottom round: roast, braise, poach, sauté (slices)
Eye of round: roast, grill
Rump roast: roast, stir-fry
Top round: roast, grill, poach, stew

Brisket
Brisket: braise, barbecue, cure (corned beef)

Plate
Short rib: braise, poach, barbecue
Skirt steak: sauté, grill, broil

Flank
Flank steak: sauté, grill, broil

Other
Cheek: braise
Hanger steak: sauté, grill, broil
Marrowbone: poach
Oxtail: poach, braise
Shank: braise, poach
Tongue: braise, poach

Chuck

The chuck is the most complicated cut of beef because it breaks down into many muscles that go this way and that and that have varying degrees of tenderness. For the most part, the muscles from the chuck are best suited for braising, although some cuts can be grilled or sautéed. The chuck is separated from the rest of the steer by cutting between the fifth and sixth ribs. In its raw and very large form (about 100 pounds), it is called a cross-cut chuck. When the brisket is removed (about 10 pounds), the chuck is called an arm chuck. When the arm is removed, the chuck is called a square-cut chuck. The square-cut chuck has many muscles, but only four main ones. The eye of the chuck, which is sometimes labeled "chuck eye roast," is the largest of the four. Then there are two muscles, one under the shoulder blade and the other over it. These are called the under-blade steak or pot roast and chuck blade or top-blade meat, respectively; the latter is sometimes called a flat-iron roast. Both make excellent pot roasts but can also be grilled, sautéed, or quickly roasted.

Beef Stew with Onions and Beer

Known as *carbonnade à la flamande*, this Belgian stew, made with onions and Belgian beer, calls for grilling the meat before braising it. You can also brown the meat in hot oil in a sauté pan or stove-top grill pan. When you slice the onions for this dish, you may think you have cut too many, but they soften and dissolve as the dish cooks.

MAKES 6 MAIN-COURSE SERVINGS

1 chuck blade roast, about 5 pounds, trimmed
    of silver skin (see page 152) and excess fat and
    cut into 2-inch chunks
Salt
Pepper
$^1/_4$ cup canola oil, if browning the meat on the
    stove top
8 large onions, about $^3/_4$ pound each, thinly sliced
4 tablespoons butter
Bouquet garni (page 320), including
    1 cinnamon stick
Two 12-ounce bottles Belgian beer, preferably
    bière brune

Season the beef all over with salt and pepper. Prepare a hot fire for direct grilling in a grill (see page 21). Place the beef chunks on the grill rack and grill, turning as needed, until well browned on all sides. Transfer to a plate. (Alternatively, in a large skillet, heat the canola oil over high heat. When the oil begins to smoke, working in batches to avoid crowding, add the meat chunks and sear, turning as needed, until well browned on all sides. Transfer to a plate.)

In a large, heavy pot, combine the onions and butter and sweat the onions over medium heat for about 15 minutes, or until they "melt" and start to stick and brown on the bottom of the pan.

Put the meat in a medium pot and spread the onions over the top. Nestle the bouquet garni in the onions and meat, and pour in the beer. Place over high heat and bring to a simmer. Turn down the heat to low and simmer gently, covered, for about 3 hours, or until the meat is easily penetrated with a fork. (Alternatively, bring to a simmer as directed, then cover and place in a preheated 275°F oven for about 3 hours to the same end.)

continued

Remove the bouquet garni. Serve the meat in warmed shallow plates with some of the liquid and onions, or puree some of the onions and liquid with an immersion blender to thicken the pan juices slightly before serving.

VARIATIONS: This is a model stew that can serve as a prototype for many variations. Other aromatic vegetables, such as carrots and celery, can replace or augment the onions; wine, cider, vinegar, broth, or meat glaze can be used in place of the beer for the liquid; and a wide array of vegetables—from mushrooms, peas, or turnips to haricots verts, leeks, or fennel—can be cooked separately and used to garnish the stew just before serving. Root vegetables can also be cooked directly in the stew, though you will need to sort through and remove the original aromatic vegetables before serving.

Beef stew with onions and beer

1. Brown the meat in a sauté pan or stove-top grill pan or on a grill.

2. Put the onions and butter in a pot and sweat the onions gently.

3. Put the onions on top of the meat, nestle the bouquet garni in the pot, and pour in the beer.

Red Wine Daube

A daube is a traditional stew of southern France. The advantage to a daube is that you don't need to brown the meat before you braise it. You just toss it into the pot with aromatic vegetables, add wine to cover, and cook slowly. True, it does help to marinate the meat overnight, and the ultimate in finesse is to lard each of the pieces. This recipe makes a lot because it is always better the next day.

MAKES 12 MAIN-COURSE SERVINGS

1 chuck blade roast, 8 pounds

1¹/₂ pounds fatback (weight not including rind)
    or *lardo,* optional

2 cloves garlic, minced and then crushed to a paste

2 large carrots, peeled and sliced

1 large onion, quartered

1 celery stalk, halved

4 cloves garlic, crushed

3 tablespoons meat glaze (page 318), optional

1 bottle (750 ml) full-bodied red wine

Bouquet garni (page 320)

1 tablespoon flour per cup of jus, optional

1 tablespoon butter per cup of jus, optional

Choosing a Cut for Stews and Other Braises

Beef lends itself especially well to braised dishes such as pot roasts and stews. The best cuts for braising come from the chuck (shoulder). Oxtails and short ribs also make savory braises. Do not attempt to use meat from the round, which is too lean and will yield a dried-out result.

Trim away the silver skin and excess fat from the roast (see page 152). Cut the meat into strips about 1 inch wide and 2 inches long. Cut the fatback into sheets about ¹/₄ inch thick, then cut the sheets into strips, or lardons, about ¹/₄ inch on each side and about 2 inches long. In a bowl, toss together the fatback and minced garlic, cover, and marinate in the refrigerator overnight. In a large nonreactive bowl, combine the meat, carrots, onion, celery, crushed garlic, meat glaze, wine, and bouquet garni; cover and refrigerate overnight. The next day, remove the meat from the marinade, reserving the marinade, and insert a lardon into each piece of meat as shown on page 15.

Select a medium heavy pot. Place the larded meat in the pot and add the reserved marinade. Bring to a simmer, cover, and simmer gently for 3 hours, or until the meat is easily penetrated with a knife. Never allow the stew to boil.

Remove and discard the onion, celery, and bouquet garni. Skim off any fat from the surface and serve the meat in warmed soup plates surrounded by the braising liquid. If you want to concentrate the braising liquid, pour the daube into a strainer placed over a saucepan. Cover the meat and place aside in a warm spot. Skim the fat off the liquid with a ladle, then simmer, skimming off any fat or froth that rises to the surface, until reduced by one-third to one-half. If you want to thicken the liquid, measure it, make a paste (a *beurre manié*) with 1 tablespoon each flour and butter per cup of liquid, and whisk the paste into the simmering liquid. The liquid must reach the simmer for the thickening effect to take place. If necessary, reheat the meat briefly in the liquid, then serve surrounded by the liquid.

Pot Roast with Carrots and Pearl Onions

The best cut for a pot roast is a chuck blade roast, sometimes called a flat-iron roast. When you buy the roast, you might as well buy the whole thing (rather than a piece), which weighs about 5 pounds and will serve about six (the meat shrinks considerably as it cooks). Ideally, the meat should be larded to give it extra moistness, though larding is not essential because a blade roast contains plenty of internal fat. The usual braising methods should be used—an initial roasting with aromatic vegetables, followed by long, slow simmering, followed by degreasing of the braising liquid and a final glazing.

MAKES 6 MAIN-COURSE SERVINGS

1 chuck blade roast, about 5 pounds

Salt

Pepper

1 piece fatback with rind, about 2 pounds, optional

1 bunch parsley, finely chopped, if larding roast

4 cloves garlic, minced and then crushed to a paste, if larding roast

1 large onion, sliced

1 large carrot, peeled and sliced

Bouquet garni (page 320)

6 cloves garlic, crushed

1 bottle (750 ml) dry white wine

4 cups chicken broth (page 316), reduced to 2 cups

3 slender carrots, peeled and sliced

One 10-ounce package pearl onions, blanched in boiling water for 1 minute, drained, rinsed under cold water, and peeled

Trim away the silver skin and excess fat from the roast (see page 152). Season all over with salt and pepper and set aside. Cut away the rind from the fatback and reserve the rind. Cut the fatback into sheets about 1/4 inch thick, then cut the sheets lengthwise into strips, or lardons, about 1/4 inch

on each side. In a bowl, mix together the lardons, parsley, and minced garlic; cover and marinate in the refrigerator for at least 3 or 4 hours or preferably overnight.

Place the roast in a shallow bowl and add the sliced onion, sliced large carrot, bouquet garni, crushed garlic, and wine. Cover and marinate in the refrigerator for at least 3 or 4 hours or preferably overnight.

Preheat the oven to 450°F. Remove the meat and vegetables from the marinade; reserve the wine and bouquet garni. Using a hinged larding needle, lard the roast with the lardons as shown on page 15.

Select a heavy ovenproof pot just large enough to hold the meat and line the bottom with the fatback rind, skin side up. Place the vegetables from the marinade on top of the rind, and put the roast on top of the vegetables. Place the pot in the oven and roast, uncovered, for about 1 1/2 hours, or until the meat releases juices that caramelize (but don't burn) on the bottom of the pot.

Remove the pot from the oven and reduce the oven temperature to 275°F. Remove any fat from the pot with a bulb baster or large spoon, and then add the broth and the wine and bouquet garni from the marinade. Bring to a gentle simmer on the stove top. Cover the pot with a sheet of aluminum foil, pressing it down slightly in the middle so that moisture will condense on its underside and drip down onto the exposed parts of the meat, and then with a lid.

Return the pot to the oven and braise the roast for 1 1/2 hours. Check occasionally to make sure the liquid is not boiling, and if it is, turn down the heat. Turn the roast over gently, so the meat that was above the liquid is now submerged, re-cover the pot with the foil and the lid, and continue to braise for about 1 hour longer, or until the roast is easily penetrated with a knife.

Transfer the roast to a smaller ovenproof pot, moving it gently so it doesn't fall apart. Strain the braising liquid into a glass pitcher and skim off the fat with a ladle. Or, ideally, refrigerate the braising liquid at this point and then lift off the congealed fat in a single layer. Pour the degreased liquid into a saucepan, bring to a simmer, and simmer, skimming off any fat or froth that rises to the surface, for about 30 minutes, or until reduced by about half. Meanwhile, raise the oven temperature to 450°F.

Pour the reduced liquid over the meat, and add the sliced slender carrots and pearl onions. Slide the pot, uncovered, into the oven and cook the roast, basting it every 10 minutes with the liquid, for about 30 minutes, or until the roast is covered with a shiny glaze and the carrot slices and pearl onions are tender.

Remove the roast from the oven. Using two spoons, serve in warmed soup plates surrounded with the braising liquid and topped with the carrot slices and pearl onions.

VARIATIONS: You can vary this recipe by using additional or different aromatic vegetables, such as onions or turnips; using cider, beer, or broth in place of the wine for the braising liquid; trading out the thyme for marjoram in the bouquet garni; or garnishing with mushrooms, haricots verts, leeks, or other vegetables in place of the carrot slices and pearl onions.

Pot roast with carrots and pearl onions

1. Trim off excess fat and silver skin from the chuck blade roast.

2. Marinate the roast with wine, aromatic vegetables, and a bouquet garni.

3. Marinate the lardons with garlic and parsley.

4. Line the braising pot with the fatback rind, placing it skin side up.

5. Arrange the aromatic vegetables from the marinade on top of the rind.

6. Place the larded roast on top of the vegetables.

7. Roast until the juices caramelize on the bottom of the pot.

8. Add the broth and the wine and bouquet garni from the marinade to the pot. Braise until the roast is tender.

9. Degrease the braising liquid. Here, the liquid has been refrigerated so that the fat congeals on the surface. Reduce the liquid for about 30 minutes.

Sauerbraten

Essentially a pot roast in which the meat is marinated and braised in vinegar, the quality of your sauerbraten will depend largely on what kind of vinegar you use. Unless you make your own wine vinegar (highly recommended), your best bet is sherry vinegar, preferably aged. There is also excellent *vinaigre de Banyuls* from southwestern France, but it is hard to find and expensive. Ideally, the meat should be larded, but if you use a chuck roast with plenty of marbling you can get by without larding.

MAKES 6 MAIN-COURSE SERVINGS

1 chuck blade roast, about 5 pounds

Salt

Pepper

1 cup red wine vinegar, sherry vinegar,
    or Banyuls vinegar

1 cup full-bodied red wine

10 juniper berries, crushed under a saucepan

1 piece fatback with rind, about 2 pounds, optional

1 bunch parsley, finely chopped, if larding roast

4 cloves garlic, minced and then crushed to a paste,
    if larding roast

1 large onion, sliced

1 large carrot, peeled and sliced

6 cloves garlic, crushed and peeled

Large bouquet garni (page 320)

4 cups chicken broth (page 316), reduced to 2 cups

3 slender carrots, peeled and sliced

One 10-ounce package pearl onions, blanched
    in boiling water for 1 minute, drained, rinsed
    under cold water, and peeled

Trim away the silver skin and excess fat from the roast as shown on the facing page. Season all over with salt and pepper. Place in a shallow bowl and add the vinegar, wine, and juniper berries. Cover, and marinate in the refrigerator for 24 hours.

Cut away the rind from the fatback and reserve the rind. Cut the fatback into sheets about 1/4 inch thick, then cut the sheets lengthwise into strips, or lardons, about 1/4 inch on each side. In a bowl, mix together the lardons, parsley, and minced garlic; cover and marinate in the refrigerator for 24 hours.

Preheat the oven to 450°F. Remove the meat from the marinade, reserving the marinade. Using a hinged larding needle, lard the roast with the lardons as shown on page 15.

Select a heavy ovenproof pot just large enough to hold the meat and line the bottom with the fatback rind, skin side up. Place the sliced onion, sliced large carrot, and crushed garlic on top of the rind and put the roast on top of the vegetables. Place the pot in the oven and roast, uncovered, for about 1 1/2 hours, or until the meat releases juices that caramelize (but don't burn) on the bottom of the pot.

Remove the pot from the oven and reduce the oven temperature to 275°F. Remove any fat from the pot with a bulb baster, and then add the marinade, bouquet garni, and the broth. Cover the pot with a sheet of aluminum foil, pressing it down slightly in the middle so that moisture will condense on its underside and drip down onto the exposed parts of the meat, and then with a lid.

continued

Return the pot to the oven and braise the roast for 1¹/₂ hours. Check occasionally to make sure the liquid is not boiling; if it is, turn down the heat. Turn the roast over gently, so the meat that was above the liquid is now submerged, re-cover the pot with the foil and the lid, and continue to braise for about 1 hour longer, or until the roast is easily penetrated with a knife.

Transfer the roast to a smaller ovenproof pot, moving it gently so it doesn't fall apart. Strain the braising liquid into a glass pitcher and skim off the fat with a ladle. Or, ideally, refrigerate the braising liquid at this point and then lift off the congealed fat in a single layer. Pour the strained liquid into a saucepan, bring to a simmer, and simmer, skimming off any fat or froth that rises to the surface, for about 30 minutes, or until reduced by about half. Meanwhile, raise the oven temperature to 450°F.

Pour the reduced liquid over the meat, add the sliced slender carrots and pearl onions, and place the pot, uncovered, in the oven. Cook the roast, basting it every 10 minutes with the liquid, for about 30 minutes, or until the roast is covered with a shiny glaze and the carrot slices and pearl onions are tender.

Remove the roast from the oven and slice it thickly. Serve in warmed soup plates surrounded with the braising liquid and topped with the carrot slices and pearl onions.

Poblano Chili con Carne

Most people think of chili as consisting mostly of beans, but in New Mexico and Texas, chili is made by stewing meat with chiles. Because many cooks don't have access to the wide variety of chiles found in the Southwest, this recipe calls for the easily found poblano, which can range from mild to hot.

MAKES 6 MAIN-COURSE SERVINGS

8 poblano chiles

3 pounds boneless beef stew meat from the chuck, cut into 1-inch cubes

Salt

Pepper

5 tablespoons olive oil, or as needed

1 large onion, sliced

4 cloves garlic, minced

10 tomatoes, about 5 pounds total weight, peeled, seeded, and chopped

1 tablespoon dried oregano

1 tablespoon ground cumin

1 chipotle chile in adobo sauce, rinsed, seeded, and chopped

3 tablespoons chopped fresh cilantro

Sour cream

If you have a gas stove, put the poblano chiles over the flame and turn as needed to blacken evenly. If you don't have a gas stove, preheat the broiler, put the poblano chiles on a sheet pan, slip under the broiler, and broil, turning as needed to blacken evenly. Transfer the chiles to a bowl, cover with plastic wrap, and let stand for about 15 minutes to steam to simplify peeling. Rinse the peppers under cold running water and peel away the skin with your fingertips. Scrape off any stubborn patches with a small knife. Seed the chiles and cut lengthwise into 1/4-inch-wide strips.

Season the meat all over with salt and pepper. In a heavy sauté pan, heat 3 tablespoons of the olive oil over high heat. When the oil begins to smoke, working in batches if needed to avoid crowding, add the beef and brown well on all sides. Transfer the beef to a plate. Pour the fat out of the pan.

In a pot just large enough to hold the meat, heat the remaining 2 tablespoons olive oil over medium heat. Add the onion and garlic and sweat them, stirring occasionally, for about 15 minutes, or until the onion and garlic have softened. Add the browned meat, tomatoes, oregano, and cumin to the pot and stir well. Cover, adjust the heat to maintain a gentle simmer, and cook for about 1 1/2 hours, or until the meat is just tender.

Add the poblanos, re-cover, and simmer for 30 minutes longer, or until the meat is easily penetrated with a fork. Add the chipotle chile and cilantro and stir well. Spoon the chili into warmed soup plates and serve. Pass the sour cream at the table.

Preparing poblano chiles

1. Blacken the chiles on the stove top or under the broiler.

2. Put the chiles in a bowl and cover with plastic wrap to steam. Peel off the skins.

3. Cut lengthwise into narrow strips.

Short Ribs

The short ribs are the section of the rib left over after the ribs chops have been cut off, or they are taken from the chuck (the shoulder) or the plate (part of the breast, below the rib). They come in three basic forms: in thin, crosswise slices; in 2- to 3-inch slices; and in pieces 4 to 6 inches long. Most recipes for short ribs can use any of these forms. Short ribs are best braised or barbecued.

Braised Short Ribs with Sauerkraut

This is one of the most satisfying meat dishes made anywhere. When the meat is properly cooked and the braising liquid thoroughly degreased, the meat melts in your mouth and leaves a long, lingering savor. Nothing requires you to serve sauerkraut with this dish—it's just that it's awfully good. Its tart crispness is the perfect foil for the rich fattiness of the meat. Other vegetables, such as carrots, turnips, pearl onions (or larger boiling onions), parsnips, or potatoes, will work, too. Mashed potatoes are also a good foil and a good way to eat the magnificent braising liquid. Although short ribs contain a good amount of fat, a lot of the fat is rendered and eliminated in the braising process. If you can't find the shape and size of short ribs called for here, just buy the equivalent weight. This dish is best made the day before serving, to allow the flavors to develop.

MAKES 6 MAIN-COURSE SERVINGS

2 short-rib sections, each with 3 or 4 ribs and about
    6 inches long (about 5 pounds total)
Salt
Pepper
1 large onion, sliced
1 large carrot, peeled and sliced
Three 12-ounce bottles Belgian beer, preferably
    bière brune
$1/4$ cup meat glaze (page 318), optional
Bouquet garni (page 320)

Four 1-pound bags sauerkraut, well drained
$1/2$ cup water

Preheat the oven to 400°F. Season the short ribs all over with salt and pepper. Place the onion and carrot on the bottom of an ovenproof pot just large enough to hold the short ribs, and place the short ribs on top. Place in the oven and roast, uncovered, for about $1^1/2$ hours, or until the short ribs release juices that caramelize (but don't burn) on the bottom of the pot.

Remove from the oven and reduce the oven temperature to 275°F. Remove any fat from the pot with a bulb baster. Pour in the beer and add the meat glaze and bouquet garni. Bring to a gentle simmer on the stove top. Cover the pot with a sheet of aluminum foil, pressing it down slightly in the middle so that moisture will condense on its underside and drip down onto the exposed parts of the meat, and then with a lid.

Return the pot to the oven and braise the short ribs for $1^1/2$ hours. Check occasionally to make sure the liquid is not boiling; if it is, turn down the heat. Turn the ribs over gently, so the meat that was above the liquid is now submerged, re-cover the pot with the foil and the lid, and continue to braise for about $1^1/2$ hours longer, or until a knife slides easily in and out of the meat.

continued

Braised short ribs with sauerkraut

1. Uncooked short ribs.

2. Place onion, carrot, and short ribs in a pot in which the ribs just fit and roast until the juices caramelize on the bottom of the pot.

3. Add beer, meat glaze, and a bouquet garni; cover the pot with aluminum foil and its lid, and braise.

4. Pour the braising liquid into a tall, narrow pitcher and skim off the fat.

5. Or, chill the liquid overnight and pull off and discard the congealed fat.

6. Put the short ribs in a clean pot and pour the braising liquid on top. Bring to a simmer on the stove top and then slide into the oven.

7. Baste every 10 minutes until the short ribs are covered with a shiny glaze.

Transfer the roast to a smaller ovenproof pot, moving it gently so it doesn't fall apart. Strain the braising liquid into a glass pitcher and skim off the fat with a large ladle. Or, refrigerate the liquid overnight and remove the fat in a single congealed layer. Pour the braising liquid over the meat and bring to a simmer on the stove top. Meanwhile, raise the oven temperature to 450°F.

Slide the pot, uncovered, into the oven and cook the ribs, basting them every 10 minutes with the liquid, for about 30 minutes, or until the meat is covered with a shiny glaze.

Meanwhile, in a large saucepan, combine the sauerkraut and water, place over low heat, and cover the pan so the sauerkraut steams. Cook gently for about 30 minutes.

When the sauerkraut is hot, arrange it in a mound on a platter. Put the short ribs on top. Pass the braising liquid in a sauceboat.

What are Kobe and Wagyū Beef?

Most of us have heard of the legendary Kobe beef, produced from steers that are fed beer and regularly treated to a massage. It is the product of a certain breed of black Wagyū cattle, in a single prefecture of Japan, that is given special treatment; it is rated using a system of A1 to A5, with A5 the highest rating. Wagyū beef comes from several different breeds of Wagyū cattle, all of them characterized by intense marbling due to their genetic makeup. Wagyū cattle are also raised in the United States, Australia, and New Zealand. In these countries, the Wagyū meat is rated using a system of 1 to 12, with 12 the most marbled. To grasp how intensely marbled Wagyū meat is, you need only compare it to American prime beef, which, if rated using the same system, would rank at about 5. One characteristic of Wagyū beef is that the fat has a particularly low melting point—around 77°F—so that it literally melts in the mouth.

Prime Rib

The prime rib comes from the section at the back of the animal that includes the ribs. It is the most expensive and, along with the tenderloin and strip or shell, the most tasty and tender of the beef cuts in general. When buying prime rib, look for meat from the loin end, which contains a single muscle, rather than the shoulder end, which has a complex of several muscles. Count on one rib for every two servings. You can ask the butcher to bone your prime rib to make carving easier, though the meat will have less flavor. You can also grill-roast a prime rib the same way you grill-roast a strip (page 160).

Roast Prime Rib

The only tricky thing about roasting prime rib is making sure you don't overcook it. Remember, if you bring it to the table underdone, you can always remedy the situation by sticking it back into the oven. Overcook it and there is no going back. Overcooking should not be a problem if you have a reliable thermometer. If you're planning on serving your prime rib rare, you won't have much in the way of drippings to make a jus, so you may want to make an "artificial jus" (page 171). If you have not cooked your prime rib rare, you may have enough juices in the pan to make a jus, in which case you can follow the directions on page 161. Don't base the cooking time for your prime rib on the weight of the roast. A large roast takes only slightly more time than a small one.

A Word about Salt

When salt is applied to raw meat it draws out water and makes the surface of the meat wet. It also penetrates the meat and flavors it. For this reason, it is always best to season meat a couple of hours before cooking it and then pat the meat dry just before cooking. A lot is made about the best variety of salt to use for cooking. The truth is that any salt will work in a pinch. Sea salt, however, is ideal.

MAKES 4 TO 16 SERVINGS

1 prime rib, 2 to 7 ribs
Salt
Pepper

If you're buying dry-aged beef, the fat covering the meat will be delicious and should be left on. Otherwise, trim off excess fat so the meat is covered with only a thin layer. Season the meat all over with salt and pepper and let it come to room temperature. Preheat the oven to 450°F.

Put the roast in a heavy roasting pan just large enough to hold it (or stack 2 sheet pans) and slide it into the oven. Roast for about 20 minutes, then turn down the oven temperature to 300°F. Roast for about 20 minutes more, then start checking the temperature with an instant-read thermometer, inserting it into the center of the roast without touching bone. Roast to 120°F for rare, 125°F for medium-rare, or 130°F for medium. (Keep in mind that the temperature will rise 5°F as the roast rests.)

Transfer the roast to a large cutting board (preferably one with a moat to catch the juices), tent loosely with aluminum foil, and let rest for 20 minutes before carving.

Cut the whole loin muscle away from the ribs and then cut the loin crosswise into slices of the desired thickness. Or, cut between the loin and ribs, freeing only as much meat as you plan to serve, then cut the loin crosswise into slices.

Strip or Shell

The shell is the loin section of the steer—essentially, the lower back—with the tenderloin removed and the back of the loin cut out and used for top butt sirloin and bottom butt sirloin. When the bones are removed from the shell, it becomes a strip. A whole strip can be grilled or roasted (a well-kept secret), but it is usually cut into steaks called strip steaks or New York cut steaks (see Steak, page 181). Depending on how thickly you cut the strip, you will get from 10 to 14 steaks out of it.

Grill-Roasted or Oven-Roasted Strip

When buying a strip for roasting, count on about $1/2$ pound per serving, or a little more if you have big eaters. If the butcher presents you with a whole strip, ask for the section from the rib end. A strip of hard, gristly tissue runs through the sirloin end. Meat from the strip needs only salt and pepper for seasoning. Don't be tempted to disguise its natural flavor with a marinade.

MAKES 4 TO 10 SERVINGS

1 section strip (New York cut), 2 to 5 pounds, cut from the rib end

Salt

Pepper

If the meat is covered with a thick layer of fat, trim it so that only a thin layer remains. Don't trim it all off or the meat will dry out during cooking. Let the meat come to room temperature. Season all over with salt and pepper.

Prepare a hot fire for direct grilling in a grill (see page 21). Place the strip, meat side down, on the grill rack. (If you start the strip fat side down, you will have a lot of flare-ups because the coals will be quite hot.) After about 20 minutes, turn the strip over, fat side down, and grill for about 15 minutes longer, or until an instant-read thermometer inserted into the thickest part reads 120°F for rare, 125°F for medium-rare, or 130°F for medium. (Keep in mind that the temperature will rise 5°F as the roast rests.)

Alternatively, preheat the oven to 450°F. Place the strip, fat side up, in a heavy roasting pan and slide it into the oven. Roast for about 15 minutes, then turn down the oven temperature to 300°F. Roast for 20 to 40 minutes more, or until the internal temperature reaches 120°F for rare, 125°F for medium-rare, or 130°F for medium.

Transfer the roast to a large cutting board (preferably one with a moat to catch the juices), tent loosely with aluminum foil, and let rest for 15 minutes before carving. Cut into slices about $1/4$ inch thick or, if you're being decadent, as thick as 1 inch. Pass the juices that collect in the moat of the cutting board at the table.

Roasts

A whole steer provides a plethora of roasts. The most famous of them is the prime rib, which consists of 7 or fewer center-cut ribs roasted in a single piece. Further back along the animal is the strip, which also makes an elegant roast. Less glamorous roasts include the top sirloin or the whole top round. These latter roasts—the tougher cuts—should be sliced relatively thinly to disguise any impression of toughness.

Tenderloin

Because it is so tender, the tenderloin is one of the most desirable and expensive beef cuts. It is easy to buy steaks cut from the tenderloin, but it often makes good economic sense to buy a whole tenderloin and break it down yourself. Once you trim it and remove the silver skin (see photos on page 162), you have an elongated muscle made up of three parts. The thick end, called the butt end, can be tied together and roasted or sliced into steaks. The center section, the heart of the tenderloin, can be roasted whole (in which case it is called chateaubriand) or sliced into perfectly round steaks called tournedos. The thin end of the tenderloin can be sliced into small rounds called filets mignons and used for the recipe on page 166.

Roast Whole Tenderloin with Jus

Most tenderloin is sold these days with the fat removed, but if you encounter one with fat, just peel the fat off in one big piece. Remove the "chain," trim off the silver skin, and tie half of the butt end to the tail end to create a roast of even thickness throughout its length.

MAKES 8 TO 12 MAIN-COURSE SERVINGS

1 whole beef tenderloin, about 4 pounds, trimmed as shown on page 162 and tied (see note)
2 tablespoons olive oil
Salt
Pepper
3 cups chicken broth (page 316)

Slice off a section from along the butt end of the tenderloin and tie it to the tail of the roast so that the whole roast is of even thickness.

Bring the beef to room temperature. Preheat the oven to 500°F.

Rub the tenderloin with the olive oil and season it liberally all over with salt and pepper. Cut the chain into small pieces and spread them over the roasting pan, preferably an oval roasting pan just large enough to hold the roast. Place the roast on top.

Slide the pan, uncovered, into the oven and roast the tenderloin for 15 to 25 minutes, or until well browned and an instant-read thermometer inserted into the center reads 120°F for rare or 125°F for medium-rare. (Don't ever cook tenderloin beyond medium-rare or it will be dry. The temperature will rise 5°F as the roast rests.)

Transfer the roast to a platter or cutting board, tent loosely with aluminum foil, and let rest for 15 minutes before carving.

While the roast is resting, make the jus. Put the roasting pan on the stove top over high heat and stir around the pieces of meat until the meat is browned and any juices have caramelized on the bottom of the pan. Deglaze the pan with 1 cup of the broth, scraping up any brown bits on the bottom of the pan with a wooden spoon. Boil down the broth until it caramelizes into a crusty brown layer with a layer of clear fat on top. Pour out the fat, return the pan to high heat, and deglaze the pan with a second cup of broth, again boiling it down. Deglaze the pan with the remaining 1 cup broth, stirring until the crust has dissolved in the liquid, and then strain the liquid through a fine-mesh strainer into a warmed sauceboat.

Carve the tenderloin into slices 1/2 inch thick. Pass the jus at the table.

Beef tenderloin

1. Whole beef tenderloin in Cryovac.

2. Whole tenderloin before trimming.

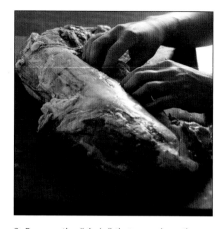
3. Remove the "chain" that runs along the side of the tenderloin.

4. Using a sharp knife, trim off the fat and silver skin.

5. Trimmed whole tenderloin.

6. Tenderloin divided into butt end, center (chateaubriand), and filets mignons.

Roast whole tenderloin with jus

1. Snip the string around the tail end of the roast.

2. Carve the tenderloin into slices about 1/2 inch thick.

3. Finished tenderloin with jus.

Beef Wellington

The secret to successful beef Wellington is to surround the meat with a duxelles (sautéed finely chopped mushrooms) that has been cooked down until completely dry. It will absorb any liquid released by the meat and prevent the crust from becoming soggy. If you don't make your own puff pastry, try to find a brand that is made with butter only. They do exist, though they are expensive.

MAKES 8 MAIN-COURSE SERVINGS

1 center-cut beef tenderloin section, about 8 inches long and 2^1/$_2$ pounds, trimmed of fat and silver skin as shown on the facing page

Salt

Pepper

4 tablespoons butter or olive oil

2 pounds cremini mushrooms, finely chopped by hand or in a food processor

1 pound store-bought all-butter puff pastry, thawed in the refrigerator if frozen

1 egg, beaten with a pinch of salt

Season the tenderloin liberally all over with salt and pepper and reserve at room temperature while you prepare the other ingredients.

In a large sauté pan, melt the butter or warm the oil over high heat. When the butter froths or the oil ripples, add a large handful of the mushrooms and toss and stir for about 1 minute. Continue adding the mushrooms, a handful at a time, and cook, stirring occasionally, for about 10 minutes, or until any liquid they release evaporates and they are nicely browned and dry. Season with salt and pepper and set aside to cool.

Preheat the oven to 425°F. If it has a convection feature, turn it on.

Roll the pastry out into a rectangle just large enough to enclose the tenderloin completely.

Sprinkle a sheet pan with cold water, and transfer the pastry to the pan. Spread the cooled duxelles over the pastry as shown on page 164. Place the tenderloin near one long edge of the pastry, then roll up the meat in the pastry to enclose it completely. Make sure that the wrapped tenderloin is seam side down, and then seal the open ends by folding them under. Place the wrapped tenderloin on the pan. Using a sharp knife, cut a series of diagonal slashes, about ^{1}/$_2$ inch apart, along the top of the roll, being careful not to cut into the meat. Brush the pastry with the egg wash.

Bake for about 40 minutes, or until the pastry is golden brown and an instant-read thermometer inserted into the center of the tenderloin reads 120°F for rare or 125°F for medium-rare. (The temperature will rise 5°F as the roast rests.)

Transfer to a platter, tent loosely with aluminum foil, and let rest for 20 minutes before serving. Using a sharp knife, cut into 1-inch-thick slices to serve.

VARIATIONS: Beef Wellington can be made with brioche dough instead of puff pastry. The duxelles can be made with wild mushrooms (it's a good use for stems saved up in the freezer), or you can replace the duxelles with crepes, which will also absorb liquid released by the roast. If you want to accompany the dish with a sauce, make the Bordelaise Sauce on page 189.

Beef Wellington

1. Cook chopped mushrooms down to form a duxelles.

2. Spread the duxelles over a rectangle of puff pastry.

3. Place a tenderloin over one side of the pastry.

4. Roll up the meat in the pastry to enclose it completely.

5. Position the roll seam side down on the pan. Make a series of slashes along the top of the pastry, being careful not to cut into the meat.

6. Finished beef Wellington.

Chateaubriand with Béarnaise Sauce

The chateaubriand, a roast taken from the center of the tenderloin, is roasted in the same way as a whole tenderloin (see page 161). You can serve it with a jus as you do the whole tenderloin, or with its classic accompaniment, béarnaise sauce. You can also substitute the butt end of the tenderloin for the chateaubriand.

MAKES 6 MAIN-COURSE SERVINGS

1 tenderloin section, about 6 inches long and
    2 pounds, cut from the center or the butt
    end and trimmed of fat and silver skin as
    shown on page 162
Salt
Pepper
2 tablespoons olive oil
Béarnaise Sauce (right)

Preheat the oven to 500°F. Season the tenderloin liberally all over with salt and pepper. In an ovenproof sauté pan just large enough to hold the meat, heat the olive oil over high heat. Add the meat and brown well on all sides. Do not brown the ends.

Transfer the pan to the oven and roast for about 15 minutes, or until you see the slightest trace of juices in the pan.

Transfer to a cutting board, tent loosely with aluminum foil, and let rest for 10 minutes before carving. Cut into thick slices to serve. Pass the sauce at the table.

Béarnaise Sauce

This rich, buttery sauce should have the thickness of mayonnaise, which makes it easy to dollop on tasty cuts of meat. The acidity in the sauce—from vinegar—delivers an irresistible tang that offsets the richness of the sauce and meat. If you have a Windsor pan (a saucepan with a narrow bottom and flared sides), use it for making the sauce.

To make béarnaise sauce, in a small saucepan, combine $1/3$ cup white wine vinegar; 1 shallot, minced; 5 peppercorns, crushed; and 3 tarragon sprigs. Place over medium heat and boil down until reduced to 3 tablespoons liquid. Remove from the heat and set aside.

Combine 3 tablespoons cold water and 3 egg yolks in a Windsor pan or a heatproof bowl and whisk briefly just until fluffy. Set the pan over medium heat, or the bowl over (not touching) simmering water in a saucepan. Whisk rapidly until the mixture froths up and then loses a little volume and you see deep traces on the bottom of the pan. This will take about 3 minutes. Immediately remove from the heat and whisk in 1 cup (2 sticks) butter, clarified (see page 6) and melted, about 1 tablespoon at a time, until a thick, emulsified sauce forms. Strain the vinegar mixture through a fine-mesh strainer into the sauce and whisk to combine. Season with salt and pepper. Makes about 1 cup, enough for 6 servings.

Tenderloin Sandwiches

These elegant little sandwiches are a great party snack. The trick is to make white bread toast the same size as the meat, and then garnish the sandwiches with the condiments you would use for hamburgers.

MAKES 8 SMALL SANDWICHES

16 slices dense-crumb white bread
1 center-cut beef tenderloin section, about 3 inches long and 1 1/4 pounds, trimmed of fat and silver skin as shown on page 162
Salt
Pepper
Olive oil for sautéing
Tomato slices
Mustard
Ketchup
Relish

Toast the bread on both sides. Cut the tenderloin into 8 perfectly round slices, each about 1/3 inch thick, and season on both sides with salt and pepper. Using a cookie cutter the same diameter as the tenderloin slices, cut out a round from each slice of toast. Set the toast rounds aside.

If you are grilling the tenderloin slices, prepare a hot fire for direct grilling in a grill (see page 21). Place the slices on the grill rack as close to the heat source as possible and grill, turning once, for about 1 minute on each side, or until rare or medium-rare. Do not cook them any longer or they will be dry. If you are sautéing the tenderloin slices, in a sauté pan, heat the olive oil over high heat until it begins to smoke. Working in batches to avoid crowding, add the slices and sauté, turning once, for about 1 minute on each side, or until rare or medium-rare.

Transfer the tenderloin slices to a warmed platter, and serve with the toast rounds, tomato slices, mustard, ketchup, and relish. Let diners assemble their own sandwiches.

Filets Mignons Rossini

This is a derivative of the famous tournedos Rossini, in which hot foie gras is placed on top of relatively large medallions of beef tenderloin and then the stack is covered with a truffle sauce. Here, I've replaced the truffle sauce with a Madeira sauce (to which you can, if you so wish, add truffles) and use the small medallions at the end of the tenderloin instead of the tournedos. If you want to make the authentic version, use tenderloins cut from the center of the filet.

MAKES 4 MAIN-COURSE SERVINGS

1 beef tenderloin section, about 5 inches long and 1 1/2 pounds, taken from the narrow end but not including the ragged tip, trimmed of fat and silver skin as shown on page 162
Salt
Pepper
3-inch-thick piece Terrine of Foie Gras (page 310) or Foie Gras au Torchon (page 312)
4 tablespoons clarified butter (page 6) or olive oil
1/2 cup Madeira
3 tablespoons meat glaze (page 318)
1 black winter truffle, peeled, thinly sliced, and peels chopped (optional)
3 tablespoons cold butter, cut into 3 slices

Cut the tenderloin section in half crosswise, then cut each half in half again crosswise. Cut each piece into 3 slices, for a total of 12 slices. Season all over with salt and pepper and reserve. Slice the foie gras into 12 slices, each 1/4 inch thick. Reserve.

Just before serving, heat 2 tablespoons of the clarified butter in a heavy sauté pan over high heat until it begins to smoke. Add the beef medallions and sear, turning once, for about 30 seconds on each side, or until nicely browned. Transfer to paper towels briefly to absorb the fat, then arrange on warmed individual plates and place in a warm spot. Pour the fat out of the pan.

Return the pan to high heat, and add the remaining clarified butter. When the butter just begins to smoke, one at a time, add the foie gras slices to heat them in the fat. Then, almost as soon as you add a slice, remove it from the pan so it doesn't melt away. Place a slice on top of each medallion. Pour the fat out of the pan.

Return the pan to high heat, and add the Madeira. Deglaze the pan, scraping up any brown bits on the bottom of the pan with a wooden spoon. Add the meat glaze and boil down the liquid until a lightly syrupy consistency develops. Add the truffle slices and chopped truffle peels, simmer for about 2 minutes, and then whisk in the cold butter until emulsified. Do not allow the sauce to boil. Season with salt and pepper.

Spoon the sauce over the medallions and serve.

VARIATION: If you like, cut out rounds of bread the same size as the medallions and brown them in clarified butter to use as stands for the medallions. If you're serving a tasting menu, you can get by with serving only one of the medallions.

Top Round

The top round is the large (about 10 pounds), dome-shaped muscle found in the middle of the leg. The meat is very lean and can be somewhat tough. It is best roasted and then thinly sliced for sandwiches, or cut into cubes and used for kebabs.

Roast Top Round

If you are making sandwiches for a big picnic or get-together for a crowd, roast a whole top round or part of a top round.

MAKES ENOUGH MEAT FOR 12 TO 20 SANDWICHES

1 piece top round of beef, about 5 pounds
Salt
Pepper

Let the beef come to room temperature. Season all over with salt and pepper.

Preheat the oven to 300°F. Place the meat in a heavy roasting pan just large enough to hold it.

Slide the pan into the oven and roast for about 1 hour, or until an instant-read thermometer inserted into the center reads 120°F for rare, 125°F for medium-rare, or to desired doneness. (The temperature will rise 5°F as the roast rests.)

Transfer to a cutting board, tent loosely with aluminum foil, and let rest for 20 minutes before slicing. Or, let cool completely, cover tightly, and store in the refrigerator for up to 5 days before using.

Grilled Shish Kebabs

You can slide just about anything onto a skewer and grill it, but here I use peppers, onions, and mushrooms, along with beef cubes. If you're using wooden skewers, soak them for an hour in cold water to cover before you use them, and make sure you press the ingredients together so they are just touching and no wood is exposed. Otherwise, the skewers can burn. You might also wrap the ends of the skewers in aluminum foil to prevent burning.

MAKES 12 KEBABS, OR 6 MAIN-COURSE SERVINGS

3 pounds top round of beef, cut into 3/4-inch cubes
4 bell peppers, in different colors, seeded and cut into 1-inch squares
1 pound cremini mushrooms, halved vertically
3 small onions, quartered through the stem end

Prepare a medium fire for direct grilling in a grill (see page 21). Thread the beef and vegetables onto 12 skewers, alternating the ingredients and colors as you go.

Place the loaded skewers on the grill rack and grill, turning as needed, for about 12 minutes, until the beef is browned on the exterior and the vegetables are softened and nicely charred. Transfer to individual plates and serve.

Bottom Round

Sometimes called the rump, the bottom round is a 14-pound cut that needs long braising or poaching to bring out its flavor and texture. Because it has a uniform rectangular shape, it yields slices that are the same size, making it an ideal cut for roulades. Also known as *paupiettes* by the French or *rollini* by the Italians, roulades can be braised or, if the meat is thinly sliced, sautéed or fried.

Herb and Onion Beef Roulades

These roulades can be filled with nearly any ingredient or mixture of ingredients you like. Ground meat, hard-boiled eggs, cheese, herbs, scallions, and bacon are just some of the possibilities.

MAKES 8 ROULADES, OR 4 MAIN-COURSE SERVINGS

1 piece beef bottom round, about 2 1/4 pounds
4 tablespoons butter
4 onions, sliced
1 teaspoon chopped fresh thyme
Salt
Pepper
3 tablespoons olive oil
2 cups chicken broth (page 316)

Cut the meat into 8 uniform slices as shown on page 170 and reserve.

In a large sauté pan, melt the butter over medium heat. Add the onions and cook, stirring occasionally, for about 30 minutes, or until they shrink and soften. Add the thyme and season with salt and pepper. Remove from the heat and let cool.

Season the meat slices on both sides with salt and pepper. Put about one-eighth of the onion mixture near the edge of a meat slice, then, starting from a short end, roll up the slice into a tight cylinder. Tie the roll in two directions, crosswise and lengthwise, with kitchen string.

Preheat the oven to 275°F. In an ovenproof sauté pan or pot just large enough to hold the roulades in a single layer, heat the olive oil over high heat. When the oil ripples, add the roulades in a single layer and brown well on all sides, turning them as needed. Pour the fat out of the pan.

Return the pan with the roulades to high heat. Add any remaining onions to the pan to complement the braise. Pour in the broth and bring to a gentle simmer. Cover the pan and slide it into the oven. Braise for about 3 hours, or until the roulades are easily penetrated with a small knife or skewer.

Snip the strings around the roulades, and gently divide the roulades among warmed soup plates. Spoon the braising liquid over and around the roulades and serve.

Herb and onion beef roulades

1. Cut off thin slices of beef from the bottom round.

2. Roll up cooked onions in the beef slices.

3. Tie the roulades.

4. Brown the roulades in oil.

5. Braise the roulades in broth.

6. Finished roulades.

Eye of the Round

The eye of the round looks similar to the tenderloin but is not nearly as tender. Eye of the round can be sliced and then pounded to make minute steaks, but it is better roasted whole and served thinly sliced.

Roast Eye of the Round

A whole eye of the round makes a suitable roast for an informal dinner. The jus, which is actually an artificial jus (see below), is optional.

MAKES 8 MAIN-COURSE SERVINGS

1 whole beef eye of the round, about 3 pounds
Salt
Pepper
1 pound beef stew meat, cut into $^1/_2$-inch cubes (optional)
1 small onion, coarsely chopped (optional)
1 small carrot, peeled and sliced (optional)
4 cups beef broth (page 316), optional

Let the beef come to room temperature. Season all over with salt and pepper.

Preheat the oven to 450°F. Place the beef in a heavy roasting pan just large enough to hold it. Surround the beef with the stew meat and the vegetables.

Slide the pan into the oven and roast, uncovered, for about 30 minutes, or until well browned. Turn down the oven temperature to 300°F and continue to roast for about 10 minutes longer, or until an instant-read thermometer inserted into the center of the roast reads 130°F for medium.

Transfer the roast to a platter or cutting board, tent loosely with aluminum foil, and let rest for 20 minutes before carving.

If you have used the stew meat, make a jus. Put the roasting pan on the stove top over high heat and add 1 cup of the broth. Deglaze the pan, scraping up any brown bits on the bottom with a wooden spoon. Boil down the broth until it caramelizes into a crusty brown layer with a layer of clear fat on top. Pour out the fat, return the pan to high heat, and deglaze the pan with a second cup of broth, again boiling it down. Repeat the process with a third cup, again boiling down the broth. Deglaze the pan with the remaining 1 cup broth, stirring to dissolve the crust with the liquid, and then strain the liquid through a fine-mesh strainer into a warmed sauceboat.

Carve the roast into thin slices to serve. Pass the jus at the table.

Artificial Jus

Often when roasting meat, especially if you are cooking it rare, you will end up with few, if any, drippings in the roasting pan for making a jus. To fake a jus, you need a little vegetable oil; about 2 pounds meat, cut into small cubes; and 4 cups good chicken or beef broth (page 316). In a skillet over medium-high heat, brown the meat thoroughly in the oil. Deglaze the pan with 1 cup of the broth, scraping up any brown bits on the bottom of the pan with a wooden spoon. Boil down the broth until it caramelizes into a crusty brown layer with a layer of clear fat on top. Pour out the fat and deglaze the pan with a second cup of broth, again boiling it down. Repeat the process with a third cup, again boiling down the broth. Deglaze the pan with the final cup of broth, stirring until the crust has dissolved in the liquid, and then strain the liquid through a fine-mesh strainer. This is your jus.

Chicken Fried Steak

A chicken fried steak is simply a steak that is fried like fried chicken. Traditionally, an onion-flavored béchamel is used to top the steaks, but here a piquant mayonnaise is used instead. An inexpensive cut, often from the round or chuck, is typically used and must be tenderized by thorough pounding.

MAKES 4 MAIN-COURSE SERVINGS

4 slices beef eye of the round, 6 ounces each
$1/2$ cup milk
Salt
Pepper
Flour
Vegetable oil for frying
Mayonnaise (below) flavored with extra mustard
    for serving

Trim the beef slices of any obvious fat or gristle (there probably won't be any). Flatten each slice by pounding it with the side of a cleaver or a meat pounder until it is about $1/4$ inch thick. Pour the milk into a shallow bowl, and season generously with salt and pepper. Put some flour in a second shallow bowl. One at a time, dip the beef slices in the seasoned milk and then coat with the flour, patting off the excess.

Pour the oil to a depth of 3 inches into a deep, heavy pot wide enough to hold all the beef slices in a single layer and heat over high heat until hot (350°F). To test if the oil is ready, dip a corner of a coated beef slice in the oil. If the oil starts bubbling immediately, it is ready. Gently lower the coated slices into the hot oil and fry, turning once, for about 2 minutes per $1/2$ inch of thickness, or longer if you like your meat well done.

Transfer the beef slices to paper towels to drain, then serve. Pass the mayonnaise at the table.

Homemade Mayonnaise

A traditional mayonnaise is made by adding oil very slowly to raw egg yolks. The beginning of the process can be tricky because the yolk and oil can easily separate. A fail-safe method is to start with a small amount of bottled mayonnaise instead of, or in addition to, one or more egg yolks. The bottled mayonnaise facilitates the establishment of the emulsion. If you opt for adding an egg yolk, it will mostly deliver color.

To make mayonnaise, in a bowl, whisk together 2 tablespoons bottled mayonnaise, 1 egg yolk (optional), and 2 teaspoons fresh lemon juice. Slowly add $3/4$ cup canola oil in a thin, steady stream while whisking constantly. Season to taste with salt. Makes 1 cup.

Brisket

Brisket is part of the breast of the steer and can weigh up to 15 pounds. It is divided into two parts, separated by a thick layer of fat, called the first cut and the second cut. The first cut is larger and leaner; the second cut, because it contains more marbling, is particularly juicy. If you are dealing with a kindly butcher, you can specify the cut you want. Either cut can be braised and served with its braising liquid.

Barbecued Brisket

Barbecuing a brisket is akin to braising, with the low heat of the covered grill providing the same gentle heat used for braising meat in its own juices in the oven. Here, the brisket is actually barbecued in a baking dish so no juices are lost. The juices are then finished with a small amount of vinegar and a very small amount of ketchup to make the sauce. You can cook as large a brisket as you like, depending on the size of your crowd and the size of your grill, though be careful that no more than half of the grill rack is covered. This recipe is unusual in that no rub or sauce is applied before or during braising. This lets the pure beefy flavor of the brisket shine through.

MAKES 8 MAIN-COURSE SERVINGS

1 first-cut or second-cut brisket, about 5 pounds
Salt
Pepper
2 tablespoons good-quality red or white wine
    vinegar or cider vinegar
2 tablespoons ketchup
1 tablespoon Worcestershire sauce
1 tablespoon light corn syrup

Prepare a fire for indirect grilling in a covered grill (see page 21). Sprinkle the coals with a handful of soaked wood chips, or put a small sheet of aluminum foil over the coals and top with a handful of sawdust. (If using a gas grill, put unsoaked chips in a special smoker box, or in a perforated foil packet and place directly over the heat.) Season the brisket all over with salt and pepper and place it in a baking dish that will fit in the grill. Place the dish over the cool side of the grill and cook for about 6 hours, or until the meat is easily cut with the side of a fork. Add soaked chips or sawdust and lighted charcoal to the coals (or unsoaked chips or sawdust to the smoker box or foil packet) every 30 minutes or so to keep the fire and the smoke going.

Transfer the meat to a cutting board. Transfer the drippings in the baking dish to a saucepan. Using a large spoon, skim off any fat from the drippings. Whisk in the vinegar, ketchup, Worcestershire sauce, and corn syrup. Season with salt and pepper and bring to a simmer. Taste and adjust the seasoning with more vinegar and/or ketchup. Pour into a warmed sauceboat.

Cut the brisket into slices about $1/2$ inch thick to serve. Pass the sauce at the table.

Brisket with Pomegranate Juice

This recipe was inspired by one in Jayne Cohen's *Jewish Holiday Cooking*. The acidity of the pomegranate juice is a perfect foil for the richness of the beef.

MAKES 8 MAIN-COURSE SERVINGS

1 first-cut or second-cut brisket, about 5 pounds, trimmed of fat

Salt

Pepper

4 tablespoons olive oil

2 onions, coarsely chopped

2 leeks, white part only, sliced

6 large cloves garlic

1 celery stalk, sliced

2 cups pomegranate juice

2 cups chicken broth (page 316), or as needed

2 tablespoons meat glaze (page 318), optional

Bouquet garni (page 320)

Season the brisket all over with salt and pepper. In a large sauté pan, heat 2 tablespoons of the olive oil over high heat. When the oil begins to smoke, add the brisket and brown well on all sides, turning as needed. Transfer the brisket to a heavy ovenproof pot just large enough to hold it. Pour the fat out of the pan.

Return the pan to medium heat and add the remaining 2 tablespoons olive oil. Add the onions, leeks, garlic, and celery and cook, stirring occasionally, for about 15 minutes, or until the vegetables soften. Remove from the heat and pour the vegetables over the brisket. Pour in the pomegranate juice and then add enough broth to come halfway up the sides of the brisket. Add the meat glaze, nestle in the bouquet garni, and bring to a simmer.

Preheat the oven to 275°F. Cover the pot with a sheet of aluminum foil, pressing it down slightly in the middle so that moisture will condense on its underside and drip down onto the exposed parts of the meat, and then with a lid. Slide the pot into the oven and braise the brisket, basting it every 30 minutes with the braising liquid, for about 4 hours, or until it is easily penetrated with a knife.

Transfer the brisket to a smaller ovenproof pot (or clean the pot you used for braising). Strain the braising liquid into a glass pitcher and skim off the fat with a ladle. Or, ideally, refrigerate the braising liquid at this point and then lift off the congealed fat in a single layer. Pour the degreased liquid into a saucepan, bring to a simmer, and simmer, skimming off any fat or froth that rises to the surface, for about 30 minutes, or until reduced by about half. Meanwhile, raise the oven temperature to 400°F.

Pour the reduced liquid over the meat. Slide the pot into the oven and cook the brisket, basting it every 10 minutes with the liquid, for about 30 minutes, or until the brisket is covered with a shiny glaze.

Remove the brisket from the oven and cut it into slices about 1/2 inch thick. Serve on warmed plates surrounded with the braising liquid.

Corned Beef

Corned beef is made by soaking beef brisket in a salt brine for several days. The word *corned* came about because the salt crystals used at one time looked like corn kernels. The characteristic rosy color of traditional corned beef is the result of including saltpeter or nitrites. Because some cooks are concerned about the possible health risks of these chemicals, I've left them out here, which means your corned beef won't be rosy.

Do not confuse this corned beef with the ready-to-eat corned beef sold in many delicatessens for sandwich making. This one must be cooked before eating. You can use it in the recipe for New England Boiled Dinner (page 176) or in any recipe calling for a corned beef brisket. For a simple supper of cooked corned beef, soak the brined brisket in water to cover overnight in the refrigerator, then drain and place in a pot; add 3 bay leaves, 1 cup white wine, and water to cover, and simmer for about 3 hours, then discard the cooking liquid and serve.

MAKES 1 CORNED BEEF BRISKET, ENOUGH FOR 8 SERVINGS

2 pounds (7 cups) sea salt or kosher salt

1 pound (2 firmly packed cups) dark brown sugar

7 quarts water

2 imported bay leaves

7 thyme sprigs

20 juniper berries, crushed under a saucepan

25 peppercorns, crushed under a saucepan

1 first-cut or second-cut brisket, about 5 pounds

Brine for corned beef.

In a large pot, combine the salt, sugar, water, bay leaves, thyme, juniper berries, and peppercorns. Place over medium-high heat and bring to a simmer, stirring to dissolve the salt and sugar. Continue to simmer, stirring, until the salt and sugar are fully dissolved. Remove from the heat, let cool completely, and pour into a nonreactive container large enough to submerge the brisket fully.

Add the brisket to the brine, then top the brisket with a plate or other nonreactive object to keep it submerged. Cover and refrigerate for 4 days, then remove the brisket and discard the brine. Cook the corned beef as directed in individual recipes.

New England Boiled Dinner

The New England boiled dinner belongs to the same family of dishes as the French pot-au-feu (opposite) and the Italian *bollito misto* (page 178). The differences are that a single meat, rather than mixed meats are used, and the poaching liquid is discarded (it becomes too salty).

MAKES 10 SERVINGS

Corned Beef (page 175), or 1 purchased corned beef brisket, about 5 pounds

3 large carrots, peeled and cut into 1¹/₂-inch sections

3 large parsnips, peeled and cut into 1¹/₂-inch sections

20 walnut-sized onions, peeled

20 red or white baby waxy potatoes

3 turnips, peeled and cut into wedges as shown on page 10 (optional)

1 head Savoy cabbage, cut into quarters through the core

10 small beets

Mustard for serving

Salt for serving

Pepper for serving

Rinse the corned beef under cold running water and soak in water to cover overnight in the refrigerator.

Drain the corned beef and put it in a pot just large enough to hold it. Add water to cover, place over medium-high heat, and bring to a simmer, skimming off any froth that rises to the surface. Reduce the heat to very low and simmer uncovered for about 3 hours, or until easily penetrated with a small knife.

If you like, cut the carrot sections lengthwise into wedges and cut out the core from each wedge as shown on page 11. Cut the parsnips, potatoes, the same way. In a pot, combine the carrots, parsnips, potatoes, onions, and turnips with water to cover and bring to a boil. Reduce the heat to maintain a steady simmer and cook for about 20 minutes, or until half-cooked. Add the cabbage and simmer for 20 minutes longer, or until all the vegetables are tender. Add the beets and simmer for 5 minutes, or until the beets are heated through.

Transfer the corned beef to a cutting board and discard the braising liquid. Cut the corned beef into thick slices. Remove the vegetables from their cooking liquid, and cut each cabbage wedge into at least 3 pieces. Serve each diner a slice of meat and an assortment of vegetables. Spoon a little of the broth from cooking the vegetables over each serving. Pass mustard and salt and pepper at the table.

Pot-au-Feu

A pot-au-feu is essentially a pot of different cuts of beef that have been poached with aromatic vegetables. The cuts should ideally be tough pieces of meat that will gradually tenderize with long cooking. Beef shank, short ribs, and brisket are particularly good choices. You can enhance a pot-au-feu by briefly poaching a tender cut with the tough cuts and then slicing it and serving it rare with the long-cooked meats and vegetables. Any tender cut can be used, such as a large piece of tenderloin, which will be ready in about 12 minutes. You can even include cuts from other animals, such as duck breasts. A pot-au-feu is traditionally served with little sour gherkins (cornichons), mustard, and coarse salt, but you can also accompany it with the *mostarda di Cremona* (page 180) and the *salsa verde* (page 180) traditionally served with *bollito misto*.

MAKES 10 MAIN-COURSE SERVINGS

4 short ribs in one piece, about 6 inches wide and
    6 inches long

5 beef shank rounds, each about 1^1/$_2$ inches thick

1 first-cut or second-cut brisket, about 5 pounds

4 cups chicken broth (page 316), or as needed

3 large carrots, peeled and cut into 1-inch sections

2 turnips, peeled and each cut into 6 wedges as
    shown on page 10

1 large onion, stuck with 1 whole clove

Bouquet garni (page 320)

Mustard for serving

Sour gherkins (cornichons) for serving

Coarse salt for serving

Put the short ribs, shank rounds, and brisket in a large pot and pour in the broth to cover. Bring to a gentle simmer and skim off any fat or froth that rises to the surface. Simmer in this way for about 1 hour.

Meanwhile, using a paring knife, cut each of the carrot sections lengthwise into 3 to 5 wedges, depending on the size of the sections, and cut out the core from each wedge as shown on page 11. Add the carrots, turnips, onion, and bouquet garni to the pot and continue to simmer, regularly skimming off any fat or froth that rises to the surface, for about 2 hours longer, or until the meats are easily penetrated with a knife.

Lift the meats from the pot. Carve the meats—pull the meat away from those cuts with bones—and divide them among warmed soup plates. Divide the carrots and turnips among the plates. Discard the onion and bouquet garni and spoon some of the broth around and over each serving. Accompany with the mustard, gherkins, and coarse salt.

Cryovac

Until the 1980s, beef was delivered in primal and subprimal cuts and was broken down into smaller cuts by the local butcher. But as slaughterhouses and large-scale butcheries became more mechanized, they began sending out meat in individual cuts, and instead of the cuts being kept dry, they were sealed in transparent plastic called Cryovac, which secured all the juices and moisture inside the package. Meat packed in Cryovac will keep for relatively long periods and doesn't require the special humidity-controlled conditions that dry-aged beef needs. However, meat does not age in Cryovac with any advantage to the meat. Simply put, any claims of aging that include the term *wet aging* are meaningless. Only authentic dry aging brings about significant changes in flavor.

Bollito Misto

Even though *bollito misto* comes from northern Italy, especially Piedmont, it is served in fine restaurants throughout the country. It is similar to a pot-au-feu but contains a greater variety of meats, including *cotechino* (fresh pork sausage), tongue, veal shank, and beef brisket. It's traditionally served with two sauces—*salsa verde* and *mostarda di Cremona*. Because it's time-consuming to make and takes a lot of forethought to gather all the ingredients, this recipe feeds twelve.

MAKES 12 MAIN-COURSE SERVINGS

1 first-cut or second-cut beef brisket, about
    3 pounds
4 veal shank rounds, each $1^1/_2$ to 2 inches thick,
    or 1 whole veal shank (see page 246)
3 beef cheeks (see page 207)
1 beef tongue, about 2 pounds (see page 206)
4 quarts beef broth (page 316) or water, or as
    needed
2 large carrots
2 fennel bulbs
1 small capon
1 *cotechino* sausage or 1 pound sweet Italian sausage
3 large onions, quartered through the stem end
1 celery stalk
Bouquet garni (page 320)
Mostarda di Cremona (page 180)
Salsa Verde (page 180)

Put the brisket, shank rounds, beef cheeks, and tongue in a large pot with cold water to cover and bring to a simmer. Simmer for 5 minutes and drain in a colander. Rinse well with cold running water. Put the meats back in the pot, add the broth to cover, and bring to a simmer, skimming off any fat or froth that rises to the surface. Reduce the heat to very low and simmer gently, uncovered, for $2^1/_2$ hours.

Meanwhile, peel the carrots and cut into 1-inch sections. Using a paring knife, cut each of the carrot sections lengthwise into 3 to 5 wedges, depending on the size of the sections, and cut out the core from each wedge as shown on page 11. Cut off the stalks from the fennel bulbs and reserve for another use; discard any bruised outer leaves. Cut each bulb in half lengthwise, then cut each half into 3 wedges with some core attached.

Add the capon, sausage, onions, carrots, fennel, celery, and bouquet garni to the pot of simmering meats. Add broth or water and continue to simmer for 1 hour more, or until the meats are easily penetrated with a small knife.

Remove the meats, capon, and sausage from the pot. Discard the bouquet garni and celery. Using a small, sharp knife, trim off any fat or gristle from the base of the tongue, then remove and discard any bones. Using the knife and your fingers, carefully peel away and discard the skin. Slice the tongue; pull the meat off the shank rounds; slice the cheeks, brisket, and sausage; and carve the capon. Serve everything, including the vegetables, in warmed soup plates surrounded with the broth. Pass the sauces at the table.

Bollito misto

Beef tongue.

Brisket.

Veal shank.

Mostarda di Cremona

This sauce dates from the sixteenth century, when sugar first became widely available in Italy. Although it is traditionally served with *bollito misto*, it goes with nearly any type of leftover meat, hot or cold. Prepare it in the summer when the fruits are in season, and keep it in tightly sealed jars in the refrigerator. Store-bought *mostarda* is hard to find and expensive, so making it yourself is the ideal remedy. **MAKES ABOUT 6 CUPS**

2 underripe pears, peeled, cored, and cut
    lengthwise into wedges
1 large apple, peeled, cored, and cut lengthwise
    into wedges
3 cups sugar
2 cups white wine vinegar or sherry vinegar
2 cups cherries, pitted
5 apricots, halved and pitted
1 large peach, peeled, pitted, and cut into wedges
9 large figs, stemmed and halved vertically
1 tablespoon powdered mustard, or to taste

In a nonreactive pot, combine the pears, apple, sugar, and vinegar and bring slowly to a simmer, stirring to dissolve the sugar. Continue to simmer gently, uncovered, for about 25 minutes, or until the fruits are soft. Add the cherries, apricots, peach, and figs, cover, and simmer for 20 minutes, or until the second batch of fruits softens. From time to time, uncover and use a wire skimmer or large slotted spoon to push the fruits down into the liquid so they are all submerged.

Using the wire skimmer or slotted spoon, transfer the fruits to a bowl. Simmer the liquid, uncovered, for about 20 minutes, or until it is thick and syrupy. Stir in the mustard until well mixed, then taste and adjust with more mustard if needed.

Return the fruits to the pot, along with any liquid they have released, and simmer for 5 minutes more. Ladle the fruits and syrup into hot, sterilized jars, cap tightly, let cool, and refrigerate. The sauce will keep for several months.

Salsa Verde

This sauce goes together in just a few minutes if you use bottled mayonnaise for the base. And once you have added additional olive oil and vinegar, no one will ever know you started out with store-bought mayonnaise. If you opt not to include the chervil and/or sorrel, add more of any of the other herbs to the same measure. **MAKES ABOUT 2 CUPS**

3 tablespoons chopped capers
3 tablespoons minced fresh chives
3 tablespoons chopped fresh parsley
2 tablespoons chopped fresh tarragon
2 tablespoons chopped fresh chervil, optional
3 tablespoons chopped fresh sorrel, optional
1 tablespoon Dijon mustard
1 tablespoon wine vinegar, or as needed
$1/4$ cup mayonnaise, homemade (page 172)
    or bottled
1 cup extra virgin olive oil
Salt
Pepper

In a bowl, whisk the capers, all the herbs, the mustard, vinegar, and mayonnaise. Add the olive oil in a slow, steady stream while whisking constantly. Then, using an immersion blender, puree on high speed for about 1 minute. Or, transfer to a stand blender and puree on high speed for about 1 minute. (This pureeing step is optional, but it brings out the flavor and color of the herbs.) Season with salt and pepper.

Steak

When buying a steak, you'll have better luck if you purchase a less expensive cut from an expensive butcher than an expensive cut from the supermarket, and you'll end up paying about the same price.

Steaks can come from the chuck (shoulder), rib section, loin section, and the leg (round). The best steaks come from the "middle" of the animal, in other words, between the shoulder and the hind leg. Ideally, a steak will be tender and well marbled, which is to say striated with a fine filigree of white fat. This fat gives the meat flavor and a satisfying feel in the mouth. Whether sautéing, grilling, or broiling, start your steaks on very high heat and brown them. Further cooking can be accomplished on lower heat. Tougher steaks, such as flank or cuts labeled "London broil," should be served sliced across the grain to minimize their chewy texture.

Steaks from the rib section can be taken from any of seven ribs in the section. After the rib seciton comes the loin, which is divided into the short loin, the source of what many consider the finest steaks, and the sirloin. The first steak in the short loin is the Delmonico, which has no tenderloin or other muscles attached. Farther back is the T-bone, which includes part of the tenderloin; and then comes the porterhouse, which contains a much larger portion of the tenderloin. Pin-bone, flat-bone, full-cut (or round-bone), wedge-bone, and short steaks follow, all cut from the sirloin and all quite large. They are the result of cutting across the whole loin and also include tender, flavorful "smaller" cuts, such as the tenderloin and New York cut or sirloin strip. The latter is also known as a strip steak when boneless and a shell steak when the bone is intact. The steaks from the sirloin are often a bargain, especially when taken from dry-aged beef.

The shell hip, which is the final cut of the loin, contains two cuts, the top butt sirloin, which is usually made into steaks, and the bottom butt sirloin, which is often broken down into three smaller muscles, the circle, the flap, and the triangle. Each of these muscles can be used in a different way: the circle can be cooked whole or cut into cubes for sautés, fondue, or kebabs; the flap can be used as London broil, ground, or, like the circle, cubed; and the triangle can be cut into miniature steaks called tri-tip steaks, or in New York at least, Newport steaks.

Steaks from the leg include round steaks, top sirloin, and eye of the round. Because they are quite tough, they are best served like London broil, that is, sliced. Finally, flank, skirt, and hanger are three little-known steaks that deserve more attention. They are slightly tougher than the cuts from the tenderloin because they come from the part of the steer that works harder. The payoff, however, is in the flavor. Typically this trio is sautéed or grilled, though the skirt steak is often braised as well, as in the Bolognese Sauce on page 200 and the Steak and Kidney Pie on page 201.

Determining the Doneness of Steaks

First, bring the meat to room temperature before you cook it. That way, it will heat through evenly. When cooking meat to black-and-blue or very rare, cook it just long enough to brown it on both sides; it should feel fleshy when you press on it. For rare, cook a minute or two longer on both sides. For medium-rare, cook until you feel the first sign of the meat becoming firm to the touch and red juices just begin to rise to the surface. For medium, cook it until it is completely firm to the touch and it is releasing more red juices. For medium-well, cook it until the juices released are brown.

Steak doneness

Black-and-blue

Rare

Medium-rare

Medium

Medium-well

Well done

Chuck Round Steaks with Béarnaise Sauce

Chuck round steaks are taken from the center of the chuck and are surprisingly tender and tasty. They're also a good value, so grab them when you see them. If you're concerned about the butter in the sauce, replace it with olive oil and you'll end up with something called *sauce tyrolienne*.

MAKES 4 MAIN-COURSE SERVINGS

4 chuck round steaks, 6 to 8 ounces each
Salt
Pepper
2 tablespoons olive oil
Béarnaise Sauce (page 165)

Let the steaks come to room temperature. Season on both sides with salt and pepper.

In a sauté pan just large enough to hold the steaks without crowding (or working in batches), heat the oil over high heat until it begins to smoke. Add the steaks and cook, turning once, until browned on both sides and cooked to the desired doneness. Plan on about 3 minutes on each side for rare, 5 minutes for medium-rare, or 7 minutes for well done, lowering the heat if necessary to prevent burning before the steaks are done to your liking.

Let rest for 3 minutes before serving. Accompany with the sauce.

Chuck round steaks with béarnaise sauce

1. Uncooked chuck round steak.

2. Browning the steaks.

3. Finished steaks with béarnaise sauce.

Grilled Rib Steak

In French, the rib steak is known as the *entrecôte*, literally "between the ribs." You can buy rib steaks without the bone, but they are more impressive if the bone is intact. Ideally, the butcher leaves you a couple of inches of bone that you—or the butcher—can french (trim off the meat and fat), resulting in a dramatic caveman-looking steak. When buying rib steaks, ask for them from the loin end, which has a single neat muscle. Here, the steaks are cooked on a charcoal or gas grill, but you can also cook them in a stove-top grill pan over high heat.

MAKES 4 MAIN-COURSE SERVINGS

4 rib steaks, about $3/4$ pound each if bone-in,
    or 10 ounces each if boneless
Salt
Pepper

Let the steaks come to room temperature. Season on both sides with salt and pepper.

Prepare a hot fire for direct grilling in a grill (see page 21). Place the steaks on the grill rack and grill for 2 minutes. Rotate the steaks 90 degrees to create a crosshatch pattern, and then grill for 2 to 3 minutes longer. Using tongs, turn the steaks over, and grill for 2 to 3 minutes. Rotate the steaks 90 degrees to create a crosshatch pattern, and then grill for 2 to 3 minutes longer, or until juices barely begin to form on the surface of the meat (medium-rare) or until done to your liking.

Let rest for 3 minutes before serving.

Rib Steak with Green Peppercorn Sauce

This adaptation of the classic steak au poivre, in which a steak is coated with cracked black peppercorns, has a more subtle, pinelike fragrance and flavor. Green peppercorns come in two forms, freeze-dried and in brine, and either can be used in this recipe.

MAKES 2 MAIN-COURSE SERVINGS

1 bone-in rib steak, 24 to 30 ounces and about
    $1^1/2$ inches thick
Salt
Pepper
20 green peppercorns
3 tablespoons olive oil
1 shallot, minced
$1/2$ cup red vermouth or port
$1^1/2$ tablespoons meat glaze (page 318)
4 tablespoons cold butter, cut into 3 or 4 slices

Ask the butcher to french 1 inch of the rib bone, or do it yourself as shown on the facing page. Let the steak come to room temperature. Season on both sides with salt and pepper.

If using brine-packed peppercorns, drain well; if using freeze-dried peppercorns, soak them a spoonful of water until rehydrated, then drain off any excess water. On a cutting board, crush the peppercorns with the side of a knife, then chop and reserve.

In a sauté pan just large enough to hold the steak, heat the olive oil over high heat until it begins to smoke. Add the steak and cook until well browned. Turn down the heat to medium and cook for a total of about 5 minutes for rare, 7 minutes for medium-rare, or 10 minutes for well done. Using tongs, turn the steak over and cook the same way on the second side. Transfer the steak to a platter, pat off the oil with a paper towel, and let rest in a warm spot for 10 minutes while you make the sauce. Pour the fat out of the pan.

Return the hot pan to high heat. Add the shallot and stir it around for about a minute, or until it smells toasty. Add the vermouth, stir in the meat glaze, and then add the peppercorns. Cook down until the sauce has a lightly syrupy consistency. If it is too thick, add water, a tablespoon at a time, until thinned to a good consistency. Whisk in the cold butter until emulsified. Do not allow the sauce to boil.

Divide the steak in half and place on warmed plates. Spoon the sauce over the steak and serve immediately.

Rib steak with green peppercorn sauce

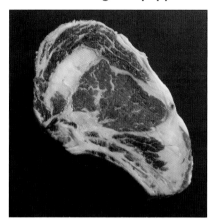

1. Uncooked bone-in rib steak.

2. French the last inch of the bone (remove the meat and fat).

3. Crush the green peppercorns.

4. Brown the steak well on both sides.

5. Stir shallots around in the hot pan and add red vermouth.

Compound Butters

Compound butters are butters that have been flavored with such ingredients as herbs, reconstituted dried mushrooms, pickles, capers, anchovies, or shallots. Parsley butter, or *beurre maître d'hôtel*, is one of the simplest to make. Montpelier butter, which is lightened with olive oil, is more complex, but if you don't have all of the ingredients on hand, you can just adjust the amounts of the ingredients you do have upward. *Marchand de vin* is a bit like a cold bordelaise sauce. All of them are classic garnishes for steaks.

PARSLEY BUTTER: On a cutting board, coarsely chop the leaves from 1 bunch parsley with a large, sharp knife. Add 1/2 cup (1 stick) butter, slightly softened, to the parsley and chop together until both ingredients are finely chopped and evenly combined. Add 2 tablespoons fresh lemon juice and work it into the mixture until evenly incorporated. If you want the butter to be perfectly smooth and more subtle, pass it through a drum sieve or fine-mesh strainer. Using the knife blade, shape the butter mixture into a rough cylinder on a sheet of parchment paper or waxed paper, positioning it near the edge. Fold the parchment over the butter, and roll up the parchment, shaping the flavored butter into a tight cylinder. Twist the ends of the parchment in opposite directions to secure. Refrigerate until serving, then cut into disks to serve. Makes 6 servings.

MONTPELIER BUTTER: Bring a saucepan filled with water to a boil. Add the leaves from 1/2 bunch each parsley, watercress, chervil, chives, and tarragon and a handful of stemmed spinach leaves and blanch for 30 seconds. Drain well, rinse under cold running water, and spin or pat perfectly dry. In a food processor, combine the blanched herbs and spinach; 2 sour gherkins (cornichons), cut up; 1 heaping tablespoon capers, rinsed; 1 clove garlic; and 4 anchovy fillets. Process until finely chopped. Add 2 raw egg yolks, 2 hard-boiled egg yolks, and 1/2 cup (1 stick) butter, slightly softened and cut into 4 slices, and process until smooth. Pass the mixture through a drum sieve or a fine-mesh strainer held over a bowl. Using a wooden spoon, work in 1/2 cup extra virgin olive oil. Cover and refrigerate until serving. Makes 8 to 12 servings.

MARCHAND DE VIN: In a small saucepan, combine 1 cup full-bodied red wine; 1 shallot, minced; and 1 tablespoon meat glaze (page 318). Place over medium heat, bring to a simmer, and simmer, skimming off any froth that forms on the surface, until reduced to a syrup consistency (about 2 tablespoons). Remove from the heat. In a bowl, work the reduction, 1 tablespoon finely chopped fresh parsley, and 2 teaspoons fresh lemon juice into 1/2 cup (1 stick) butter, slightly softened, until evenly incorporated. Transfer to a sheet of parchment paper or waxed paper and wrap as described for parsley butter. Refrigerate until serving, then cut into disks to serve. Makes 6 servings.

Parsley butter

1. Chop together the parsley and butter.

2. Work the mixture through a drum sieve.

3. Scrape the butter from the bottom of the drum sieve.

4. Roll up the butter in a sheet of parchment paper, shaping it into a cylinder.

5. Twist the ends of the cylinder in opposite directions to tighten. Chill.

6. Strip steak with parsley butter.

Carpaccio

This dish of thin slices of raw beef was first featured at Harry's Bar in Venice, where it was named after the fifteenth-century Venetian painter Vittore Carpaccio. While tenderloin is often the cut of choice for carpaccio, at Harry's they use New York strip, which has a much fuller flavor. Be sure to choose meat with a lot of fatty marbling, which will give the finished dish a better flavor. Steak like this is hard to slice thinly by hand, so if your butcher has a meat slicer, you might ask him or her to slice it for you. Explain that you will be serving the beef raw, so that the slicer will be properly cleaned before it is used on your purchase.

MAKES 6 FIRST-COURSE SERVINGS

1 New York strip steak, 1^1/$_2$ pounds
1 cup homemade mayonnaise (page 172)
2 tablespoons Worcestershire sauce

Put the meat in the freezer for about 30 minutes, or until it is quite firm. Using a razor-sharp knife, cut the meat as thinly as possible against the grain, and arrange the slices attractively on individual large plates.

In a small bowl, stir together the mayonnaise and Worcestershire sauce. Transfer the mixture to a plastic sandwich bag, cut a tiny corner off the lower end of the bag, and make a Jackson Pollock series of streaks and lines with the mayonnaise mixture on each serving of beef. Serve immediately.

Porterhouse or T-Bone Steak with Bordelaise Sauce

Many steak aficionados consider the porterhouse the king of steaks. It includes two muscles—the larger sirloin strip and the smaller tenderloin—divided by a T-shaped bone. A porterhouse differs from a T-bone in that it contains a significant section of tenderloin and a T-bone does not. If you are serving porterhouse, don't try to buy individual steaks, unless you are feeding gargantuan appetites. It's better to buy a larger steak for as many as four people and then carve it at the table, being sure to give everyone a piece or more of each muscle. A high-quality porterhouse will have enough flavor and be sufficiently tender to not require a marinade, which would only disguise its natural beefy flavor. If some guests like their porterhouse cooked longer, carve off and keep warm the rarer pieces while you cook the rest of the meat longer, or cook two steaks to different degrees of doneness.

MAKES 4 MAIN-COURSE SERVINGS

1 porterhouse or T-bone steak, about 2 inches thick
Salt
Pepper
3 tablespoons olive oil
Bordelaise Sauce (opposite)

Let the steak come to room temperature. Season on both sides with salt and pepper.

If you are sautéing the steak, in a sauté pan or stovetop grill pan just large enough to hold the meat, heat the olive oil over high heat until it begins to smoke. Add the steak and cook for 2 to 3 minutes. If using a grill pan, rotate the steak 90 degrees to create a crosshatch pattern, and then cook for about 2 minutes longer. Using tongs, turn the steak over and cook for 2 minutes. Rotate the steak 90 degrees to create a crosshatch pattern, and then cook for 2 to 3 minutes longer, or until juices barely begin to form on the surface of the meat (medium-rare) or until done to your liking.

If you are grilling the steak, prepare a hot fire for direct grilling in a grill (see page 21). Rub the steak on both sides with the olive oil.

Place the steak on the grill rack and grill for 2 minutes. Rotate the steak 90 degrees to create a crosshatch pattern, and then cook for about 2 minutes longer. Using tongs, turn the steak over and cook for 2 minute. Rotate the steak 90 degrees to create a crosshatch pattern, and then cook for 2 to 3 minutes longer, or until juices barely begin to form on the surface of the meat (medium-rare) or until done to your liking.

Let the steak rest for 10 minutes in a warm place before carving (see page 190). Spoon the sauce over the steak.

Bordelaise Sauce

Unlike other red wine sauces that are typically finished with butter, bordelaise sauce is finished with marrow. Select a full-bodied red without a lot of tannin or acid. Wines from South America are particularly good for cooking and can be found at decent prices.

To make bordelaise sauce, in a saucepan, combine 1½ cups full-bodied wine; 2 tablespoons meat glaze (page 318), 2 shallots, minced; 3 thyme sprigs; and 1 imported bay leaf. Place over medium heat, bring to a simmer, and simmer for about 15 minutes, or until the mixture has a lightly syrupy consistency that coats the back of a spoon. Remove from the heat.

Strain the mixture into a clean saucepan. Add the marrow from a 3-inch marrowbone, soaked overnight in salty water in the refrigerator (see page 190) and sliced into rounds. Bring to a simmer and serve immediately. (If the sauce sits, the marrow melts and turns to oil.) Makes about 1 cup, or enough for 4 servings.

1. Uncooked porterhouse.

2. Grilling porterhouse.

3. Carve the loin and tenderloin muscles off the bone and cut each into slices.

How to Remove Marrow from Marrowbones

Marrow, the fatty tissue found inside bones, is a classic component of bordelaise sauce. Marrow aficionados like to cook the bones and then remove the marrow and spread it on toast. When buying marrow-bones, look for pieces that have been cut from the center of the bone, not from the ends. The center contains neat cylinders of marrow that are easy to extract.

If possible, when using marrow in a recipe, remove it from the bone and soak it overnight in salty water in the refrigerator to remove the blood, which will otherwise turn gray when the marrow cooks. To extract the marrow, stand a bone on one end on a cutting board and give it a quick whack with a meat cleaver to split it. Hold the cleaver so that you strike only the bone and don't cut into the marrow. Turn the bone onto the opposite end and strike it the same way. Now, pull the bone away from the marrow.

Steak Tartare

Although steak tartare isn't something to serve guests whose preferences are unknown, those who unite around it do so with a true carnivore's relish. You don't need to use an expensive cut, but you do need to make sure the beef is fresh, rather than a day away from the sell-by date. Tenderness is not an issue, only the flavor of the meat is, so opt for round steak or rump or, if need be, sirloin. Don't go for tender cuts or for cuts like the shank that are too tough even when ground. Mix together the ingredients for the steak tartare at the table.

MAKES 6 FIRST OR LIGHT MAIN-COURSE SERVINGS

2 pounds lean steak such as round, rump, or sirloin
2 egg yolks
1 onion, minced, or 4 shallots, minced
2 bunches parsley, chopped at the last minute
$1/4$ cup capers, drained
16 anchovies, rinsed and chopped to a paste

Seasonings
Salt
Pepper
Hot sauce
Mustard
Fresh lemon juice
Worcestershire sauce

Trim the meat of all gristle and connective tissue. Using a meat grinder fitted with the coarse blade of a food processor, grind the meat, being careful not to grind it too fine. Put it in a large bowl.

At the table, stir in the egg yolks, onion, parsley, capers, and anchovies. Serve the mixture on chilled plates, or pass the bowl at the table and let people help themselves. Pass the seasonings at the table. (Alternatively, divide the egg yolks, onion, parsley, capers, and anchovies among individual plates with a serving of meat as shown below.)

Steak tartare

1. Chop the raw meat; here, the meat is chopped by hand.

2. Serve the steak tartare with lemon, parsley, capers, chopped onion, mustard, and raw egg yolks.

Grilled or Sautéed Top Sirloin Steak

Remember the axiom that it is always better to buy an inexpensive cut from a good butcher who ages his or her own beef than it is to buy a more expensive cut from the supermarket? Top sirloin, located just above the knee of the steer, is proof of that maxim. An especially good bargain, it has a lot of flavor and is relatively tender. Do not confuse it with sirloin proper, which comes from the haunch of the steer.

MAKES 4 MAIN-COURSE SERVINGS

1 top sirloin steak, about 2 pounds and 1 inch thick
Salt
Pepper
2 tablespoons olive oil

Let the steak come to room temperature. Season on both sides with salt and pepper.

If you are sautéing the steak, in a sauté pan just large enough to hold the meat, heat the olive oil over high heat until it begins to smoke. Add the steak and cook until well browned. Turn down the heat to medium and cook for a total of 3 to 5 minutes for rare, 7 minutes for medium-rare, or 10 minutes for well done. Using tongs, turn the steak over and cook the same way on the second side.

If you are grilling the steak, prepare a hot fire for direct grilling in a grill (see page 21). Rub the steak on both sides with the olive oil. Place the steak on the grill rack and grill for 2 minutes. Rotate the steak 90 degrees to create a crosshatch pattern, and then grill for 2 to 3 minutes longer. Using tongs, turn the steak over and grill for 2 minutes. Rotate the steak 90 degrees to create a crosshatch pattern, and then grill for 2 to 5 minutes longer, or until juices barely begin to form on the surface of the meat (medium-rare) or until done to your liking.

Let the steak rest for 5 minutes in a warm spot before carving and serving.

Grilled Tri-Tip Steak

Triangular and embedded in the sirloin, the tri-tip steak, also known as the Newport steak, is one of the great bargains of the butcher's counter. It will cook best if you butterfly it first. Here, I grill it, but you can also easily sauté it in olive oil over high heat.

MAKES 4 MAIN-COURSE SERVINGS

1 tri-tip steak, about $1^1/_2$ pounds and
    $1^1/_2$ inches thick
Salt
Pepper
1 tablespoon olive oil

To butterfly the steak, place it on a cutting board, with a long side facing you. Using a long, sharp knife, carefully cut the steak in half horizontally, stopping just short of the opposite side, so the steak can be opened flat, like a book (see page 195). Season the steak on both sides with salt and pepper and let come to room temperature.

Prepare a hot fire for direct grilling in a grill (see page 21). Rub the steak on both sides with the olive oil. Place on the grill rack and grill, turning once, for about 4 minutes on each side for rare, or 5 minutes for medium-rare.

Let the steak rest for 5 minutes in a warm place, then slice across the grain to serve.

Marinades

Despite frequent claims to the contrary, most marinades do very little to tenderize meat. If the marinade contains raw papaya, mango, or pineapple, it will indeed tenderize, but it also can make the meat mushy. The primary role of marinades is to provide flavor, and they are best used for less delicately flavored cuts whose natural flavor will not be buried by the marinade. In other words, don't marinate an aged porterhouse because you want its inherent flavor to shine through. On the other hand, hanger, chuck, flank, tri-tip, or other steaks made from tough (and flavorful) cuts benefit from a marinade that augments, but does not compete with, their flavor.

Marinades can be simple. In fact, one of my favorite marinades calls for just four ingredients: soy sauce, olive oil, fresh thyme, and garlic. Any herb can be used instead of thyme—marjoram is especially good—and shallots can supplement or replace the garlic. Most marinades contain oil, though it isn't necessary unless you are using it for its flavor. Extra virgin olive oil is an example. Many cooks mistakenly believe the addition of an acidic element, such as lemon or vinegar, will help tenderize the meat. But such acids have little effect on tenderness and should be used only when their flavor is welcome.

Meat can be marinated for an hour or so or as long as overnight. However, when using a marinade containing tropical fruits (see above), don't marinate for more than an hour or the meat will turn mushy. Avoid using wine in marinades for steaks or other meats that are cooked to a low internal temperature. The heat won't cook off the alcohol and the taste of raw alcohol in rare meat is unpleasant. That said, wine is delicious in the marinade for a pot roast or stew. In fact, the best marinade for a braised dish of any sort is made up of the aromatic ingredients used in the braise—in other words, the wine, carrots, onions, and bouquet garni that usually form the basis of a braise. Don't use distilled spirits in any kind of marinade, as they give meat an unpleasant gaminess.

London Broil with White Wine and Shallot Sauce

Originally, the term *London broil* always meant flank steak, but nowadays flank steak has become relatively expensive, so London broil can be just about any cut, including less common, less expensive cuts such as those from the chuck. Unlike steaks, which are served whole or carved into thick slices at the table, London broil is always served thinly sliced, usually across the grain, which attenuates the impression of toughness. Despite the name, London broil does not have to be broiled and in fact is best sautéed, so you end up with some juices in the pan. The marinade provides plenty of flavor (the soy sauce adds umami but no distinct Asian flavor), but if you are in a rush, you can skip it. You can also opt to rub the steak with the olive oil, grill it over a hot charcoal or gas fire (see page 21), and serve it without the sauce.

MAKES 4 MAIN-COURSE SERVINGS

1 tri-tip, flank, chuck, or sirloin steak,
   1 1/2 to 2 pounds
1/4 cup soy sauce
1 teaspoon fresh thyme leaves
2 cloves garlic, minced
1/4 cup olive oil
Pepper

Sauce
2 shallots, minced
1/2 cup dry white wine
1/2 cup beef broth (page 316) or other broth
2 tablespoons meat glaze (page 318), optional
2 tablespoons cold butter, cut into 2 slices
Salt
Pepper

If using a tri-tip steak, butterfly it as shown on the facing page.

In a shallow dish, stir together the soy sauce, thyme, garlic, 2 tablespoons of the olive oil, and several grinds of pepper. If you're using flank steak, poke tiny holes in it with the tip of a knife. Add the steak to the marinade, turn to coat, cover, and marinate at room temperature for at least 4 hours or in the refrigerator for up to overnight.

In a sauté pan just large enough to hold the steak, heat the remaining 2 tablespoons olive oil over high heat until it begins to smoke. (Making sure the pan is hot enough is especially important if the steak is thin. If the pan is not hot enough at the beginning, the steak won't brown before it overcooks.) Remove the steak from the marinade, add it to the pan, and cook until well browned. Turn down the heat to medium and cook for a total of 4 minutes for rare, 5 minutes for medium-rare, or 7 minutes for well done. Using tongs, turn the steak over and cook the same way on the second side. Transfer the steak to a cutting board and let rest in a warm spot while you make the sauce. Pour the fat out of the pan.

To make the sauce, return the pan to high heat. Add the shallots and stir around for about 1 minute, or until they smell toasty. Add the wine and broth, bring to a boil, and deglaze the pan, scraping up any brown bits on the bottom of the pan with a wooden spoon. Stir in the meat glaze and cook down until the sauce has a lightly syrupy consistency. Whisk in the butter until emulsified. Do not allow the sauce to boil. Season with salt and pepper.

Slice the steak into long strips across the grain and arrange on warmed plates. Spoon the sauce over the top.

London broil with white wine and shallot sauce

1. Whole tri-tip steak.

2. Using a long, thin-bladed, sharp knife, butterfly the tri-tip, cutting in half horizontally and stopping just short of the opposite side.

3. Open the steak and flatten it.

4. Sautéed tri-tip.

5. To get the widest slices, cut the tri-tip across the grain on the diagonal.

6. Tri-tip steak with white wine and shallot sauce.

Hanger Steak with Mushrooms and Red Wine

Each animal has only one hanger steak, a cut that "hangs" within the rib cage. Tender and with a deep beefy flavor, most hanger steaks weigh about 3/4 pound and make a generous serving for one or a "normal" serving for two. Don't be shocked by the number of mushrooms in this recipe. They shrink considerably. I have grilled the steaks here, but you can sauté them in olive oil in a sauté pan over high heat or on a stove-top grill pan.

MAKES 4 MAIN-COURSE SERVINGS

2 hanger steaks, about 3/4 pound each

Salt

Pepper

4 tablespoons butter

1 1/4 pounds cremini mushrooms, quartered
   vertically

1 tablespoon olive oil

3/4 cup full-bodied red wine

2 tablespoons meat glaze (page 318), optional

Let the steaks come to room temperature. Season on both sides with salt and pepper.

Prepare a hot fire for direct grilling in a grill (see page 21).

In a large sauté pan, melt the butter over high heat. When the butter froths and then begins to subside, add a handful of the mushrooms, stir or toss for a minute or two, and add another handful of mushrooms. Continue in this way until you have added all the mushrooms and they have browned and any liquid they released has evaporated. This will take about 10 minutes total.

Meanwhile, rub the steaks on both sides with the olive oil. Place on the grill rack and grill, turning once, for about 4 minutes total for rare, 5 minutes for medium-rare, or 8 minutes for well done.

Let the steaks rest for 5 minutes in a warm spot while you finish the sauce. Add the wine and meat glaze to the mushrooms and boil for a few minutes until the liquid develops a saucelike consistency.

Slice the steaks and place on warmed plates. Spoon the mushroom sauce over the steaks.

Hanger steak with mushrooms and red wine

1. Two uncooked hanger steaks.

2. Sauté mushrooms until any liquid they release evaporates.

3. Hanger steak with mushroom sauce.

Grilled Flank Steak Salad

A flank steak comes from the strip of meat that hangs down the side of the animal, literally forming its flank. If you put your hands on each side of your abdomen, the underlying muscles are your flank steaks. In the past, this was an inexpensive cut, but no longer. However, it is one of the tastiest cuts on the steer and worth the cost. Look at a flank steak and you'll see a distinct grain that runs its length. When you serve it, always slice it across that grain to ensure tenderness. Here, it is served tossed with greens in a simple salad ideal for lunch or a light supper.

MAKES 4 MAIN-COURSE SERVINGS

1/4 cup soy sauce

3 cloves garlic, crushed

Leaves from 5 sprigs marjoram or thyme

4 tablespoons olive oil

Pepper

1 flank steak, about 1 1/2 pounds

2 teaspoons Dijon mustard

Salt

1 tablespoon red wine vinegar

3 tablespoons extra virgin olive oil

1/2 pound assorted lettuces such as Boston, romaine, arugula, and/or frisée

Tomatoes, cut into wedges, hard-boiled eggs, cut into wedges, or avocado, sliced

In a shallow dish, stir together the soy sauce, garlic, marjoram, olive oil, and several grinds of pepper. Poke tiny holes in the flank steak with the tip of a knife. Add the steak to the marinade, turn to coat evenly, cover, and marinate at room temperature for at least 4 hours or in the refrigerator for up to overnight.

Prepare a hot fire for direct grilling in a grill (see page 21). Remove the steak from the marinade, place on the grill rack, and grill, turning once, for about 3 minutes on each side for rare, or 4 minutes for medium-rare, moving it to a cooler area of the grill if it starts to brown too much. Let the steak rest for 5 minutes in a warm spot before slicing.

Meanwhile, to make the vinaigrette, in a small bowl, whisk together the mustard, 1/2 teaspoon salt, 1/4 teaspoon pepper, and the vinegar. Slowly whisk in the extra virgin olive oil, whisking until emulsified. Place the lettuces and other salad ingredients in a bowl, drizzle with the vinaigrette, and toss to coat evenly.

Cut the steak across the grain on the diagonal into thin slices as shown on page 198. Divide the salad among individual plates. Arrange the steak slices on top. Sprinkle with salt and grind over pepper, then serve.

Grilled flank steak salad

1. Uncooked flank steak

2. Marinate the steak

3. To serve, cut the steak across the grain on the diagonal into thin slices.

Fajitas

1. Uncooked skirt steaks.

2. Cut each flank steak into 4 pieces and then grill.

Fajitas

This Tex-Mex favorite of grilled meat wrapped in tortillas calls for skirt steak, an underappreciated, tasty, long, thin cut from the plate, or belly, of the steer. When shopping for skirt steak, keep in mind that two types are sold, the inside and the outside. The inside is thinner and generally smaller and is considered the more desirable of the two, primarily because it contains less tough membrane.

MAKES 6 MAIN-COURSE SERVINGS

2 skirt steaks, about 1 pound each

3 tablespoons red wine vinegar or fresh lime juice

Salt

Pepper

2 bell peppers, seeded and cut lengthwise into narrow strips

$1/2$ pound shiitake mushrooms, stems removed and caps sliced

1 onion, thinly sliced

1 Cuban or poblano chile, seeded and cut lengthwise into narrow strips

2 jalapeño chiles, seeded and chopped

3 tablespoons chopped fresh cilantro

Olive oil

6 flour tortillas, 8 inches in diameter

Sour cream for serving

Salsa for serving

Cut each steak crosswise into 4 pieces. In a shallow bowl, combine the vinegar and a generous pinch each salt and pepper. Add the steaks, turn to coat, and marinate at room temperature for up to 1 hour or in the refrigerator for up to 4 hours.

Place a stove-top grill pan over high heat and heat until hot. Add the bell peppers, mushrooms, onion, and chiles and grill, turning all the while, for about 10 minutes, or until nicely browned. Transfer the vegetables to a bowl, add the cilantro, season with salt and pepper, and toss to mix. Cover to keep warm.

Remove the steaks from the marinade. With the grill pan still over high heat and working in batches to avoid crowding, add the steaks and cook for about 4 minutes, or until well browned. Turn the steaks over and continue to cook for about 3 minutes longer, or until well browned on the second side and firm to the touch. The steaks should be medium-rare. Transfer to a plate and let rest in a warm spot.

Coat a small skillet with a light film of olive oil and place over medium heat. One at a time, add the tortillas and heat, turning once, for about 1 minute on each side, or until very lightly browned but still flexible. As each tortilla is ready, transfer to a plate and cover to keep warm.

Cut the steaks into long, thin slices across the grain on the diagonal. Divide the meat evenly among the tortillas. Top the meat with the grilled vegetables, again dividing evenly. Roll up the tortillas and place a rolled tortilla on each warmed plate. Serve at once. Pass the sour cream and salsa at the table.

Skirt Steak Rolled with Prosciutto and Sage

Tender, flavorful skirt steak is used to make these small rolls. I have grilled them here, but you can also broil them, using the same timing. Be sure they are close enough to the heat source to brown nicely. Look for *prosciutto di Parma* or another high-quality imported prosciutto for the best result.

MAKES 6 MAIN-COURSE SERVINGS

2 skirt steaks, about 1 pound each
6 large, thin slices prosciutto, cut in half crosswise
12 fresh sage leaves
Salt
Pepper
Olive oil or melted butter

If using wooden skewers, soak them in water to cover for 1 hour before loading.

Prepare a hot fire for direct grilling in a grill (see page 21).

Cut each skirt steak crosswise into 6 pieces of equal size. Place a half slice of prosciutto on each steak piece, and top the prosciutto with a sage leaf. Roll up each piece of beef into a snug cylinder, then slide the roll onto 2 metal or wooden skewers, piercing the roll once near each end. Repeat to top and roll the remaining 11 pieces of steak, putting 6 rolls on each pair of skewers (or fewer if you have only small skewers). Season the rolls with salt and pepper and brush with olive oil.

Place the skewers on the grill rack and grill, turning as needed and brushing with additional oil, for about 10 minutes total, or until the rolls are nicely browned and the meat is medium-rare.

Slide the rolls off the skewers onto a warmed platter or individual plates to serve.

Bolognese Sauce

This famous sauce is often made with skirt steak, which is both flavorful and needs some time to tenderize. Toss it with fettuccine or other long pasta, or spoon it atop ravioli.

MAKES ENOUGH SAUCE FOR 4 PASTA SERVINGS

3 tablespoons olive oil
1 pancetta slice, $1/4$ inch thick, cut into $1/4$-inch cubes
1 carrot, peeled and chopped
$1/2$ stalk celery, chopped
1 onion, chopped
$1^1/2$ pounds skirt steak, cut into $1/4$-inch dice
$3/4$ cup dry white wine
3 tablespoons tomato paste
5 tomatoes, peeled, seeded, and chopped
$1/2$ cup heavy cream
Salt
Pepper

In a heavy pot, heat the olive oil over medium heat. Add the pancetta, carrot, celery, and onion and sweat the vegetables, stirring often, for about 10 minutes, or until they have softened. Add the steak and continue to cook, stirring occasionally, for about 20 minutes, or until the meat begins to brown. (The meat will release liquid, which must be boiled down until it caramelizes on the bottom of the pan.) Add the wine, tomato paste, tomatoes, and cream and stir well. Simmer gently, uncovered, for about $1^1/2$ hours, or until the meat yields when pressed with the back of a fork. If the sauce begins to get too thick before the flavors have married and the meat is tender, add water, a little at a time, as needed to thin to a good consistency. Season with salt and pepper.

Steak and Kidney Pie

As in the Bolognese Sauce on the facing page, the skirt steak used here is braised to ensure tenderness. The pairing of beef and kidneys is traditional in this iconic pie of the British dinner table, but if you don't like kidneys, just leave them out.

MAKES 8 MAIN-COURSE SERVINGS

Pastry
4 cups flour
1¹/₄ cups (2¹/₂ sticks) cold butter, sliced
2 eggs
1 teaspoon salt
1 tablespoon water, or as needed

1¹/₂ pounds skirt steak, cut against the grain into strips 1¹/₂ inches long
Salt
Pepper
Olive oil for sautéing
1 onion, chopped
1 large carrot, peeled and chopped
3 cloves garlic, minced
2 cups dry red wine
3 tablespoons meat glaze (page 318), optional
Bouquet garni (page 320)
2 tablespoons butter
2 tablespoons flour
2 veal kidneys, about ³/₄ pound each
1 pound cremini mushrooms, quartered vertically
1 egg, beaten with a large pinch of salt

To make the pastry, in a food processor, combine the flour, butter, eggs, and salt and process for about 1 minute, or until the dough comes together in a ragged mass. If it doesn't come together, add the water and continue processing. Gather the dough, shape it into a ball, and then flatten it into a disk. Wrap in plastic wrap and set aside in a cool place.

Unless the kitchen is very warm, avoid placing it in the refrigerator, which makes it too cold and hard to roll out.

Cut the skirt steak across the grain into strips about 1¹/₂ inches long, ¹/₂ inch wide, and ¹/₂ inch thick. Season well with salt and pepper. In a large sauté pan, heat 2 tablespoons olive oil over high heat. When the oil begins to smoke, add the beef strips, a few at time, and cook, turning as needed, for 1 to 2 minutes on each side, or until nicely browned. Using a slotted spoon, transfer the meat to a plate. Pour the fat out of the pan.

Return the pan to medium heat and add 2 table-spoons olive oil. Add the onion, carrot, and garlic and sweat the vegetables, stirring occasionally, for about 15 minutes, or until they have softened. Return the meat to the pan and pour in the wine. Stir in the meat glaze and add the bouquet garni. Cover the pan and simmer gently on the stove top for about 3 hours, or until the meat is easily

continued

penetrated with a fork. (Alternatively, slide the covered pan into a 275°F oven and cook for about 3 hours to the same end.)

In a small bowl, work together the butter and flour with the back of a fork to make a smooth paste, or *beurre manié*. Return the pan to the stove top if it has been in the oven. Discard the bouquet garni. Whisk the paste into the simmering liquid and simmer until thickened to a nice stewlike consistency. Season with salt and pepper. Strain the stew and reserve the solids and braising liquid separately.

Pull and/or cut off any fat clinging to each kidney, then cut out any excess fat and gristle at the center of the kidney, being careful not to cut the kidney apart (see page 255). Season the kidneys all over with salt and pepper. In a sauté pan just large enough to hold the kidneys in a single layer, heat 2 tablespoons olive oil over high heat until the oil begins to smoke. Add the kidneys and sauté, turning as needed, for about 10 minutes total, or until well browned on both sides. Transfer to a plate. Pour the fat out of the pan and wipe out the pan.

Return the pan to high heat and add 2 tablespoons olive oil. When the oil is hot, add a handful of the mushrooms, stir or toss for a minute or two, and add another handful of mushrooms. Continue in this way until you have added all the mushrooms and they have browned and any liquid they released has evaporated. This will take about 10 minutes total. Season with salt and pepper.

Slice the kidneys.

Preheat the oven to 375°F. Cut the pastry dough in half. On a lightly floured work surface, roll out each half into a round about 13 inches in diameter. Drape one round on the rolling pin and then unroll it over a 10-inch pie plate, easing it into the bottom and sides. Spoon the stew meat into the pastry-lined plate. Arrange the kidney slices and mushrooms over the top. Drape the second pastry round on the rolling pin and unroll it over the pie. Trim the top and bottom crusts so they extend about 3/4 inch beyond the rim. Fold the edges under and crimp or flute decoratively around the rim. Brush the top of the pie with the beaten egg. Use a pastry bag tip to make a hole in the center of the top crust and pour in the braising liquid. Using a sharp knife, make about 6 slits in the crust to allow steam to escape. If you like, decorate the pie with leaves cut from the pastry trimmings and brush the leaves with beaten egg. Place the pie plate on a sheet pan to prevent drips in the oven.

Slide the sheet pan into the oven and bake the pie for about 1 hour, or until the crust is golden brown and you can see the filling bubbling through the slits. Let cool for about 10 minutes before serving.

Steak and kidney pie

1. Slice the skirt steak into strips.

2. Sweat mirepoix (onion, carrot, and garlic).

3. Brown the kidneys on both sides in hot oil.

4. Line the bottom of a pie pan with pastry dough and put in the stew.

5. Arrange the kidney slices over the stew.

6. Put the mushrooms on top.

7. Unroll the top crust over the pie and trim off the excess.

8. Pour the braising liquid through a hole in the top crust of the pie.

9. Finished pie.

Beef Stroganoff

This classic dish is traditionally finished with sour cream, but American sour cream has such a low butterfat content that it curdles if it gets too hot. Crème fraîche makes an excellent alternative and won't curdle. Once you have browned the meat and cooked the sauce, you can set both elements aside for up to a few hours, and then add the meat to the sauce and reheat just before serving. Serve with rice or egg noodles.

MAKES 4 MAIN-COURSE SERVINGS

$1^1/_2$ pounds tenderloin, sirloin, tri-tip, strip, or
    other tender steak
Salt
Pepper
3 tablespoons olive oil
3 tablespoons butter
1 small onion, minced
2 tablespoons flour
$1^1/_2$ cups beef broth (page 316) or other flavorful
    broth
$^1/_4$ cup dry sherry
10 ounces fresh cremini or white mushrooms,
    quartered vertically
$^1/_2$ cup crème fraîche or sour cream

Cut the meat across the grain into strips about 2 inches long, $^1/_2$ inch wide, and $^1/_2$ inch thick. Season well with salt and pepper. In a large sauté pan, heat the olive oil over high heat. When the oil begins to smoke, add the beef strips, a few at time, and cook, turning as needed, for 1 to 2 minutes on each side, or until nicely browned on the outside and still rare inside. Using a slotted spoon, transfer to a platter, spreading the strips in a single layer. (Do not heap them or they'll overcook.) When all of the beef strips are browned, pour the fat out of the pan.

Return the pan to low heat and melt the butter. Add the onion and cook, stirring occasionally, for about 10 minutes, or until translucent. Stir in the flour and cook, stirring, for about 2 minutes to cook away its starchy flavor. Whisk in the broth and then the sherry, and then add the mushrooms and simmer for about 10 minutes. Add the crème fraîche and simmer gently for about 5 minutes, or until the mixture thickens slightly. (If you are using sour cream, make sure the mixture does not boil or it will curdle.)

Add the beef strips and stir briefly to mix well and heat evenly. Serve at once.

Beef Sautés

Most beef stews are made by slowly cooking tough cuts of meat in a sauce until they are tenderized. But some dishes, the best known of which is beef Stroganoff, are made by quickly cooking tender cuts, such as sirloin, tenderloin, tri-tip, or strip steaks, in a sauce to emulate a stew. The trick is not to over-cook the meat, so that when your guests bite into a piece expecting a stewlike texture, they instead find themselves eating tender, rare, juicy beef. Creating a sauce for these quick-cooked stews, which are more properly called sautés, that is as tasty as the sauce of a long-cooked stew is difficult. Short of making an authentic stew and using the braising liquid for the sauté, there is no easy solution. The best method is to reduce flavorful broth as much as you dare, thicken it with a roux, and finish it with cream or butter. Beef sautés are also an excellent way to use leftover meat from roasts. Just don't brown the meat as you do for the Beef Stroganoff recipe.

Stir-Fried Beef with Bell Peppers, Mushrooms, and Snow Peas

Stir-fries are easy to improvise with whatever vegetables you have on hand. Here, I use onion, mushrooms, bell peppers, and snow peas, but you might also try green beans, bok choy, carrots, or cabbage. For stir-frying, be sure to use a tender cut, such as sirloin or the round steak used here. Tough cuts will remain so.

MAKES 4 MAIN-COURSE SERVINGS

Marinade

$^1/_4$ cup soy sauce

2 teaspoons toasted sesame oil

2 cloves garlic, minced

3 tablespoons peeled and grated fresh ginger

1 tablespoon cornstarch

1 teaspoon sugar

$1^1/_2$ pounds round or rump steak

3 tablespoons canola oil

1 onion, thinly sliced

2 celery stalks, thinly sliced

2 bell peppers, seeded and cut lengthwise into narrow strips or crosswise into narrow rounds

One 8-ounce can water chestnuts, drained and quartered

10 ounces white mushrooms or shiitake mushrooms, tough stems removed and caps sliced

$^1/_2$ pound snow peas, ends trimmed

2 tablespoons water or chicken broth (page 316)

1 bunch cilantro, finely chopped

To make the marinade, in a bowl, combine the soy sauce, sesame oil, garlic, ginger, cornstarch, and sugar and stir until the cornstarch and sugar dissolve. Cut the steak across the grain on the diagonal into strips about $^1/_2$ inch wide, 3 inches long, and

$^1/_2$ inch thick. Add to the marinade and toss to coat evenly. Let stand for 30 minutes.

Remove the meat from the marinade and pat it dry on paper towels (do not let it sit on the paper or it will stick to it). Reserve the marinade.

In a wok or large skillet, heat the canola oil over high heat until it begins to smoke. Add the meat and stir-fry for about 2 minutes, or until nicely seared. Using a wire skimmer or slotted spoon, transfer the meat to a plate.

Add the onion, celery, bell peppers, water chestnuts, mushrooms, and snow peas and stir-fry for 3 to 5 minutes, or until the vegetables are tender-crisp. Return the meat to the pan and add the reserved marinade and the water. Sprinkle in the cilantro and stir-fry for about 1 minute, or until the liquid thickens and coats the vegetables and meat. Serve immediately.

Tongue

Because they are quite tough, tongues must be braised or poached (as in Bollito Misto on page 178) until meltingly tender. Ideally, they are larded so they stay nice and moist, though that step is not essential. In general, try to find the largest tongue you can to make cooking it worth the effort and for heightened drama when you present it at the table.

Tongue with Madeira Sauce

Here, I call for two tongues because tongues from American steers can be quite small.

MAKES 8 MAIN-COURSE SERVINGS

2 or 3 beef tongues, about 4 pounds total weight

1 pound fatback (weight not including rind)
  or *lardo,* optional

1 large carrot, peeled and cut into $1/2$-inch-thick
  slices

1 large onion, quartered

1 cup dry or medium-dry Madeira

4 cups beef broth (page 316) or chicken broth
  (page 316)

2 tablespoons meat glaze (page 318), optional

Bouquet garni (page 320)

Rinse the tongues under cold running water. If you want to lard the tongues, cut the fatback into sheets about $1/4$ inch thick, then cut the sheets into strips, or lardons, about $1/4$ inch on each side and 6 inches long or longer. Using a hinged larding needle, pull the strips through each tongue on a diagonal. Put the tongues in a pot, add cold water to cover, and bring to the simmer. Simmer for 5 minutes, then drain in a colander. Rinse well with cold running water.

Preheat the oven to 400°F. Put the tongues in an ovenproof pot just large enough to hold them and add the carrot and onion. Slide the pot, uncovered, into the oven and roast the tongues for about

1 hour, or until golden brown and the juices they release caramelize on the bottom of the pot.

Remove from the oven, place on the stove top over high heat, and add the Madeira, broth, meat glaze, and bouquet garni. Bring to a simmer, turn down the heat to low, cover, and simmer gently for about 2 hours, or until the tongues are easily penetrated with a knife. (Alternatively, slide the pot into a 275°F oven and cook for about 2 hours to the same end.)

Remove the tongues from the braising liquid. Using a small, sharp knife, trim off any fat or gristle from the base of each tongue. Using the knife and your fingers, carefully peel away and discard the skin. Put the tongues in an ovenproof pot just large enough to hold them (they will have shrunk).

Strain the braising liquid into a glass pitcher and skim off the fat with a ladle. Or, ideally, refrigerate the braising liquid at this point and then lift off the congealed fat in a single layer. Pour the strained liquid into a saucepan, bring to a simmer, and simmer, skimming off any fat or froth that rises to the surface, for about 20 minutes, or until reduced by about half. Meanwhile, raise the oven temperature to 400°F. Pour the reduced liquid over the tongues and place the pot, uncovered, in the oven. Cook the tongues, basting them every 10 minutes with the liquid, for about 30 minutes, or until they are covered with a shiny glaze.

Transfer the tongues to a platter or cutting board and cut crosswise into slices $1/4$ inch thick. Serve in warmed soup plates with the braising liquid spooned around the edges.

Cheek

If you're lucky enough to track them down, beef cheeks, the well-worked muscles found on the steer's cheekbones, make the perfect stew meat: they are well marbled with fat and yield a moist, tender, juicy result when slowly braised. Use them in Bollito Misto on page 178, the daube on page 149, or in the stew that follows here.

Beef Cheeks Braised with Julienned Vegetables

Here, the aromatic vegetables that were braised with the cheeks are cut into julienne and served with the cheeks. The result is an impressive tangle of flavorful vegetables and meltingly tender meat. This recipe calls for a lot of meat because it shrinks by about half.

MAKES 6 MAIN-COURSE SERVINGS

5 pounds beef cheeks (6 cheeks, each weighing
    a scant 1 pound)
Salt
Pepper
3 tablespoons olive oil, or as needed

1 cup dry white wine
4 cups beef broth (page 316) or other broth
    or water
Bouquet garni (page 320)
1 large carrot, peeled and cut into julienne
    (see page 11)
1 turnip, peeled and cut into julienne
1 small celeriac, peeled and cut into julienne
    (optional)
4 leeks, white part only, cut into julienne

Pat the beef cheeks dry, then season all over with salt and pepper. Select a heavy pot just large enough to hold the cheeks snugly and the julienned vegetables. Add the olive oil and heat until the oil begins to smoke. Working in batches to avoid crowding, add the beef cheeks and brown

continued

Beef cheeks braised with julienned vegetables

1. Uncooked beef cheek.

2. Brown the beef cheeks in olive oil.

well on both sides, adding more oil as needed, then transfer to a plate. Pour the fat out of the pan.

Return the cheeks to the pot. Pour in the wine and the broth to cover, and add the bouquet garni. Bring to a gentle simmer. Cover the pot with a sheet of aluminum foil, pressing it down slightly in the middle so that moisture will condense on its underside and drip down into the pot, and then with a lid.

Simmer gently on the stove top for 1 hour. (Alternatively, slide the pot into a 275°F oven and cook for 1 hour.) Uncover and add the carrot, turnip, celeriac, and leeks. Re-cover with the foil and lid and continue braising on the stove top or in the oven for about 1½ hours longer, or until the meat is easily penetrated with a knife.

Remove the beef cheeks from the pot and thickly slice them. Serve in warmed soup bowls with the tangled vegetables. Spoon the broth over and around the meat and vegetables.

Shank

Beef shanks, the lower portion of the steer's legs, are a lean, tough cut that benefit from moist cooking. That means they are good in stews and are delicious in a pot-au-feu. They can also be cut into 1 1/2- to 2-inch-thick rounds for braising. I have always found rear shanks to be meatier than front shanks.

Braised Beef Shanks with Saffron, Ginger, Preserved Lemon, and Cilantro

Four ingredients—saffron, ginger, preserved lemons, and cilantro—give this braise a decided Moroccan character, making it a candidate for the term *tagine*.

MAKES 6 MAIN-COURSE SERVINGS

6 beef shank rounds, each 1 1/2 to 2 inches thick
Salt
Pepper
5 tablespoons olive oil, or as needed
1 onion, chopped
1 carrot, peeled and sliced
3 tablespoons peeled and grated fresh ginger
2 cloves garlic, minced
3 cups beef broth (page 316) or water,
   or as needed
Bouquet garni (page 320)
Pinch of saffron threads, soaked in 1 tablespoon
   hot water for 30 minutes
1 preserved lemon, cut into 1/4-inch dice
2 tablespoons chopped fresh cilantro

Season the shank rounds all over with salt and pepper. Select a heavy ovenproof pot just large enough to hold the shank rounds snugly in a single layer. Add 3 tablespoons of the olive oil and heat until the oil begins to smoke. Working in batches to avoid crowding, add the shank rounds and cook, turning once, for about 5 minutes on each side, or until well browned, adding more oil as needed. Transfer to a plate. Pour the fat out of the pan.

Return the pan to medium heat and add the remaining 2 tablespoons oil. Add the onion, carrot, ginger, and garlic and sweat them, stirring occasionally, for about 10 minutes, or until the onion is translucent. Arrange the shanks in the pot in a single layer, pour in the broth to cover by about 1/2 inch, and add the bouquet garni. Bring to a gentle simmer. Cover the pot with a sheet of aluminum foil, pressing it down slightly in the middle so that moisture will condense on its underside and drip down into the pot, and then with a lid.

Simmer gently on the stove top for about 3 hours, or until a knife slides easily in and out of the shank meat. (Alternatively, slide the pot into a 275°F oven and cook for about 3 hours to the same end.)

Preheat the oven to 400°F. Gently transfer the shank rounds to a platter. Strain the braising liquid into a glass pitcher and skim off the fat with a ladle. Or, ideally, refrigerate the braising liquid at this point and then lift off the congealed fat in a single layer. Return the shank rounds to the pot, and pour the degreased liquid over them. Bring to a simmer on the stove top and slide the pot, uncovered, into the oven. Cook the shank rounds, basting them every 10 minutes with the liquid, for about 30 minutes, or until they are covered with a shiny glaze.

Return the pot to the stove top, add the saffron and its soaking water, the preserved lemon, and the cilantro, and bring to a simmer. Serve the shank rounds in warmed soup plates with the braising liquid spooned over and around them.

Beef Shanks with Red Wine and Mushrooms

This classic French method of preparing beef shanks is easy and sure to satisfy. It's also inexpensive, except for the wine.

MAKES 6 MAIN-COURSE SERVINGS

6 beef shank rounds, each 1½ to 2 inches thick

Salt

Pepper

5 tablespoons olive oil

1 whole clove

2 onions, halved through the stem end

2 carrots, peeled and cut into 1-inch sections

1 head garlic, halved through the equator

Bouquet garni (page 320)

3 cups full-bodied red wine

3 cups chicken broth (page 316) or water

3 tablespoons meat glaze (page 318), optional

1 pound cremini mushrooms, left whole if small
    or quartered vertically if large

Season the shank rounds all over with salt and pepper. In a large, heavy sauté pan, heat the olive oil over high heat until it begins to smoke. Working in batches to avoid crowding, add the shank rounds

and cook, turning once, for about 5 minutes on each side, or until well browned, adding more oil as needed. Transfer the shanks to an ovenproof pot in which they fit snugly.

Stick the clove in an onion half, and then nestle all the onion halves, the carrots, garlic, and the bouquet garni in the pot. Pour in the wine and then enough broth to cover, and add the meat glaze. Bring to a gentle simmer. Cover the pot with a sheet of aluminum foil, pressing it down slightly in the middle so that moisture will condense on its underside and drip down into the pot, and then with a lid.

Simmer gently on the stove top for 2 to 3 hours, or until a knife slides easily in and out of the shank meat. (Alternatively, slide the pot into a 275°F oven and cook for 2 to 3 hours to the same end. Remove from the heat or the oven.)

Gently transfer the shank rounds to a platter. If you like, you can also remove and reserve the carrots. Strain the braising liquid into a glass pitcher and skim off the fat with a ladle. Or, ideally, refrigerate the braising liquid at this point and then lift off the congealed fat in a single layer. Pour the degreased liquid into a saucepan, bring to a simmer, and simmer, skimming off any fat or froth that rises to the surface, for about 30 minutes, or until reduced by about half. Meanwhile, preheat the oven to 400°F.

Return the shank rounds to the pot (or put into a clean pot), add the carrots, if saved, and pour the reduced liquid over the top. Bring to a simmer on the stove top, sprinkle the mushrooms over the top so they will cook along with the meat, and slide the pot, uncovered, into the oven. Cook the shanks, basting every 10 minutes with the liquid, for about 40 minutes, or until the shanks and mushrooms are covered with a shiny glaze.

Serve the shanks in warmed soup plates. Spoon the mushrooms (and carrots) and a few tablespoons of the braising liquid over and around them.

Oxtail

Ideally, the oxtail should come from a large steer so the sections are nice and big. If you can pick out your own rounds of tail, select the larger pieces. Oxtail is a bony cut and must be braised or poached for a long time for it to render its flavor and gelatin. When it does, it is a delicious choice for the table.

Oxtail Soup

A century ago, oxtail soup was a standard of the American dinner table. It deserves to have that same status today. Be sure to use authentic Spanish sherry and not an ersatz one from the United States. This version is unusual in that it contains fennel, which adds a lovely freshness. It is by no means essential, however.

MAKES 6 FIRST-COURSE SERVINGS

Bouquet garni (page 320)
4 pounds oxtail rounds
1 onion, halved through the stem end
1 carrot, peeled and sliced
$1/2$ stalk celery
Handful of chopped fennel stalk, optional
2 cups dry sherry
Salt
Pepper

Put the bouquet garni in a pot, and put the oxtails on top. Add the onion, carrot, celery, fennel, and sherry, and then add water as needed to cover. Bring to a gentle simmer, skimming off any froth that rises to the surface. Then simmer gently, skimming off any fat or froth that rises to the surface, for 5 hours, or until the meat is falling off the bone.

Using a slotted spoon, transfer the oxtails to a platter. When cool enough to handle, pick the meat from the oxtails and discard the bones. Strain the braising liquid through a fine-mesh strainer into a saucepan. Return the meat to the braising liquid and heat until piping hot. Season with salt and pepper and ladle the soup into warmed bowls.

Oxtail Stew with Grapes

Grapes give this dish a sweet flavor, which counteracts the richness and gelatinous quality of the sauce. The oxtails are marinated, browned, and braised with the usual aromatic vegetables, but a generous measure of grapes are added along with the vegetables. At serving time, the vegetables are discarded and the stew is served with the grapes as a garnish.

MAKES 6 MAIN-COURSE SERVINGS

6 pounds oxtail rounds, as large as possible
Salt
Pepper
2 onions, quartered through the stem end
2 carrots, peeled and sliced
1 bottle (750 ml) full-bodied red wine
Bouquet garni (page 320)
$1/4$ cup olive oil
3 pounds seedless grapes

Season the oxtails all over with salt and pepper and place in a large bowl. Add the onions, carrots, wine, and bouquet garni. Cover and marinate in the refrigerator for at least 4 hours or up to overnight.

Remove the oxtails from the marinade and pat dry. Reserve the marinade. Preheat the oven to 275°F. Select a heavy ovenproof pot large enough to hold the oxtails in one or two layers. Add the olive oil and heat over high heat until the oil begins to smoke. Working in batches to avoid crowding, add the oxtail rounds and brown, turning once, for

continued

about 5 minutes on each side, or until well browned. Transfer to a plate. Pour the fat out of the pan.

Return the oxtails to the pot, and pour the marinade, including the aromatic vegetables and bouquet garni, over the top. Bring to a gentle simmer on the stove top. Cover the pot with a sheet of aluminum foil, pressing it down slightly in the middle so that moisture will condense on its underside and drip down into the pot, and then with a lid.

Slide the pot into the oven and braise for 2 hours. Uncover and add the grapes. Re-cover and braise for 2 hours longer, or until a knife slides easily in and out of the meat.

Gently lift out the grapes and reserve in a bowl. Let the oxtails cool to room temperature in the pot, then cover and refrigerate overnight. The next day,

lift off the congealed fat from the surface with a spoon. The braising liquid will have set into a jelly. Unmold the cold oxtails from the jelly and pick out the rounds. (Working with the oxtail rounds when they are cold keeps them from falling apart.) Transfer the jelly and the vegetables to a saucepan, place over medium heat, and heat until the jelly melts. Remove from the heat, strain the liquid, and return it to the saucepan. Bring to a simmer and simmer, skimming off any fat or froth that rises to the surface, for about 30 minutes, or until reduced by about half.

Just before serving, reheat the oxtails and grapes in the reduced braising liquid. Serve the oxtails in warmed soup plates surrounded with the braising liquid and topped with the grapes.

Oxtail stew with grapes

1. Brown the drained marinated oxtails in oil.

2. Cover the oxtails with the wine and marinade vegetables.

3. Braise for 2 hours, until the marinade vegetables soften.

4. Put the grapes into the pot and continue braising.

5. Remove as much fat as possible from the chilled oxtails.

6. Unmold the congealed oxtails.

7. Take the oxtails out of the congealed braising liquid.

8. Melt the jelly with the aromatic vegetables.

9. Strain the liquid.

Marrowbone

Don't confuse marrowbones with knucklebones. The latter are used to make broth, while marrowbones are prized for their marrow. Marrowbones can be poached (they are often included in a pot-au-feu) or roasted and the marrow spread on toast for a light dinner. The marrow is also used in some sauces, mixed in near the end to add richness (see Bordelaise Sauce on page 189). To prepare marrow to use in this way, take it out of the bones and soak it overnight in salty water in the refrigerator (see page 190). The salt pulls out blood that would otherwise turn gray once the marrow is hot.

Roast Marrowbones

Marrow tastes best when the bones have been roasted in a low oven, so the heat penetrates them evenly. Allow the marrowbones to come to room temperature before roasting. Remember to buy long marrow bones and not knucklebones. Extract the cooked marrow from the bones with demitasse spoons (teaspoons are too large).

MAKES 4 LIGHT MAIN-COURSE SERVINGS

**4 large marrowbones, each about 4 inches long,
     at room temperature**
Toasted baguette slices for serving
Salt for serving
Pepper for serving

Put the bones in a baking dish, slide the dish into the oven, and turn the oven to 300°F (there is no need to preheat). Bake for about 20 minutes, or until the marrow has a translucent appearance.

Gently transfer the bones to plates and serve hot with the toast and salt and pepper for sprinkling.

Ground Beef

Many of us make the mistake of buying ground meat that is too lean. The rich, beefy flavor of a good hamburger comes from fat in the meat. When you buy ground chuck, ground round, or ground sirloin, you are not necessarily buying meat taken from those cuts. Often times, trimmings from various parts of the animal—from the chuck, to the plate, to the sirloin—are combined and ground to make ground beef. Ground chuck typically has the most fat, and ground sirloin the least. If these ground meats were actually made from the cuts whose labels they bear, they would all be very lean. If you want hamburger that is perfectly lean, go to a good butcher, pick out some steaks or a roast from an inexpensive cut (round is good), and have it ground or take it home and grind it yourself in a food processor. The advantage to having meat ground in this way, other than knowing exactly what you are getting, is that the surface bacteria, which are worked into the meat during grinding, have less time to establish themselves within the meat. Unlike a steak, whose surface bacteria are killed during cooking, bacteria in a rare hamburger are not killed. So having meat ground, or grinding it just before you use it, is a healthful option for anyone who likes their hamburgers rare.

Hamburgers

There's really nothing to hamburgers except choosing the meat (I recommend ground chuck), forming it into patties, and putting them on the grill or in the sauté pan. The secret to good cheeseburgers is to use the best cheese. Try Gruyère or real English or Vermont Cheddar. Blue cheese aficionados should look for Roquefort, Gorgonzola, or Stilton. Serve buns and the usual condiments and let everyone build their own burgers.

MAKES 6 MAIN-COURSE SERVINGS

2¹/₂ pounds ground chuck
Salt
Pepper
6 slices flavorful cheese (see note)
6 hamburger buns, split

Condiments
Lettuce leaves
Tomato slices
Onion slices
Pickles
Relish
Mustard
Ketchup

Divide the meat into 6 equal portions and shape each portion into a patty about 4 inches in diameter and ³/₄ inch thick. Season on both sides with salt and pepper.

Prepare a hot fire for direct grilling in a grill (see page 21), or preheat a large skillet over medium heat. Place the patties on the grill rack or in the pan and cook for about 2 minutes for rare or 4 minutes for medium. Using a spatula, turn the patties and top each patty with a cheese slice. Continue to cook for about the same time on the second side. If you are grilling the burgers, toast the buns, cut side down, on the grill rack.

Transfer to individual plates and let diners assemble their own burgers with the buns and condiments.

Meat Loaf

A meat loaf is more or less a rough-hewn pâté. Ground meat is typically mixed with seasonings, some raw onion, and one or more herbs and then shaped into a loaf and baked. Some meat loaf recipes include pork and/or veal, but many standard meat loaves are made with ground beef alone. Eggs are usually included to bind the meat loaf together.

MAKES 8 MAIN-COURSE SERVINGS

2 tablespoons olive oil or butter, plus more for
    the pan

1 onion, minced

$^1/_4$ pound cremini mushrooms, finely chopped

1 teaspoon chopped fresh thyme, or 1 tablespoon
    chopped fresh marjoram

3 slices dense-crumb white bread, crusts removed

$^1/_4$ cup milk

$^1/_2$ pound ground chuck

$^3/_4$ pound ground pork shoulder

$^3/_4$ pound ground veal

1 egg, beaten

1$^1/_2$ tablespoons salt

1$^1/_2$ teaspoons pepper

8 slices bacon

Grease a roasting pan that is about 12 inches long.

In a medium sauté pan, heat the olive oil over medium heat. Add the onion and sauté for about 10 minutes, or until lightly browned. Raise the heat to high, add the mushrooms, and cook, stirring the mushrooms every couple of minutes until all the water they release evaporates. This should take about 5 minutes. Add the thyme and remove from the heat.

In a large bowl, combine the bread and milk and work together to form a paste. Add the cooked mushroom mixture, ground meats, egg, salt, and pepper and work together with your hands until all the ingredients are evenly distributed. Form the mixture into a loaf about 10 inches long and 4 inches wide. Wrap the bacon slices crosswise around the loaf, tucking the ends of the slices under the loaf then place the loaf in the prepared pan.

Slide the pan into the oven, turn on the oven to 350°F (there is no need to preheat), and bake the meat loaf for about 1$^1/_4$ hours, or until an instant-read thermometer inserted into the center of the loaf reads 145°F. Do not cook it any longer or the meat will dry out.

Transfer to a platter and let rest for 15 minutes. Cut into slices $^1/_2$ inch thick and serve the slices wrapped with the bacon.

Meat loaf

1. Sauté onion and mushrooms until dry.

2. Combine the ground meats and the rest of the ingredients.

3. Shape the meat loaf in an oiled roasting pan.

4. Wrap the meat loaf in bacon.

5. Tuck the bacon under the meat loaf.

6. Finished meat loaf.

Meatballs

Mixtures for making meatballs are much the same as mixtures for making meat loaves: ground meat, bread, eggs, and herbs. The meatballs are then sautéed in oil or simmered in broth, salted water, or some kind of sauce. Shape the Meat Loaf mixture (opposite) into balls in whatever size appeals to you, then cook as desired. Serve them in broth or in Bolognese Sauce (page 200) or another sauce, or accompany them with a dipping sauce, such as yogurt and mint, sweet and sour, or *romesco*. Makes 8 main-course servings.

Spaghetti and meatballs in Bolognese sauce (page 200).

VEAL

In 1950, the average American ate seven pounds of veal per year; nowadays, it's down to just one pound. No doubt much of the decrease is due to the ugly stories describing how most calves are raised: away from their mothers, restricted in their movement, and on a diet purposely low in iron so their muscles don't turn red. You can avoid contributing to these practices by buying veal from a reputable farm—or from a butcher whose stock comes from a responsible source—that you know practices humane husbandry.

Veal is a magnificent meat with a mild, yet deeply satisfying flavor. It lends itself to nearly all the cooking methods, including roasting, sautéing, and braising, yielding particularly delicious pot roasts, stews, and luxurious roasts. Because the calf is a small animal, speaking of it in terms of primal cuts is less common than it is with beef. But you do need to understand the overall structure of the calf to make the best decisions on which cooking methods to use with which retails cuts.

The shoulder includes cuts that can be roasted or braised. Cuts from the loin, in contrast, are always roasted or sautéed. The veal breast, which lies below the shoulder, rack, and loin, and between the shank and flank, is typically braised, in small pieces or large. The leg contains many different muscles, which can be roasted, braised (with thorough larding), poached, or stewed. The back of the animal boasts two magnificent cuts, the saddle and the rack, which can be cut into chops or roasted whole.

Veal also provides some delicious organ meats, all of which have a more delicate flavor than the same organs taken from older animals. In Europe, organ meats tend to be the most expensive items on the menu, but in the United States, most of these meats, though easy to cook, are rarely eaten.

VEAL CUTS

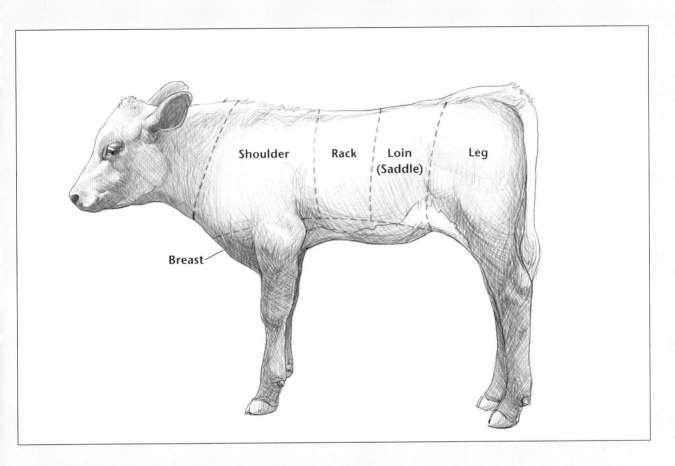

Shoulder
Shoulder chop: sauté, grill, broil, stew
Shoulder clod: roast, braise

Rack
Rack: roast
Rib chop: sauté, grill, broil
Rib roast: roast

Loin (Saddle)
Loin chop: sauté, grill, broil
Saddle: roast

Leg
Eye of the round: roast (thin slices), grill,
    stew (*blanquette de veau*)
Top round: roast, sauté (scaloppine), grill

Breast
Breast: braise

Other
Brains: poach, sauté (slices)
Kidney: roast, sauté
Liver: roast, sauté (slices), broil (slices)
Shank: braise
Sweetbreads: braise, sauté
Tripe: braise

Shoulder

The whole shoulder includes the shoulder clod; the neck meat; the Scotch tender (which resembles a miniature tenderloin and is, in fact, tender); and the foreshank. The clod, which usually weighs about 5 pounds, is a large, meaty group of muscles that is easily tied for roasting or braising. All the remaining shoulder cuts are used for stew meat.

Roast Veal Shoulder Clod

To ensure a tender result, roast the veal shoulder clod to 135°F, or medium. The clod usually comes already tied from the butcher, so all you need to do is season it and slide it into the oven.

MAKES 8 TO 10 MAIN-COURSE SERVINGS

1 veal shoulder clod, about 5 pounds, tied
Salt
Pepper
**2 cups veal broth or chicken broth (page 316)
   or water**

Let the veal come to room temperature. Season all over with salt and pepper.

Preheat the oven to 400°F. Put the veal in a heavy roasting pan just large enough to hold it and slide it into the oven. Roast for about 50 minutes, or until an instant-read thermometer inserted into the center of the veal without touching bone reads 135°F.

Transfer the roast to a large cutting board (preferably one with a moat to catch the juices, tent loosely with aluminum foil, and let rest for 15 minutes before carving.

While the roast is resting, make the jus. Put the roasting pan on the stove top over high heat and boil down any juices until they have caramelized on the bottom of the pan. Discard the fat and return the pan to high heat. Deglaze the pan with 1 cup of the broth, scraping up any brown bits on the bottom of the pan with a wooden spoon and boiling down the broth until it caramelizes into a crusty brown layer. Deglaze the pan with the remaining 1 cup broth, stirring and scraping until the crust has dissolved in the liquid, and then strain the liquid through a fine-mesh strainer into a warmed sauceboat.

Snip the strings on the veal and cut into slices 1/4 to 1/2 inch thick. Pass the jus at the table.

Veal Shoulder Clod Pot Roast

This elegant veal pot roast was de rigueur on the eighteenth-century French table. It is cooked *à la cuillière*, literally "to the spoon," which means it is cooked to the point of falling apart—soft enough to be scooped up with a pair of spoons for serving. I recommend thorough larding of the veal for the best result, but it will still be good if you skip this step. When larded and braised in this manner, this dish is called a *fricandeau*. Ideally, you have veal broth on hand, which is made by simmering bones from a breast of veal for 6 hours (see Creamy Veal Stew, page 225). But any kind of broth or even water can be used.

MAKES 8 MAIN-COURSE SERVINGS

1 veal shoulder clod, about 5 pounds
Salt
Pepper
**2 pounds fatback (weight not including rind)
   or *lardo***
2 cloves garlic, minced and then crushed to a paste

1 onion, coarsely chopped

1 carrot, peeled and coarsely chopped

6 cups veal broth (see note), beef broth
    (page 316), chicken broth (page 316), or water,
    or as needed

Bouquet garni (page 320)

$^1/_4$ cup meat glaze (page 318), optional

If the veal clod is tied, snip and remove the string. Season all over with salt and pepper and let it rest overnight in the refrigerator. Cut the fatback into sheets about $^1/_4$ inch thick, then cut the sheets lengthwise into strips, or lardons, about $^1/_4$ inch on each side. Using a hinged larding needle, lard the veal with the lardons as shown on page 224. Using kitchen string, tie the meat lengthwise and then crosswise at intervals, as shown on page 224, creating a compact sausage-shaped bundle.

Preheat the oven to 400°F. Select a heavy ovenproof pot just large enough to hold the veal, and spread the garlic, onion, and carrot on the bottom. Place the veal on top. Slide the pot, uncovered, into the oven and roast for about 90 minutes, or until the roast is well browned and any juices released caramelize (but don't burn) on the bottom of the pot.

Remove from the oven and reduce the oven temperature to 275°F. Add enough broth to come halfway up the sides of the meat and nestle in the bouquet garni. Bring to a gentle simmer on the stove top. Cover the pot with a sheet of aluminum foil, pressing it down slightly in the middle so that moisture will condense on its underside and drip down onto the exposed parts of the meat, and then with a lid.

Return the pot to the oven and braise the roast for about 2 hours. Check occasionally to make sure the liquid is not boiling, and if it is, turn down the heat. Turn the roast over gently, so the meat that was above the liquid is now submerged, re-cover the pot with the foil and the lid, and continue to braise for about 1 hour longer, or until the roast is easily penetrated with a knife.

Transfer the roast to a smaller ovenproof pot, moving it gently so it doesn't fall apart. Strain the braising liquid into a glass pitcher and skim off the fat with a ladle. Or, ideally, refrigerate the braising liquid at this point and then lift off the congealed fat in a single layer. Pour the degreased liquid into a saucepan, bring to a simmer, and simmer, skimming off any fat or froth that rises to the surface, for about 30 minutes, or until reduced by about half. Meanwhile, raise the oven temperature to 400°F.

Pour the degreased and reduced liquid over the veal and add the meat glaze. Place the pot, uncovered, in the oven. Cook the veal, basting it every 10 minutes with the liquid, for about 30 minutes, or until the braising liquid is syrupy and the veal is covered with a shiny glaze.

Remove the veal from the oven and snip the strings. Spoon out portions or slice it thickly, and place the servings in warmed soup plates. Ladle the braising liquid around and over the meat and serve.

VARIATIONS: Meat glaze can be added to the pot at the same time as the broth, so the braising liquid is more syrupy at the end. Stir some heavy cream into the braising liquid just before serving to give it a richer flavor and consistency and also to stretch it. Heat reconstituted dried morels or porcini in the braising liquid and spoon them over each serving of veal.

Veal shoulder clod pot roast

1. Lard the veal shoulder clod thoroughly.

2. Tie the roast lengthwise once, then crosswise at intervals, starting at the center.

3. Select a pot in which the roast just fits and include aromatic vegetables. Roast and then braise.

4. Strain the braising liquid.

5. Baste the veal with the reduced braising liquid.

6. Snip the strings on the veal.

7. Slice the veal or serve it with a spoon.

8. Finished veal pot roast.

Breast

The breast of veal is the least expensive cut of veal, but it is large and can be cumbersome to handle. Some butchers will sell a half breast, which is easier to manage, but even a half breast weighs almost 10 pounds. A whole 20-pound breast of veal contains about 7 pounds of bones and 4 pounds of fat, leaving just 9 pounds of meat.

There are two approaches to cooking breast of veal. For both methods, the breast must be boned and the excess fat trimmed off. The first method calls for cutting the meat into pieces and making a stew. A classic veal stew simmers in a white broth (broth made without browning the meat) and is finished with cream. For the second method, you roll up half the breast and braise it like a pot roast. For either method, the best approach is to bone the breast and make a broth with the bones by first blanching (they throw off an enormous amount of gray scum) and rinsing them and then simmering them gently for at least 6 hours. This broth—the bones from a whole breast will yield about 2 quarts—can then be used to braise the meat. In a pinch, just use whatever broth is on hand.

Recipes in most American cookbooks for veal breast are based on European recipes and suggest roasting the breast. They don't take into account that a veal breast bought in the United States weighs at least 15 pounds. Ignore any suggestion to roast this cut. A veal breast needs to be braised.

Creamy Veal Stew

To make this stew, you can use a half veal breast or the equivalent amount of veal stew meat. The advantage to using the veal breast is that it includes the bones, which can be used for making a broth for braising the meat. Traditionally, the braising liquid from a veal stew is thickened with roux and egg yolks. Here, it is finished with cream and left relatively thin, for serving in soup plates.

MAKES 6 MAIN-COURSE SERVINGS

$1/2$ breast of veal, about 7 pounds, or 4 pounds veal stew meat

1 whole clove

1 large onion, halved

1 large carrot, peeled and cut into 4 sections

Bouquet garni (page 320)

4 cups chicken broth (page 316), or as needed, if not making veal broth

3 tablespoons butter

3 tablespoons flour

10 ounces cremini mushrooms, quartered vertically

One 10-ounce package pearl onions, blanched in boiling water for 1 minute, drained, rinsed under cold water, and peeled

1 cup heavy cream

Salt

White pepper

continued

If you are using breast of veal, bone it, trim it of fat, and cut the meat into strips about 3 inches long and $1/2$ inch thick or into 2-inch cubes as shown on the facing page. Put the meat and bones in a pot, add water to cover, and bring to a boil. Boil for 2 minutes, then drain in a colander and rinse thoroughly with cold water. (This blanching is essential for eliminating froth and scum that would otherwise cloud the broth.) Cover the meat and refrigerate until needed. Return the bones to the pot, add water to cover, bring just to a boil, adjust the heat to maintain a gentle simmer, and simmer, uncovered, for 6 hours. Add water as needed to keep the bones covered. Strain the broth through a fine-mesh sieve.

If you are using veal stew meat, cut into 2-inch cubes and blanch for 2 minutes as described above, then drain and rinse.

Stick the clove in an onion half. In a pot, combine the meat, onion halves, carrot, and bouquet garni. Add enough broth to cover the meat. (If you are short of broth, add water.) Bring to a gentle simmer, cover, and braise for about 2 hours, or until the meat is easily penetrated with a fork. (Alternatively, bring to a gentle simmer on the stove top, cover, slide the pot into a 275°F oven, and braise for about 2 hours to the same end.)

Drain the stew in a colander set over a bowl (to save the braising liquid), and pick out and discard the bouquet garni and the vegetables. Reserve the meat. Skim off the fat from the braising liquid with a ladle. In the same pot, melt the butter over medium heat. Whisk in the flour and cook, whisking constantly, for about 3 minutes, or until the mixture is smooth and smells toasty. Whisk in the braising liquid and bring to a gentle simmer, whisking constantly. Simmer gently, skimming off any fat or froth that rises to the surface, for 15 minutes.

Return the meat to the pot along with the mushrooms and pearl onions and bring to a gentle simmer. Cover and cook for about 20 minutes, or until the onions are tender.

Gently stir in the cream and heat through. Season with salt and pepper. Spoon into warmed soup plates to serve.

Creamy veal stew

1. Blanch the veal.

2. After blanching, simmer the veal with aromatic vegetables and a bouquet garni.

Preparing a breast of veal

1. Whole breast of veal.

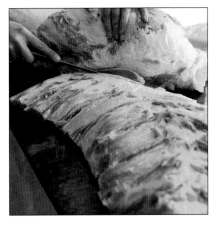

2. Trim the meat away from the bones.

3. Separate the bones by cutting through the small strip of cartilage that separates them.

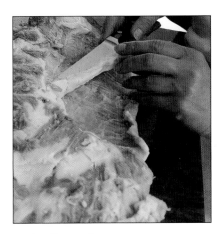

4. Trim off excess fat.

5. Cut the veal breast in half.

6. For stew, cut one half veal breast into strips or cubes

7. For pot roast, season one half veal breast, roll up the roast, and tie it.

Breast of Veal Stew with Porcini and Morel Mushrooms

Here, I flavor a rich stew with dried porcini mushrooms, but you can also include fresh mushrooms sautéed in butter or other dried mushrooms such as morels. When buying dried porcini, you should be able to smell their aroma through the bag. Look for large, even slices, not little pieces. Serve the stew with rice.

MAKES 6 MAIN-COURSE SERVINGS

$1/2$ breast of veal, about 7 pounds

1 whole clove

1 large onion, halved

1 large carrot, peeled and cut into 1-inch sections

2 tablespoons butter

2 tablespoons flour

Handful of dried porcini mushrooms, soaked in warm water just to cover for 1 hour

1 cup ($1/2$ ounce) dried morels, soaked in warm water just to cover for 1 hour (optional)

1 cup heavy cream

Salt

Pepper

Bone the veal breast, trim it of fat, and cut the meat into strips about 3 inches long and $1/2$ inch thick as shown on page 227. Put the meat and bones in a pot, add water to cover, and bring to a boil. Boil for 2 minutes, then drain in a colander and rinse thoroughly with cold water. (This blanching is essential for eliminating froth and scum that would otherwise cloud the broth.) Cover the meat and refrigerate until needed. Return the bones to the pot, add water to cover, bring to a boil, adjust the heat to maintain a gentle simmer, and simmer, uncovered, for 6 hours. Add water as needed to keep the bones covered. Strain the broth through a fine-mesh sieve.

Stick the clove in an onion half. In a pot, combine the meat, onion halves, carrot, and broth to cover. Bring to a gentle simmer, cover, and braise for about 2 hours, or until the meat is tender when you bite into a piece. (Alternatively, bring to a gentle simmer on the stove top, cover, slide the pot into a 275°F oven, and braise for about 2 hours to the same end.)

Drain the stew in a colander set over a bowl (to save the braising liquid), and pick out and discard the vegetables. Reserve the meat. Skim off the fat from the braising liquid with a ladle. In the same pot, melt the butter over medium heat. Whisk in the flour and cook, whisking constantly, for about 3 minutes, or until the mixture is smooth and smells toasty. Whisk in the braising liquid and bring to a gentle simmer, whisking constantly. Simmer gently, skimming off any fat or froth that rises to the surface, for about 20 minutes, or until reduced to about 2 cups.

Lift the mushrooms out of their soaking water and squeeze them gently to release any water back into the bowls. Add the cream and the mushrooms to the simmering liquid, then carefully pour in the mushroom soaking water, leaving any grit behind in the bowls. Simmer the sauce until it has the consistency you like.

Stir the meat into the sauce and simmer gently for about 5 minutes to heat through. Season to taste with salt and pepper and serve.

Breast of Veal Pot Roast

A half breast of veal makes a perfect pot roast. As with any pot roast, the cooking time is long but the results are worth it, and there is actually little active cooking time. Here, the breast is braised with dry sherry and the broth is made from the bones. The braising liquid is then finished with cream and used to baste the finished roast. This recipe calls for braising the pot roast in the oven, but you can instead simmer it gently on the stove top for about the same amount of time. No garniture is included, but the addition of mushrooms would deliver a delightful contrast of texture and boost the flavor. Wild mushrooms—sautéed and added at the end, or cooked with the roast during the final basting—are celestial.

MAKES 6 MAIN-COURSE SERVINGS

$1/2$ breast of veal, about 7 pounds
Salt
Pepper
1 large onion, sliced
1 large carrot, peeled and sliced
Big bouquet garni (page 320)
1 cup dry sherry
1 cup heavy cream

Bone the veal breast and trim it of fat as shown on page 227. Refrigerate the meat until needed. Put the bones in a pot, add water to cover, and bring to a boil. Boil for 2 minutes, then drain in a colander and rinse thoroughly with cold water. (This blanching is essential for eliminating froth and scum that would otherwise cloud the broth.) Return the bones to the pot, add water to cover, bring to a boil, adjust the heat to maintain a gentle simmer, and simmer, uncovered, for 6 hours. Add water as needed to keep the bones covered. Strain the broth through a fine-mesh sieve.

Preheat the oven to 400°F. Season the breast all over with salt and pepper, then roll it up and tie as shown on page 227. Season the tied roast all over with salt and pepper. Select a heavy ovenproof pot just large enough to hold the meat, and put the onion, carrot, and bouquet garni on the bottom. Set the veal on the vegetables. Slide the pot, uncovered, into the oven and roast for about 1 hour, or until the roast is well browned and any juices released caramelize (but don't burn) on the bottom of the pot. If the juices start to caramelize before the roast has heated through, add 2 cups of the broth to the pot to keep the juices from burning.

Remove the pot from the oven and reduce the oven temperature to 275°F. Remove any fat from the pot with a bulb baster or by pouring it off. Add the sherry and then add enough broth to come halfway up the sides of the meat. Bring to a simmer on the stove top. Cover the pot with a sheet of aluminum foil, pressing it down slightly in the middle so that moisture will condense on its underside and drip down onto the exposed parts of the meat, and then with a lid.

continued

Return the pot to the oven and braise the roast for 1½ hours. Check occasionally to make sure the liquid is not boiling, and if it is, turn down the heat. Turn the roast over gently, so the meat that was above the liquid is now submerged, re-cover the pot with the foil and the lid, and continue to braise for about 1 hour longer, or until the roast is easily penetrated with a knife.

Transfer the roast to a smaller ovenproof pot. Raise the oven temperature to 450°F. Strain the braising liquid into a glass pitcher and skim off the fat with a ladle. Or, ideally, refrigerate the braising liquid at this point and then lift off the congealed fat in a single layer. Pour the degreased liquid back into the pot.

Place the pot, uncovered, in the oven. Cook the veal, basting it every 10 minutes with the liquid, for about 30 minutes, or until the veal is covered with a shiny glaze. Pour the cream over the veal and continue to baste for 10 minutes longer.

Remove the veal from the oven. Snip the strings and slice the veal thickly. Serve in warmed soup plates with the braising liquid spooned around the sides and over the top.

Breast of veal pot roast

1. Place the roast on a bed of aromatic vegetables.

2. Roast until the juices released by the meat caramelize on the bottom of the pan.

3. Baste the pot roast with the degreased braising liquid until glazed and shiny.

Saddle

A whole saddle of veal, suitable for serving eight to twelve, is an unusual roast because most people either don't know about it or can't stomach the expense. Also, because the veal saddle is essentially the veal loin, virtually all saddles are broken down into loin chops, so you don't see them for sale. This is truly a grand and unforgettable roast that none of your guests is likely to have ever been served. That said, you must expect to pay well over a hundred dollars for it.

You will have to special order a veal saddle. If you aren't sure your butcher knows what you are talking about, ask him or her for cut no. 331, which is the number given the cut in the meat buyer's guide that all butchers use. Be sure to specify that you don't want it trimmed. You want to trim it yourself so you have the trimmings for making a jus and for saving for stew. When you get the saddle, it's going to weigh about 30 pounds, but by the time you trim off the flaps on the sides, it will weigh closer to 15 pounds. The flaps—the equivalent to flank steaks in beef butchery—should be trimmed of excess fat, cut into strips, and then roasted in the roasting pan destined for the saddle for about 30 minutes before the saddle goes into the oven. You can also save the trimmings (the flank) to make the veal stew on page 225.

Veal Roasts

The shoulder clod, the rack, the saddle, and the top round all make lovely—and extravagant—veal roasts that are perfect for special occasions. They are best served with a natural jus, which, depending on the roast, may be possible only if you include trimmings in the pan. It's imperative that these veal roasts not be overcooked—don't let them get above 135°F—as they dry out quickly.

Roast Saddle of Veal with Jus

The saddle is the whole lower back of the animal, and when you buy it untrimmed, as I suggest you do here, you will get the flaps, which will contribute to the jus, and sometimes also the kidneys (see page 255 for ideas on serving the kidneys). If you have veal broth left over from preparing the veal breast recipes on pages 225–229, use it here. If not, chicken broth is a good substitute.

MAKES 8 TO 12 MAIN-COURSE SERVINGS

1 saddle of veal, untrimmed, about 30 pounds
1 onion, sliced
1 carrot, peeled and sliced
3 cloves garlic, crushed
Salt
Pepper
4 cups veal broth (see note), chicken broth (page 316), or water

Pull out the white fat on the inside of the saddle and the kidneys, if they have been left attached. Using a sharp knife, trim the flaps off the saddle where they join the loin muscles, being careful not to cut into the muscles. (You can also ask your butcher to do this.) Trim the excess fat from the flaps and cut the flaps into strips about 1/2 inch wide. Slide the knife carefully under the 1 or 2 ribs that are customarily left attached to the saddle, cutting them away from the meat without cutting into it. Twist the ribs away from the vertebrae. Let the saddle come to room temperature.

Spread the flap strips on the bottom of a large roasting pan with the onion, carrot, and garlic. Slide the pan into the oven and turn on the oven to 450°F (no need to preheat). Roast for about 2 hours, turning every 30 minutes or so, or until the juices released into the pan are beginning to caramelize.

Season the saddle all over with salt and pepper. Place it, with the smaller tenderloin muscles down, on top of the meat and vegetables. Roast for 20 minutes, then turn down the oven to 350°F and continue to roast for about 40 minutes longer, or until an instant-read thermometer inserted into one of the loin muscles reads 130°F. (The final temperature should be 135°F, but the temperature will rise while the roast rests.) Turn the saddle over and continue to roast for 10 minutes longer to finish cooking the tenderloins. If at any point the meat and vegetables threaten to burn, add 1 to 2 cups water to the roasting pan.

Transfer the roast to a platter, tent loosely with aluminum foil, and let rest for 15 minutes before carving.

While the roast is resting, make the jus. Put the roasting pan on the stove top over high heat and stir around the trimmings until any juices caramelize on the bottom of the pan. Discard the fat and return the pan to high heat. Deglaze the pan with 2 cups of the broth, scraping up any brown bits on the bottom of the pan with a wooden spoon. Boil down the broth until it caramelizes into a crusty brown layer with a layer of clear fat on top. Pour off the fat, return the pan to medium to high heat, and deglaze the pan with the remaining 2 cups broth, stirring until the crust has dissolved into the liquid, then strain the liquid through a fine-mesh strainer into a warmed sauceboat. The cooked trimmings can be moistened with broth or water and made into stew or used to make broth.

Carve the roast as shown for saddle of lamb on page 280, slicing it lengthwise or crosswise. Pass the jus at the table.

Rack

The rack is one of the most luxurious cuts on the calf and makes an exquisite roast. Most of the rib cage—there are eight ribs on each side—is contained in the rack. Ask the butcher for a split rack; otherwise you may get the double rack, which includes all sixteen ribs. You can, however, have a rack cut to any size you like—specified by the number of ribs—from three ribs up to all eight. If you're buying fewer than eight ribs, specify that you want the section from the loin end, not the shoulder end. The loin end muscles are neater. Make sure the butcher cuts the chine bone off the rack, so you can easily cut between the ribs when it comes time to carve. Also, ask him or her to french the rack for you and ask that all the trimmings be saved. Or, if you want to do it yourself, follow the directions for a rack or pork on page 125.

Roast Rack of Veal

Typically, a rack is carved between the ribs, with each diner getting a whole rib. This is a large portion, however. If you like, slice away the ribs and then carve the loin muscle into slices. Despite requests in pretentious restaurants for how you want your veal done, veal is always cooked to medium—opaque with just a trace of pink translucency.

MAKES 3 TO 8 MAIN-COURSE SERVINGS

1 rack of veal, with 3 to 8 ribs, chine bone removed, ribs frenched (page 125), and trimmings saved
Salt
Pepper
1 small onion, sliced
1 small carrot, peeled and sliced
3 cloves garlic, crushed
4 cups veal broth, chicken broth (page 316), or water

Let the rack come to room temperature. Season all over with salt and pepper. Spread the trimmings, chine bone, onion, carrot, and garlic on the bottom of a roasting just large enough to hold the rack. Slide the pan into the oven and turn on the oven to 450°F (no need to preheat). Roast for about 30 minutes, or until the juices released into the pan are starting to caramelize and the trimmings are well browned.

Place the rack on top of the trimmings and vegetables and roast for about 45 minutes, or until an instant-read thermometer inserted into the center of the roast without touching bone reads 130°F. If at any point the meat and vegetables threaten to burn, add 1 to 2 cups water to the roasting pan. (The final temperature should be 135°F, but the temperature will increase while the roast rests.)

Transfer the rack to a platter, tent loosely with aluminum foil, and let rest for 15 minutes before carving.

While the roast is resting, make the jus. Put the roasting pan on the stove top over high heat and stir around the trimmings until any juices caramelize on the bottom of the pan. Deglaze the pan with 2 cups of the broth, scraping up any brown bits on the bottom of the pan with a wooden spoon. Boil down the broth until it caramelizes into a crusty brown layer with a layer of clear fat on top. Pour off the fat, return the pan to medium to high heat, and deglaze the pan with the remaining 2 cups broth, stirring until the crust has dissolved into the liquid, then strain the liquid through a fine-mesh strainer into a warmed sauceboat.

Carve the roast by slicing between the ribs or by slicing away the whole loin muscle and then slicing the loin either lengthwise or into rounds. Pass the jus at the table.

Chops

Veal chops come in only three types: rib chops, loin chops, and shoulder chops. The difference between rib and loin chops is easy to recognize: the rib chop, which comes from the rack, contains the rib and the loin, and the loin chop, which comes from the saddle, includes both the relatively large loin muscle and the tenderloin, like a miniature T-bone steak. In the United States, most loin chops are cut from a single side of the saddle only, but it is possible to get double chops by cutting across the whole rack. When cutting a rack into rib chops, french the rack first (follow the directions for a rack of pork on page 125) so the rib bone on each chop will show up dramatically.

The method for sautéing rib chops and loin chops is the same. The variation comes in choosing the sauce to make from the pan drippings. Shoulder chops are best braised much like pork shoulder chops (page 113).

Sautéed Veal Chops

Veal chops are usually cut fairly thick for sale, especially rib chops that must each contain a rib, so they should be sautéed over medium heat. Remember, the thinner the meat being sautéed, the higher the heat.

MAKES 4 MAIN-COURSE SERVINGS

4 loin or rib veal chops, about 3/4 pound each
Salt
Pepper
2 tablespoons butter
2 tablespoons olive oil

Let the veal chops come to room temperature. Season on both sides with salt and pepper.

Place a sauté pan just large enough to hold the chops without crowding over medium heat. (Alternatively, sauté the chops in batches or use two pans.) Melt the butter with the olive oil in the pan. When the butter begins to froth, add the chops and cook for about 5 minutes on the first side. Turn the chops over and continue to cook for about 5 minutes, or until an instant-read thermometer inserted through the side into the center reads 130°F or they just begin to feel firm to the touch.

Transfer the chops to a plate, tent loosely with aluminum foil, and let rest for 10 minutes before serving. Pour the fat out of the pan and deglaze the pan to make one of the sauces on the facing page.

Transfer the chops to warmed plates and spoon the sauce over them.

Sauces for Sautéed Veal Chops

Veal's gentle flavor is easily accompanied with any number of tasty sauces. For roast veal, rely on a jus, but for sautéed veal chops, make a pan sauce; see page 7 for more information about pan-deglazed sauces. Each of the following recipes makes enough sauce to serve 4.

PRUNE AND WHITE WINE SAUCE: The ideal wine for this sauce is something slightly sweet, such as a Vouvray demi-sec or a Moscato d'Asti. The prunes are pitted and soaked in the wine to soften them, and then cooked long enough in the sauce to cook out any raw wine flavor. Soak 16 pitted prunes in $1/2$ cup semisweet white wine for 1 hour, turning the prunes around in the wine every 20 minutes. Deglaze the pan with the soaking liquid from the prunes, boil down by half, and add $1/2$ cup heavy cream and the prunes. Simmer until the sauce has a lightly syrupy consistency. You can also add 1 tablespoon meat glaze (page 318) for extra body. Season with salt and pepper.

FRESH TOMATO AND TARRAGON SAUCE: Deglaze the pan with $1/2$ cup dry white wine, then add 3 peeled, seeded, and chopped tomatoes, and 1 tablespoon chopped fresh tarragon. Simmer until nicely thickened, then finish with 2 tablespoons cold butter, whisking until emulsified. Season with salt and pepper.

DRIED PORCINI AND PROSCIUTTO SAUCE: Soak a handful of dried porcini in warm water just to cover for 1 hour, then lift the mushrooms out of their soaking water and squeeze them gently to release any water back into the bowl. Chop the mushrooms coarsely, and reserve the mushrooms and soaking water separately. Cut 1 thin slice prosciutto into narrow strips. Deglaze the pan with the mushroom soaking water, pouring carefully to leave any grit behind in the bowl. Add the mushrooms, prosciutto, and $1/2$ cup heavy cream and simmer until a saucelike consistency forms. Season with salt and pepper.

WHITE WINE–HERB SAUCE: Deglaze the pan with $3/4$ cup dry white wine and then add 1 tablespoon chopped fresh herbs (tarragon, marjoram, or thyme are good choices). If you like, enrich the sauce with 2 tablespoons meat glaze (page 318), and finish the sauce with 3 tablespoons cold butter, whisking until emulsified.

VERMOUTH AND MUSTARD SAUCE: After you have discarded the burnt fat, add 1 shallot, minced, and $1/2$ teaspoon fresh thyme leaves, chopped, to the hot pan and stir for about 1 minute, or until they release their aroma. Add $3/4$ cup dry white vermouth and, if you like, 2 tablespoons meat glaze (page 318) and deglaze the pan. Boil down the liquid by about two-thirds, or until the sauce has a syrupy consistency. Whisk in 1 tablespoon Dijon mustard, or to taste, and then whisk in 2 tablespoons cold butter until emulsified. Season with salt and pepper.

Veal Chops en Papillote

Sealing meats in a parchment-paper pouch for cooking (*en papillote*) is a good idea when you want to trap the fragrance of an aromatic ingredient, such as wild mushrooms or truffles, that you are cooking with the meats. It also makes sense when you are pairing the meats with certain herbs, such as tarragon. If you like, you can brown the chops and sauté the mushrooms and refrigerate them for up to 4 hours before encasing them in parchment. Increase the baking time to about 15 minutes.

MAKES 4 MAIN-COURSE SERVINGS

4 loin or rib veal chops, about $3/4$ pound each
Salt
Pepper
$1^1/2$ pounds wild mushrooms such as chanterelle, morel, porcini, or black trumpet, alone or in combination
6 tablespoons butter
$1/2$ teaspoon fresh thyme leaves
$1/4$ cup port
1 egg white, lightly beaten

Let the veal chops come to room temperature. Season on both sides with salt and pepper

Quickly rinse the mushrooms in a colander and pat dry. If using large chanterelles, cut them in half or in quarters, following their contours so the pieces maintain their shape. If they are small, leave them whole. If the porcini are large, cut them into thick slices. Morels and black trumpets are usually small enough to leave whole. Set the mushrooms aside.

Place a sauté pan just large enough to hold the chops without crowding over high heat. (Alternatively, sauté the chops in batches or use two pans.) Before the pan gets hot, add 4 tablespoons of the butter to the pan. When the butter begins to froth, add the chops and cook on the first side for about 5 minutes, or until well browned. Turn the chops over and brown on the second side the same way. Transfer the chops to a plate and pour the fat out of the pan.

Return the pan to high heat and add the remaining 2 tablespoons butter. When the butter froths, add a large handful of the mushrooms and toss and stir for 1 minute. Continue adding the mushrooms, a handful at a time, and cook, stirring occasionally for about 10 minutes, or until any liquid they release evaporates and they are browned and fragrant. Season with salt and pepper and remove from the heat.

Preheat the oven to 450°F. Place 1 chop in the center of one-half of a large rectangle of parchment paper. Spoon one-fourth of the mushrooms on top of the chop, sprinkle with one-fourth of the thyme, and drizzle with 1 tablespoon of the port. Brush the edges of the parchment with the egg white, and fold the uncovered half over the chop. Brush the three open edges of the folded parchment and fold over the edges to seal. Repeat with the remaining ingredients and 3 more rectangles of parchment.

Divide the pouches between 2 rimmed sheet pans. Bake for about 12 minutes, or until the parchment puffs up.

To serve, put each pouch on a warmed rimmed plate or soup plate, to trap any liquid that spills when the pouches are cut open. Pass a pair of scissors at the table.

Veal chops en papillote

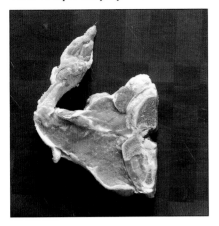

1. Veal loin chop.

2. Sauté the veal chop until well browned.

3. Sauté the mushrooms adding a handful at a time.

4. Veal chop with mushrooms on top.

5. Brush the parchment paper with egg white and fold the edges.

6. The finished pouch.

7. The opened pouch after cooking.

8. Finished veal chop and mushrooms.

Top Round

The top round is found in the leg and looks somewhat like a flattened football. If you are buying a whole veal top round, which typically weighs about 2 pounds, be aware that it is sometimes sold "cap on." The cap is a layer of muscle that covers the round, and it must be removed (easy to do by following the muscle with the knife) before you use the round. Once you have the whole round, you can roast it whole (below) or slice it into scaloppine (see page 240).

Butter-Roasted Top Round of Veal

When ordering your top round of veal, ask for cut no. 349A (from the meat buyer's guide that all butchers use). The A is important because it means "cap off." The top round is one of the leanest cuts of meat there is, which means you must not overcook it by a second or it will be dry. The best approach is to brown it on the stove top in clarified butter and then finish it in a low oven, basting it regularly with clarified butter and its juices as it roasts.

MAKES 6 TO 8 MAIN-COURSE SERVINGS

1 top round of veal with cap removed, about 3¹/₂ pounds
Salt
Pepper
¹/₂ pound (2 sticks) butter, clarified (page 6)

Let the veal come to room temperature. Season all over with salt and pepper.

Preheat the oven to 300°F. In a sauté pan, heat 4 tablespoons of the clarified butter over high heat. Add the veal and brown well on both sides until golden. Transfer the roast to a small round roasting pan or ovenproof sauté pan just large enough to hold it, and pour the remaining clarified butter over the top.

Slide the pan into the oven and roast for about 40 minutes, basting every 10 minutes or so with the butter, or until an instant-read thermometer inserted into the center reads 130°F or the roast feels firm, rather than fleshy, to the touch. (The final temperature should be 135°F, but the temperature will rise while the roast rests.)

Transfer the roast to a cutting board, tent loosely with aluminum foil, and let rest for 15 minutes before carving. Pour the butter and juices in the pan into a warmed sauceboat.

Cut the roast across the grain into slices and serve. Pass the jus at the table.

Leg

It's unlikely that you'll encounter a whole leg of veal at your butcher shop. Nowadays, butchered calves are generally quite large, which means their legs are too large to sell whole to retail customers. If you are able to find a small leg—25 pounds or so—you can roast it whole to a temperature of 130°F, which will rise to 135°F—the temperature of perfect roast veal—after it rests. If you're stuck with a large whole leg (they reach almost 100 pounds), you should break it down by following the natural separation of the muscles. You'll end up with a shank, a top round, an eye of the round, the bottom round, the sirloin, the rump, and lots of trimmings for stew.

Butter-roasted top round of veal

1. Whole top round of veal.

2. Brown the veal round on both sides in clarified butter.

3. Roast until firm to the touch or to an internal temperature of 130°F. Let rest.

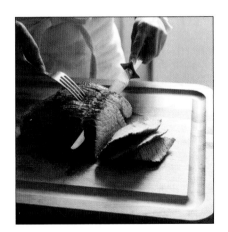

4. Slice the veal round into thick slices.

5. Serve the veal with its jus.

Saltimbocca

In this classic Italian preparation, the scaloppine are dusted with flour before cooking. Buy high-quality prosciutto or Spanish *serrano* ham and ask for it sliced thin, but not paper thin.

MAKES 4 MAIN-COURSE SERVINGS

4 veal scaloppine cut from the top round, about 6 ounces each

Salt

Pepper

Flour

4 tablespoons clarified butter (page 6) or olive oil

$1/_2$ cup (1 stick) butter

4 fresh sage leaves

4 thin slices *prosciutto di Parma* or *serrano* ham

Veal Scaloppine

The best scaloppine—thin slices of veal—are taken from the top round, though butchers sometimes also take them from other cuts. The most extravagant way to make scaloppine is by pounding medallions cut from the loin. The least expensive approach is to use muscles from the leg, such as the eye of the round.

Don't cut your scaloppine too thin or they will dry out during cooking. Slice them across the grain and on an angle so you exploit the shape of the top round and get the largest slices. Hold one hand against the top and side of the round while you slice with the other hand. By placing one hand firmly on the meat, you are better able to control the thickness of the slices as you cut.

Just before sautéing, season the scaloppine on both sides with salt and pepper. Spread some flour on a plate. Working with 1 veal slice at a time, coat evenly on both sides with the flour, then shake off the excess.

Select a skillet or sauté pan just large enough to hold the scaloppine in a single layer and preferably nonstick. Place over high heat and heat the clarified butter just until it begins to smoke. Add the veal slices one at a time, waiting about 15 seconds after each slice is added before adding the next one so the pan stays hot. Cook each slice for 15 to 30 seconds on the first side, or until golden. Turn the slices, again one at a time, and cook on the second side for 15 to 30 seconds, or until they are golden and feel just firm to the touch. Transfer the scaloppine to a warmed platter and pat them dry.

Pour the fat out of the pan, let the pan cool for 1 minute, and then return the pan to medium heat and add the $1/_2$ cup butter and the sage leaves. When the butter has melted, heat for a minute or two until the sage releases its fragrance and the butter froths and smells nutty. Divide the scaloppine among warmed plates and top each one with a slice of prosciutto. Place a sage leaf on top of each serving and spoon the butter over the top. Serve at once.

Saltimbocca

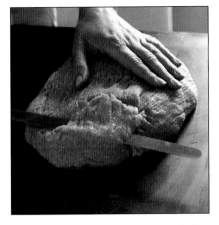

1. Slice the scaloppine off the top round of veal.

2. Season the scaloppine on both sides with salt and pepper.

3. Coat the veal with flour.

4. Brown the veal in clarified butter on both sides over high heat.

5. Heat butter and sage in the sauté pan and spoon over the veal.

6. Finished saltimbocca.

Sautéed Veal Scaloppine with Butter and Sage

Here, the scaloppine are breaded with fresh bread crumbs. Most sauces for breaded scaloppine are added at the last minute, so they don't make the breading soggy. Because the sauce for this dish is composed almost entirely of butter, it won't cause sogginess.

MAKES 4 MAIN-COURSE SERVINGS

4 slices slightly stale, dense-crumb white bread, crusts removed

Flour

1 egg

Salt

Pepper

4 veal scaloppine cut from the top round, about 6 ounces each

4 tablespoons clarified butter (page 6)

4 tablespoons butter

4 fresh sage leaves

Sautéed Veal

The best veal cuts for sautéing are from the tender muscles: rib chops, loin chops, boneless loin medallions, or top round. Other muscles, such as the eye of the round from the leg, can be cut into medallions, but these can be tough and must be pounded into scaloppine. Unlike with beef and pork, the veal tenderloin is rarely sold whole, because half is left attached to the leg and the other half is left attached to the loin. When sautéing thinly sliced veal or pounded veal, it is impossible to brown the veal without overcooking it. The solution is to bread thin slices before cooking.

Tear the bread into pieces, place in a food processor, and pulse to form crumbs. If desired, pass the crumbs through a fine-mesh strainer or a drum sieve so the crumbs are uniformly fine. Spread the crumbs on a plate. Spread some flour on a second plate. In a shallow bowl, beat the egg until blended, then season generously with salt and pepper.

Working with 1 veal slice at a time, coat evenly on both sides with the flour, shaking off the excess. Next, dip the slice in the egg, and then, holding the slice above the bowl by one end, wipe off the excess egg by sliding the thumb and index finger along its length. Finally, lay the slice on the bread crumbs, turn to coat both sides, and transfer to a plate. Repeat with the remaining scaloppine.

Select a skillet or sauté pan just large enough to hold the scaloppine in a single layer and preferably nonstick. Place over medium heat and heat the clarified butter. Gently place the breaded scaloppine in the pan—don't use tongs; use your fingers so as not to tear through the breading—in a single layer. Cook, moving the pan every minute or so to ensure the scaloppine cook evenly, for about 3 minutes, or until golden brown. Using a spatula or your fingertips, turn the scaloppine over and cook for about 3 minutes on the second side, or until golden brown and just firm to the touch. Transfer the scaloppine to warmed plates and set aside in a warm spot.

Pour the fat out of the pan, let the pan cool for 1 minute, and then return the pan to medium heat and add the 4 tablespoons butter and the sage leaves. When the butter melts, heat for a minute or two until the sage releases its fragrance and the butter froths and smells nutty.

Place a sage leaf on each veal slice and spoon the butter over the top. Serve at once.

Veal Piccata

This is a hallowed restaurant classic that, unlike many of its counterparts, is actually quite good. And nothing could be simpler: just lightly flour the veal, sauté it briefly, and finish it with butter and lemon juice.

MAKES 4 MAIN-COURSE SERVINGS

**4 veal scaloppine cut from the top round,
    about 6 ounces each**
Salt
Pepper
Flour
3 tablespoons clarified butter (page 6) or olive oil
4 tablespoons butter
1 tablespoon fresh lemon juice

Just before sautéing, season the scaloppine on both sides with salt and pepper. Spread some flour on a plate. Working with 1 veal slice at a time, coat evenly on both sides with the flour, shaking off the excess.

Select a skillet or sauté pan just large enough to hold the scaloppine in a single layer and preferably nonstick. Place over high heat and heat the clarified butter just until it begins to smoke. Add the veal slices one at a time, waiting about 15 seconds after each slice is added before adding the next one so the pan stays hot. Cook each slice for 15 to 30 seconds on the first side, or until golden. Turn the slices, again one at a time, and cook on the second side for 15 to 30 seconds, or until they are golden and feel just firm to the touch. Transfer the scaloppine to a warmed platter and pat them dry.

Pour the fat out of the pan, let the pan cool for 1 minute, and then return the pan to medium heat and add the 4 tablespoons butter and the lemon juice. Heat for just a minute or two until the butter froths. Divide the scaloppine among warmed plates and spoon the butter over the top.

Veal Scaloppine with Madeira Sauce

When buying Madeira for this dish, buy Rainwater or Malmsey Madeira. Rainwater Madeira is slightly sweet; a Malmsey is even more so.

MAKES 4 MAIN-COURSE SERVINGS

**4 veal scaloppine cut from the top round,
    about 6 ounces each**
Salt
Pepper
Flour
3 tablespoons clarified butter (page 6) or olive oil
$1/2$ cup Madeira
2 tablespoons meat glaze (page 318)
3 tablespoons cold butter, cut into 3 slices

Just before sautéing, season the scaloppine on both sides with salt and pepper. Spread some flour on a plate. Working with 1 veal slice at a time, coat evenly on both sides with the flour, shaking off the excess.

Select a skillet or sauté pan just large enough to hold the scaloppine in a single layer and preferably nonstick. Place over high heat and heat the clarified butter just until it begins to smoke. Add the veal slices one at a time, waiting about 15 seconds after each slice is added before adding the next one so the pan stays hot. Cook each slice for 15 to 30 seconds on the first side, or until golden. Turn the slices, again one at a time, and cook on the second side for 15 to 30 seconds, or until they are golden and feel just firm to the touch. Transfer the scaloppine to a warmed platter and pat them dry.

Pour the fat out of the pan, return the pan to medium heat, and add the Madeira. Deglaze the pan, scraping up any brown bits on the bottom of the pan with a wooden spoon. Add the meat

continued

glaze, turn up the heat to high, and boil down the Madeira until a lightly syrupy consistency develops. Whisk in the cold butter until emulsified. Do not allow the sauce to boil. Season with salt and pepper.

Divide the scaloppine among warmed plates and spoon the sauce over the top.

Braised Veal Rolls

Scaloppine can be stuffed with an amazing array of (often improvised) fillings and then braised in broth or in tomato sauce. Stuffed scaloppine can also be grilled. Here, I have created a stuffing with pine nuts, raisins, cheese, prosciutto, and eggs, but countless other ingredients, such as bread crumbs, bacon, pancetta, dried currants, sage, and milk, can be used.

MAKES 6 MAIN-COURSE SERVINGS

12 very thin scaloppine cut from the top round, about 3 ounces each

$^1/_2$ cup pine nuts, toasted

$^1/_3$ cup raisins

$^1/_2$ cup grated Parmigiano-Reggiano cheese

$^1/_4$ pound *prosciutto di Parma* or other high-quality prosciutto, sliced $^1/_8$ inch thick and then cut into $^1/_8$-inch cubes

Leaves from 1 bunch parsley, finely chopped

2 cloves garlic, minced and then crushed to a paste

2 eggs, lightly beaten

Salt

Pepper

2 cups veal broth or chicken broth (page 316)

Butter

If the scaloppine are not very thin, use the side of a cleaver to pound them until they are a uniform $^1/_8$ inch thick. Reserve the veal in the refrigerator until needed.

To make the stuffing, in a bowl, stir together the pine nuts, raisins, cheese, prosciutto, parsley, garlic, and eggs, mixing until well combined. Season generously with salt and pepper.

Preheat the oven to 400°F. Lay the veal slices on a work surface. Put about one-sixth of the stuffing near the edge of each veal slice. Then, one at a time and starting from a short end, roll up each slice into a tight cylinder. Tie each roll in two directions, crosswise and lengthwise, with kitchen string.

Arrange the veal rolls in a baking dish just large enough to hold them in a single layer. Pour over the broth and sprinkle with salt and pepper. Butter a sheet of parchment paper or aluminum foil large enough to cover the dish, and then place it, buttered side down, over the dish. Slide the baking dish into the oven and cook, basting the rolls every 10 minutes with the broth, for about 35 minutes, or until the rolls feel firm to the touch.

Snip the strings on the rolls, and gently divide the rolls among warmed soup plates. Spoon the braising liquid over and around the rolls and serve.

Eye of the Round

The eye of the round is a cylindrical muscle from the leg that looks a lot like a tenderloin. Unfortunately, it can be quite tough. The best approach is to roast it whole (it is lean, so don't overcook it even a second) and serve it thinly sliced, or to slice it into medallions about $1/4$ inch thick, pound the medallions with side of a cleaver to make them thinner and to tenderize them, and then sauté them in butter or olive oil.

Roast Veal Eye of the Round

When properly roasted (which is to say not overcooked), the eye of the round releases little in the way of juices. If you like, surround the roast with pieces of veal stew meat, a little onion, and a little carrot to provide flavorful juices for making a jus.

MAKES 4 MAIN-COURSE SERVINGS

1 veal eye of the round, about $1^1/2$ pounds
Salt
Pepper
1 pound veal stew meat, cut into $1/2$-inch cubes (optional)
1 small onion, coarsely chopped (optional)
1 small carrot, peeled and coarsely chopped (optional)
4 cups veal broth or chicken broth (page 316), optional

Let the veal come to room temperature. Season all over with salt and pepper.

Preheat the oven to 450°F. Select a heavy oven-proof pan just large enough to hold the veal (an oval roasting pan is ideal). Place the veal in the pan and surround it with the stew meat, onion, and carrot. Slide the pot into the oven and roast for about 30 minutes, or until the veal is well browned. Reduce the oven temperature to 300°F and roast for about 10 minutes longer, or until an instant-read thermometer inserted into the center of the roast reads 130°F. (The final temperature should be 135°F, but the temperature will rise while the roast rests.)

Transfer the roast to a platter, tent it loosely with aluminum foil, and let rest for 15 minutes.

If you have used the stew meat, put the pan on the stove top over high heat. If the stew meat has not thoroughly browned, stir it around until it browns and any juices caramelize on the bottom of the pan. Deglaze the pan with 1 cup of the broth, scraping up any brown bits on the bottom of the pan with a wooden spoon. Boil down the broth until it caramelizes into a crusty brown layer with a layer of clear fat on top. Pour off the fat, return the pan to high heat, and deglaze the pan with a second cup of broth, again boiling it down. Repeat the process with a third cup of broth. Deglaze the pan with the remaining 1 cup broth, stirring until the crust has dissolved into the liquid, and then strain the liquid through a fine-mesh strainer into a warmed sauceboat.

Thinly slice the roast to serve and pass the jus at the table.

Shank

The back leg shank, sometimes labeled "osso buco," is usually sold cut into rounds about $1^1/2$ inches thick. One round is a perfect single serving. You can also request a whole veal shank, braise it, and then carve it at the table to serve four. A whole veal shank is also used in Bollito Misto on page 178.

Osso Buco with Fennel and Leeks

You can braise osso buco with virtually any root vegetable, but a mixture of fennel and leeks imparts a delicate flavor that is perfectly suited to veal.

MAKES 4 MAIN-COURSE SERVINGS

4 veal shank rounds, each $1^1/2$ inches to
   2 inches thick
Salt
Pepper
2 tablespoons olive oil
3 tablespoons butter
1 fennel bulb, trimmed and thinly sliced
6 leeks, white and pale green parts only, sliced
1 cup dry white wine
2 cups chicken broth (page 316) or water
Bouquet garni (page 320)

Season the shank rounds all over with salt and pepper. Select a sauté pan with high sides and a lid just large enough to hold the shank rounds in a single layer. Heat the olive oil in the pan over high heat, add the shank rounds, and brown well on both sides. Transfer the shank rounds to a plate. Pour the fat out of the pan.

Return the pan to low to medium heat and add the butter, fennel, and leeks. Sweat the vegetables for about 10 minutes, or until they soften slightly. Transfer to a bowl. Place the shank rounds in the pan, and pour in the wine and broth. Spoon the vegetables over and add the bouquet garni. Cover the pot with a sheet of aluminum foil, pressing it down slightly in the middle so that moisture will condense on its underside and drip down into the pot, and then with a lid.

Simmer gently on the stove top for about 2 hours, or until the veal is easily penetrated with a knife. (Alternatively, slide the pot into a 275°F oven and cook for about 2 hours.)

Transfer the shank rounds to a plate, cover, and set aside in a warm spot. Remove and discard the bouquet garni, then simmer the braising liquid, with the vegetables, until reduced to about $1^1/2$ cups. Season with salt and pepper.

Divide the shank rounds among warmed soup plates. Spoon the reduced liquid and vegetables over the top.

Osso buco

1. Uncooked veal shank rounds.

2. Brown the shank rounds on both sides.

3. Sweat the fennel and leeks.

4. Pour wine and broth into the pan with the shanks.

5. Cover the shanks with cooked leeks and fennel and add the bouquet garni.

6. Finished osso buco with fennel and leeks.

Brain

Bad press often surrounds the eating of calves' brains because of the threat of bovine spongiform encephalopathy (mad-cow disease), but little or no evidence exists to consider their consumption a danger in the United States. Brains are the most delicate of all the organ meats (both in texture and flavor) and are hard to dislike. Their texture is reminiscent of softly scrambled eggs and they typically take on the flavor of whatever ingredients are prepared with them. They are best poached in a light broth or salted water and then served with a little frothy butter, or with butter, capers, and lemon juice like the sweetbreads on page 251. They are also delicious paired with scrambled eggs. Brains can also be sliced and sauteed—breaded or not—in clarified butter.

Calf's Brain with Butter and Lemon

It's ideal to have some vegetable broth (court bouillon) on hand for poaching the brains, but don't bother making it if you don't have it; just use salted water instead.

MAKES 4 MAIN-COURSE SERVINGS

1¹/₂ pounds veal brains

8 cups vegetable broth or salted water, or as needed

6 tablespoons butter

1 tablespoon fresh lemon juice

To remove any excess blood, peel the membrane off the brains and rinse the brains under running cold water to wash away bits of blood. If you're not going to use the brains right away, soak them in salted water. This removes additional blood which is harmless but can cause the brains to turn gray once cooked.

In a large pot, bring the broth to a simmer. Add the brains and simmer gently, uncovered, for about 10 minutes, or until the brains stiffen and feel slightly firm to the touch. Using a wire skimmer, transfer the brains to warmed plates or a platter and cover to keep warm. Discard the cooking liquid.

In a small sauté pan, melt the butter over medium heat until it turns frothy and then the froth begins to subside. Let cool slightly and add the lemon juice. Pour over the brains and serve at once.

Sweetbreads

The most luxurious of veal organ meats, sweetbreads are white and have a delicate texture and flavor. After a preliminary blanching, trimming and weighting, they are best braised or sautéed with a light bread crumb coating.

When buying sweetbreads, notice that there are two shapes: a round flattened ball, which the French call the *noix*, or "nut," and a long, ragged piece, which the French call the *gorge*, or "throat." In the animal, these two parts are connected and form the thymus gland, which is part of the body's immune system and gradually shrinks as the animal matures. If you have a choice, pick the round pieces; they are better to look at and cook more evenly. Cook sweetbreads within a day of purchase, as they are highly perishable.

Braised Sweetbreads with Prosciutto and Thyme

Like all braises, there is a classic method that involves sweating onions and carrots and then cooking the sweetbreads with this mixture along with a little broth. The amount of broth (braising liquid) should be kept to a minimum so the flavor of the sweet-breads is concentrated. Here, I include prosciutto to round out the flavor of the dish and balance the presence of fresh thyme.

MAKES 4 MAIN-COURSE SERVINGS

2$^{1}/_{2}$ to 3 pounds sweetbreads, preferably round *noix* pieces (see page 250)
1 carrot, peeled and finely chopped
1 onion, finely chopped
1 thin slice *prosciutto di Parma* or other high-quality prosciutto, cut into strips 1 inch long and $^{1}/_{8}$ inch wide
$^{1}/_{2}$ teaspoon fresh or $^{1}/_{4}$ teaspoon dried thyme leaves
1 imported bay leaf
6 tablespoons butter
1 cup veal broth or chicken broth (page 316)
Bouquet garni (page 320)
2 tablespoons meat glaze (page 318), optional
Salt
Pepper

In a pot, combine the sweetbreads with water to cover and bring to a boil over high heat. Drain immediately (the water should not boil for more than a second), place the sweetbreads on a small sheet pan or other shallow pan, and trim off any unsightly veins or pieces of tissue. Put a cutting board on top of the sweetbreads and top the board with a weight. Cover and refrigerate for at least 5 hours or up to overnight.

continued

Braised sweetbreads with prosciutto and thyme

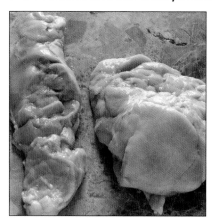
1. Notice the difference between the so-called *gorge* (left) and the *noix* (right).

2. Sweated aromatic vegetables for braising.

3. Sweetbreads on top of sweated aromatic vegetables set for braising.

Preheat the oven to 350°F. In an ovenproof pan just large enough to hold the sweetbreads in a single layer, combine the carrot, onion, prosciutto, thyme, and bay leaf with 2 tablespoons of the butter and sweat the vegetables over medium heat for about 10 minutes, or until they are slightly softened and the mixture is fragrant.

Arrange the sweetbreads in the pan, pour the broth over them, and add the bouquet garni and meat glaze. Cover loosely with a sheet of parchment paper or aluminum foil. Bake for about 25 minutes, or just until the sweetbreads feel firm to the touch, no longer.

Transfer the sweetbreads to warmed plates, cover, and set aside in a warm place. Discard the bouquet garni. Return the pan to the stove top and boil down the braising liquid to thicken it to a lightly syrupy consistency. Or, if it is already too thick, thin it with a little broth or water. Cut the remaining 4 tablespoons butter into 3 or 4 slices and whisk into the sauce until emulsified. Do not allow the sauce to boil. Season with salt and pepper.

Slice the sweetbreads on the diagonal into slices $1/3$ inch thick. Divide among warmed soup plates. Spoon the sauce over the sweetbreads and serve.

VARIATIONS: Try different herbs in the braising liquid and try adding finely chopped parsley, chervil, or tarragon at the end. The sauce can also be finished with cream. Sweetbreads are excellent with wild mushrooms (reconstituted dried porcini or morels are particularly tasty) and truffles. For a decorative touch, cut carrots, onions, and celery into fine dice (about $1/8$ inch, called *brunoise*) or less fine dice (about $1/4$ inch, called *macedoine*) and sweat them in a little butter before spooning them over the sweetbreads and braising. This is the method shown above.

Sautéed Sweetbreads with Lemon, Parsley, and Capers

Sweetbreads are delicious breaded and sautéed in butter, ideally clarified. The sauce can be just some frothy butter, or butter with lemon and capers.

MAKES 4 MAIN-COURSE SERVINGS

2¹/₂ to 3 pounds sweetbreads, preferably round
   noix pieces (see page 250)

6 slices slightly stale, dense-crumb white bread,
   crusts removed

Flour

2 eggs

Salt

Pepper

4 tablespoons clarified butter (page 6)

4 tablespoons butter

2 tablespoons capers

2 tablespoons fresh lemon juice

1 tablespoon finely chopped fresh parsley

In a pot, combine the sweetbreads with water to cover and bring to a boil over high heat. Drain immediately (the water should not boil for more than a second), place the sweetbreads on a small sheet pan or other shallow pan, and trim off any unsightly veins or pieces of tissue. Put a cutting board on top of the sweetbreads and top the board with a weight. Cover and refrigerate for at least 5 hours or up to overnight.

Tear the bread into pieces, place in a food processor, and pulse to form crumbs. Pass the crumbs through a fine-mesh strainer or a drum sieve so the crumbs are uniformly fine. You should have about 1¹/₂ cups. Spread the crumbs on a plate. Spread some flour on a second plate. In a shallow bowl, beat the eggs until blended, then season generously with salt and pepper.

continued

Sautéed sweetbreads with lemon, parsley, and capers

1. Slicing sweetbreads for sautéing.

2. Saute the breaded sweetbreads.

3. Finished sweetbreads

Slice the sweetbreads on the diagonal into long slices about $1/2$ inch thick. Working with 1 slice at a time, coat evenly on both sides with the flour, shaking off the excess. Next, dip the slice in the egg, and then, holding the slice above the bowl by one end, wipe off the excess egg by sliding the thumb and index finger along its length. Finally, lay the slice on the bread crumbs, turn to coat both sides, and transfer to a plate. Repeat with the remaining sweetbread slices.

Select a skillet or sauté pan, preferably non-stick, that is just large enough to hold the sweetbread slices in a single layer (or work in batches). Place over medium heat and melt the butter. Gently place the breaded slices in the pan—don't use tongs; use your fingers so as not to tear through the breading—in a single layer. Cook, moving the pan every minute or so to ensure the slices cook evenly, for about 3 minutes, or until golden brown on the first side. Using a spatula or your fingertips, turn the slices over and cook for about 3 minutes on the second side, or until golden brown. Transfer to warmed plates, cover, and set aside in a warm place. Pour the fat out of the pan.

Return the pan to medium heat and add the butter, capers, lemon juice, and parsley and heat until the butter is frothy and smells nutty. Spoon the sauce over the sweetbreads and serve.

VARIATIONS: Omit the bread crumbs and coat the sweetbreads with $1/2$ cup finely chopped fresh herbs or summer truffles (or even winter truffles) for a dramatic effect. (You will need about 2 large truffles.) If you are feeling extravagant, you can also shave white truffles over the finished sweetbreads to serve them *tartufati* style.

Liver

Veal liver, often labeled "calf's liver," is the most delicate of all the large-animal livers and shouldn't be confused with baby beef liver, which has a stronger taste. If you buy a whole liver, be sure to pull away the thin membrane that covers it before cooking it either whole or sliced. If the membrane is left on and the liver is sliced, the slices will curl in the pan. If you have purchased slices of liver and the membrane is still intact on each slice, make several slits around the edge of each slice through the membrane, so that when the membrane contracts, the slice won't curl.

Sautéed Calf's Liver with Vinegar and Onions

In this dish, the natural sugar in the onions becomes highly concentrated during cooking and rebounds off the acidity of the vinegar, creating a flavor reminiscent of an Italian *salsa agrodolce*, or sweet-and-sour sauce.

MAKES 4 MAIN-COURSE SERVINGS

4 tablespoons butter

4 large onions, thinly sliced

1 cup veal broth or chicken broth (page 316)

2 tablespoons meat glaze (page 318), optional

$1/4$ cup sherry vinegar or balsamic vinegar

4 slices calf's liver, 6 to 8 ounces each

Salt

Pepper

Flour

3 tablespoons olive oil

In a large, heavy pot, melt the butter over medium heat. Add the onions and cook, stirring almost constantly. When the onions release their water, after about 10 minutes, turn up the heat to high to evaporate the liquid, watching carefully to make sure the onions don't burn. Turn down the heat to medium and continue to cook the onions, stirring often, for about 10 minutes, or until they form a brown crust on the bottom and sides of the pot. Add the broth, glaze, and vinegar, bring to a gentle simmer, and simmer for about 10 minutes, or until the mixture takes on a saucelike consistency. Remove from the heat and cover to keep warm.

If the membrane is intact on the liver slices, make several slits around the edge of each slice through the membrane to prevent the slice from curling. Pat the slices dry, then season on both sides with salt and pepper. Spread some flour on a plate, then coat each slice evenly on both sides with the flour, shaking off the excess.

Select a sauté pan large enough to hold the slices in a single layer. (Alternatively, use 2 pans, or work in batches and keep the first 2 slices warm in the oven while you sauté the second 2 slices.) Place the pan over high heat and add the olive oil. When the oil begins to smoke, gently place the slices in the pan one at a time, waiting for about 30 seconds after adding each slice before adding the next one. (This prevents the pan from cooling off.) Cook the slices for about 3 minutes on the first side, or until well browned. Turn the slices and cook for about 3 minutes on the second side, or until well browned and the liver feels just barely firm to the touch. Again, wait for about 30 seconds after turning each slice before turning the next one.

Transfer the slices to a warmed platter lined with paper towels to absorb any oil, and pat off the burnt oil from the tops with more paper towels. Transfer to warmed plates, spoon the onion sauce over the top, and serve.

Roast Calf's Liver

If you have access to authentic calf's liver, this is a dramatic way to show it off—by roasting it whole or by buying a large section. Livers can weigh as much as 12 pounds, so be sure to ask for a piece that is the size you need.

MAKES 8 MAIN-COURSE SERVINGS

1 whole liver or piece of liver, about 5 pounds
Salt
Pepper
3 tablespoons olive oil

Preheat the oven to 375°F.

Peel the membrane off the liver as shown below. Season the liver all over with salt and pepper. In an ovenproof nonstick sauté pan just large enough to hold the liver, heat the oil over high heat until it begins to smoke. Add the liver and brown well on both sides. Slide the pan into the oven and roast for about 35 minutes, or until an instant-read thermometer inserted into the center of the liver reads 135°F or it feels just firm to the touch.

Transfer the liver to a platter, tent loosely with aluminum foil, and let rest for 15 minutes. Carve into long, thin slices to serve.

Roast calf's liver

1. Pull off the membrane that covers the liver.

2. Season the liver and brown on both sides in a nonstick sauté pan.

3. Roast until just firm to the touch, or until a thermometer reads 135°F.

4. Slice the roast liver.

5. Finished roast liver.

Kidney

On restaurant menus in France, kidneys are often among the most expensive items. Their high cost is for two reasons: the French like flavorful meats, and each animal has only two kidneys. Kidneys do indeed have a strong flavor that is off-putting to some people and appealing to others. They are also one of the few meats in which the juices that are released in cooking are not used to make a sauce. You can roast kidneys whole—brown them first in a small pan—or you can slice them and lightly sauté them plain or coated with bread crumbs. They are also great with mustard, either dipped in it before flouring or served with a sauce that incorporates it. Kidneys are sold pretty much ready to cook. Occasionally, they are covered with a layer of fat, which you can trim off completely or trim to a thin layer. The only other preparation necessary is to remove the fat and gristle at the center of each kidney, working carefully not to cut away too much or the kidney will fall apart.

Kidneys with juniper sauce (recipe follows)

1. Uncooked kidney.

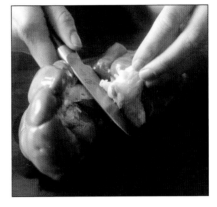

2. Remove excess fat and gristle from the connective tissue that holds the kidney together, but do not cut the kidney apart.

3. Brown the kidneys on all sides, then roast until firm to the touch, or until a thermometer reads 140°F.

4. Slice the kidney.

Kidneys with Juniper Sauce

This sauce is purposely made a bit acidic to cut through the strong flavor and richness of the kidneys.

MAKES 4 MAIN-COURSE SERVINGS

4 veal kidneys, about 3/4 pound each

Salt

Pepper

2 tablespoons olive oil

10 juniper berries, crushed under a saucepan

1 shallot, minced

1 small clove garlic, minced

1 cup dry white wine

2 tablespoons meat glaze (page 318), optional

4 tablespoons cold butter, cut into 3 or 4 slices

Preheat the oven to 450°F. Pull off and/or cut off any fat clinging to each kidney, then cut out any excess fat and gristle at the center, being careful not to cut the kidney apart (see page 255). Season the kidneys all over with salt and pepper.

In an ovenproof sauté pan just large enough to hold the kidneys in a single layer, heat the oil over high heat until it begins to smoke. Add the kidneys and brown well on all sides. Slide the pan into the oven and cook for about 25 minutes, or until an instant-read thermometer inserted into the center of a kidney reads 135°F or the kidneys are just firm to the touch.

Meanwhile, in a small saucepan, combine the juniper berries, shallot, garlic, and wine over high heat and boil down until reduced by half. Add the meat glaze and boil for about 2 minutes, or until the sauce has a lightly syrupy consistency. Strain through a fine-mesh strainer into a clean saucepan and whisk in the butter until emulsified. Do not allow the sauce to boil. Season with salt and pepper. Keep warm.

When the kidneys are ready, transfer to a cutting board and cut on the diagonal into slices about 1/3 inch thick. Arrange the slices on warmed plates and spoon the sauce over the top.

VARIATIONS: Kidneys are also complemented by port and mustard. Boil down about 1 1/2 cups ruby or tawny port until reduced by half, whisk in 1 or 2 tablespoons meat glaze, and simmer until a lightly syrupy consistency forms. Whisk in a spoonful or two of Dijon mustard, and then whisk in 3 or 4 tablespoons cold butter until emulsified.

Tripe

Tripe, the collective term for the four stomachs of a ruminant, or cud-chewing, animal, is almost always sold well cleaned and often partially cooked, requiring only additional long, slow cooking to tenderize it and to temper its sometimes aggressive flavor. Keep in mind that there are several kinds of tripe, including honeycomb tripe (the easiest to find), thick-seam tripe, bible tripe (sometimes found in Asian markets), and reed tripe. If you find the flavor of tripe too strong, try eating it cold, made into a terrine as described in the variation that follows the recipe.

Tripe Stew with Cider

Tripe can be braised in just about any liquid. In Normandy, cider is the traditional medium, though beer, wine, or even broth will work.

MAKES 8 MAIN-COURSE SERVINGS

5 pounds honeycomb tripe

1 whole clove

1 onion, halved

2 carrots, peeled and cut into 1-inch sections

1 celery stalk, halved

4 cups hard cider, or 2 cups each apple cider and
    cider vinegar, or as needed

Bouquet garni (page 320)

$^1/_4$ cup Calvados, optional

Cut the tripe into strips about 3 inches long and $^3/_4$ inch wide. Put them in a pot, add water to cover, bring to a simmer, and simmer for 5 minutes. Drain into a colander and rinse well under cold running water. Drain again.

Stick the clove in an onion half. In a pot, combine the tripe, onion halves, carrots, and celery and add cider to cover. Nestle the bouquet garni in the pot. Bring to a gentle simmer, cover, and cook for about 4 hours, or until the tripe is easily penetrated with a knife or skewer. (Alternatively, bring to a gentle simmer on the stove top, cover, slide the pot into a 275°F oven, and cook for about 4 hours.) Remove from the heat and add the Calvados. Simmer for 5 minutes to cook the alcohol out of the Calvados.

Spoon the tripe, vegetables, and braising liquid into warmed soup plates to serve.

VARIATION: Drain the tripe, reserving the braising liquid. Pick through the tripe and toss out the vegetables. Put the tripe in a porcelain terrine and pour the braising liquid over the top. Let cool, then cover and refrigerate until the liquid has set (it is very gelatinous). Slice and serve cold with mustard and sour gherkins (cornichons).

LAMB AND GOAT

Americans are not big lamb eaters, consuming only about one-half pound per person per year. Most observers attribute this low consumption rate to the fact that the United States has little tradition of sheep farming. Despite that lack of history, I find it surprising that lamb—which, unlike pork, has not lost its flavor to a national campaign to produce leaner meat—is not more popular on the country's dinner tables.

Lamb has a rich, slightly musky flavor that makes it adaptable to all sorts of treatments. Most contemporary scholars believe that sheep were first domesticated about ten thousand years ago in what is modern-day Kurdistan. Sheep husbandry quickly spread to areas in the Mediterranean, including Sardinia, Corsica, and Crete. Nowadays, lamb is especially appreciated in kitchens around the Mediterranean, throughout the Middle East and Central Asia, and in India. Even though it is at the heart of a wide variety of dishes, many of which can be complex, it often tastes best simply sautéed, braised, or roasted, depending on the cut.

Lamb is one of the easier animals to understand anatomically because it is relatively small. When butchered, it is not cut in half lengthwise, the way a steer or a hog is. Instead, it is cut crosswise into four pieces: the shoulder, the double rack (the ribs), the saddle (double loin), and the legs (most of the forelegs remains connected to the shoulder). The shoulder is best braised, in large pieces, as chops, or in small pieces for stew. The legs can also be braised, but in general all the cuts except for the shoulder are ideally roasted. The rack and saddle can also be cut crosswise into chops for sautéing.

Don't confuse a baby lamb with spring lamb. Baby lambs, which weigh about twenty pounds each, are available in the spring around Easter and are traditionally roasted whole. Spring lambs are born in the spring and best eaten in the fall, not in the spring.

Keep in mind, too, that lamb cuts from Australia or New Zealand are considerably smaller than their equivalent American cuts. A rack of American lamb will serve four, but a rack of New Zealand lamb will only serve two. Also, shoulders from New Zealand or Australian lamb can be roasted—there is no need for braising.

I have also included goat in this chapter, which has an even smaller culinary profile than lamb in the United States, but it fits well here because it's anatomically similar to lamb and cooked in much the same way.

LAMB CUTS

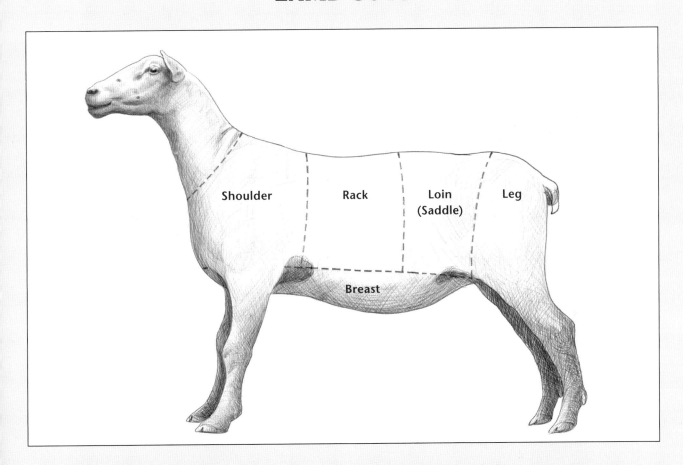

Shoulder
Shank: braise, poach, stew
Shoulder: braise, poach, stew, roast
Shoulder chop: sauté, grill, stew, broil

Rack
Rack: sauté (chops), roast, grill
Rib chop: sauté, grill, broil

Loin (Saddle)
Saddle: sauté (chops), roast
Loin chop: sauté, grill, broil

Leg
Leg: braise, roast, grill (butterfly)
Shank: braise, poach, stew

Breast
Breast: braise, roast

Whole Lamb

While it is unlikely you will ever have to butcher a whole lamb, it helps to see one broken down so you understand its anatomy and, for that matter, the anatomy of most four-legged animals.

Breaking down a whole lamb

1. Poke a hole into the carcass between the thirteenth and fourteenth ribs. (In other words, the last rib is left to the rear and the remaining ribs to the front.)

2. Move the knife along the length of the rib toward the backbone.

3. Turn the carcass around and repeat on the other side.

4. Cut through the backbone with a hacksaw.

5. Hindquarter with loin section connected to the "baron," which is what the group of two legs is called.

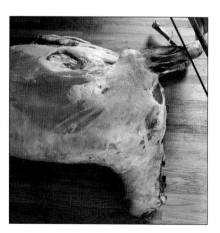

6. Cut the "nubs" off the forequarters.

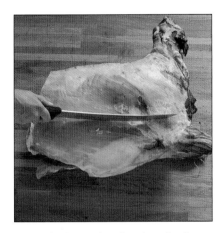

7. Use a knife to make a line along the ribs.

8. Saw through the rib section.

9. Cut the rack off the forequarter.

10. Cut through the spine with a saw.

11. Rack of lamb.

12. Saw the saddle off the hindquarter.

Shank

Lamb shanks (shins) traditionally come from the forelegs of the animal, with each one an individual-serving cut. But shanks have become so popular that nowadays the hind shanks are sometimes treated the same way. (The hind shanks can also be cut crosswise into thick slices, or boned and the meat used for stews.) Shanks are the toughest cut of the lamb and must be braised for a long time to tenderize. The best approach is to brown them in the oven with aromatic vegetables (onions, carrots, celery, turnips) until they have released their juices, moisten them with some wine and broth, and then braise them in the usual way.

Lamb Shanks Braised with Shallots

Here, I braise lamb shanks with carrot, onion, a bouquet garni, and red wine for a few hours. I then strain and degrease the braising liquid, reunite the shanks with the liquid, add the shallots, and braise the dish in the oven for an hour to cook the shallots. You can also trade out the shallots for other vegetables, such as garlic cloves, turnips, carrots, or potatoes (see Variations).

MAKES 6 MAIN-COURSE SERVINGS

6 American lamb shanks, about 1 pound each,
    or 12 Australian or New Zealand lamb shanks,
    about $1/2$ pound each
Salt
Pepper
1 large onion, coarsely chopped
1 large carrot, peeled and coarsely chopped
4 cups chicken broth (page 316), or 2 cups water
    combined with $1/4$ cup meat glaze (page 318)
3 cups dry red wine
Bouquet garni (page 320)
24 shallots, peeled but left whole

Season the shanks all over with salt and pepper and bring to room temperature. Preheat the oven to 450°F.

Put the shanks in a roasting pan just large enough to hold them in a single layer and sprinkle the onion and carrot on top. Place the pot in the oven and roast, uncovered, for about 30 minutes, or until the shanks release juices that caramelize (but don't burn) on the bottom of the pan. Meanwhile, in a saucepan, bring the broth to a boil and simmer until reduced to 2 cups.

Gently transfer the shanks to a clean ovenproof pot. Place the roasting pan on the stove top over high heat, pour in the wine, and deglaze the pan, scraping up any brown bits on the bottom of the pan with a wooden spoon. Pour the liquid over the shanks, nestle in the bouquet garni, add the broth (or diluted meat glaze), and bring to a simmer. Cover the pot with a sheet of aluminum foil, pressing it down slightly in the middle so that moisture will condense on its underside and drip down into the pot, and then with a lid. Simmer gently for about 3 hours, or until a knife slides easily in and out of the shanks. (Alternatively, slide the pot into a 275°F oven for about 3 hours to the same end.)

Gently lift the shanks out of the pot and transfer them to a plate. Strain the braising liquid in a glass pitcher and skim off the fat with a ladle. Or, ideally, refrigerate the braising liquid at this point and then lift off the congealed fat in a single layer. Put the shanks back in the pot, pour in the degreased liquid, add the shallots, and bring to a simmer on the stove top. Re-cover the pot with foil and a lid, slide it into a 300°F oven, and cook for about 1 hour, or until the shallots are tender.

Transfer the shanks to warmed soup bowls, dividing them evenly. Divide the shallots evenly among the bowls, placing 4 shallots in each. Spoon the braising liquid over and around the shanks and serve.

VARIATIONS: Substitute 4 heads garlic, cloves separated and peeled, for the shallots. You can puree the cooked cloves of garlic and use to thicken the braising liquid, adding the puree at the end. You can also add root vegetables, sectioned and shaped; whole or sectioned mushrooms; or cooked artichoke hearts to the braising liquid for the last 5 minutes of cooking. To give the braising liquid a Moroccan twist, flavor it with ginger and saffron, and garnish the shanks with olives and diced preserved lemon.

Lamb shanks braised with shallots

1. Put the shanks in a roasting pan with aromatic vegetables on top. Roast to release the juices, then braise in the oven or on the stove top.

2. Add the degreased braising liquid, which here was chilled to remove the fat, to the braised shanks.

3. Add the shallots to the shanks.

Shoulder

Because lamb, unlike beef or pork, is not split in half lengthwise, the shoulder, at the wholesale level, contains both the right and left shoulders. For most dishes, it is practical to have only half of this primal cut, or a single shoulder, which is what is labeled a "whole shoulder" in a butcher shop. Once you get the single shoulder home, boning it is a simple matter of following your nose and of keeping the knife always against the bone.

The shoulder is better suited for making stew, for tying and braising, or, if the lamb is young and the shoulder small, for roasting. The photos on the facing page show how to bone a single whole shoulder and then tie it for braising or roasting.

A lamb shoulder is sometimes cut into chops, but the chops have a lot of connective tissue, fat, and gristle, which is why they are best braised. There are two kinds of shoulder chops: blade chops and arm chops. The arm chops are cut crosswise against the foreleg and have a single bone surrounded by relatively lean meat. Blade chops are cut perpendicular to the foreleg; they look a little like rib chops, but they have a lot more fat and gristle.

Breaking down a double whole lamb shoulder

1. Double lamb shoulder.

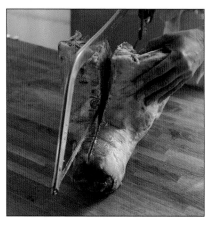

2. Cutting the double shoulder into two single whole shoulders with a saw.

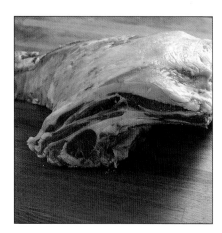

3. Whole lamb shoulder with bones.

Boning and tying a single whole lamb shoulder

1. Whole lamb shoulder.

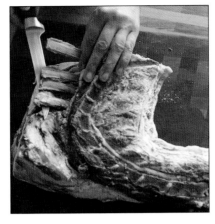

2. Slide the knife under the rib bones.

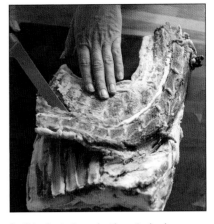

3. Slide the knife under the spinal column.

4. Detach the spinal column.

5. Take out the shoulder blade.

6. Cut around the joint and remove the remaining bones.

7. Cut away the long nerve that runs along where the spinal column was attached.

8. Finished boned lamb shoulder.

9. Tie the shoulder into a round shape.

Braised Lamb Shoulder

You'll have to buy a single whole shoulder to make this recipe and bone it yourself, unless you're lucky enough to have a cooperative butcher. Then, to braise it, you will need to tie it into a round shape, known as *en ballon* in French.

MAKES 6 MAIN-COURSE SERVINGS

1 single whole lamb shoulder, about 6 pounds, boned as shown on page 267

Salt

Pepper

1 onion, coarsely chopped

1 carrot, peeled and cut into 3-inch sections

1 small turnip, peeled and quartered

6 cups chicken broth (page 316), or 3 cups water combined with 3 tablespoons meat glaze (page 318)

1 cup dry white wine

Bouquet garni (page 320)

Lay the boned shoulder, with the "inside" up, on a work surface, season with salt and pepper, and then tie into a balloon shape as shown on page 267. Season the outside with salt and pepper and let the shoulder come to room temperature. Preheat the oven to 400°F.

Put the onion, carrot, and turnip in an ovenproof pot just large enough to hold the shoulder, and place the shoulder on top of the vegetables. Slide the pot, uncovered, into the oven and roast for about 1 hour, or until the lamb is well browned and releases juices that caramelize (but don't burn) on the bottom of the pot. If the juices start to caramelize and threaten to burn before the roast has begun to release the lion's share of its juices, add $1/2$ to 1 cup water to the pot. Meanwhile, in a saucepan, bring the broth to a boil and simmer until reduced to 3 cups.

When the lamb is well browned and the juices have caramelized, pour in the wine and broth (or diluted meat glaze); the liquid should come halfway up the sides of the shoulder. If it doesn't, add broth or water as needed. Nestle the bouquet garni in the pot and bring to a simmer on the stove top. Cover the pot with a sheet of aluminum foil, pressing it down slightly in the middle so that moisture will condense on its underside and drip down onto the exposed parts of the meat, and then with a lid. Simmer gently for about 1 hour. Turn the lamb over gently so the meat that was above the liquid is now submerged, re-cover the pot with the foil and the lid, and continue to simmer gently for 1 hour longer, or until a knife slides easily in and out of the roast. (Alternatively, slide the pot into a 275°F oven for about 2 hours, turning in the same way.)

Preheat the oven to 400°F. Transfer the shoulder to a smaller ovenproof pot (or clean the pot you used for braising). Strain the braising liquid into a glass pitcher and skim off the fat with a ladle. Or, ideally, refrigerate the braising liquid at this point and then lift off the congealed fat in a single layer. Pour the degreased braising liquid over the roast and slide the pot, uncovered, into the oven. Cook the shoulder, basting it every 10 minutes with the liquid, for about 30 minutes, or until the liquid becomes lightly syrupy and the shoulder is covered with a shiny glaze.

Remove the shoulder from the oven and snip the strings. Spoon out portions of the meat into warmed soup plates. Ladle the braising liquid around and over the meat and serve.

VARIATION: Sautéed wild mushrooms are a delightful garnish for this braised shoulder. Sauté them in butter and scent them with herbs and/or aromatics, such as garlic, lavender, hyssop, thyme, or marjoram.

Braised lamb shoulder

1. Place the shoulder on a bed of aromatic vegetables in a pot.

2. Roast the shoulder until the juices caramelize.

3. Pour in enough liquid to come halfway up the sides of the shoulder.

4. Cover the pot with a sheet of aluminum foil, and then the lid, and braise.

5. Finished braised lamb shoulder.

Roast Lamb Shoulder

If you have a small American lamb shoulder or a lamb shoulder from New Zealand, where they are smaller, bone it and tie it as you would for braising, but roast it instead. Larger shoulders, such as those from American lamb, should be braised.

MAKES 4 TO 6 MAIN-COURSE SERVINGS

1 small single whole American lamb shoulder,
    3 to 4 pounds, boned as shown on page 267
Salt
Pepper

Lay the boned shoulder, with the "inside" up, on a work surface, season with salt and pepper, and then tie into a balloon shape as shown on page 267. Season the outside with salt and pepper and let the shoulder come to room temperature. Preheat the oven to 400°F.

Put the lamb in a heavy roasting pan just large enough to hold it and slide it into the oven. Roast for about 30 minutes, or until an instant-read thermometer inserted into the center reads 135°F. The temperature will rise to 140°F while it rests.

Transfer the roast to a platter, snip the strings, and tent loosely with aluminum foil. Let rest for 15 minutes before slicing.

Lamb Tagine with Raisins, Almonds, and Saffron

The lamb *tagines* (stews) of Morocco come in almost infinite variety. Raisins are commonly added, as are prunes, apples, saffron, ginger, almonds, apricots, dates, and honey—primarily sweet elements that contrast well with the rich meat. Serve this aromatic *tagine* with couscous or rice.

MAKES 6 MAIN-COURSE SERVINGS

4 pounds boneless lamb shoulder meat, cut into
    1½-inch chunks
Salt
Pepper
¼ cup olive oil
4 tablespoons butter
1 large onion, chopped
3 cloves garlic, minced and then crushed to a paste
3 tablespoons peeled and grated fresh ginger
½ teaspoon cayenne pepper
3 tomatoes, peeled, seeded, chopped
2 cups chicken broth (page 316) or other broth
    or water
Small pinch of saffron threads, soaked in
    1 tablespoon hot water for 30 minutes
½ cup blanched almonds, toasted for about
    15 minutes in a 300°F oven until fragrant
    and golden
¾ cup raisins, soaked in warm water to cover
    until plumped, then drained
Harissa (page 26) for serving

Season the lamb all over with salt and pepper. In a large, heavy sauté pan, heat the oil over high heat. When the oil begins to smoke, add half of the meat and cook, turning as needed, until well browned on all sides. Transfer to a plate and repeat with the remaining meat. Pour the fat out of the pan.

Return the pan to medium heat and melt the butter. Add the onion, garlic, ginger, and cayenne and cook, stirring occasionally, for about 20 minutes, or until the onion softens and caramelizes. Return the lamb to the pan and add the tomatoes and broth. Cover and simmer gently for about 2 hours, or until the meat is easily penetrated with a skewer.

Add the saffron and its soaking water, the almonds, and the raisins and return the mixture to a simmer. Serve the *tagine* in warmed soup plates. Pass the *harissa* at the table.

Irish Stew

The genius of Irish stew is using potato as a thickener. Some recipes call for two types of potatoes: starchy ones such as russets for thickening the braising liquid and waxy potatoes such as Yukon Gold as part of the garniture

MAKES 8 MAIN-COURSE SERVINGS

5 pounds boneless lamb shoulder meat

Salt

Pepper

2 teaspoons mixed chopped fresh thyme and
marjoram, in equal parts (or only thyme
if marjoram is unavailable)

1 large russet potato, peeled and sliced

2 large onions, thinly sliced

Bouquet garni (page 320)

2 quarts chicken broth (page 316) or water,
or as needed

3 tablespoons meat glaze (page 318), optional

2 pounds Yukon Gold or Yellow Finn potatoes,
peeled and quartered

Cut the meat into pieces about 1 inch by 2 inches. Season all over with salt and pepper. Layer the meat, herbs, russet potato, and onions in alternating layers in a narrow, heavy pot and nestle in the bouquet garni. Pour in broth to cover, and stir in the meat glaze. Bring to a gentle simmer and simmer, uncovered, for about 1¹/₂ hours or until the potato falls apart easily.

Stir vigorously to break up the russet potato slices, then add the Yukon Gold potatoes and continue to simmer for about 40 minutes longer, or until the potatoes are tender and the lamb is easily penetrated with a knife.

Discard the bouquet garni. Serve the stew in warmed soup plates.

Irish stew

1. When the potato slices are cooked, stir the stew to break up the potatoes.

2. Add waxy potatoes and simmer until they are done and the lamb is tender.

3. Finished Irish stew.

Lamb Stew with Spring Vegetables

Lamb shoulder can be used to make countless kinds of stews that differ only in the moistening liquid, the aromatics and other vegetables simmered along with the meat (for example, an Irish stew contains potatoes), and the final garniture. Among the most famous lamb stews is the French *navarin*, a basic stew garnished with spring vegetables. For this recipe, it's handy to have an assortment of baby vegetables—turnips, carrots, potatoes—but if you don't have them, older vegetables can be sectioned and shaped.

MAKES 8 MAIN-COURSE SERVINGS

1 whole lamb shoulder, about 6 pounds,
    or 5 pounds boneless lamb shoulder meat
Salt
Pepper
3 tablespoons olive oil
1 whole clove
1 large onion, quartered
1 large carrot, peeled and thickly sliced
Bouquet garni (page 320)
1 cup dry white wine
4 cups chicken broth (page 316) or water,
    or as needed
18 baby carrots, or 2 large carrots
18 baby turnips, or 2 large turnips
5 tablespoons butter
18 baby white or red waxy potatoes or small
    potatoes such as fingerlings or Rattes
$1/2$ pound haricots verts or regular green beans,
    trimmed
1 tablespoon flour
2 tablespoons chopped fresh parsley

If you are using a whole shoulder, bone it as shown on page 267. (Ideally, make a broth with the bones. Brown the bones on the stove or in the oven, add water to cover, and simmer uncovered for 3 hours. Strain the broth through a fine-mesh sieve. Use in place of the chicken broth.) Cut the meat into 1-inch cubes and season all over with salt and pepper. In a large, heavy sauté pan, heat the olive oil over high heat. When the oil begins to smoke, add half of the meat and cook, turning as needed, until well browned on all sides. Transfer to a plate and repeat with the remaining meat. Pour the fat out of the pan.

Put the meat in a pot. Stick the clove into an onion quarter and add the onion quarters to the pot along with the carrot slices and the bouquet garni. Return the sauté pan to medium heat, add the wine, and deglaze the pan, scraping up any brown bits on the bottom of the pan with a wooden spoon. Pour the wine over the meat and add enough broth just to cover the meat. Bring to a gentle simmer and cook, covered, at the barest simmer (you want only a bubble or two to break on the surface every few seconds) for about 3 hours, or until a knife easily penetrates a piece of meat. (Alternatively, slide the pot into a 275°F oven and cook for about 3 hours to the same end.)

Remove from the heat. Strain the braising liquid into a glass pitcher. Pick out and discard the vegetables and the bouquet garni from the strainer and set the meat aside. Skim off the fat from the liquid with a ladle. Or, ideally, refrigerate the braising liquid at this point and then lift off the congealed fat in a single layer. Pour the degreased liquid into a saucepan, bring to a simmer, and simmer, skimming off any fat or froth that rises to the surface, for about 30 minutes, or until reduced to about 2 cups.

While the braising liquid is simmering, peel the baby or large carrots and turnips (if using baby vegetables, a razor works well because less flesh is wasted). If using large carrots and turnips, cut them into sections and turn the turnips as shown on pages 10 and 11. If using baby carrots and turnips, leave whole. Spread the carrots and turnips in a single layer in a wide pan. Add water to come halfway up the sides of the vegetables and 2 tablespoons of the butter, cover the pan loosely with aluminum foil, and simmer for about 20 minutes, or until all the liquid evaporates and the vegetables are coated with a shiny glaze. At the same time, in a saucepan, combine the potatoes with water to cover (start them out in cold water so they cook evenly), bring to a simmer, and simmer for about 10 minutes to cook partially, then drain. In a large sauté pan, melt 2 tablespoons of the butter over medium-high heat, add the potatoes, and cook for about 15 minutes, or until nicely browned and tender. Bring a saucepan filled with water to a boil, add the haricots verts, and boil for about 5 minutes, or until tender, then drain. Season all the vegetables with salt and pepper and set aside in a warm spot.

In a pot large enough to hold the lamb later, melt the remaining 1 tablespoon butter over medium heat. Whisk in the flour and cook, whisking constantly, for about 3 minutes, or until the mixture is smooth and smells toasty. Whisk in the reduced braising liquid, bring to a gentle simmer, and cook, whisking constantly, until lightly thickened.

Add the lamb to the thickened braising liquid and reheat until hot. Stir in the vegetables and heat briefly. Stir in the parsley, spoon the stew into warmed soup plates, and serve.

Braised Lamb Shoulder Chops with White Wine and Aromatics

A whole lamb shoulder can be broken down into bone chops from the arm end and blade chops from the rib section as shown on page 274. Shoulder chops have too much sinew to sauté, but they are delicious braised in white wine and a little broth.

MAKES 4 MAIN-COURSE SERVINGS

4 blade or arm lamb shoulder chops,
    6 to 8 ounces each
Salt
Pepper
5 tablespoons olive oil
1 onion, chopped
1 carrot, peeled and chopped
3 cloves garlic, minced
Bouquet garni (page 320)
1 cup dry white wine
2 cups chicken broth (page 316) or water
2 tablespoons meat glaze (page 318), optional
4 tablespoons cold butter, cut into 3 or 4 slices,
    optional

Season the chops on both sides with salt and pepper. Select a heavy, ovenproof sauté pan with a lid just large enough to hold the chops in a single layer. Add 2 tablespoons of the olive oil and heat over high heat. When the oil begins to smoke, add the chops and cook, turning once, for about 3 minutes on each side, or until well browned. Transfer to a plate. Pour the fat out of the pan.

Return the pan to medium heat and add the remaining 3 tablespoons oil. Add the onion, carrot, and garlic and sweat the vegetables, stirring occasionally, for about 10 minutes, or until the onion is translucent. Return the chops to the pan, nestling

continued

them in the vegetables, and add the bouquet garni, wine, broth, and meat glaze. Bring to a gentle simmer. Cover the pan with a sheet of aluminum foil, pressing it down in the center so it almost touches the surface of the chops, and top with the lid. Simmer gently for about 2 hours, or until a knife slides easily in and out of the chops with no resistance.

Preheat the oven to 400°F. Transfer the chops to a plate. Strain the braising liquid into a glass pitcher and skim off any fat with a ladle. Or, ideally, refrigerate the braising liquid at this point and then lift

off the congealed fat in a single layer. Return the chops to the sauté pan, add the degreased braising liquid, and slide the pan into the oven. Cook the chops, basting every 10 minutes with the liquid, for about 30 minutes, or until they are covered with a shiny glaze.

Transfer the chops to warmed plates. Whisk the butter into the braising liquid until emulsified. Spoon the liquid over and around the chops and serve.

Lamb shoulder chops

Arm chop.

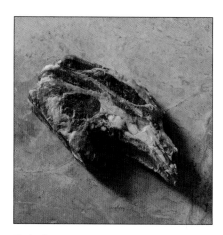

Blade chop.

Braised Lamb Shoulder Chops with Root Vegetables, Marsala, and Sherry Vinegar

Shoulder lamb chops are the least expensive of all the lamb chops, but they have the most flavor and best texture when they are cooked properly. Here, the sweet-and-sour flavors of vinegar and wine are perfect foils for the rich cut.

MAKES 4 MAIN-COURSE SERVINGS

4 large blade or arm lamb shoulder chops, 6 to 8 ounces each

Salt

Pepper

6 tablespoons olive oil

1 small turnip, peeled and cut into $1/4$-inch cubes

1 carrot, peeled and cut into $1/4$-inch cubes

1 small onion, chopped

Bouquet garni (page 320)

$1/2$ cup sherry vinegar or other wine vinegar

$1/2$ cup sweet Marsala, sweet sherry, or sweet Madeira

3 tablespoons meat glaze (page 318)

Season the chops on both sides with salt and pepper. Select a heavy sauté pan with a lid just large enough to hold the chops in a single layer. Add 3 tablespoons of the olive oil and heat over high heat. When the oil begins to smoke, add the chops and cook, turning once, for about 3 minutes on each side, or until well browned. Transfer to a plate. Pour the fat out of the pan.

Return the pan to medium heat and add the remaining 3 tablespoons oil. Add the turnip, carrot, and onion and sweat the vegetables, stirring occasionally, for about 15 minutes, or until they just start to brown. Return the chops to the pan, nestling them in the vegetables, and add the bouquet garni, vinegar, wine, and meat glaze. Bring to a gentle simmer. Cover the pan with a sheet of aluminum foil, pressing it down in the center so it almost touches the surface of the chops, and top with the lid. Bring to a gentle simmer, cover, and cook for about 2 hours, or until a knife slides easily in and out of the chops.

Transfer the chops to warmed soup plates, cover, and set aside in a warm spot. Skim the fat off the braising liquid with a large spoon, then boil down the liquid, skimming off any fat or froth that rises to the surface, until it has a lightly syrupy consistency. Spoon the braising liquid and vegetables over the chops and serve.

VARIATION: If you don't want to take the time to cut the turnip and carrot into perfect cubes, you can just chop them and strain them out of the braising liquid—or you can even leave them in.

Breast

The breast of lamb, like the equivalent breast of veal (see pages 225 to 230), is something you are likely to encounter only if you break down a whole animal yourself or if you frequent a top-notch butcher shop, especially if you want a whole breast. Quality butchers sell the whole breast either bone-in or boneless. Sometimes you will also see lamb ribs from the breast for sale. They can be quite fatty but are tasty and relatively inexpensive and are delicious marinated and grilled.

In the recipe below, I roast a boneless rolled breast of lamb, but you can roast a trimmed breast without boning or rolling it, and then cut between the ribs with a cleaver or knife to serve.

Rolled Breast of Lamb with Sage

You may have to special order the whole breast from your butcher. Be sure you ask for an American breast, which will be larger than a New Zealand or Australian lamb breast. I have provided instructions for trimming and boning the breast. Try to remove as much surface fat and membranelike connective tissue as possible to ensure the best result.

MAKES 4 MAIN-COURSE SERVINGS

1 whole breast of American lamb, about 3 pounds
Salt
Pepper
3 fresh sage leaves
2 cups chicken broth (page 316) or water

Following the directions on the facing page, trim off the fat and remove the bones from the breast. Season on both sides with salt and pepper, arrange the sage leaves on top, and then roll it up and tie it.

Place the breast in an ovenproof saucepan, sauté pan, or roasting pan just large enough to hold it, and slide the pan into the oven. Roast for about 45 minutes, or until an instant-read thermometer inserted into the center reads 135°F or the meat feels firm when you press it with a fingertip.

Transfer the breast to a cutting board, tent loosely with aluminum foil, and let rest for 10 minutes.

While the breast is resting, make the jus. Pour the fat out of the pan and put the pan on the stove top over high heat. Add 1 cup of the broth and deglaze the pan, scraping up any brown bits on the bottom of the pan with a wooden spoon. Boil down the broth until it caramelizes into a crusty brown layer with a layer of clear fat on top. Pour off the fat, return the pan to high heat, and deglaze with the remaining 1 cup broth, stirring until the crust has dissolved into the liquid. Strain the liquid through a fine-mesh strainer into a warmed sauceboat.

Snip the strings on the rolled breast and carve into thick slices to serve. Pass the jus at the table.

VARIATION: Add fresh lemon juice to the jus to help cut the richness of the meat.

Rolled breast of lamb with sage

1. Breast of lamb.

2. Cut away the sheet of meat covering the breast and freeze it for making artificial jus (page 171).

3. Trim off excess fat from the breast.

4. With a knife, push the meat around the sides of the bones, and then pull the bones out with a towel.

5. Lay the sage leaves on the meat and roll up the breast.

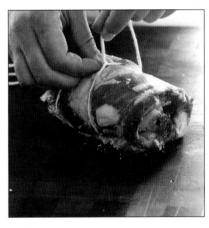

6. Tie up the breast.

7. Roast the breast.

8. Slice the breast.

Saddle

The saddle is one of the great underrated lamb cuts. It includes the whole loin section, which means it comes with flaps (what would be flank steaks on a steer), tenderloins, and loin muscles, and it is usually cut into loin chops. But a whole saddle makes an eye-catching roast and is typically less expensive than buying two racks of lamb, which would yield the same number of servings as a single saddle. And, unlike the rack, the saddle contains the tenderloin muscles from both sides of the lamb.

Roast Saddle of Lamb

Part of the drama of a whole saddle of lamb is how it is carved. It can be carved in two ways: lengthwise into strips, by first slicing the loin and then turning the saddle over and slicing the tenderloin; or into rounds, by cutting away the loin and then the tenderloin and cutting both of them crosswise into slices.

MAKES 8 MAIN-COURSE SERVINGS

**1 untrimmed saddle of lamb (including flaps),
    about 8 pounds**
Salt
Pepper
$^1/_2$ onion, coarsely chopped
2 cups chicken broth (page 316)

Let the saddle come to room temperature. Preheat the oven to 450°F.

Working carefully to avoid damaging the loin muscle, cut the flaps off the saddle as shown on the facing page. Trim the excess fat from the flaps, then cut the meat into strips about $^1/_2$ inch wide. Trim the excess fat off the saddle, leaving a thin layer of fat covering the meat. Season the saddle all over with salt and pepper. Spread the flap strips and onion in a roasting pan just large enough to hold the saddle. Place the saddle, fat side up, on top.

Slide the pan into the oven and roast the saddle for about 30 minutes, or until an instant-read thermometer inserted into the center without touching bone reads 125°F or the meat feels firm when you press both ends of the saddle. Check the tenderloins on the bottom in the same way to make sure they are done, too. If not, turn the saddle over and roast for a few minutes longer.

Transfer to a platter, tent loosely with aluminum foil, and let rest for 15 minutes before carving.

While the saddle is resting, make the jus as shown on page 280. Put the roasting pan on the stove top over high heat and stir around the pieces of meat until the meat is browned and any juices have caramelized on the bottom of the pan. Discard the fat and return the pan to high heat. Deglaze the pan with 1 cup of the broth, scraping up any brown bits on the bottom of the pan with a wooden spoon. Boil down the broth until it caramelizes into a crusty brown layer with a layer of clear fat on top. Pour off the fat, return the pan to high heat, and deglaze the pan with the remaining 1 cup of broth while scraping up the crust until it dissolves in the liquid. Strain the liquid through a fine-mesh strainer into a warmed sauceboat.

To carve the roast lengthwise, cut through the loin muscles halfway up the saddle, cutting them in half lengthwise, then slice each section lengthwise with the knife held sideways, as shown on page 280. Turn the roast over and carve the tenderloins the same way. (Alternatively, cut the loin and tenderloin away from the chine bone and slice crosswise.) Pass the jus at the table.

VARIATIONS: Like any roast, this dish can be varied by infusing different elements into the jus just before serving. Lemon juice and zest; orange juice and zest; saffron; and herbs such as chervil, tarragon, or basil can all be infused in the jus. One dramatic way to serve the roast is to infuse the jus with a chiffonade (narrow, small strips) of basil before it is allowed to cool and set, and then slice the cold roast and spread the cold, perfumed *gelée* over the strips of meat.

Trimming and roasting saddle of lamb

1. Saddle of lamb.

2. Cut the flaps off each side of the saddle where they meet the loin, being careful not to cut into the loin.

3. Trim excess fat off the saddle.

4. Season the saddle.

5. Place the saddle on a bed of its trimmings in a roasting pan.

6. Roast to an internal temperature of 125°F. The fat covering the loin should be crispy.

Making jus for saddle of lamb

1. Boil down any juices that remain in the pan. When the juices caramelize, discard the fat. Deglaze the pan with broth.

2. Boil down the broth until it caramelizes on the bottom of the pan.

3. Deglaze the pan a second time.

Carving roast saddle of lamb

1. Slide a knife along the backbone, alongside the loin, until you reach more bone, then work around the next small ridge of bone.

2. Trim the fat off the top of the loin.

3. Holding the knife blade parallel to the cutting board, slice through the loin to obtain long, rectangular strips.

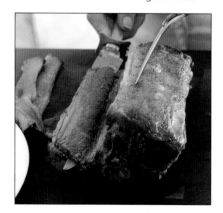

4. Continue slicing the loin until no meat is left.

5. Turn the saddle over and carve lengthwise along the tenderloins or cut them away from the bone and slice them crosswise.

6. Chine bone of saddle of lamb with all meat removed.

Rack

A rack is one of the most luxurious cuts from the lamb and makes a dramatic roast. Count on two ribs per person (four servings per rack) if you're using American lamb and four ribs per serving if you're using New Zealand or Australian lamb. When carving, alternate sides as you serve the ribs so one person isn't stuck with the "seconds," the ribs from the shoulder end of the rack.

If you have a double rack of lamb, split it as shown on page 282. This removes the chine bone automatically. If you have a single rack, make sure the butcher trims off the chine bone so you can carve the rack easily. French the rack and remove the layer of fat that covers the half of the rack on the shoulder end as shown on pages 282 to 283. This helps the meat to cook evenly.

Roast Rack of Lamb

You will save time in the kitchen if your butcher has frenched the ribs for you. But if the rack isn't frenched, don't skip the step. A frenched rack is a stunning sight on the dinner table.

MAKES 4 MAIN-COURSE SERVINGS

1 American rack of lamb (8 chops) or 2 New Zealand racks of lamb (16 chops total), about 1¹/₂ pounds, ribs frenched

Salt

Pepper

1 pound lamb stew meat or trimmings, cut into ¹/₂-inch strips

¹/₂ onion, coarsely chopped

2 cups chicken broth (page 316)

Let the rack(s) come to room temperature and season all over with salt and pepper. Preheat the oven to 450°F.

Spread the stew meat and onion on the bottom of a roasting pan just large enough to hold the rack(s). Place the rack(s) on top. Slide the pan into the oven and roast for about 25 minutes, or until an instant-read thermometer inserted into the center of the roast without touching bone reads 125°F to 130°F

or until the meat feels firm when you press both ends of the rack(s).

Transfer the rack(s) to a platter or cutting board, tent loosely with aluminum foil, and let rest for 15 minutes before carving.

While the rack(s) are resting, make the jus. Put the roasting pan on the stove top over high heat and stir around the pieces of meat until the meat is browned and any juices have caramelized on the bottom of the pan. Discard the fat and return the pan to high heat. Deglaze the pan with ¹/₂ cup of the broth, scraping up any brown bits on the bottom of the pan with a wooden spoon. Boil down the broth until it caramelizes into a crusty brown layer with a layer of clear fat on top. Pour off the fat, return the pan to high heat, and deglaze the pan with a second ¹/₂ cup broth, again boiling it down. Deglaze the pan with the remaining 1 cup broth, stirring until the crust has dissolved into the liquid, and then strain the liquid through a fine-mesh strainer into a warmed sauceboat.

Carve the rack(s), cutting between the ribs as shown on page 283. Pass the jus at the table.

VARIATION: The rack(s) can also be carved lengthwise, much like the saddle of lamb shown on the facing page.

Breaking down and trimming a double rack of lamb

1. Double rack of lamb.

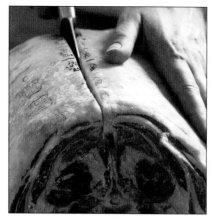

2. Cut along one side of the spinal bones that protrude to the back. Cut all the way down to where the ribs join the spine.

3. Cut along the other side of the spinal bones.

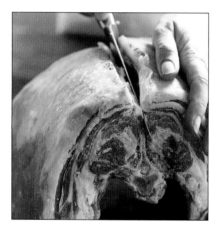

4. Use a cleaver to cut through the ribs where they join the chine bone, freeing one rack.

5. Cut the second rack off the chine bone.

6. Single racks of lamb with chine bone removed.

7. Slide a knife into the shoulder side of the rack and cut out the shoulder blade.

8. Find the small muscle surrounded by fat that sits just above the loin muscle. With a knife, score a line along the back of the rack just above the small muscle. Using the line as a guide, cut between the ribs.

9. Press against the fat that separates the ribs with the side of a knife. Some of the rib bones may come free of the membrane.

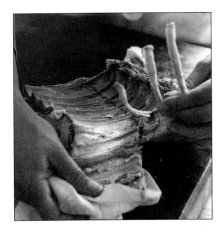

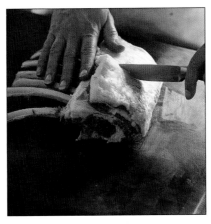

10. In one piece, peel off the strip of fat and any meat that covers the ribs.

11. Cut off the deckle (the thick layer of fat and meat) that covers the shoulder side of the rack. This helps both ends of the rack to cook in the same amount of time.

12. Trim off fat from the loin end of the rack.

Roasting and carving a rack of lamb

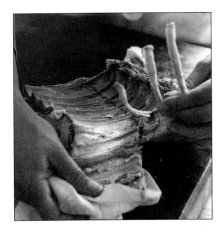

1. Season the lamb, place in a roasting pan with the trimmings and chopped onion, and roast.

2. To carve, cut between the ribs or between each pair of ribs.

3. Finished carved rack of lamb with jus.

Chops

Lamb chops come in three types: shoulder chops, which have a considerable amount of gristle and fat and are best braised; rib chops, which come from the rack and include the rib and loin; and loin chops, which come from the saddle and include the loin and the tenderloin. Rib chops demand the highest price because everyone wants a chop with a pretty rib; loin chops are often a better value. Shoulder chops are cheaper than their cousins, but because they must be braised like nearly all the shoulder cuts, they are included with the other shoulder cuts on page 266.

Rib chops and loin chops are commonly sautéed, usually over high heat in a little oil (the thinner the chop, the higher the heat), and should be served between rare and medium-rare. You can cut your own rib chops by ordering a rack of lamb, having the chine bone cut out, and then slicing between the ribs. Or, you can break down the double rack yourself (see page 282). Loin and rib chops are almost always interchangeable in recipes, so here I have included a basic recipe for sautéed loin or rib chops. For an outline and ideas for making a pan-deglazed sauce, see page 7.

Slicing and sautéing rib lamb chops

1. If cutting chops from a rack of lamb, cut between each rib (or every other rib if the rack is small) to divide into chops.

2. Brown the chops on both sides in hot oil. Usually a minute or two on each side suffices.

3. Whisk in butter to enrich the pan sauce.

Sautéed Lamb Chops with Marjoram and White Wine

For those who have never had marjoram, this dish will come as a revelation. You can substitute thyme, savory, sage, or rosemary; if using rosemary, use only about $1/2$ teaspoon because its flavor is strong.

MAKES 4 MAIN-COURSE SERVINGS

8 loin or rib American lamb chops, or 16 loin or
    rib New Zealand or Australian lamb chops
Salt
Pepper
3 tablespoons olive oil
1 clove garlic, minced and then crushed to a paste
2 teaspoons finely chopped fresh marjoram
$3/4$ cup dry white wine
2 tablespoons meat glaze (page 318)
2 tablespoons cold butter, cut into 2 slices

Season the chops on both sides with salt and pepper. Let the chops come to room temperature. If you are using rib chops, for a more elegant presentation, french the bones on the chops.

In a sauté pan large enough to hold the chops in a single layer, heat the olive oil over high heat. When the oil begins to smoke, add the chops. If the chops are thin, leave the heat on high; if they are thick, reduce the heat slightly. Cook for 1 or 2 minutes on the first side if the chops are thin, or about 4 minutes on the first side if the chops are thick. Turn the chops and sauté for the same amount of time on the second side, or until the lamb just begins to feel firm to the touch. The chops will be a nice medium-rare.

Transfer the chops to a paper towel–lined plate to absorb the fat, pat the tops dry with paper towels, and let rest in a warm spot while you make the sauce. Pour the fat out of the pan.

Return the pan to high heat. Add the garlic and marjoram and stir them around for about 30 seconds to bring out their flavor. Add the wine, bring to a boil, and deglaze the pan, scraping up any brown bits on the bottom of the pan with a wooden spoon. Stir in the meat glaze and cook down until the sauce has a lightly syrupy consistency. Whisk in the cold butter until emulsified. Do not allow the sauce to boil. Season with salt and pepper.

Place the chops on warmed plates. Spoon the sauce over the top and serve.

Leg

A leg of lamb is a good option when you want to serve a special cut, but don't want to buy a more costly rack or saddle. The leg can be roasted or braised. If braising, you will need to lard it or it will dry out. If you are roasting the leg, you can skip this step. If you buy a leg of lamb that hasn't been trimmed, you'll have to remove the "fell," the thin layer of tissue that covers the fat. It is pulled away with little effort. It is also a good idea to remove the pelvic bone and the aitchbone (hipbone) to ease carving.

Roast Leg of Lamb

Leg of lamb is sometimes sold cut in half, which means you can be offered the shank end or the butt end (the shank end is easier to carve). Of course, you can also buy a whole leg of lamb, which will likely yield some delicious leftovers. Whole bone-in legs typically weigh between 10 and 15 pounds.

MAKES 10 MAIN-COURSE SERVINGS

1 bone-in leg of lamb, about 12 pounds

Salt

Pepper

5 cloves garlic, crushed and then minced to a paste, optional

1 onion, coarsely chopped

2 carrots, peeled and cut into 3-inch sections

1 turnip, peeled and quartered

1 pound lamb trimmings and/or lamb stew meat, cut into 1/2-inch chunks

2 cups chicken broth (page 316)

Let the leg come to room temperature. Preheat the oven to 400°F.

Remove the fell and bones and trim the leg as shown on the facing page, reserving any meaty trimmings. Lay the leg, inside up, on a work surface and season with salt and pepper and the garlic, then tie the leg as shown.

Spread the onion, carrots, turnip, and lamb trimmings in a roasting pan just large enough to hold the leg. Place the leg on top. Slide the pot, uncovered, into the oven and roast for about 40 minutes, or until golden brown. Turn down the oven to 300°F and continue to roast for about 40 minutes, or until an instant-read thermometer inserted into the center reads 120°F.

Transfer the roast to a platter or cutting board, tent loosely with aluminum foil, and let rest for 15 minutes before carving.

While the roast is resting, make the jus. Put the roasting pan on the stove top over high heat and stir around the pieces of meat until the meat is browned and any juices have caramelized on the bottom of the pan. Discard the fat and return the pan to high heat. Deglaze the pan with 1/2 cup of the broth, scraping up any brown bits on the bottom of the pan with a wooden spoon. Boil down the broth until it caramelizes into a crusty brown layer with a layer of clear fat on top. Pour off the fat, return the pan to high heat, and deglaze the pan with a second 1/2 cup broth, again boiling it down. Deglaze the pan with the remaining 1 cup broth, stirring until the crust has dissolved in the liquid, and then strain the liquid through a fine-mesh strainer into a warmed sauceboat.

Snip the strings and carve the lamb as shown on page 288. Pass the jus at the table.

Breaking down and boning a leg of lamb

1. Peel the fell off the leg of lamb.

2. Remove the pelvic bone by following the irregular bones, including the section of tail bone, with the tip of a knife.

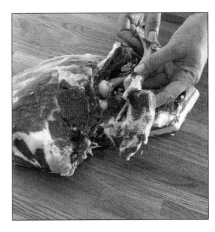

3. Remove the aitchbone, or hip bone, by cutting along its contours.

4. Cut out the small piece of fat that rests against the large dome-shaped bottom round muscle.

5. Remove the small musk gland.

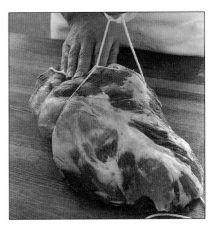

6. Trim away the excess fat, leaving a thin layer. Tie the lamb into an ovoid shape.

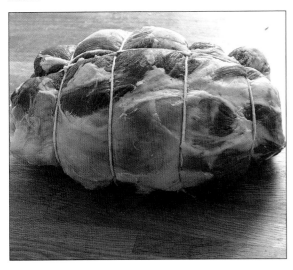

7. Boned and tied leg of lamb.

Roasting and carving a leg of lamb

1. Place the lamb on a bed of aromatic vegetables and trimmings, season the lamb, and roast to an internal temperature of 120°F.

2. To make a jus, put the roasting pan on the stove top and boil down all the juices until they caramelize on the bottom.

3. Pour off or spoon off the fat and discard.

4. Deglaze the pan with broth, scraping up any brown bits with a wooden spoon, then strain the jus.

5. Carve the meat lengthwise in slices about 1/3 inch thick.

6. Finished sliced lamb with jus.

Braised Leg of Lamb

One of the most famous dishes of old-fashioned French cooking is *gigot de sept heures*, or "seven-hour leg of lamb." Even though this recipe is cooked for a much shorter time, the final flavor and texture of the lamb is reminiscent of that long-braised French classic. Because the leg is lean, it's best to lard it when you are braising it, so that it stays moist during the long cooking. When the lamb is done, the meat should be so tender that you can serve it with two spoons. The juices are especially delicious.

MAKES 10 MAIN-COURSE SERVINGS

1 pound fatback (weight not including rind)
    or *lardo*
1 bone-in leg of lamb, 10 pounds or larger
2 cloves garlic, minced and then crushed to a paste
Salt
Pepper
1 onion, quartered
1 large carrot, peeled and thickly sliced
1 cup dry white wine
4 cups chicken broth (page 316), or as needed
2 tablespoons meat glaze (page 318), optional
Bouquet garni (page 320)

Cut the fatback into sheets about 1/4 inch thick, then cut the sheets lengthwise into strips, or lardons, about 1/4 inch on each side. In a bowl, toss the lardons with the garlic and marinate for at least 1 hour at room temperature or preferably overnight in the refrigerator.

Let the lamb come to room temperature. Preheat the oven to 400°F.

Pull away the fell and remove the pelvic bone and aitchbone from the leg as shown on page 287. Trim off the excess fat but don't expose the meat. Using a hinged larding needle, lard the leg with the lardons as shown on page 15. Season the lamb all over with salt and pepper. Tie the boned-out end of the lamb together with kitchen string.

Put the lamb in an ovenproof pot in just large enough to hold it snugly—an oval pot is ideal—and surround it with the onion and carrot. Slide the pot, uncovered, into the oven and roast for about 1 hour, or until the lamb releases juices that caramelize (but don't burn) on the bottom of the pot.

Remove from the oven and reduce the oven temperature to 275°F. Add the wine and enough broth to come halfway up the sides of the lamb. Bring to a gentle simmer on the stove top. Add the meat glaze and nestle in the bouquet garni. Cover the pot with a sheet of aluminum foil, pressing it down slightly in the middle so that moisture will condense on its underside and drip down onto the exposed parts of the meat, and then with a lid.

Return the pot to the oven and braise the lamb for about 4 hours, or until a knife slides easily in and out of the lamb. Check occasionally to make sure the liquid is not boiling, and if it is, turn down the oven temperature.

Transfer the lamb to a smaller pot (it will have shrunk). Strain the braising liquid into a glass pitcher and skim off the fat with a ladle. Or, ideally, refrigerate the braising liquid at this point and then lift off the congealed fat in a single layer. Pour the degreased liquid into a saucepan, bring to a simmer, and simmer, skimming off any fat or froth that rises to the surface, for about 30 minutes, or until reduced by about half. Meanwhile, raise the oven temperature to 400°F.

Pour the reduced liquid over the lamb. Slide the pot, uncovered, into the oven and cook the lamb, basting the meat every 10 minutes with the braising liquid, for about 30 minutes, or until the lamb is covered with a shiny glaze.

Remove the lamb from the oven. Snip the strings and slice the lamb thickly or portion it with two spoons. Serve in warmed soup plates with the braising liquid spooned around the sides and over the top.

Goat

Goat is a popular meat in many parts of the world, including the Caribbean, Mexico, India, and much of Europe. It has a delicate flavor (less strong than lamb) and can be cooked like young lamb, which is to say, the leg, shoulder, rack, and loin can all be roasted. The shoulder can be boned whole, tied, and braised, much like the lamb shoulder on page 268. It can also be cut into cubes and used in a stew. Goat tastes best when young and, ideally, milk fed.

Curried Goat Stew

This stew is made in the same way as most stews except the meat isn't browned first. Make sure that your curry powder is fresh and fragrant; when you buy a new container, use it within a year. Experiment with different brands (or with blending your own) until you find one with the flavor you like. Serve this simple stew with steamed jasmine or basmati rice.

MAKES 4 MAIN-COURSE SERVINGS

1 whole double goat shoulder, about 2 pounds
Salt
Pepper
1 large onion, chopped
2 carrots, peeled and sliced
3 cloves garlic, minced
$1/4$ cup olive oil
1 tablespoon curry powder
1 cup dry white wine
2 cups chicken broth (page 316) or water
Bouquet garni (page 320)

Bone the shoulder and cut the meat into roughly 1-inch cubes. Season with salt and pepper.

In a heavy pot just large enough to hold the goat, combine the onion, carrots, garlic, and olive oil and sweat the vegetables over medium heat for about 15 minutes, or until the onion turns translucent. Add the curry powder and cook, stirring occasionally, for 1 minute more. Add the goat cubes, wine, broth, and bouquet garni. Bring to a simmer and simmer gently, covered, for about 2 hours, or until a piece of meat is easily crushed between your thumb and forefinger.

Pour the stew into a colander set over another pot. Discard the bouquet garni and set aside the meat and vegetables. Place the pot off center on a burner over medium heat so the liquid boils on only one side and pushes the fat to the other side (this makes it easier to skim). Simmer, regularly skimming off any fat or froth that floats to the surface, for about 30 minutes, or until the liquid is reduced to about 2 cups.

Add the meat and vegetables to the reduced liquid and simmer gently until the meat is heated through. Serve the stew in warmed soup plates.

Roast Leg of Goat

A goat leg is roasted in much the same way as a leg of lamb, but goat is typically roasted to medium, while lamb is usually roasted rare to medium-rare. Goat meat is said to resemble veal, and in appearance it does. Its flavor, however, is much more assertive—gamey but not in an unpleasant way (unless you got an old goat). Here, I don't make a jus because it tends to concentrate the gamey flavors and make them too strong.

MAKES 4 MAIN-COURSE SERVINGS

1 bone-in leg of goat, about 3 pounds
Salt
Pepper

Let the leg come to room temperature. Preheat the oven to 450°F.

Remove the pelvic bone if it is still in place. Season the meat all over with salt and pepper. Tie the leg lengthwise with kitchen string, and then tie it crosswise with 3 or 4 lengths of string. Place the leg in a roasting pan just large enough to hold it. Slide the pan into the oven and roast for about 40 minutes, or until an instant-read thermometer inserted into the center of the roast without touching bone reads about 130°F.

Transfer the leg to a cutting board, tent loosely with aluminum foil, and let rest for 10 minutes before carving in the same way as for a roast leg of lamb (see page 288).

SAUSAGES

O nce you get the knack of it, sausage making can be addictive, probably because it's so versatile. For a basic sausage, use two parts lean pork meat (from the shoulder) to one part pork fatback. You can grind the meat and fat using a meat grinder, the grinding attachment on a stand mixer, or a food processor. For the best result, cut the meat and fatback into cubes and partially freeze them before grinding. You can also finely chop them by hand.

It is easy to flavor this base of pork and pork fat with herbs (thyme, marjoram, or oregano is a good choice), spices (especially *quatre épices*, see page 308), and/or vegetables such as fennel. You can also give the sausage a handmade character by adding small cubes of various meats or other ingredients, such as duck or squab breast, pistachios, foie gras, prosciutto, *lardo*, or fatback. For an even more sophisticated result, marinate each of the components in a different wine and with a different herb or spice. This will keep the flavors changing in the mouth, which makes more interesting sausage than one in which the ingredients have simply been ground together.

Once you have made the sausage mixture, the simplest thing to do is to form it into patties for cooking. If you can find caul fat (a thin, lacy, fatty membrane that surrounds the organs of cows, sheep, and pigs; pork caul is the most commonly available), wrap each patty in it to keep it moist during cooking, though its use is by no means essential. You can also stuff your sausage filling into casings, which come in various sizes. This can be done with a stand mixer with a sausage stuffer attachment or with a pastry bag outfitted with a large plain tip. But for the smoothest stuffing experience, you need to invest in a sausage stuffer (see www.sausagemaker.com for options in all price ranges).

In this chapter, I have included directions for making just eight types of fresh sausage. Countless additional kinds of fresh, cooked, and semidry and dry (or cured) sausages can be made or purchased. Brief descriptions of some well-known sausages appear in the box on page 300.

How to Select and Clean Sausage Casings

Most European shoppers can choose from a wide selection of casings, from different animals and in different sizes. In this country, we are limited primarily to hog casings ($1/2$ inch to 2 inches in diameter), which are used for the classic thin link sausages, and beef middle casings ($2^1/4$ to $2^1/2$ inches in diameter), which are ideal for larger sausages, about the size of most salami. You can sometimes find sheep casings, which are good for making small sausages.

Most butchers sell hog casings, though you will probably need to buy a minimum of 1 pound, which is a lot. However, they come packed in salt and keep indefinitely in the refrigerator. When you are ready to use them, cut off the length you need and soak it in cold water to cover for about 5 minutes, swirling it around every now and again. Then, attach one end to the kitchen tap and very slowly turn on the cold water. Unwrap any crimps in the casing as it begins to fill. Once the water is running completely through the casing, let it run for about 2 minutes to rinse out the salt.

How to Stuff Sausage Casings

Stuffing sausage meat into casings can be tricky. The casings can tear, and the stuffer can be resistant and hard to push. But with a little practice, you'll get the knack of it. After rinsing the casings thoroughly as described above, roll the entire length of the casing up on the tube that extends from the stuffer. Tie a small knot in the end of the casing to seal it. Then, as you gently press down on the stuffer, pull out a short length of casing from the tube allowing it to fill with sausage mixture. When you have the length you want, twist the sausage around about five times to form the link. If you're worried about the sausages coming unraveled, tie a short length of kitchen string around each twist. Continue in this way until you have used all the sausage mixture.

Sausage making

1. Load the sausage filling into the sausage stuffer.

2. Slide the sausage casing up on the shaft of the stuffer.

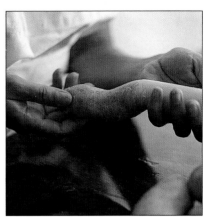

3. Force the sausage into the casings with the stuffer.

How to Cook Fresh Sausages

Fresh sausages in casing can be cooked in simmering water. Pierce them in several places with the tip of a knife and place them in a pan with water to cover, bring to a simmer, and cook until heated through, about 20 minutes.

Most fresh sausages in casing are also delicious sautéed or grilled. It is best, but not necessary, to first simmer them until heated through as described above, and then brown them in a small amount of oil in a sauté pan over medium-high heat or directly over a medium-hot to hot fire on a grill. This way, the sausages won't scorch in the time it takes them to fully cook.

If you have opted to shape the sausage mixture into patties instead of stuffing it into casings, sauté or grill them without first simmering them. Add a little oil to the pan to prevent sticking and cook over medium-high heat or directly over a medium-high fire until nicely browned and cooked through.

Basic Pork Sausage

If you are set on making this sausage and are unable to find fatback, you can use Italian *lardo* in its place. Make the filling as directed but leave out the kosher salt. Shape a nugget of the filling into a small patty, sauté it in a little olive oil, and taste it, then add salt to the filling mixture as needed. The *lardo* has the advantage of providing great flavor to the sausage mixture, but the disadvantage of being a pricy addition to the shopping list.

MAKES 12 PATTIES OR 10 SAUSAGE LINKS (ABOUT 5 OUNCES EACH)

2^1/$_2$ pounds boneless pork shoulder, cut into
    1-inch cubes
1 pound fatback (weight not including rind)
    or *lardo*, cut into 1-inch cubes
2 cloves garlic, minced
1 tablespoon kosher salt, if using fatback (see note)
2 teaspoons pepper
1 tablespoon fennel seeds or aniseeds, finely
    chopped
^{1}/$_2$ teaspoon ground nutmeg
2 teaspoons chopped fresh marjoram,
    or 1 teaspoon chopped fresh thyme
3 feet hog casings, rinsed (see page 294), optional

Spread the meat and fatback on a sheet pan (don't combine them). Slide the pan into the freezer for about 20 minutes, or until the meat and fat are partially frozen. Grind the meat into ^{1}/$_4$-inch pieces in a food processor or with a meat grinder or stand mixer fitted with the coarse grinding attachment. Grind the fatback into ^{1}/$_8$-inch pieces.

Place the meat and fatback in a bowl and add the garlic, salt, pepper, fennel seeds, nutmeg, and marjoram. Work the ingredients together with clean hands until they are evenly distributed. Sauté a small patty of the mixture, taste for salt, and adjust if needed.

Divide the mixture into 12 equal portions and form each portion into a patty about ^{1}/$_2$ inch thick. Or, stuff into casings as described on page 294.

To serve, cook the sausages as described on page 295.

Italian-Style Pork Sausage with Marjoram

This sausage gets its flavor from garlic and marjoram. If you can't find fresh marjoram, use 1^1/$_2$ teaspoons chopped fresh thyme

MAKES ABOUT 10 SAUSAGE LINKS (ABOUT 5 OUNCES EACH)

2 pounds Boston butt (weight not including rind)
1 pound fatback (weight not including rind)
    or *lardo*
^{1}/$_2$ pound prosciutto end
2 teaspoons salt, if using fatback
2 teaspoons pepper
2 teaspoons ground anise or fennel
1 tablespoon chopped fresh marjoram
2 garlic cloves, minced
1 cup fresh bread crumbs
^{1}/$_2$ cup dry white wine
4 feet hog casings, rinsed (see page 294)

Cut the pork and the fatback into ^{3}/$_4$-inch cubes and place in a large bowl. Cut the prosciutto end into ^{1}/$_4$-inch cubes and add to the bowl. Add the salt, pepper, anise, marjoram, and garlic and mix well with clean hands until all the ingredients are evenly distributed. In a small bowl, mix together the bread crumbs and wine to make a smooth paste. Work the paste into the meat mixture, distributing it evenly. Grind in a food processor or with a meat grinder or stand mixer fitted with the coarse grinding attachment. The mixture should have the consistency of coarse hamburger meat.

Stuff into casings as described on page 294.

To serve, cook the sausages as described on page 295.

Turkey Sausage

Although some people believe that eating turkey sausage is a way to avoid consuming pork, most often they will discover that pork fat is part of the mix because it is what keeps the filling moist. Sometimes cream can be used in place of the pork, as in the recipe on page 298. Here, as in the Basic Pork Sausage on the facing page, *lardo* can be substituted for the fatback, with the same caveat applied: Because the saltiness of *lardo* varies, make the filling as directed but leave out the kosher salt. Shape a nugget of the filling into a small patty, sauté it in a little olive oil, and taste it, then add salt to the filling mixture as needed. This recipe calls for thyme, but other herbs, such as marjoram or oregano, would be delicious in its place. If using marjoram, use 2 teaspoons; if using oregano, use $1/2$ teaspoon dried or 2 teaspoons fresh.

MAKES 12 PATTIES OR 10 SAUSAGE LINKS (ABOUT 5 OUNCES EACH)

2 pounds boneless, skinless turkey breast, cut into 1-inch cubes

1 pound fatback (weight not including rind) or *lardo*, cut into 1-inch cubes

2 cloves garlic, minced

1 tablespoon kosher salt, if using fatback

2 teaspoons pepper

$1/2$ teaspoon nutmeg

1 teaspoon chopped fresh thyme

3 feet hog casings, rinsed (see page 294), optional

Spread the turkey and fatback on a sheet pan (don't combine them). Slide the pan into the freezer for about 20 minutes, or until the turkey and fat are partially frozen. Grind the turkey in a food processor or with a meat grinder or stand mixer fitted with the coarse grinding attachment until it has the consistency of hamburger meat. Grind the fatback to a consistency somewhat finer than the turkey.

Place the turkey and fatback in a bowl and add the garlic, salt, pepper, nutmeg, and thyme. Work the ingredients together with clean hands until they are evenly distributed. Sauté a small patty of the mixture, taste for salt, and adjust if needed.

Divide the mixture into 12 equal portions and form each portion into a patty about $1/2$ inch thick. Or, stuff into casings as described on page 294.

To serve, cook the sausages as described on page 295.

Sausage Safety Tips

When working with sausage meat, make sure your hands are immaculately clean—wash them often—and the sausage meat is always cold. Use only the freshest ingredients, including garlic, which some of us use when it has become too stale. Never taste the raw sausage mixture. If you want to check the seasonings, sauté a small patty and taste it. Store fresh sausages in the refrigerator for up to 3 days and in the freezer for up to 3 months. Always wash your equipment as soon as you have finished using it. Don't leave it sitting all day without cleaning and then start using it again later in the day.

Creamed Turkey Sausage

This is the perfect sausage to make if you're trying to avoid pork. Essentially a turkey mousse, this sausage is delicate, smooth, and perfectly white.

MAKES 12 SAUSAGE LINKS (ABOUT 6 OUNCES EACH)

2 pounds boneless, skinless turkey breast, cut into
    1-inch cubes
4 egg whites
3 1/2 to 4 cups heavy cream
1 tablespoon salt
1/4 teaspoon ground nutmeg
1/2 teaspoon white pepper
7 feet hog casings, rinsed (see page 294)

In a food processor, combine the turkey and egg whites and puree until smooth. Transfer the mixture to a large bowl, cover with plastic wrap, pressing it directly onto the surface of the mixture, and chill for 3 hours in the refrigerator or over a bowl of ice for 30 minutes.

Work the cream into the turkey mixture, a little at a time; the mixture should be thick enough to hold its shape (you may not need to add the full amount of cream). Chill again for 3 hours in the refrigerator or for 30 minutes over a bowl of ice. Finally, work in the salt, nutmeg, and pepper until well mixed.

Stuff into casings as described on page 294, forming sausages about 6 inches long and tying them off with a small length of kitchen string.

To serve, cook the sausages as described on page 295.

Kielbasa

To most Americans, a kielbasa is a hearty garlic-infused smoked pork, or pork and beef, sausage with Polish origins. But the word *kielbasa* is actually the most common Anglicization for a wide variety of sausages—made from beef and/or pork, fresh, smoked, or dried—found throughout eastern Europe and Russia. Here is my take on this rich tradition.

MAKES ABOUT 10 PATTIES OR 10 SAUSAGE LINKS
(ABOUT 4 OUNCES EACH)

3/4 pound lean beef such as chuck
1 1/4 pounds Boston butt (weight not including rind)
1/2 pound fatback (weight not including rind)
    or *lardo*
2 cloves garlic, minced and then crushed to a paste
2 teaspoons salt, if using fatback
2 teaspoons pepper
1/2 teaspoon ground cumin
1/2 teaspoon fresh thyme leaves, chopped
4 feet hog casings, rinsed (see page 294), optional

Cut the beef, pork, and fatback into 1-inch cubes. Spread them on a sheet pan, slide the pan into the freezer for about 20 minutes, or until the meat and fat are partially frozen. Grind the meats and fat in a food processor or with a meat grinder or stand mixer fitted with the coarse grinding attachment to the consistency of pickle relish. Transfer to a bowl and add the garlic, salt, pepper, cumin, and thyme and mix well. Sauté a small patty of the mixture, taste for salt, and adjust if needed.

Divide the mixture into 10 equal portions and form each portion into a patty about 1/2 inch thick. Or, stuff into casings as described on page 294.

To serve, cook the sausages as described on page 295.

Chorizo

Chorizo comes in many styles, depending on where it is made—Spain, Portugal (*chouriço*), Mexico, Central America, South America—and whether it is fresh, cooked, or cured. In Spain, it is typically made from a mixture of coarsely chopped pork and pork fat and flavored with smoked paprika (*pimentón*), with many regional variations, both smoked and not. This is an adaptation of the popular Spanish sausage.

MAKES ABOUT 10 PATTIES OR 10 SAUSAGE LINKS (ABOUT 4 OUNCES EACH)

2 pounds boneless Boston butt (weight not including rind)

$1/2$ pound fatback (weight not including rind) or *lardo*

$3/4$ teaspoon salt, if using fatback

2 teaspoons black pepper

1 teaspoon cayenne pepper

1 teaspoon cumin

2 cloves garlic, minced and then crushed to a paste

1 teaspoon chopped fresh thyme

$1/4$ cup sweet or hot smoked Spanish paprika (*pimentón*) or other sweet or hot paprika

4 feet hog casings, rinsed (see page 294), optional

Cut the pork and fatback into 1-inch cubes. Spread them on a sheet pan and slide the pan into the freezer for about 20 minutes, or until the pork and fat are partially frozen. Grind the pork and fat in a food processor or with a meat grinder or stand mixer fitted with the coarse grinding attachment to the consistency of pickle relish. Transfer to a bowl and add the salt, black pepper, cayenne pepper, cumin, garlic, thyme, and paprika and mix well. Sauté a small patty of the mixture, taste for salt, and adjust if needed.

Divide the mixture into 10 equal portions and form each portion into a patty about $1/2$ inch thick. Or, stuff into casings as described on page 294.

To serve, cook the sausages as described on page 295.

Duck Sausage with Pistachios

Here, I have used the mixture for a classic duck terrine to make a batch of flavorful sausages. The filling includes pork for bulk and a meaty backdrop. The meat from the duck legs is ground, but duck breast meat and the fatback are cut into small cubes to give the sausages an interesting texture and an appealing appearance. Pistachios are added for color and crunch.

MAKES 12 SAUSAGE LINKS (5 TO 6 OUNCES EACH)

Ingredients for Duck Terrine (page 307)
5 feet beef middle casings, rinsed (see page 294)

Prepare the mixture for the terrine as directed. Do not be tempted to grind the ingredients together as you do for the other sausages in this chapter, or the unique quality of these sausages will be lost. Stuff into casings as described on page 294.

To serve, cook the sausages as described on page 295.

White Veal Sausage

In France at Christmas time, *boudins blancs*—white veal sausages—begin to appear in charcuterie windows. In fancier places, they have black spots from the truffles they contain. These classic sausages are a great way to use extra meat from the leg or shoulder of veal. They are delicious served with sauerkraut or sautéed cabbage.

MAKES 12 SAUSAGE LINKS (ABOUT 6 OUNCES EACH)

2 pounds veal leg or shoulder meat, trimmed of all fat and gristle (weight before trimming)

4 egg whites

3¹/₂ to 4 cups heavy cream

1 tablespoon salt

¹/₄ teaspoon ground nutmeg

7 feet hog casings, rinsed (see page 294)

Cut the veal into 1-inch pieces. In a food processor, combine the veal and egg whites and puree until smooth. Transfer the mixture to a large bowl and cover with plastic wrap, pressing it directly onto the surface of the mixture, and chill for 3 hours in the refrigerator or for 30 minutes over a bowl of ice.

Work the cream into the meat mixture, a little at a time; it should be thick enough to hold its shape (you may not need to add the full amount of cream). Chill again for 3 hours in the refrigerator or for 30 minutes over a bowl of ice. Finally, work in the salt and nutmeg until well mixed.

Stuff into casings as described on page 294, forming sausages about 6 inches long and tying them off with a small length of kitchen string.

To serve, cook the sausages as described on page 295.

A World of Sausages

For centuries, sausage making was seen as a practical way to use up any meat scraps, fat, or innards that remained after the butchering of a hog. The sausages were usually smoked or salted and air-dried for long keeping. Nowadays, fresh sausages are as common as cured sausages, all kinds of meat are used, and sausage making is considered an art, rather than a way to use up scraps. Here are twenty well-known sausages that are usually (but not always) cooked—typically gently simmered, sautéed, or grilled—before eating.

ANDOUILLE: Two kinds of andouille exist, French and American. French andouille sausages are made from pork intestines and stomach and have a rather strong flavor that some find disagreeable. A smaller version is called *andouillette*. American andouille sausages, which are especially popular in the Cajun kitchens of Louisiana, are made from pork, garlic, and spices and are commonly smoked over pecan or hickory wood.

BANGER: This fat, white British sausage, usually made from pork, bread crumbs, herbs, and spices, is often eaten for breakfast and is a standard pub item, traditionally paired with mashed potatoes. Bangers are known to burst during cooking, so be sure to poke them with a pin in several places before simmering.

BAUERWURST: A coarse-textured German sausage flavored with mustard seeds.

BOCKWURST: This popular German sausage is traditionally made from a mixture of veal and pork seasoned simply with salt, pepper, and paprika. Nowadays, it is often made with other meats and is sometimes smoked.

BOUDIN: This term is used for a wide variety of sausages in the kitchens of France and in the Cajun and Creole kitchens of the American South. *Boudin blanc* is made from pork or veal, and includes rice in the American version and milk in the more delicate French version. *Boudin noir* is made from a mixture of pork and pork blood. In Normandy and Paris, boudin is served hot with sautéed apples.

BRATWURST: Sometimes smoked and usually a mixture of veal and pork, these spicy sausages are among Germany's most popular.

BUTIFARRA: These Spanish sausages are made from pork and almost always need to be cooked. They come in many varieties including, white (popular in Catalonia) and black (blood sausages).

CERVELAS DE LYON: Originally made from brains, these sausages are now made with pork and bacon and are often flavored with truffles and pistachios.

CHAURICE: Similar to Spanish chorizo, this highly seasoned, chile-hot pork sausage is used in Creole and Cajun cooking.

CHIPOLATA: Thin and short, this pork sausage, which varies from country to country (though it originated in Italy), is richly flavored with herbs and spices and is usually sautéed or grilled.

CHORIZO: Popular in Spain, in much of Latin America, and in parts of the Caribbean, chorizos are made from pork and vary—fresh or smoked, fiery or mild—according to their place of origin.

COTECHINO: Made from pork, fatback, and pork rind, this lightly spiced, large fresh sausage is a specialty of Modena, Italy. It is de rigueur in *bollito misto* (page 178) and is traditionally paired with lentils for New Year's eve supper.

HAGGIS: Sometimes called a savory pudding, rather than a sausage, and made by stuffing sheep's innards, rolled oats, onions, and spices into a sheep's stomach and then poaching or steaming it, haggis is a traditional dish of Scotland and an acquired taste beyond its borders.

ITALIAN SAUSAGE: In the United States, this term typically refers to a so-called sweet pork sausage flavored with plenty of fennel and garlic.

KNACKWURST: Also spelled knockwurst, this short, plump, highly spiced precooked German sausage is made from pork and beef or veal. Lightly smoked and pure beef kosher versions are also available.

LINGUIÇA: Seasoned with garlic, paprika, pepper, and vinegar, this long, thin, lightly smoked Portuguese pork sausage has a mild flavor.

LUGANEGA: A specialty of northern Italy, but found throughout the boot, *luganega* is commonly made from the cheek and neck meat of the pig and is often flavored with spices, such as cinnamon or nutmeg, and sometimes with Parmigiano-Reggiano cheese.

MERGUEZ: From North Africa, the *merguez* is a thin, fresh sausage made from lamb or beef, or a mixture, and seasoned with garlic, paprika, and cayenne.

WEISSWURST: Made primarily from veal, and flavored with parsley, onion, and spices, this fresh, white sausage is a specialty of Munich.

ZAMPONE: Made by stuffing the boned foreleg of a pig with a lightly spiced mixture of pork, pork fat, and pork rind, *zampone* has a flavor similar to that of *cotechino* and must be poached or steamed.

PÂTÉS, TERRINES, AND FOIE GRAS

Nowadays, the terms *pâté* and *terrine* are used almost interchangeably, but traditionally a pâté has a crust—today often called a *pâté en croûte*, despite the redundancy—and a terrine is a pâté mixture without a crust baked in a mold of the same name. A mousse is similar to a terrine, but has a smooth, homogenous texture.

The simplest pâtés and terrines are made by grinding meat and other ingredients, as though making sausages, and then baking the mixture in a mold, traditionally an ovoid vessel for a pâté and a rectangular one for a terrine. Better pâtés and terrines, those with a more interesting texture and an attractive cross section when sliced, contain ingredients that have been layered in the vessel by hand. These can include such items as pieces of meat, strips of fat, pistachio nuts, or truffles. It also adds drama to grind the meat for a pâté to different textures. For example, make one finely ground mixture and use it to hold together a second coarsely chopped mixture.

You can use nearly any type of meat for making pâtés and terrines, but pork fat should almost always be part of the mixture to ensure a melting texture. Don't try to cut down the fat in a recipe or the pâté will be dry. Unfortunately, pork fat, in its unsalted form fatback, can be hard to find. For this reason, I recommend Italian *lardo*, pork fat cured with salt and herbs, as an alternative. Its drawback is that it is expensive and salty.

Foie gras is the enlarged liver of a goose or duck—a size made possible by feeding the animal copious amounts of grain with the aid of a funnel. Some claim that this is a cruel process, and they will want to skip the three recipes for foie gras I have included in this chapter. Those who opt to try them may need some tips on purchasing and cooking this extravagant food. First, you have a choice of duck or goose foie gras, though duck is far more common. You can buy raw whole foie gras, cooked foie gras terrine (either a whole liver or a large chunk, either fully cooked or lightly cooked), and foie gras mousse (which is made from trimmings). Finally, when cooking fresh foie gras, you must not let your mind stray. Because it has both a high fat and high water content, foie gras melts quickly when exposed to heat, and you will end up with a puddle of fat in what seems like seconds if you don't pay close attention.

Hot Foie Gras

Most cooks prepare hot foie gras by sautéing (or sometimes grilling) slices of the fresh whole liver. The disadvantage to this is that whole livers contain a lot of water that immediately renders. For a richer, more substantial effect, sauté or grill slices of Terrine of Foie Gras (page 310) or Foie Gras au Torchon (page 312) instead of using raw liver. Because hot foie gras is very rich, it is often best to use it to garnish other foods, rather than make it the main attraction.

Country Pâté

A country pâté (or, really, a terrine since it has no crust) can be made, much like meat loaf, with a combination of ground meats, with a predominance of pork. It also must contain a high percentage of fat. If you try to reduce the fat, the pâté will be dry. Liver, traditionally pork though chicken will work, too, is usually included. The mixture is seasoned with herbs, often thyme or marjoram; with plenty of garlic; and with spices. Some recipes include shallots, usually lightly sweated in butter, as well as bread crumbs soaked in milk, which have a lightening effect.

MAKES 10 FIRST-COURSE SERVINGS

1 pound boneless pork shoulder, cut into 1-inch cubes

3/4 pound fatback (weight not including rind)
or *lardo*, cut into 1-inch cubes

1/2 pound chicken livers, trimmed of any
membranes and green patches

2 eggs

3 cloves garlic, minced and then crushed to a paste

1 tablespoon finely chopped fresh thyme,
or 1 1/2 tablespoons fresh marjoram

2 teaspoons salt, if using fatback

2 teaspoons pepper

1/2 teaspoon ground cloves

1/2 teaspoon ground ginger

1/4 teaspoon ground nutmeg

1 tablespoon olive oil

1/2 pound fatback, *lardo*, or prosciutto, thinly sliced,
for lining the terrine

Spread the pork on a sheet pan and slide the pan into the freezer for 20 minutes, or until the pork is partially frozen. Transfer to a food processor and grind to the consistency of pickle relish. Transfer to a bowl. Add the fatback cubes and chicken livers to the food processor and process until smooth. Add the liver mixture to the pork, then add the eggs, garlic, thyme, salt, pepper, cloves, ginger, and nutmeg and mix well. Make a small patty of the

mixture, then sauté it in the olive oil in a small sauté pan. Taste the patty and adjust the seasoning accordingly.

Preheat the oven to 350°F. Line a 1-quart terrine or similar mold with the thin slices of fatback, leaving enough overhanging the sides of the mold to cover the top. Pack the pork mixture into the lined mold, then fold the overhang over the top, covering it completely. Cover the pâté with a piece of parchment paper and then with a triple layer of aluminum foil, creasing it tightly around the edges of the mold.

Put the filled mold into a roasting pan, and add hot water to come about halfway up the sides of the mold. Place the roasting pan in the oven and bake the pâté for about 1 1/4 hours, or until an instant-read thermometer inserted into the center reads 145°F.

Remove the pâté from the water bath. Place a cutting board or other flat weight on the still-covered pâté to weight it and let cool to room temperature. Remove the weight and refrigerate for at least 4 hours before serving. To serve, run a knife around the edges of the pâté to loosen it, then cut into slices.

Lining Molds for Terrines or Pâtés

Thin sheets of fatback (unsalted pork fat) are the traditional lining for a pâté or terrine mold. But fatback poses a problem. Pork is now leaner than in the past, which means that finding fatback in solid, thick chunks can be difficult. Most of the time, it comes in a large sheet with a rind and a rather thin layer of fat, and getting the fat off in thin sheets is nearly impossible. In the past, a butcher could slice the fatback on a slicer, but now the fatback is too thin. Alternatives to fatback include caul fat—the netlike sheets of fat that hold the innards of an animal in place— prosciutto slices, blanched leek greens, and Italian *lardo*.

Hot Pâté en Croûte

A hot pâté is best baked in a crust, which helps to hold it together when it is sliced and served. Traditionally, the crust would be a pie pastry made with lard, but more refined versions (and easier, too, because you can buy the pastry) are made with puff pastry.

MAKES 12 FIRST-COURSE SERVINGS

3/4 pound boneless pork loin or tenderloin, cut into 1/4-inch cubes

3/4 pound boneless veal from the loin, round, or bottom round, cut into 1/4-inch cubes

1/2 cup dry white wine

1 clove garlic, minced

Salt

1 teaspoon pepper

1 pound boneless pork shoulder, cut into 1-inch cubes

1/2 pound fatback (weight not including rind), cut into 1-inch cubes

1/2 pound chicken livers, trimmed of any membranes and green patches

2 eggs

1 teaspoon fresh thyme leaves, chopped

1/4 teaspoon ground nutmeg

1/4 teaspoon ground cloves

1/2 teaspoon ground ginger

1 pound store-bought all-butter puff pastry, thawed in the refrigerator if frozen

In a bowl, toss together the pork loin and veal cubes, wine, garlic, 1 tablespoon salt, and the pepper. Cover and refrigerate for at least 4 hours or up to overnight.

In a food processor, combine the pork shoulder, fatback, chicken livers, and 1 of the eggs and process until smooth. Transfer to a bowl and work in the thyme, nutmeg, cloves, and ginger until evenly distributed. Drain the meat cubes and fold them into the ground pork mixture.

Preheat the oven to 400°F. Divide the pastry in half. On a lightly floured board, roll out each half into a 13-by-10-inch rectangle. Lightly sprinkle a sheet pan with water (to keep the pastry from burning), and place 1 of the rectangles on the pan. Spread the filling evenly over the rectangle, leaving a 1-inch border uncovered on all sides. In a small bowl, beat the remaining egg with a pinch of salt. Bring the uncovered border of pastry up around the filling on all sides, then brush the turned-up pastry with the beaten egg. Place the remaining rectangle of pastry on top of the filling, and press the overhang down around the sides, sealing it to the base pastry. Cut diagonal slashes about 1/2 inch apart across the top of the pâté, being careful not to cut into the filling. Then make an equal number of slashes in the opposite direction, to create a crosshatch pattern.

Bake the pâté for about 40 minutes, or until an instant-read thermometer inserted through one of the slashes into the center reads 135°F. If at any point the pastry starts to get too dark, turn down the oven temperature to 300°F.

Remove the pâté from the oven and let rest for about 20 minutes before slicing. Serve warm.

Duck Terrine

Any full-flavored bird can be used in this same way to make a terrine. The meat from the thighs is ground with the forcemeat, and the meat from the breasts is cut into cubes that contribute an attractive pattern when the terrine is cut. Cubes of fatback or *lardo* are added for texture and moistness, and pistachios deliver both bright color and a nice crunch. If the terrine is well sealed with foil, it will keep well for several months in the refrigerator. In fact, its flavor will improve.

MAKES ABOUT 12 SERVINGS

1 Pekin duck, about 5 pounds

3 slices dense-crumb white bread, crusts removed

$1/4$ cup milk

$3/4$ pound boneless pork shoulder, cut into
   1-inch cubes

$1/4$ pound chicken livers, trimmed of any
   membranes and green patches

1 egg

$1/4$ pound fatback (weight not including rind) or
   lardo, cut into large cubes, for the forcemeat

$2^1/2$ teaspoons salt, or 2 teaspoons, if using *lardo*

2 teaspoons ground pepper

$2^1/2$ teaspoons ground ginger

$3/4$ teaspoon ground nutmeg

$1/4$ teaspoon ground cloves

1 tablespoon dried thyme, chopped fine

3 large cloves garlic, minced and then crushed
   to a paste

$1/4$ pound fatback (weight not including rind)
   or *lardo*, cut into $1/4$-inch cubes

$1/4$ pound prosciutto, sliced $1/8$ inch thick and
   cut into $1/8$-inch dice

$1/3$ cup pistachio nuts, blanched for 1 minute,
   drained, rinsed with cold water, and skins
   removed

1 tablespoon olive oil

About 12 thin slices fatback, prosciutto, or *lardo*
   for lining the terrine

Cut up the duck as shown on page 74. Strip the meat off the thighs, cut it into roughly 1-inch cubes, and reserve. Skin and bone the breasts, cut the meat into $1/4$-inch cubes, and reserve. Reserve the liver. In a small bowl, work together the bread and milk to make a smooth paste.

Place a few of the pork shoulder cubes in a food processor and process until smooth, adding more cubes, a few at a time, as the first ones break down. Then add the duck thigh cubes, a few at a time, again processing until smooth. Add the bread paste, the chicken livers (and the duck liver if it was included with the duck), the egg, the large fatback cubes, the salt, pepper, ginger, nutmeg, cloves, thyme, and garlic and continue to process for about 2 minutes, or until the mixture is smooth and creamy.

Transfer the contents of the food processor to a large bowl. Add the duck breast cubes, the $1/4$-inch fatback cubes, the prosciutto, and the pistachios and mix well. Make a small patty of the mixture, then sauté it in the olive oil in a small sauté pan. Taste the patty and adjust the seasoning accordingly.

Preheat the oven to 350°F. Line a 12-by-4-by-3-inch terrine with the fatback slices as shown for the foie gras terrine on page 311, leaving enough overhanging the sides of the mold to cover the top. Pack the duck mixture into the lined mold, then fold the overhang over the top, covering it completely. Cover the terrine with a rectangle of parchment paper and then with a triple layer of aluminum foil, creasing it tightly around the edges of the mold.

Put the filled mold into a roasting pan, and add hot water to come about halfway up the sides of the mold. Place the roasting pan in the oven and bake the terrine for about 1 hour, or until an instant-read thermometer inserted into the center reads 140°F.

continued

Remove the terrine from the water bath. Place a cutting board or other flat weight on the still-covered terrine to weight it and let cool to room temperature. Remove the weight and refrigerate for at least 6 hours before serving.

To serve, run a knife around the edges of the terrine to loosen it, then cut into slices. (Alternatively, unmold the terrine: loosen the sides as directed, then invert a platter over the mold, invert the mold and the platter together, and lift off the mold.)

Duck Rillettes

To make a quick pâté for spreading on baguette slices, shred the meat from confit duck legs and combine it with duck fat and spices. Traditionally, *rillettes* contain a high percentage of fat to ensure a moist, melting texture. But they can still be wonderfully satisfying when made with less fat, as they are here.

MAKES 6 HORS D'OEUVRE SERVINGS

4 confit Pekin duck legs, or 3 confit Moulard duck legs (page 79)

²/₃ cup rendered duck fat, melted and cooled to room temperature

Salt

1¹/₂ teaspoons *quatre épices* (see below)

Thin baguette slices, toasted if desired

Sour gherkins (cornichons)

Pull off and discard the skin from the duck legs, then pull the meat away from the bones and discard the bones. Using your fingers, pull the meat into shreds, so that you end up with a pile of stringy meat. Place the meat in a bowl

Using a wooden spoon, work the duck fat into the meat until combined. Add ¹/₂ teaspoon salt and the *quatre épices* and stir to mix thoroughly. Taste and adjust the seasoning with more salt if needed. Cover and refrigerate until well chilled.

To serve, spoon into a shallow serving bowl and surround with the baguette slices and gherkins.

Quatre Épices

Pâtés and French sausages often call for *quatre épices* ("four spices") for a distinct and aromatic note that balances the rich, dense flavor of the meats. Because recipes don't call for much of the spice blend and the spices do eventually stale, I recommend making only small amounts. Store the mixture in a tightly sealed jar in the freezer.

To make *quatre épices*, in a small bowl, stir together 2¹/₂ teaspoons freshly ground white pepper, ³/₄ teaspoon ground ginger, ³/₄ teaspoon ground nutmeg, and ¹/₄ teaspoon ground cloves until well combined. Makes about 1¹/₂ tablespoons.

Duck rillettes

1. Pull the skin away from confit duck legs and discard.

2. Pull the meat away from the legs and pull into shreds. Place in a bowl.

3. Pour duck fat onto the meat, add salt and spices, and mix well.

Chicken liver mousse (recipe follows)

1. Chicken livers.

2. Sauté the livers.

3. Deglaze the pan with vermouth.

4. Puree the sautéed livers with butter.

5. Work the liver mixture through a drum sieve or strainer.

6. Combine the liver mixture and whipped cream. Chill.

Chicken Liver Mousse

This creamy mousse is a great way to showcase chicken livers. At its best, it's reminiscent of foie gras. Serve it with crackers or toasted baguette slices.

MAKES 8 HORS D'OEUVRE SERVINGS

Sautéed Chicken Livers with Thyme (page 62)
6 tablespoons cold butter, cut into 6 slices
3/4 cup heavy cream
Salt
Pepper

Sauté the chicken livers and prepare the sauce as directed in the recipe, but do not add the butter to the sauce. Let the chicken livers and the sauce cool.

In a food processor, combine the cooled chicken livers and sauce and the butter and process until smooth. Using a rubber spatula, the back of a wooden spoon, or a plastic pastry scraper, work the mixture through a drum sieve or a fine-mesh strainer held over a bowl.

In a bowl, using a whisk or mixer, whip the cream until medium-firm peaks form. Fold the cream into the liver mixture until thoroughly combined and smooth. Season with salt and pepper. Cover and chill well before serving.

Terrine of Foie Gras

You will need to find a source for whole fresh foie gras for this luxurious terrine. Traditionally, it is baked in a porcelain mold lined with fatback, but prosciutto or *lardo* is a good substitute. Serve this bread with white toast. Don't serve brioche, which will be too rich.

MAKES ABOUT 12 FIRST-COURSE SERVINGS

1 large or 2 small fresh whole foie gras (about 3 pounds total)

About 12 thin slices prosciutto, *lardo*, or fatback for lining the terrine
Salt
Pepper

Separate the two lobes of the liver(s). Follow the veins on each lobe with a paring knife, and then pull them away from the lobe with your fingers. Don't worry if the lobes break up a bit.

Preheat the oven to 300°F. Line a 12-by-4-by-3-inch terrine with the fatback slices, leaving enough overhanging the sides of the mold to cover the top. Press the lobes into the terrine, seasoning each layer with salt and pepper. Mound the lobes so they rise above the rim of the mold (they shrink as they cook). Fold the overhang over the top. Cover the top with a rectangle of parchment paper and then with a triple layer of aluminum foil, creasing it tightly around the edges of the mold.

Put the filled mold into a roasting pan, and add hot water to come about halfway up the sides of the mold. Put a pan or other heavy object that is ovenproof on top of the terrine to weight it. Place the roasting pan in the oven and bake the terrine for about 1 hour, or until an instant-read thermometer inserted into the center reads 130°F.

Remove the weight from the terrine, and remove the terrine from the water bath. Let cool to room temperature. Refrigerate the still-covered terrine overnight before serving. If you want to save the fat rendered by the terrine, pour the water from the water bath into a bowl, let it cool, and then refrigerate overnight. Pull off the congealed fat. The fat is useful for making omelets or for finishing emulsified sauces such as béarnaise sauce.

To serve, run a knife around the edges of the terrine to loosen it, then cut into slices. (Alternatively, unmold the terrine: loosen the sides as directed, then invert a platter over the mold, invert the mold and the platter together, and lift off the mold.)

Terrine of foie gras

1. Fresh whole foie gras.

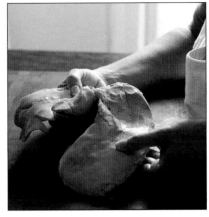

2. Pull apart the two lobes.

3. Follow the veins with a knife and pull them out with your fingers.

4. The deveined liver.

5. Line a terrine with prosciutto slices. Leave enough overhanging the sides to cover the top.

6. Put the liver into the mold in layers.

7. Season each layer with salt and pepper.

8. Mound the liver and then press down firmly.

9. Fold the overhanging prosciutto over the top of the terrine.

continued

10. Cover the terrine with parchment paper, and then with a triple layer of aluminum foil.

11. Put the filled mold in a roasting pan, and fill the pan with hot water to come halfway up the sides of the mold.

12. Top the terrine with a heavy object to weight it, then bake.

Foie Gras au Torchon

In the French kitchen, a *torchon* is a kitchen towel or, when being less polite, an old rag. Here, the old towel is put to use by wrapping fresh foie gras in it and poaching the swaddled liver for just a few minutes in hot salted water. Then, the towel is tightened around the liver and the packet is chilled overnight so the foie gras holds its shape.

MAKES ABOUT 12 FIRST-COURSE SERVINGS

1 large or 2 small fresh whole foie gras (about 3 pounds total)
Salt
Pepper

Separate the two lobes of the liver(s). Follow the veins on each lobe with a paring knife, and then pull them away from the lobe with your fingers. Don't worry if the lobes break up a bit; they will be sealed together in the towel. Season the foie gras all over with salt and pepper.

Place a sheet of parchment paper on a work surface. Place the lobes of foie gras in a line along the center of the paper, and then roll the parchment around them, pressing firmly to form the liver into a sausage shape about 10 inches long. Place the parchment-wrapped foie gras on a kitchen towel and roll it up tightly in the towel. Twist the two ends in opposing directions, and then tie each end tightly with kitchen string, keeping them snug against the end of the "sausage."

Bring a large pot of water to a boil, then reduce the heat to a simmer. Add the wrapped foie gras, cover the pot, and poach gently for exactly 4 minutes.

Remove the foie gras from the pot. Twist the ends again (they will have loosened because the liver will have rendered some of its fat and shrunk), snugging them up against the ends of the roll, and tie each end with a new piece of string (don't bother removing the original string). Make sure the wrapping is as taut as possible around the foie gras so it holds its sausagelike shape. Place on a platter, let cool completely, and refrigerate overnight.

The next day, snip the strings, unwrap the towel, and peel away the parchment. Cut into thin slices to serve.

Sautéed Foie Gras with Calvados and Apples

Calvados is distilled hard cider, or apple brandy, from the coastal region of Normandy, in northern France. The best Calvados has been aged for at least two decades in oak casks, which yields a smooth spirit with the subtle flavor of apple. If you can't find Calvados or another apple brandy (also known as applejack in America), use hard apple cider.

MAKES 4 FIRST-COURSE SERVINGS

4 slices Terrine of Foie Gras (page 310) or Foie Gras
    au Torchon (opposite), each $1/3$ inch thick
Salt
Pepper
3 tablespoons rendered duck fat or butter
2 large apples, peeled, halved, cored, and each half
    cut into 6 wedges
1 tablespoon sugar
$1/2$ cup Calvados or other apple brandy or hard
    cider
3 tablespoons meat glaze (page 318), optional
1 tablespoon cold butter

Season the foie gras slices on both sides with salt and pepper and keep covered in the refrigerator until needed.

In a large sauté pan (preferably nonstick), heat the duck fat over medium heat. Add the apple wedges and sprinkle them with the sugar. Sauté for about 10 minutes, or until nicely browned on the first side. Turn the wedges over and continue to cook for about 5 minutes longer, or until browned on the other side. Remove from the heat and cover to keep warm.

Select a sauté pan just large enough to hold the foie gras slices and heat over high heat until intensely hot. Place 1 foie gras slice in the pan, wait for about 15 seconds, turn it, and wait for 15 seconds more. The idea is to brown the foie gras without melting it. You'll have to get a sense of how the foie gras is browning and melting in order to regulate the exact time. Sauté the remaining foie gras slices the same way.

Transfer the foie gras slices to warmed plates and keep warm. Check the juices left in the pan. If they are tasty (that is, they are not too dark or burned), pour in the brandy and deglaze the pan over medium heat (stand back, the brandy can flare up), scraping up any brown bits from the bottom of the pan with a wooden spoon. If they are not tasty, pour the brandy into a clean pan over medium heat, standing back to avoid flare-ups. Add the meat glaze, stir well, and simmer until a nice sauce consistency forms. If it becomes too thick, thin with a little water or broth. Whisk in the butter until the sauce is emulsified.

Arrange the apples next to the foie gras. Spoon the sauce over the foie gras.

Extra Foie Gras

If you find you have extra raw foie gras, use it to make a mini foie gras terrine: press it into a heatproof bowl or ramekin—season each layer with salt and pepper—cover with parchment paper and aluminum foil, place it in a water bath, and bake it as directed for a large foie gras terrine (see page 310). Let cool and refrigerate overnight. Save any fat that runs into the water bath by pouring the water into a bowl and refrigerating it overnight. Pull off the fat in the morning and use it in any of the ways described in the terrine recipe. Slice and serve the mini terrine.

BROTHS AND CONSOMMÉS

Good broths are essential to good braises, sauces, soups, and other dishes. Most cooks make their broths from bones, but if you can figure out an economical way to make them from meat, the result will be much more satisfying. One way to do that is to make Pot-au-Feu (page 177) or Bollito Misto (page 178) and reserve the broth for other uses.

There are two basic kinds of broth, white and brown. The difference between them is that the bones and/or meat for a brown broth are browned in the oven or on the stove top before they are simmered in water, and the bones and/or meat for a white broth are not, though they are sometimes blanched before they are simmered. The blanching is necessary when using the meat or bones of young animals such as veal because they release large amounts of albumin, which clouds the broth and gives it a soapy taste. Brown broths are more flavorful than white broths and are also easier to keep clear because any albumin and other soluble protein is denatured before it is moistened. They are especially good for adding to braises and for reducing for sauce making. A white broth is useful when you are adding broth to a light soup, a white sauce, or other preparation that must remain pale.

Homemade broths are easy to make, but a handful of tips will ensure success. First, if the broth is made from bones alone, make sure you have browned or blanched them before you combine them with water. Ideally, use a narrow, tall pot to facilitate skimming, and add only enough water to cover the bones and/or meat. If you add too much water, the broth will be weak and thin. Start with cold water and bring it slowly to a simmer. If hot water is used, the bones and/or meat will release proteins that will cloud the broth before a simmer is even reached. Keep the broth at a bare simmer throughout the cooking, ideally with a bubble or two gently rising every second or so on one side of the pot only (move the pot slightly off center of the burner, which makes it is easier to skim away impurities). Meat in a broth not only contributes flavor but also helps clarify any cloudiness. That's because proteins and fat are slowly released into the liquid as the meat cooks, and as the proteins gradually coagulate, they trap minute particles, forming a froth on top. Keep an eye on the broth as it cooks and regularly skim it with a ladle so the froth and fat don't accumulate. Never allow a broth to boil. If it boils, the proteins and fat will be churned into it, clouding it and giving it a greasy flavor. Finally, don't add salt to a broth as it cooks. If you decide to reduce it later for a sauce, the salt will intensify, making your sauce too salty.

You can also make a highly concentrated broth by using broth to make broth. For example, you can make a beef broth by simmering beef knucklebones and/or shanks in beef broth. Or, you can create this same degree of concentration by simmering down, or reducing, broth.

<hr>

A consommé is a perfectly clear concentrated broth. Most cooks make a rich broth and then use a clarification mixture that includes eggshells, egg whites, ground meat, and aromatic vegetables. I have found that you can make a consommé more easily by simply making a double broth: make a meat broth and then use that broth as the base for a second broth. If you skim your broth carefully as it cooks and never let it boil, you can strain it through a fine-mesh strainer and it will be perfectly clear. If the consommé still has specks, line the strainer with a tightly wrung wet kitchen towel and strain the consommé a second time. Consommé may be seasoned with salt after it is clarified, but pepper should never be added to the finished soup; it will leave unsightly specks. If you want the flavor of pepper, crush about 20 peppercorns with the bottom of a saucepan, wrap them in cheesecloth, and infuse them in the broth for about 10 minutes before straining. Consommés are typically served as the soup course at the beginning of a formal dinner or as an intermezzo between courses.

Chicken Broth

Here is a great all-purpose brown broth that uses relatively inexpensive chicken drumsticks, which are ideal here because they carry a lot of flavor and natural gelatin. If you want to make a white broth, skip the browning step.

MAKES ABOUT 5 QUARTS

10 pounds chicken drumsticks
2 carrots, peeled and cut into 1-inch sections
1 onion, quartered through the stem end
Bouquet garni (page 320)

Preheat the oven to 450°F. Spread the drumsticks in a heavy roasting pan just large enough to hold them in a single layer, and sprinkle the carrots and onion over the top. Roast for about 45 minutes, or until the drumsticks are well browned and have released all their juices and the juices have caramelized on the bottom of the pan.

Transfer the drumsticks and vegetables to a pot, and put the roasting pan on the stove top over high heat. Pour about 4 cups water into the roasting pan, bring to a boil, and deglaze the pan, scraping up any brown bits on the bottom of the pan with a wooden spoon. Pour the liquid over the drumsticks. Add cold water to the pot to cover the drumsticks by about 2 inches, and nestle the bouquet garni in the center.

Bring to a gentle simmer, starting over high heat and reducing the heat to low once a simmer is reached. Move the pot slightly off center of the burner and adjust the heat so the liquid bubbles gently on one side (a bubble rises only every second or two). Simmer gently, uncovered, for 3 hours, skimming off the fat and froth with a ladle as they accumulate on the surface. Add water as needed to keep the drumsticks covered.

Remove from the heat, lift out and discard the drumsticks, and strain the liquid through a fine-mesh strainer into a storage container. Let cool for 1 hour or so at room temperature, then cover and store as directed on page 318. Lift off and discard the fat congealed on the surface before using.

The Ultimate Beef Broth

You can make beef broth from bones (get knucklebones, not marrowbones) or from meat (beef shanks) but your broth will be much better if both meat and bones are used. The bones supply the gelatin and the meat the savor. The quandary, of course, is that bones take 24 hours to release all their gelatin and by then the meat is spent and inedible. The best solution is to make the broth in two steps, the bone broth first and then the meat broth, using the bone broth as the base of the latter. That way the meat will still be edible, delicious served hot or cold with a tasty sauce (such as Mostarda di Cremona on page 180 or Salsa Verde on page 180). You will need a couple of days to make this super-broth, but the results will be worth it. An easier solution, as mentioned in the introduction to this chapter, is to make Pot-au-Feu (page 177) or Bollito Misto (page 178), serve the meats, and reserve the

Duck Broth and Duck Glaze

If you find yourself confronted with at least a couple of duck carcasses, it will be worthwhile to make duck broth. Break up the carcasses with a cleaver (they are tougher than chicken carcasses), place them in a pot with aromatic vegetables and water (or chicken broth) to cover as you do for chicken broth (see above) and simmer for 3 hours. If you want to make duck glaze, simmer down the duck broth as directed for meat glaze (see page 318).

broth for other uses. Or, make only the bone broth or the meat broth; you will still have a respectable broth for adding to your braises and sauces.

EACH BROTH RECIPE MAKES ABOUT 5 QUARTS

Bone Broth

10 pounds beef knucklebones
3 carrots, peeled and cut into 1-inch sections
2 onions, quartered through the stem end
Bouquet garni (page 320)

Preheat the oven to 450°F. Spread the bones in a heavy roasting pan just large enough to hold them in a single layer, and sprinkle the carrots and onions over the top. Roast for about 1 hour, or until the bones are well browned and any drippings have caramelized on the bottom of the pan.

Transfer the bones and vegetables to a pot, and put the roasting pan on the stove top over high heat. Pour about 4 cups water into the roasting pan, bring to a boil, and deglaze the pan, scraping up any brown bits on the bottom of the pan with a wooden spoon. Pour the liquid over the bones. Add enough cold water to cover the bones by about 3 inches, and nestle the bouquet garni in the center.

Bring to a gentle simmer, starting over high heat and reducing the heat to low once a simmer is reached. Move the pot slightly off center of the burner and adjust the heat so the liquid bubbles gently on one side (a bubble rises only every second or two). Simmer gently, uncovered, for a total of 24 hours, skimming off the fat and froth as they accumulate on the surface whenever it is convenient to do so. Add water as needed to keep the bones covered.

Remove from the heat, lift out and discard the bones, and strain the liquid through a fine-mesh strainer into a storage container. Let cool for 1 hour or so at room temperature, cover, and refrigerate, then lift off and discard the fat congealed on the surface and

use the broth to make the meat broth. Or, cover and store as directed on page 318 and use the broth as is, discarding the congealed fat before using.

Meat Broth

10 pounds beef shank, cut into 1-inch-thick rounds
3 carrots, peeled and cut into 1-inch sections
2 onions, quartered through the stem end
Bone broth (preceding recipe) and/or water
Bouquet garni (page 320)

Preheat the oven to 450°F. Spread the shanks in a heavy-bottomed roasting pan just large enough to hold them in a single layer, and sprinkle the carrots and onions over the top. Roast for about 1 hour, or until the shanks are well browned and any juices they have released have caramelized on the bottom of the pan.

Transfer the shanks and vegetables to a pot, and put the roasting pan on the stove top over high heat. Pour about 4 cups water into the roasting pan, bring to a boil, and deglaze the pan, scraping up any brown bits on the bottom of the pan with a wooden spoon. Pour the liquid over the shanks. Add enough bone broth and/or water to cover the shanks by about 3 inches, and nestle the bouquet garni in the center. Bring to a gentle simmer, starting over high heat and reducing the heat to medium once a simmer is reached. Move the pot slightly off center of the burner and adjust the heat so the liquid bubbles gently on one side (a bubble rises only every second or two). Simmer gently, uncovered, for 4 hours, skimming off the fat and froth as they accumulate on the surface. Add water as needed to keep the shanks covered.

Remove from the heat, lift out the shanks and set aside to enjoy later, and strain the liquid through a fine-mesh strainer into a storage container. Let cool for 1 hour or so at room temperature, and then cover and store as directed on page 318. Lift off and discard any fat congealed on the surface before using.

Meat Glaze

Meat glaze is made by simmering down (reducing) broth until it has a syrupy consistency. Once you have this glaze on hand, you can use it for making sauces and giving body and flavor to braises and stews. You can reduce meat broth down to about one-fifteenth its original volume, or to a demi-glace, or you can reduce it again by half (about one-thirtieth its original volume) to get *glace*, or meat glaze. Commercial meat glaze, specifically the excellent More-than-Gourmet brand, is the equivalent of broth that has been reduced to about one-thirtieth of its original volume.

To make meat glaze, put 5 quarts beef broth (page 316) in a pot on the stove top and bring to a gentle simmer. Move the pot slightly off center of the burner and adjust the heat so the liquid bubbles gently on one side (a bubble rises only every second or two). Simmer gently, frequently skimming off the fat and froth as they accumulate with a ladle, until the broth is reduced by about half. Remove from the heat and strain through a fine-mesh strainer into a smaller pot. Return the broth to the stove top and continue reducing the same way. When it is again reduced by half, strain it into a smaller pot and continue reducing until you have about $2/3$ cup. Transfer to a jar or plastic container, let cool, cover, and refrigerate for up to 3 months or freeze indefinitely. If you prefer to make and use demi-glace, only reduce the broth to $1^1/3$ cups and use twice as much in recipes calling for meat glaze.

Many cookbooks recommend putting broth in ice-cube trays and freezing it for quick use in sauces and even soups. The problem with this idea is that you need bagfuls of cubes to give body to a sauce or to make a soup. Instead, follow the directions for making meat glaze, but reduce the broth only until it is about one-eighth its original volume. (If you start with about 5 quarts, you will have about $2^1/2$ cups.) Pour the reduced broth into ice-cube trays and freeze. One cube is just about perfect for a sauce that yields four servings.

Storing Broth

Broth can be stored in a tightly covered container in the refrigerator for up to 5 days. At that point, you can bring the broth back to a boil, let it cool, and store it for up to 5 days longer. This can be repeated indefinitely. You can also store the broth in the freezer for up to 1 year. If you have reduced broth to the demi-glace or *glace* stage (see Meat Glaze, above), it will last even longer (up to 6 months in the refrigerator or up to 2 years in the freezer) and will eventually develop mold rather than turn sour. If the mold is superficial, you can scrape it off and still use the glaze.

Pork Broth

The trick to making pork broth is finding a cheap source of meat and bones. If you can find pork neck, buy 5 pounds of it, though pork neck is rarely seen in butcher shops nowadays. You will probably be stuck with using a cut from the shoulder, which isn't cheap but isn't terribly expensive, either. Plus, after you have simmered the pork for making the broth, you can serve the meat for supper, accompanied with sauerkraut and mustard.

MAKES ABOUT 5 QUARTS

1 bone-in picnic ham (picnic shoulder),
   about 7 pounds
3 carrots, peeled and cut into 1-inch sections
2 onions, quartered through the stem end
Bouquet garni (page 320)

Cut the rind off the ham and put it, skin side up, in the bottom of a pot. Cover it with the vegetables and then put the ham on top. Add water to cover by 1/2 inch and nestle in the bouquet garni. Place the pot over high heat and bring just to a simmer, then reduce the heat to low. Move the pot slightly off center of the burner and adjust the heat so the liquid bubbles gently on one side (a bubble rises only every second or two). Simmer gently, uncovered, for 4 hours, skimming off the fat and froth with a ladle as they accumulate on the surface. Add water as needed to keep the pork covered. After 4 hours, a knife or skewer should easily slide in and out of the meat, indicating it is done.

Remove from the heat and lift out the shoulder to enjoy later. Pour the liquid through a fine-mesh strainer into a storage container, let cool for 1 hour or so at room temperature, and then cover and store as directed on the facing page. Lift off and discard any fat congealed on the surface before using.

Turkey Broth

You can make turkey broth with a whole turkey, but when you consider that the leftover carcass from a roast turkey yields a comparable result, a whole turkey is an unnecessary extravagance. So, here is how to make a broth with the carcass left over from your holiday roast turkey. Remember, never add salt and pepper to a broth until just before serving: salt because you may end up reducing the broth later and the salt will intensify, and pepper because it turns acrid and hot when cooked in liquid for more than several minutes.

MAKES ABOUT 4 QUARTS

1 turkey carcass
1 carrot, peeled and cut into 1-inch sections
1 large onion, quartered through the stem end
5 cloves garlic, cut in half
Bouquet garni (page 320)

Break up the turkey carcass with a cleaver and put the pieces in a pot. Add the carrot, onion, garlic, and cold water to cover by 1 or 2 inches, and nestle the bouquet garni in the center.

Bring to a gentle simmer, starting over high heat and reducing the heat to low once a simmer is reached. Move the pot slightly off center of the burner and adjust the heat so the liquid bubbles gently on one side (a bubble rises only every second or two). Simmer gently, uncovered, for 4 hours, skimming off the fat and froth with a ladle as they accumulate on the surface.

Remove from the heat and lift out and discard the large carcass pieces. Strain the liquid through a fine-mesh strainer into a storage container, let cool for 1 hour or so at room temperature, and then cover and store as directed on the facing page. Lift off and discard any fat congealed on the surface before using.

Chicken Consommé

To capture the rich flavor of a good chicken consommé, make a white chicken broth first, and then use it as the base for making a brown chicken broth.

MAKES ABOUT 2¹/₂ QUARTS

10 pounds chicken drumsticks
2 carrots, peeled and cut into 1-inch sections
2 onions, cut into 1-inch sections
2 bouquets garnis (below)

Place 5 pounds of the drumsticks in a pot and add 1 of the carrots and 1 of the onions. Pour in cold water to cover the drumsticks by about 2 inches, and nestle 1 of the bouquets garnis in the center.

Bring to a gentle simmer, starting over high heat and reducing the heat to low once a simmer is reached. Move the pot slightly off center of the burner and adjust the heat so the liquid bubbles gently on one side (a bubble rises only every second or two). Simmer gently, uncovered, for 3 hours, skimming off the fat and froth with a ladle as they accumulate on the surface. Add water as needed to keep the drumsticks covered.

Remove from the heat, lift out and discard the drumsticks, and strain the liquid through a fine-mesh strainer into a clean container. Reserve for making the second batch of broth.

Preheat the oven to 450°F. Spread the remaining 5 pounds drumsticks in a heavy-bottomed roasting pan just large enough to hold them in a single layer, and sprinkle the remaining carrot and onion over the top. Roast for about 45 minutes, or until the drumsticks have released all their juices and the juices have caramelized on the bottom of the pan.

Transfer the drumsticks and vegetables to a pot, and put the roasting pan on the stove top over

What Is a Bouquet Garni?

A bouquet garni is a bundle of herbs that is added to braises, stews, soups, or other simmered preparations to infuse them with flavor. The ideal bouquet garni is made with fresh thyme or thyme dried on the stem, imported bay leaves, and flat-leaf parsley sprigs, tied up with a piece of kitchen string. If you use thyme leaves, rather than sprigs, you will need to secure them in a little satchel of cheesecloth.

Most cooks make their bouquets garnis too small and don't adjust the size to the amount of liquid being infused. If you are making a large pot of broth, you will need two bouquets each the thickness of a fist. For making 5 quarts broth, such as the recipes in this chapter, the bouquet garni should be as thick as your thumb and two closest fingers held together. In other words, it should contain a whole bunch of parsley, 10 thyme sprigs, and 1 bay leaf. A bouquet garni for a pot roast or similar braise should be of a similar size. In every case, make sure you use imported bay leaves, not leaves from a California bay, which have an aggressive eucalyptus flavor.

high heat. Pour about 2 cups water into the roasting pan, bring to a boil, and deglaze the pan, scraping up any brown bits on the bottom of the pan with a wooden spoon. Pour the liquid over the drumsticks. Pour in the broth from the first batch, add the remaining bouquet garni, and then simmer for 3 hours, skimming regularly, as you did the first batch.

Remove from the heat, lift out and discard the drumsticks, and strain the liquid through a fine-mesh strainer lined with a clean, damp kitchen towel into a clean container. Use immediately, or let cool to room temperature, cover, and refrigerate for up to 5 days or freeze for up to 3 months. (If refrigerated or frozen, before reheating, remove any traces of congealed fat with a spoon.)

Beef Consommé

A good beef consommé must have the rich, subtle flavor of the meat. To achieve that, you will need to prepare two batches of beef broth made with meat only. Don't be tempted to make a broth from bones, which would yield a consommé that is too gelatinous.

MAKES ABOUT 2½ QUARTS

10 pounds beef shank, cut into 1-inch-thick rounds
4 carrots, peeled and cut into 1-inch sections
2 onions, quartered through the stem end
2 bouquets garnis (opposite)

Preheat the oven to 450°F. Spread 5 pounds of the shanks in a heavy roasting pan just large enough to hold them in a single layer, and sprinkle 2 of the carrots and 1 of the onions over the top. Roast for about 1 hour, or until the shanks are well browned and any juices they have released have caramelized on the bottom of the pan.

Transfer the shanks and vegetables to a pot, and put the roasting pan on the stove top over high heat. Pour about 2 cups water into the roasting pan, bring to a boil, and deglaze the pan, scraping up any brown bits on the bottom of the pan with a wooden spoon. Pour the liquid over the shanks. Add enough water to cover the shanks by about 3 inches, and nestle 1 bouquet garni in the center.

Bring to a gentle simmer, starting over high heat and reducing the heat to low once a simmer is reached. Move the pot slightly off center of the burner and adjust the heat so the liquid bubbles gently on one side (a bubble rises only every second or two). Simmer gently, uncovered, for 4 hours, skimming off the fat and froth with a ladle as they accumulate on the surface. Add water as needed to keep the shanks covered.

Remove from the heat, lift out the shanks and set aside to enjoy later, and strain the liquid through a fine-mesh strainer into a clean container. Reserve for making the second batch of broth.

To make the second batch of broth, brown the remaining 5 pounds shanks, 2 carrots, and 1 onion the same way, transfer them to a pot, deglaze the roasting pan with 2 cups water, and pour the liquid over the shanks. Pour in the broth from the first batch, add the remaining bouquet garni, and simmer for 4 hours, skimming regularly, as you did the first batch.

Remove from the heat, lift out the shanks and set aside to enjoy later, and strain the liquid through a fine-mesh strainer lined with a clean, damp kitchen towel into a clean container. Use immediately, or let cool to room temperature, cover, and refrigerate for up to 5 days or freeze for up to 3 months. (If refrigerated or frozen, before reheating, remove any traces of congealed fat with a spoon.)

INDEX

Measurement Conversion Charts

Volume

U.S.	IMPERIAL	METRIC
1 tablespoon	½ fl oz	15 ml
2 tablespoons	1 fl oz	30 ml
¼ cup	2 fl oz	60 ml
⅓ cup	3 fl oz	90 ml
½ cup	4 fl oz	120 ml
⅔ cup	5 fl oz (¼ pint)	150 ml
¾ cup	6 fl oz	180 ml
1 cup	8 fl oz (⅓ pint)	240 ml
1¼ cups	10 fl oz (½ pint)	300 ml
2 cups (1 pint)	16 fl oz (⅔ pint)	480 ml
2½ cups	20 fl oz (1 pint)	600 ml
1 quart	32 fl oz (1⅔ pint)	1 l

Weight

U.S./IMPERIAL	METRIC
½ oz	15 g
1 oz	30 g
2 oz	60 g
¼ lb	115 g
⅓ lb	150 g
½ lb	225 g
¾ lb	350 g
1 lb	450 g

Length

INCH	METRIC
¼ inch	6 mm
½ inch	1.25 cm
¾ inch	2 cm
1 inch	2.5 cm
6 inches (½ foot)	15 cm
12 inches (1 foot)	30 cm

Temperature

FAHRENHEIT	CELSIUS/GAS MARK
250°F	120°C/gas mark ½
275°F	135°C/gas mark 1
300°F	150°C/gas mark 2
325°F	160°C/gas mark 3
350°F	180 or 175°C/gas mark 4
375°F	190°C/gas mark 5
400°F	200°C/gas mark 6
425°F	220°C/gas mark 7
450°F	230°C/gas mark 8
475°F	245°C/gas mark 9
500°F	260°C